Governmental Auditing

Cornelius E. Tierney
Certified Public Accountant
Partner

Arthur Young and Company
Washington, D. C.

Library of Congress
Catalog Number: 79-53054

About the Author

Mr. Cornelius E. Tierney, a Certified Public Accountant, is the partner-in-charge of Arthur Young & Company's federal government service practice. He has a Bachelor's Degree in Accounting and Finance and a Master's Degree in Business Administration and more than 19 years of governmental accounting, auditing and financial management experience with various federal executive, legislative and regulatory agencies, as well as with state and local governmental units.

He is a member, and holds chairmanships, of committees responsible for governmental auditing with the American Institute of Certified Public Accountants and the District of Columbia Institute of Certified Public Accountants. Additionally, he is a frequent speaker and publisher on governmental accounting and auditing subjects and has co-authored two books, published by the AICPA.

Table of Contents

PREFACE

The objective of this book is to provide a single reference and guide to the accounting and auditing practices relating to governmental organizations. This work should be of interest to practicing public accountants, financial managers, and government accountants and auditors. It is an attempt to identify auditing procedures and practices at the federal, state and local government levels. Similarities and differences in governmental financial practices are discussed, and the consistency with generally accepted auditing standards is described.

Admittedly, this effort was undertaken during a period of change; but then few, if any, observors can see or predict a period of calm and stability. A need was perceived for guidance in the conduct of audits in the governmental sector at the time the relevant bodies of governmental audit knowledge are being examined. The Municipal Finance Officers Association is making considerable progress in the revision and modernization of its *Governmental Accounting, Auditing and Financial Reporting.* The American Institute of Certified Public Accountants is continuing to provide accounting and auditing guidance to governmental accounting and auditing. The Financial Accounting Standards Board continues to issue statements on accounting practices related to the commercial sector, but has, additionally, turned its attention to governmental accounting and reporting..

Acknowledgement is given to the MFOA, AICPA, the Institute of Internal Auditors and the Pennsylvania Institute of Certified Public Accountants for permission to use and build upon the bodies of knowledge developed by them. Reliance also has been placed on the auditing procedures and practices of governmental audit organizations and the experiences of many practitioners auditing the accounts and operations of federal, state and local governments. Particular thanks must be given to the contributions, assistance, and advice provided by Thomas J. Moore, Jr., Certified Public Accountant, of Arthur

Young & Company, a professional with years of experience in the practice of governmental auditing.

No other, however, has any responsibility for the content of this book. This responsibility rests solely with the author. Additionally all views, opinions or positions expressed are the author's and do not necessarily reflect the views of others or the firm of Arthur Young & Company.

Cornelius E. Tierney

Washington, D. C.

1979

Chapter 1
Governmental Auditing

Background

Until the early 1970s, governmental accounting, financial management and auditing were practiced in anonymity by thousands of governmental executives and civil service personnel. There was minimal concern or interest expressed by legislators, the press or the general public in the need to adhere to generally accepted accounting principles and practices or to apply generally accepted auditing standards to the review and examination of financial statements of governmental units and other public organizations. Few academicians and certified public accountants were sufficiently interested in governmental accounting and auditing to publish on the subjects. It was a rare educational institution that offered a full curriculum in public sector financial management. Few texts addressed the uniqueness of governmental finance and none attempted to bridge the gap between accounting in the corporate and governmental sectors or to explain the similarities of federal, state and local governmental accounting and audit.

1

By the 1970s, about 20 percent of the working force was employed by some level of government, whose combined level of expenditure approximated 40 percent of the country's gross national product. The voters were demanding more governmental services, while reacting vigorously to increased taxes and the imposition of new taxes. By the mid 1970s, governments had almost exhausted the exploitation of taxables bases and the methods and types of taxes that could be assessed. Rates of taxation were felt by many to be approaching confiscatory levels.

Concurrent with the growing awareness that many governmental units were reaching the limits of resources, disquieting news accounts were published of some major governments being close to legal bankruptcy. Other governmental units were experiencing difficulties in selling securities to the general public. Discussions centered on governmental units defaulting on their obligations for publicly held securities.   Professional publications disclosed that governments did not issue the same types of financial statements as did corporations whose securities were publically held. Generally accepted accounting principles and auditing standards were not uniformly applied to government; many governmental units were not audited. Long exempt from the oversight of the Securities and Exchange Commission, governmental securities were sold to the public with few of the safeguards afforded to investors in securities of publicly held corporations.

Interested individuals and organizations learned that governmental financial systems were not generally designed for managing resources, but rather to insure compliance with legal or statutory requirements. Governmental fund accounting structures made it difficult for all but the most knowledgeable to assess the economy, efficiency or effectiveness of the management of governmental activities by public officials. Greater accountability was demanded; the number of audits, with differing objectives, was increased. The American Institute of Certified Public Accountants issued an industry audit guide for state and local governments. The National Council on Governmental Accounting revised its authoritative governmental guide, the publication *Governmental Accounting, Auditing and Financial Reporting.* The Comptroller General of the United States issued standards for auditing governmental units. The Secretary of the Treasury published, for the first time, consolidated financial statements for the United States Government, attempting to apply the principles of business accounting to the business of government. The Financial Accounting Standards Board commissioned a study of accounting for non-business organizations, which included governmental organizations.

Legislators incorporated the requirement for audits into new laws. Governmental agencies made audits of other governmental units and individuals to whom funds or other types of assistance were provided. A proliferation of audit guides resulted; over 100 different audit guides were issued by agencies of the federal government alone. Few audits were coordinated, and much duplication in audit coverage resulted.

The Governmental Financial Process

The development, approval and implementation of the budget has, generally, been the primary impetus to the type of accounting and reporting practiced by governmental units. Often the budget is issued in the form of laws and statutes. Controls have been established to insure compliance. Financial information is accumulated and published to provide an accounting in relation to budgets. The governmental budget is viewed simultaneously as a listing of priority activities of the government and as the plan for managing the government over a specified time period.

Historically, accounting procedures have been designed to assure that compliance with budgeted amounts is monitored on a continuous basis. Accordingly, unique structures of accounts and specific types of accounting entries were designed and practiced to insure the fiscal integrity of a governmental appropriation or fund.

The budget process, as well as the accounting for budgetary expenditures, while generally similar at the federal, state and local government levels, also differs at each level. For this reason, several chapters have been devoted to providing an overview of the financial process that forms the basis for governmental audits:

Chapter 2, "The Governmental Budget Process," describes the similarities and differences between the federal, state and local governmental budget processes. Additionally, planning and budgeting concepts that have been applied to public organizations are discussed, such as PPBS (planning, programming, budgeting systems), MBO (management by objectives), ZBB (zero based budgeting), and performance budgeting;

Chapter 3, "The Federal Government Accounting Process," summarizes the legislative requirements, the applicable accounting standards and the accounting process for federal departments and agencies;

Chapter 4, "The State and Local Government Accounting Process," summarizes the accounting principles and practices utilized by many state and local governmental units.

At all levels of government, a distinguishing and, oftimes, confusing aspect of governmental budgeting and accounting is the reliance on fund accounting concepts and the integration of budget-related journal entries with historical accounting transactions. A knowledge of these concepts is a prerequisite to the performance of governmental audits. With few exceptions, some aspects of all government audits are directed towards assessing the extent of compliance to program, management, legal or financial criteria set forth in the budget, which has been formalized in a law or statute.

Governmental Audit Standards, Criteria and Guides

Governmental organizations are typically subjected to a variety of audits by a variety of auditors. This duplication of audits, while decreasing, continues despite the efforts of federal agencies, such as the General Accounting Office and the Office of Management and Budget, which have provided policy guidelines to federal agencies and other levels of government that would permit the reduction in audits. Understanding the types of audit authority, the forms of audit organizations and the varying nature of audit responsibilities is beneficial to clarifying the existing audit system in the public sector.

The body of applicable auditing standards and criteria, defining, in part, acceptable accounting principles, consists principally of several publications:

The AICPA's *Statement on Auditing Standards,* the codification and successor to the earlier Statements on Auditing Procedures;

The AICPA's industry audit guide, *Audits of State and Local Governmental Units;*

The National Council on Governmental Accounting's *Governmental Accounting, Auditing and Financial Reporting,* the authoritative accounting principles and procedures for all governmental units except federal government and its agencies, which also includes auditing criteria;

The U.S. General Accounting Office's publications:

Accounting Principles and Standards and Internal Auditing Guidelines for guidance of federal agencies; and

Standards for Audit of Governmental Organizations, Programs, Activities and Functions;

The Financial Accounting Standards Board's several statements and interpretations on accounting matters and issues;

The federal government's contract and grant cost principles, which outline and prescribe those costs that may be properly chargeable by governmental organizations to programs for which federal assistance has been received; and

The numerous audit guides published by the several federal departments and agencies which set forth audit criteria for specific governmental programs.

Sufficient reference is made to these publications to illustrate the applicability to governmental auditing. However, it is presumed that students and practitioners have knowledge of these authoritative reference documents.

These documents must be consulted to insure full compliance with applicable audit standards, criteria and guidelines.

Several chapters are directed towards an explanation of the nature and requirements of governmental auditing:

Chapter 5, "Governmental Audits and the Nature of Audit Responsibilities," describes the principal governmental audit organizations, the general responsibilities of each and the types of audits often made of governmental units;

Chapter 6, "Governmental Auditing Standards and Guides," summarizes the audit standards and qualifying criteria that are prerequisites to the performance of satisfactory governmental audits;

Chapter 7, "Cost Principles Applicable to Federal Contracts and Grants to State and Local Governments," outlines the allowability criteria governing the acceptability of the $50 billion transferred annually from the federal government to state and local governments under contracts and grants.

Planning and Conducting Governmental Audits

In the public sector, financial statement audits are not necessarily the most significant or the most frequent type of audit performed. Because of legal or statutory requirements governing most revenues and expenditures, compliance auditing of some sort permeates the practice. Numerous contract and grant audits, which are limited scope audits, are made. A significant number of internal audits of governmental program activities and operations are performed. Recently, increased interest has been shown in the conduct of performance or operational audits.

Considerable audit effort may be wasted and much duplication may result when an audit staff fails to recognize and appropriately plan for the multidimensional aspects of governmental audits. An auditor may proceed to complete the more familiar financial statement audit, only to subsequently realize that the compliance and special-scope audit requirements could have been accomplished simultaneously as part of the detailed testing required for the financial statement audit. Auditors, on occasion, presume that the examination will require a certificate that the audit was conducted in accordance with generally accepted auditing standards, when actually a different scope audit was desired by the client.

In several chapters, examples and the process of conducting types of governmental audits are discussed:

Chapter 8, "Planning and Conducting a Government Audit," describes elements of a governmental audit and illustrates a method for developing an audit approach and budget;

Chapter 9, "Examples of Special Scope Governmental Audits," describes the many types of audits that might be made of governmental organizations;

Chapter 10, "Audits of Federally Assisted Programs," describes several areas of significance to an auditor when accepting an engagement to audit a federally supported governmental activity;

Chapter 11, "Performance Audits," highlights the nature and special considerations of performance-type audits and outlines the several elements that might comprise such audits;

Chapter 12, "Audit Test Methodology," provides an illustration of analytic review and testing concepts applied to the audit of appropriated funds.

Care must be given to the planning of a governmental audit. Since most governmental audits will be influenced by legislation, the scope of such audits will vary. Reporting on compliance with statutes or regulations affecting allowability of costs is often mandatory, and opinions concerning the results of these audits must be specific. While many of the generally accepted auditing standards are applicable, other audit criteria almost always must be met as well.

A comprehensive program for reviewing the internal controls and making a financial audit of a governmental unit, prepared by the Pennsylvania Institute of Certified Public Accountants, has been included as Appendix A.

Account Balances and Accounting Transactions

Although generally similar to the private sector, the governmental treatment of some accounts and transactions differs from generally accepted accounting procedures. While the variances are not too numerous, the effect on account balances and financial statements could be significant. It is important to know that accrual accounting may not be generally applied, values other than cost may be used for several items, not all transactions may be reflected in the central accounting records of the governmental unit, and legal or budgetary restrictions may affect the nature of the accounting practiced. These and other subjects are highlighted for accounts comprising assets, liabilities, obligations and encumbrances, fund balances and net worth, revenue and certain expenditure or costs in the following chapters:

Chapter 13, "Assets, Liabilities, and Fund Balances/Net Worth";

Chapter 14, "Revenues and Receipts";

Chapter 15, "Expenditures and Expenses (An Overview)—Part I";

Chapter 16, "Expenditures and Expenses (Personnel, Travel and Transportation)—Part II";

Chapter 17, "Expenditures and Expenses (Contracts, Grants, Interagency or Intragovernmental Transactions)—Part III."

The absence or unique treatment of accruals for certain receivables, inventories, prepaid expenses, depreciation and other types of costs have caused concern among governmental financial personnel and users of governmental financial information and reports. Additionally, expenditures related to items susceptible to personal use have caused establishment of many controls to insure the fiscal integrity of reported amounts. Until lately, compliance with budgetary and other requirements was the principal criterion of governmental accountability. More recently, the use of accounting information for general purpose financial reporting and for managing resources has received increasing emphasis.

Reporting on Governmental Activities

In the private sector, the corporation, although its operations may be dispersed among several subsidiaries and autonomous organizations, is the accounting entity. A single financial report summarizes the financial position and the results of its operations.

The reporting entity differs in the public sector. The legislatively approved budget or appropriation of monies is the accounting entity. A separate set of records or subsidiary accounts is maintained for each fund to provide for the ready identification or earmarking of revenues and expenditures for the purposes outlined in the authorizing law or statute. In some instances, the fund or appropriation may be synonymous with a single agency. In other instances, an agency may be responsible for several funds, each requiring independent accounting and financial statements.

Since the requirements for financial statements differ between the federal and state/local governments, separate chapters have been devoted to the financial reporting of both levels of government:

Chapter 18, "Illustrative Financial Statements (Federal Government Units)," and

Chapter 19, "Illustrative Financial Statements (Local Governmental Units)."

By specific exclusion, the reporting of governmental units does not come within the purview of the Securities and Exchange Commission. However, many governmental units issuing securities to the general public have voluntarily adopted a disclosure-type reporting similar to that provided by publicly held corporations. A suggested content for a disclosure statement relating to the issuance of securities to the public has been published by the Municipal Finance Officers Association. Because of the widespread adoption of many of the suggested items, the publication, *Disclosure Guidelines of*

Offerings of Securities by State and Local Governments, has been included as
Appendix B.

Use of Computers and Electronic Data Processing in Auditing

With few exceptions, the volume of financial detail related to the smallest
governmental entity is often sufficient to require the use of a computer and
some form of automated data processing. The changes in the recording,
processing and reporting of data have been dramatic in the past decade,
affecting private and governmental organizations alike. The impact and need
for examining audit techniques exist in governmental as well as in private
sector auditing.

In 1977, the Institute of Internal Auditors sponsored a comprehensive
research study on data processing audit and control practices. While this
study was directed primarily towards the work of internal auditors, the
concerns expressed over controls and over accuracy of results is no less
applicable to other fields of auditing, including governmental auditing.
Selected excerpts of the findings of this study appear in Chapter 20. One
summary observation of the study is that, while an increasing number of
auditors are using the computer, many are still auditing around the computer.

Part I
The Governmental Financial Process

The Governmental Budget Process

The Federal Government Accounting Process

The State and Local Government Accounting Process

Chapter 2
The Governmental Budget Process

Budget Period
Budget Cycle
Governmental Planning and Budget Control Concepts

An understanding of the budget process is basic to the performance of governmental audits. In governmental finance, the budget is viewed simultaneously as the listing of priority activities of the government, the plan for managing the government over a specified period of time and the financial authority for which there must be an accounting. The budget is significant in governmental finance to a far greater extent than in corporate accounting. Budgetary accounting controls have been incorporated as generally accepted accounting procedures by agencies at all levels of government. Similarly, fund accounting, the basis for much confusion and difficulty in understanding governmental financial management, is a direct result of legally mandated budgetary restraints and requirements for specific fiscal accountability.

The budget, once approved by the legislative branch and accepted by the chief executive officer, establishes the operating criteria for the governmental agencies and activities and provides the legal authority to collect revenues and make expenditures.

An evaluation of existing budgetary controls is a concept of auditing unique to governmental units. At all levels of government, the requirements of law related to the budgeting of funds (for revenue collections and disbursements) have special audit and reporting significance. The deviation from budgetary limitations or requirements may constitute statutory violations, for which there must be a reporting and accounting of the reasons for the variances.

Budget Period

The budget period is frequently a fiscal year, although biennial budget periods are common. At any level of government, though, officials are concerned with three budgetary periods:

The *budget period*—the next fiscal period for which the budget is being considered by the legislative body;

The *current fiscal period*—the fiscal period that will end with the implementation of the budget under review; and

The *budget period, plus one*—the fiscal period beyond the budget period for which preliminary plans are being developed by the executive agencies and officials.

Except for the smaller governmental units, possibly those with populations of less than 100,000, the executive involvement in the budget process is continuous. However, the legislative or budget review period varies, depending upon the laws of the governmental unit. At the federal level, there is an annual budget review and the approval period has been practically a full-time effort for the Congress for many years. In contrast, the budget periods within the states vary. In some instances, the budget is prepared for a single year; in other cases, the budget is a biennial financial plan. Typically, the review and approval phase at the state level is a part-time activity of the legislative branch. The local government legislatures, elected council or supervisors may be in session monthly for the greater part of the year, with the approval of the governmental budget occupying a designated time period—often a few months.

Budget Cycle

At each level of government, laws, statutes and regulations prohibit raising of revenues or making of expenditures of public funds unless such actions have the express and formal approval of the executive and legislative branches of government. With the possible exception of smaller governmental units, the chief executive officer (elected or appointed) generally is the initiating force in the development and submission of the budget. The legislative branch evaluates the financial plan and proposed activities, modifies the proposed budget and approves a program of revenue raising and expenditure for the executive branch.

Throughout this chapter, the following definitions have been adopted to avoid redundant explanations:

> *Chief executive officer*—the senior elected official or appointed executive head of the government (the President, a governor, mayor, county executive, city manager)
>
> *Executive agencies*—the agencies, departments, authorities, or other activities of the government charged with conducting operations and programs in accordance with the approved budget
>
> *Legislative branch*—elected or appointed officials charged with law or rule-making authority, who have the authority and responsibility to review and approve the budget of the governmental unit (Senators, Congressmen, Councilmembers, Supervisors, and others).

Each of these levels of government plays a critical role in the development and execution of a governmental budget. At all levels of government, the several phases of the budget process are similar. Exhibit 2-1 illustrates the several phases of governmental budget development that are described in the following several paragraphs.

Exhibit 2-1

Phases of Governmental Budget Process

Phases of Budget Process	Action Parties
• *Budget Call*—establishing initial goals and objectives	• Central Budget Office, usually with direction from Chief Executive Officer
• *Budget Formulation and Development*—preparing plans of activities, programs	• Executive agencies, with consultation from Central Budget Office
• *Executive Review, Approval and Submission to Legislative Branch*—development of final budget priorities	• Chief Executive Officer, with assistance of Central Budget Office
• *Legislative Review and Approval*—including revisions to proposed executive budget	• Legislative Branch
• *Budget Execution and Monitoring of Operating Plans*	• Chief Executive Officer and executive agencies
• *Review, Evaluation and Audit*	• Executive agencies and Legislative Branch

The Budget Call

The commencement of the budget formulation process generally takes the form of a budget call issued by the chief executive officer. The purpose of the budget call is to establish, on a preliminary basis, the operating criteria for the forthcoming budget period. Goals and objectives might be cited for the executive agencies. Limits on taxes and expenditures often will be described in the budget call guidelines.

The executive agencies are expected to respond by developing an operating plan that is consistent with existing or proposed legislation and with the expressed direction of the chief executive officer. Increasingly, executive agencies are requested to identify long-range goals, and to describe the short-range objectives required to achieve the goals, in their budget proposals.

This phase of the budget cycle generally requires meetings and discussions between the chief executive, agency heads and the central budget office. Because numerous key decisions and strategies must be examined, the effectiveness of programs reviewed and adjustments planned for agency operations, this phase of the budget generally begins a year or more in advance of submission of the budget to the legislative branch.

Budget Formulation and Development

In this phase, the executive agencies are concerned with obtaining the opinions of management and staff with respect to the financial and operating aspects of existing programs and to the impact of any new program initiatives proposed by the chief executive officer. During this phase, agencies often have the opportunity to propose program changes and alternatives to the chief executive officer.

Once agreement is reached between the agency heads and the chief executive officer, the mechanical steps of budget preparation begin. Many governmental units have developed budget manuals describing the procedures and forms required for the formalization of the written budget document. Consistency of forms among the several agencies and the government as a whole assists the executive branch in the final development efforts. Uniform budget presentations also considerably assist the legislative branch in its review process.

While not universal, the developed budget often relates to a single fiscal period, although two-year budgets are common. Governments do prepare projections or plans for three to five years into the future, however. This latter requirement provides a perspective on the impact of a proposed program and some indication of the government's ability to support the contemplated program as well as existing activities.

Executive Review, Approval and Submission to the Legislative Branch

During this phase, the executive branch should make a final assessment of the costs of past activities, evaluate the rate of current revenue collections and expenditures made and compare the level of projected activity to the overall guidance provided by the chief executive officer.

As the required budget submission date nears, budget priorities are crystalized. Earlier projections are reexamined, existing programs are evaluated, proposed activities are reviewed. The economy and business outlook are closely monitored for indicators that might be supportive, possibly even disruptive, of the budget being formulated. Tentative limits are established for receipts or revenue levels and expenditures or disbursements.

As the budget document develops, there is considerable interchange between the chief executive officer and the legislative branch as well as among the public and news media. It must be remembered that, while the budget is a formal operating plan, it is above all a political document. The submission and publication at most levels of government, takes the form of both an oral and a written presentation. This submission is often made to the public, as well as to the legislature, by the chief executive officer. Many governmental units adhere to a practice of publishing the proposed budget in the news media for the benefit of the general public.

With the passage of the Congressional Budget Act of 1974, the federal government established a new fiscal year, which begins on October 1 of each year. (Earlier fiscal years had begun on July 1.) A new Congressional Budget Office was established by the Act to provide assistance to the legislature in much the same manner as the federal Office of Management and Budget does to the President; and a two-phased budget submission procedure was initiated. Exhibit 2-2 summarizes the steps in the new federal budget cycle. Note that the President now must submit, by November 15, the current services budget for the federal government. The full budget, including the current services portion, is due to the Congress by the fifteenth day after Congress convenes. A similar, but less detailed, schedule of budget activity dates usually exists for governmental units at the other levels of government.

Exhibit 2-2

The Federal Budget Cycle

Budget Preparation Steps	Timing
• Executive agencies commence activities for budget	16-18 months before start of budget year
• President transmits current service budget	By November 15
• President transmits budget to Congress	By 15th day after Congress convenes
• Congressional Committees submit reports to budget committees	By March 15
• Congressional Budget Office reports to budget committees	By April 1
• Budget committees report first concurrent resolution on budget to their Houses	By April 15
• Committees report bills authorizing new budget authority	By May 15
• Congress adopts first concurrent resolution on budget	By May 15
• Congress completes actions on bills providing budget authority	By 7th day after Labor Day
• Congress completes actions on second cucurent resolution on budget	By September 15
• Congress completes action on reconciliation bill or resolution, implementing second concurrent resolution	By September 25
• Government's fiscal year begins	October 1

Source: *The United States Budget in Brief, Fiscal Year 1978,* Executive Office of the President, Office of Management and Budget.

Legislative Review and Approval

The role of the legislature in the budget process at the federal level is guaranteed by the Constitution, which states:

> No Money shall be drawn from the Treasury, but in Consequence of Appropriations made by Law; . . . [Article 1, Section 9]

An appropriation, at the federal level, is an authorization by an act of Congress to incur obligations and to make payments out of the Treasury for specified purposes. The authorization of an appropriation is not the authority to incur obligations or make payments. The Congress requires passage of a specific act, an appropriation act, which declares the amount, duration and purposes for which revenues may be raised or expenditures or obligations incurred.

While the legislative review and approval period at the state and local levels of government will vary and, generally, be considerably shorter than the time provided to the federal Congress, the steps performed in the budget approval process and the enactment of appropriation legislation are similar, often consisting of:

A defense of the submitted budget before the legislature by executive branch officials;

Hearings, attended by agency representatives, citizens and organizations having an interest in the budget, and members of the general public;

Production of special analyses and independent reviews of particular aspects, programs or other activities in the proposed budget;

Private or executive sessions on the scope and content of the budget;

Proposals for alternative programs, revenue measures, expenditure limitations, ceilings etc., and possible modification of the budget under consideration;

Development of a legislative package consisting of a single budget bill or several authorization and appropriation bills, ultimately totalling the legislature's consensus of the budget; and

Adoption of the budget through the formal enactment of appropriation ordinances or legislation.

With the possible exception of a manager-type executive form of local government, the final phase in the budget approval process is the submission of the enacted budget to the chief executive for approval and execution.

Budget Execution and Monitoring of Operating Plan

Once approved by both the legislature and the chief executive, the formal budget is viewed by governmental agencies as the operating plan for the next fiscal period.

The executive branch is primarily responsible for the conduct of governmental operations in compliance with the enacted budget. At all levels of government, agency operations may exist that are outside of the direct control of the executive branch but these are also expected to conform to governmental budget requirements. Reference is made here to operations of independent commissions, government corporations, authorities and, possibly, some agencies existing in the legislative branch.

The responsibilities of the agency head, with respect to the execution and monitoring of the budget, will include:

Raising revenues and incurring obligations or encumbering funds pursuant to the enacted appropriation ordinance or law;

Monitoring receipts and expenditures to insure compliance with budget legislation;

Reporting periodically on a comparison of actual to budgeted revenues and expenditures;

Providing for a system of allocating and allotting the appropriated budget for achievement of a designated purpose, program or activity within the specified time period;

Establishing and adhering to agency-level procedures and controls to insure that activities are supportive of legislated goals and objectives; and

Installing and maintaining those systems of internal controls, accounting and information to monitor agency performance and the degree of achievement of legislated programs' goals.

While there is a similarity to the budget preparation and approval process and to the terminology (e.g. appropriations, allocations, allotments) used in preparation and approval, there are differences. Literature does exist on the details of the budget formulation, approval and execution process, which should be examined prior to commencing a governmental audit. At the federal level, considerable insight about the federal budget process and related procedures appears in the following documents:

Office of Management and Budget Circular, A-11, *Preparation and Submission of Annual Budget Estimates*

Office of Management and Budget Circular, A-34, *Instructions Relating to Apportionments and Reports on Budget Status*

In many respects, the centralized operations of state governments parallel the federal government. Local government operations vary considerably, however, making it difficult to generalize. An authoritative publication on local government budget processes and procedures is the publication titled, *A Manual of Techniques for the Preparation, Consideration, Adoption, and Administration of Operating Budgets,* by Lennox L. Moak and Kathryn W. Killian, (Municipal Finance Officers Association, Chicago, Illinois, 1974, Fifth Printing).

Review, Evaluation, and Audit

Review, evaluation and audit are the final steps in the budget cycle. In governmental accounting, the budget or fund is a legal criteria for which there must be an accounting. The failure to comply with a legally authorized budget is a reportable event. Additionally, once enacted, the budget becomes the operating plan for the several governmental units.

Reviews and evaluations can be made in the form of special studies or analyses. Some governmental units have enacted legislation that requires management evaluations or performance audits of agency operations. Most governmental units must comply with legislation or statutory requirements that financial and compliance audits periodically be made. Additionally, the central budget office and the planning and analyses staffs generally are responsible for conducting continual reviews of the agency or department progress in meeting the objectives and complying with the financial criteria outlined in the budget.

Federal and state agencies and departments generally have staffs who perform audits of appropriated funds and monitor the compliance with statutory budget requirements. The General Accounting Office, an agency in the federal legislative branch, conducts audits of federal executive agencies and federally supported programs administered by other levels of government. The GAO reports directly to the Congress, although copies of the reports also are sent to the head of the audited agency, the Office of Management and Budget and the President. In a somewhat similar structure, several states have state auditors or auditor generals (who may be appointed or elected), who serve a similar independent audit function. Like their federal counterparts, state agencies and departments may have their own audit staffs who are concerned with conducting periodic audits of the legally appropriated funds for which the agency is responsible.

At the local government level, the auditor could be employed by either the executive or legislative branch. Most of the local government auditors appear to be appointive or to hold office under civil service. A larger city might have both a legislative and an internal auditor, the legislative auditor considered to have the more independent reporting role. Often the audit reports, regardless of the employing branch of government, are distributed to both branches.

Governmental Planning and Budget Control Concepts

In the commercial sector, profitability provides a rather clear criterion for performance. Efficiency, in a relative sense, can be measured by the size of return on investment. Possibly due to the lack of such a measurement, governments have resorted to other measures to assess economy, efficiency and effectiveness. Lacking the profit criterion, governments have borrowed various other planning and budget control concepts from industry.

The government auditor will encounter repeated references and adherence to processes such as planning, programming and budgeting systems (PPBS), management by objectives (MBO), zero based budgeting (ZBB) and performance budgeting. Each approach to planning and monitoring the resources of government serve a slightly different purpose. While the applications will not be uniform, modified versions of these processes are being used in the governmental sector.

Planning, Programming, and Budgeting Systems

The three-phased planning, programming, budgeting system (PPBS) was introduced into the civilian agencies of the executive branch of the federal government by the President in 1965. The concept had been used earlier in the Department of Defense. In summary, the phases consisted of:

Planning, or the study of agency objectives and alternatives to achieve objectives, to plan for future environments and to assess contingencies;

Programming, or the method of describing activities according to objectives and outputs and of relating these to the costs or inputs needed to produce the outputs or levels of achievement or effectiveness desired; and

Budgeting, or the activity through which funds are requested of the President and Congress, or appropriated, apportioned or accounted for.

As designed, PPBS was to be an integrated system of processes utilized by the head of an agency for decision-making and for more efficiently and effectively managing an agency's programs and operations. The several major processes that generally comprised the PPBS approach are outlined in Exhibit 2-3. PPBS, while continuous in its operation, generally is seen as a cyclical activity coinciding with the budget cycle. PPBS is a time-phased scheduling of agency funding and resources with specific events and activities, including the development of studies, evaluations and strategies. Exhibit 2-4 illustrates the generalized decision or data flow processes that an agency's PPBS might require and shows the relative relationship to the governmental budget cycle.

While desired, the implementation of PPBS was not uniform throughout the federal government. The concept did provide more structure and promoted more analyses and review of resource commitments and expenditures in relation to achievement. Adherence to PPBS was not required after 1971. Since many governmental programs were not susceptible to cost/benefit analyses and the consideration of the full range of viable alternatives, the ultimate objective of PPBS was not attainable in the governmental sector. PPBS, though, provided for increased quality of program evaluation, required the development of more refined information systems and resulted in perfecting the procedures for planning, executing, administering and monitoring agency budgets and programs. Some states and local governments adopted parts or modified versions of PPBS as integral parts of the budgetary process.

Exhibit 2-3

Processes of Planning, Programming, Budgeting Systems

Process	Activity
Planning Process	• Established agency program objectives and broad requirements to achieve objectives within specified time period
Programming Process	• Established programs consisting of time-phased action schedules and estimated funding and staff resources to achieve objectives
Budgeting Process	• Established detailed projections of funds for programs, obtains and allocates funds, balances priorities among competing resources
Program Operating Process	• System by which authorized funds and resources were spent to achieve program objectives
Progress Reporting Process	• Financial and non-financial information on status and results of program operations transmitted to appropriate levels of agency management
Program Change Process	• System and procedures by which changes were introduced to multi-year programs, financial plans, and operating plans
Evaluation Process	• Systematic reviews and examinations of accomplishments by program operations

Source: Planning, Programming, Budgeting System (PPBS), Office of Economic Opportunity, 1968.

Exhibit 2-4

Planning, Programming, Budgeting System Decision Process and Data Flow

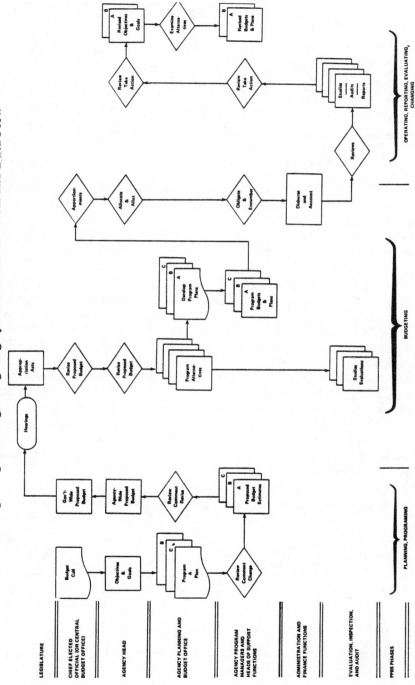

Source: Summary of flow charts of Planning, Programming, Budgeting System, Office of Economic Opportunity, 1968, Washington, D.C.

Management by Objectives

Management by objectives is a system of planning and monitoring that concentrates resources of an organization on the achievement of specific, defined objectives.

In the early 1970s, the federal government, through the Office of Management and Budget, placed emphasis on the development and utilization of management by objectives. The MBO concept was intended to be integrated into the agency's planning, budgeting and monitoring process. Agencies were required to establish or clearly describe program and activities goals and objectives to be achieved within specified time periods. Information and other tracking systems were to be established to monitor performance and permit the assessment of achievement. Unlike PPBS, no detailed reporting systems, categorization of activities and functions, or detailed accounting of program changes was required for MBO.

In theory, the sum of individual and organization MBO efforts form an integrated whole, most likely to optimize the total achievement of agency. In practice, MBO requires a process of management conferences—between the individual and superiors, between subordinate activities and higher organizations, between program managers and the head of the agency. Each subordinate element must identify objectives and major areas of responsibility for achieving agency objectives. Criteria for assessing achievement and monitoring success must be selected, and information must be accumulated, periodically. Wherever possible, objectives must be described in quantifiable terms, capable of being measured. Specific periods for accomplishment must be set at the beginning of the program to permit the determination of progress towards the defined objectives. The objectives that emerge must possess certain critical characteristics:

The objectives must be specific to provide a clear statement of what is to be accomplished—when it will be accomplished—who will accomplish it;

The objectives must be measurable to permit quantitative assessment of accomplishment; and

The objectives must be attainable to provide an atmosphere of success, within realistic standards and within the timeframe designated.

A summary of the MBO process is outlined in Exhibit 2-5.

Exhibit 2-5

Management by Objectives Process

Process	Considerations
Define organization goals and performance measures	Generally set forth in policy statements.
Objective-setting meetings	Between organizations, supervisors and employees to insure mutual agreement on objectives, performance measures, period for achievement.
Feedback on performance against established milestones	Based upon acceptable management information system; not directed towards punitive aspects; permits corrective actions and reaction to variances on current basis.
Revision of objectives	Permits the achievement of alternatives; flexibility to take corrective actions; modification of activities to be measured.
Periodic reviews of results against targeted objectives	Typically done quarterly or more frequently, supervisors must meet with employees; permits adjustments in objectives and resource allocations to optimize performance of individual and organization within the specified time period.
Overall review of organizational performance and related to initial step in process for next planning period	Usually done annually to evaluate completed year and provide inputs for development of appropriate goals and objectives for next year. Review concentrates on the achievement of overall organization.

As is evident, MBO may be applied on an exception basis and not only to the entire organization. An MBO program might be developed for those functions, activities or groupings of staff that have consistently performed in a less than adequate manner or that consistently have lower productivity averages than others. The goals and objectives may be designed to fit the problem. Performance can be measured with respect to limited goals or objectives.

Zero Based Budgeting

Another management concept relating to the accomplishment of plans within finite resources is zero based budgeting. This concept had its genesis in the commercial sector.

ZBB is a planning and budgeting concept that requires resource allocation decisions to begin at the zero level of expenditures. Periodically, under this concept, an organization's budget base must be reexamined and rejustified. The concept requires justification of all expenditures, establishment of quantifiable measures of service and determination of the effectiveness of the activity.

ZBB provides several advantages over the conventional incremental-type budgeting process, in which the past dollar bases are seldom examined. For example, ZBB:

Provides a systematic and uniform method for reviewing and evaluating existing and proposed activities of an organization;

Allows for budget revisions in a planned and systematic manner;

Identifies areas of overlap and duplication;

Increases involvement of officials in planning and priority-setting phases of public management;

Develops more complete information for executive and legislative budget decision makers;

Establishes a formal basis for other improved administration techniques such as MBO, program accountability, PPBS; and

Provides a method for allocating finite resources to the almost infinite program needs of governmental units.

The preparation of a zero based budget entails several steps:

Definition of decision units to lay the foundation for zero based budgeting. A review is made of the organization's accounting and information systems, identifying levels of responsibility and accountability.

Development of decision packages at the lowest level of accountability. A decision package is prepared for each organizational decision unit, often similar to a cost center.

Establishment of priorities and alternatives, including various levels of funding and activity.

Preparation of a detailed budget based upon the priority rankings and anticipated resources.

Basic to the implementation of zero based budgeting is the preparation of decision packages for each decision unit. The *decision package* is a description of the level of effort anticipated within a decision unit in the organization. Generally, budgets are prepared for alternative levels of effort by the unit. The terms "minimum level," "base level" and "expanded level" may be used (other levels of activity may be forecast, though):

Minimum level—lowest level that can be funded and still be economically feasible to continue the decision unit. At this level the decision is one of minimal funding or a no funding, zero level.

Base level—a similar level of effort as the prior year, unless budget is for a new unit. This level is generally the prior year's budget, plus inflationary and cost-of-living type adjustments. This is considered to be an additive package or budget; the minimum level must be funded before the base level can be considered.

Expanded level—an increased level, additive to the base level, that must be funded. Several expanded levels might be identified and decision packages developed for each.

The decision packages, once developed, then are ranked in priority order and funded to the levels possible within the resources available to the unit. Exhibit 2-6 illustrates the hierarchal process of arraying decision packages for various levels of a governmental organization.

As with MBO, zero based budgeting may be used for analyzing specific programs as well as all programs of any agency. The concept is suited to implementation by exception. Specific organizational units can be subjected to ZBB analyses for purposes of assessing the economic viability of alternative funding levels for a single organization.

Performance Budgeting

Performance budgeting is a practice that may be in a renaissance of sorts. Within the past few years, all levels of government have shown a renewed interest in quantitative analyses of activities, functions, and programs of government. Numerous governmental units have conducted work resource management studies in an attempt to determine the economy and efficiency of performance or output, particularly in relation to a specified or finite level of input resources.

This concept probably first attracted the widespread attention of governmental executives as a recommendation of the Hoover Commission on Budgeting and Accounting (i.e. the second Hoover Commission, created in July 1947, expired in June 1949). To improve the federal government's budget

Exhibit 2-6

Hierarchal Process for Development of a Zero Base Budget

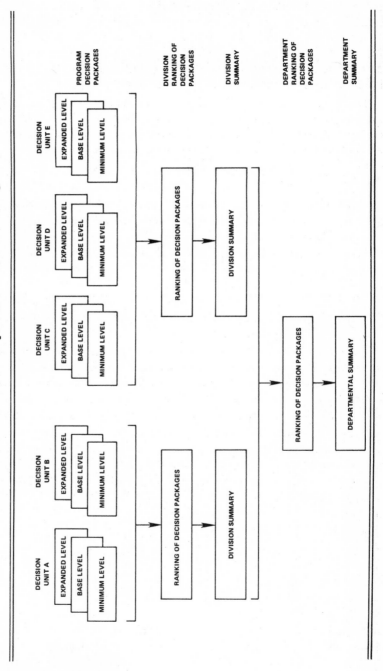

process, the Commission recommended the use of performance budgeting, placing greater emphasis on the services to be rendered rather than on items (i.e., personnel, supplies, materials, equipment) purchased with federal monies. The objective of this recommendation was to develop a budget based on functions, activities and projects to be performed and to provide historical information on performance and on what these services cost.

The general methodology for development of a performance budgeting system contains several of the essentials of PPBS, MBO, and ZBB, discussed earlier. For example, the following objectives or criteria must be established and adhered to when implementing a performance budget:

Functions, activities, and projects must be defined and management responsibilities fixed to a minimal number of organizations.

Quantifiable goals and objectives and performance criteria must be established, to the extent possible. Care must be used to establish the most meaningful work units possible.

Budget estimates must be directly identifiable with the work units. The sum of information for several work units will provide the budget of the larger organization, function or activity.

An effective and continuous program of evaluation must be supported to provide timely and relevant performance conclusions to management.

The accounting system and information or statistical reporting system should be supported, with the cost and quantitative data accumulated and reported by the performance budget items.

The work measurement, closely approximating industrial engineering techniques in application, and the detailed cost accounting requirements probably hindered the earlier applications of performance budgeting in government. However, it is precisely the questions that this type of information could answer—What was the estimate? What was the cost? What did one get?—that governments and the public are asking anew. For this reason, variants of performance budgeting may be encountered at all levels of government over the next several years as resources become increasingly limited and trade-offs of governmental services must be made.

Chapter 3
The Federal Government Accounting Process

Although the principal accounting concept at the federal level is referred to as fund accounting, the concept's definition of funds, its budgetary accounting procedures and its required costing practices vary from the fund accounting requirements generally used by state and local government agencies. The accounting practices of state and local governments are reviewed in the following chapter.

At the federal government level the responsibilities for prescribing, establishing and maintaining a system of accounting are split between the United States General Accounting Office and the individual federal agencies and departments. To a limited degree, requirements also are imposed by the Office of Management and Budget and the United States Department of the Treasury. But, by law, the General Accounting Office is responsible for

28

prescribing the required accounting principles and practices and for reviewing the accounting systems of the federal agencies. Legislation also requires that the individual agency and department heads establish and maintain an accounting system that will meet the requirements of the General Accounting Office and comply with the requirements of Congress as set forth in the agency's authorization or appropriation legislation.

A distinguishing aspect of governmental accounting, as compared to corporate-type accounting, is the reliance on fund accounting concepts and on the integration of budget-related journal entries with historical accounting transactions.

Legislative Requirement for Federal Accounting

The legislative requirements for establishing and maintaining systems of accounting within the federal government were broadly established by two acts: the Budget and Accounting Act of 1921 and the Budget and Accounting Procedures Act of 1950. By these laws, the Comptroller General (the head of the General Accounting Office) was required to prescribe: (1) the forms, systems and procedures for the administrative appropriation and fund accounting in various departments and establishments; and (2) the principles, standards and related requirements of accounting to be observed by federal agencies, including the integration of accounting between the executive agencies and the Treasury Department.

By the Act of 1950, the head of each agency or department was required to maintain the system of accounts, in accordance with the principles and standards published by the General Accounting Office, on an accrual basis to show the resources, liabilities and costs of operations.

Accounting Principles, Objectives and Standards

Accounting Principles

The requirements for accounting by federal agencies and departments have been published by the Comptroller General and have been revised over the years. The latest version, *Accounting Principles and Standards for Federal Agencies,* was issued by the General Accounting Office in August 1972. (Changes were made to this edition. These principles and standards were published, in pamphlet form and for insertion in the *GAO Manual for the Guidance of Federal Agencies,* in 1978.)

Objectives of Federal Accounting Systems

The objectives of federal agency accounting, as set forth in the published principles and in the Budget and Accounting Procedures Act of 1950, require that a financial system provide:

Full disclosure of the financial results of the agency;

Production of adequate financial information for management purposes;

Effective control of funds, property and other assets of the agency;

Reliable accounting results as a basis for preparing and supporting budget requests, controlling budget expenditures and providing financial information required by the Office of Management and Budget; and

Suitable integration of agency accounting with the central accounting and reporting activities of the Treasury Department.

While the General Accounting Office is responsible for reviewing and approving the accounting systems, the individual agencies and departments design and implement the specific procedures and practices required to comply with these general objectives and the legal requirements that might appear in legislation relating to specific Congressional appropriations.

Accounting Standards

The General Accounting Office has recognized that no single set of principles or standards will meet all of the circumstances of the numerous agencies. However, the accounting systems of federal agencies and departments must be consistent with the following general standards prescribed by the General Accounting Office:

The agency must comply with all laws relating to the accounting and administration of funds and appropriations for which it is responsible;

The accounting system must be designed to provide for (1) internal cost and other financial data needs, (2) results of performance of organizational segments, budget activities and program structures, and (3) external requirements of Congress, the President, the Office of Management and Budget and the Treasury Department;

The accounting system must conform, in all material respects, to the principles, standards and related requirements prescribed by the Comptroller General;

The data produced by the accounting system must be useful to officials for planning and controlling resources and promoting greater efficiency and economy in operations;

The structure of the accounting system must be designed to permit major assignments of responsibility or areas of activity to be readily reported on;

To the extent possible, the planning, programming, budgeting and accounting classifications must be consistent and relatable to the agency's organizational structure;

The accounting system must comprise the formal books and accounts, supporting records, documents, papers, reports and related procedures used to account for an agency's resources and operations;

The design, implementation and maintenance of the accounting systems must be in the hands of competent leadership and capable staff;

The highest standards of truthfulness and honesty must be applied in accounting for the receipt, disbursement and application of public funds;

The accounting system must be simple and readily understandable, and undue precision must not be required where estimates and judgements are a significant factor;

The accounting system must be reviewed from time to time to assure the continued utility of the system to users.

The agency accounting system must be designed to demonstrate compliance with all applicable laws to the maximum extent practicable. Under the federal standards, the agency system must account for all funds, property, assets, liabilities, obligations, receipts and revenues, expenditures, disbursements and costs. Transactions must be traceable from the originating document to summary records and financial reports.

The above standards do not require compliance with a single, uniform system of accounting. Aside from the central accounts of receipts and disbursements maintained by the Treasury Department, no government-wide system exists at the federal level.

Bases for Federal Governmental Accounting

The predominant type of accounting at the federal government level is *fund accounting.* At the federal level, fund accounting has a different connotation than at the local government level. The usage of the term at the state level more closely parallels the federal definition.

Fund Accounting

In federal accounting, the appropriation or fund approved by the Congress is the accounting entity. The appropriation is the Congressional authority to spend and must be accounted for and controlled from the enactment to the expiration of the legislation. An individual agency may, concurrently, be authorized and responsible for the control and expenditure of funds under several appropriations. Activities must be reported by the specific legislation. The sum of the several appropriations constitutes the total resources of that agency or department.

As shown in Exhibit 3-1, federal agencies may be responsible for funds derived from two sources: (1) the general taxing and revenue powers of the government or the business operations of agencies and (2) in capacities as custodian or trustee. For each of the identified funds, the Congress must pass legislation giving an agency the authority to receive or expend funds or enter into obligations on behalf of the government that will be honored by later acts of Congress.

Exhibit 3-1

Fund Structure of Federal Government

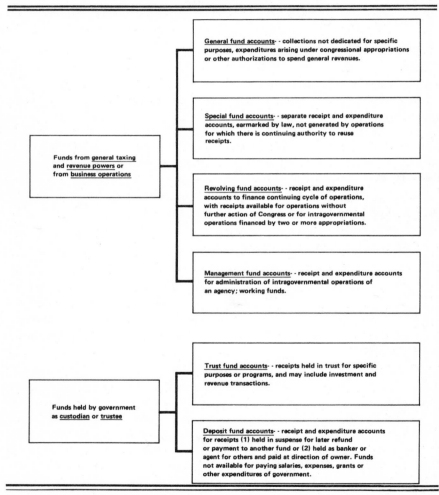

Funds from general taxing and revenue powers or from business operations

General fund accounts- - collections not dedicated for specific purposes, expenditures arising under congressional appropriations or other authorizations to spend general revenues.

Special fund accounts- - separate receipt and expenditure accounts, earmarked by law, not generated by operations for which there is continuing authority to reuse receipts.

Revolving fund accounts- - receipt and expenditure accounts to finance continuing cycle of operations, with receipts available for operations without further action of Congress or for intragovernmental operations financed by two or more appropriations.

Management fund accounts- - receipt and expenditure accounts for administration of intragovernmental operations of an agency; working funds.

Funds held by government as custodian or trustee

Trust fund accounts- - receipts held in trust for specific purposes or programs, and may include investment and revenue transactions.

Deposit fund accounts- - receipt and expenditure accounts for receipts (1) held in suspense for later refund or payment to another fund or (2) held as banker or agent for others and paid at direction of owner. Funds not available for paying salaries, expenses, grants or other expenditures of government.

Source: *Accounting Principles and Standards for Federal Agencies,* Comptroller General of the United States, Revised 1972.

The requirement to account for federal monies by appropriations is recognized in the Constitution. Article I of the Constitution states that no money shall be drawn from the Treasury, except "... in consequence of appropriations made by law." Federal agencies are guided by the provisions of the Anti-Deficiency Act, which prohibits the incurrence of obligations at a rate that will result in an appropriation deficiency later in the year. This Act also provides that no officer or employee of the federal government shall make or authorize an expenditure or incur an obligation under any appropriation in excess of the amount approved by the Congress. Knowing and willful violations are punishable by fine, imprisonment or both.

Additionally, many of the appropriation acts of the Congress have specific requirements and limitations that must be accounted for and controlled.

Accrual Accounting

The prescribed basis of accounting by federal agencies is the accrual basis. "Accrual accounting" is the recording of financial transactions in the accounts as the transactions occur—as goods and services are purchased or used or as revenues are earned—even though cash may be received or paid at other dates. Other refinements, however, are used in federal accrual accounting. For example, by GAO's definition, a transaction may be recorded over a period of time as an accrued expenditure or an applied cost.

An "accrued expenditure" is the liability incurred for goods or services that have been ordered and received.

An "applied cost" is the amount of goods or services, used or consumed by agency activity or operations, often referred to as accrued costs.

Budgetary Accounting

A concept of budgetary accounting exists within the federal government. The accounting is similar to the encumbrance procedures common in state and local governmental accounting.

The term "obligation" has both an accounting and a legal definition in federal financial management. From an accounting view, an obligation is a reservation or restriction of a previously unobligated appropriation balance. Unless the obligation is liquidated or reversed, these same funds cannot be later authorized for another expenditure. From a legal view, as explained later, the term obligation refers to the specific documentation that must exist before the federal agency may authorize or disburse funds to pay a liability or debt of the agency.

The accounting system of each federal agency provides for the recording of entries for obligations and commitments of the agency. These entries are integrated into the accounting procedures and process and often are referred to as budgetary accounts and transactions.

Accounting for Federal Appropriations

As mentioned earlier, a federal agency must comply with the laws relating to the administration of funds and appropriations for which it is responsible. The accounting system must reflect whether the agency adhered to the legal requirements to the maximum extent possible.

Appropriation Defined

In federal financial management, an "appropriation" is defined by the GAO as:

> An authorization by an act of the Congress to incur obligations and to make payments out of the Treasury for specified purposes.

It should be noted that the authorization by Congress *does not* authorize an agency to incur obligations or make payments. Historically, the Congress passed authorizing legislation for numerous programs, which were not supported by the passage of a related appropriation act. Thus, no monies were made available for expenditure.

The appropriation act generally will specify (1) the purpose for which funds are appropriated, (2) the amount of money authorized for expenditure and (3) the time period for which the obligation or expenditure authority is valid. An agency does not have the administrative discretion to incur obligations or make payments of public funds in a manner or for a purpose or period that is contrary to the provisions of the appropriation act.

Types of Appropriations

Exhibit 3-2 lists several types of appropriations. While the listed terms or descriptors are in general use, the titles are not necessarily uniformly applied throughout the federal government. Further, the appropriation descriptors are not mutually exclusive.

Exhibit 3-2

Types of Appropriations and Other Federal Obligational Authority

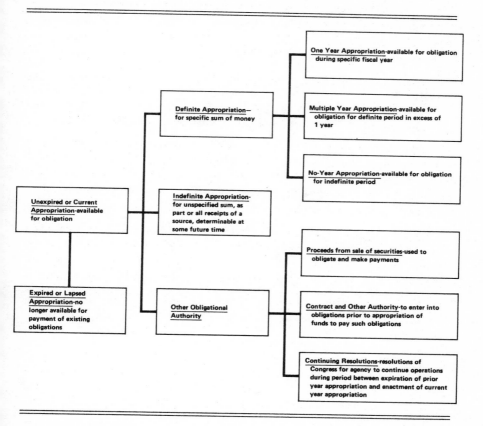

Source: *Standardized Fiscal Procedures*, GAO Manual for Guidance of Federal Agencies, Title 7, pages 7-8 to 7-10, 1967.

The *unexpired or current* appropriation is an authorization to the agency to incur obligations or make payments. An appropriation remains current or active or valid until accomplishment of its intended purpose, expenditure of the authorized money or passage of the specified period of time. After that, the appropriation is described as an expired or lapsed appropriation.

An *expired or lapsed appropriation,* while no longer available for obligation, may be available to the agency to pay for obligations incurred prior to the expiration of the authorized time period.

A *definite* appropriation is one for which Congress has specified a certain amount of funding; the duration of the appropriation can be for varying time periods. Typically, the federal agency receives a definite appropriation to support its staff and operating programs.

In contrast, an *indefinite* appropriation would not be authorized for a specified funding level. The authorized funding level would be dependent upon the level of receipts or the funds to be provided from a source designated by the Congress.

There have been other forms of *obligational authority* passed by the Congress. For example, an agency may receive the authority to sell securities and use the proceeds for support of staff expenses and program operations.

Similarly, an agency may be authorized by Congress to enter into contracts to accomplish a particular purpose. This contract authority, the amount of all legally executed contracts, then becomes the amount of the appropriation that subsequently must be authorized by the Congress.

Federal agencies, on occasion, will not receive appropriation authorization prior to the expiration of an earlier appropriation. The temporary, short-term, Congressional authorization to permit the continuance of operations is referred to as a *continuing resolution.* Under the resolution, the federal agency may not undertake any new programs or exceed the rate of expenditures permitted in the expired appropriation. If one of the Houses of Congress has passed an appropriation bill, providing for a lesser obligational authority, the agency must adhere to the rate of expenditure implicit in the lower limit, pending the passage of an appropriation act by the whole Congress.

Appropriation Accounting Requirements

The agency system must be integrated in a manner to permit simultaneous accounting for each appropriation on several bases. The system also must provide an accounting of the total resources and program activities for which an agency is legally responsible. Exhibit 3-3 illustrates, in summary, the groups of accounts that must be maintained.

Exhibit 3-3

Overview of Required Federal Agency Appropriation Accounting

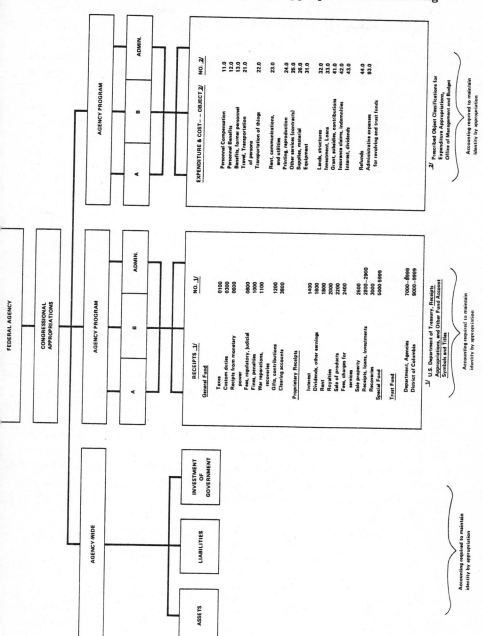

Assets, Liabilities and Investment of Government

The accounting system of a federal agency must be capable of aggregating the dollar value of assets and liabilities and the investment of the government, in total for all appropriations and for individual appropriations. The transaction coding structure must permit the summing of account balances to show the total assets and debt or investment of the government, provided through one or more appropriations and for one or more years. The amounts in these individual general ledger accounts must in turn be traceable to the authorizing appropriation.

Receipts

The Congress will assign the responsibility for the collection of receipts to specified agencies. The funds collected may or may not be available to the collecting agency for its obligation and expenditure. (For example, the Internal Revenue Service, the government's collector of income taxes, is not permitted to enter into obligations or make payments from collected amounts without specific authorization by Congress.)

The following general classification of receipts has been established by the Treasury Department for collecting agencies: general funds receipts, proprietary receipts, special fund receipts and trust funds receipts. Specific agency receipt appropriation account numbers, symbols and titles have been established by the Treasury Department.

Expenditures

Most federal agencies are not involved with or authorized to collect significant funds from the general public. An agency often receives only an expenditure appropriation from the Congress, permitting the agency to incur obligations or make payments for authorized purposes and time periods. The Treasury Department has prescribed a uniform expenditure appropriation numbering system for each agency of the government. The federal agency must maintain detailed accounts to permit the accumulation and reporting of obligations, expenditures and costs for the appropriation by the several object classes prescribed by the Office of Management and Budget. Additionally, these transactions must be segregated by the various programs, activities and functions of the agency.

Federal Accounting Period

The government's fiscal year is from October 1 through September 30. The accounting system for any federal agency concurrently provides financial information for three fiscal years—the current fiscal year and the two immediate past years. Usually, though, only the current year's appropriation is available for new obligation. Records are maintained for the two immediate prior years, but the transactions for these years generally are related to the liquidation of previously incurred obligations.

Once obligated, an agency must account for appropriation expenditures until the obligation has been liquidated or reversed or until the passage of two years after the close of the fiscal year during which the funds were obligated. The accounts for each appropriation are closed by the agency as of the end of the second fiscal year following the fiscal year or years for which the appropriation was available for obligation.

The obligated balance of the appropriation is transferred to a successor or merged ("M") account. The transferred balances then are reported by the federal agency to the Treasury Department. After transfer of the balance to the merged account, the agency appropriations are counted as a single fund; and the fund is now available, without fiscal year limitation, for the payment of properly incurred obligations chargeable against the agency's appropriations.

Federal Financial Process

There are several agencies that utilize the corporate system of accounting, like that used by commercial organizations. This system of accounting is used by such organizations as quasi-government corporations, special authorities and working capital and other business-type operations. However, the predominant financial system of federal agencies is based on fund accounting concepts, with the congressional appropriation or fund being the accounting entity. The appropriation accounting systems are used throughout the executive branch of government to account for funds received and disbursed. These financial activities are recorded in a uniform manner by agencies under a double-entry system of accounting, which concurrently provides budgetary and operating information, generally in accordance with accrual accounting principles.

Exhibit 3-4 illustrates, in summary form, the federal financial process. This exhibit and the following paragraphs provide a general description of the federal appropriation accounting system. In practice, the detailed systems are necessarily complex, since many of the systems account for annual budgets of several billions of dollars.

Exhibit 3-4
Summary of Federal Government Financial Process

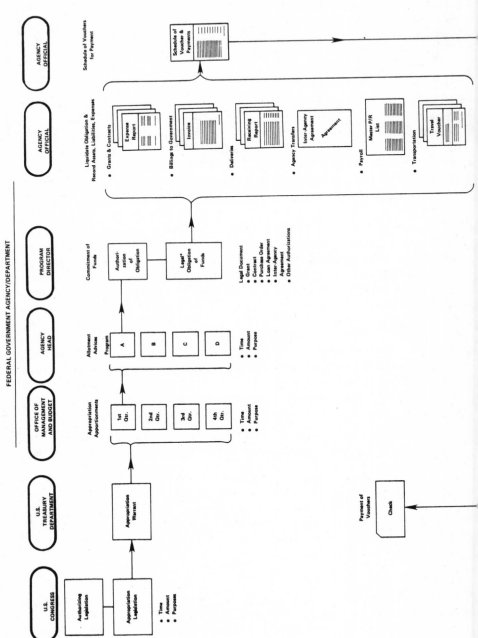

Sources of Agency Funding

As explained earlier, the basic authority of an agency to incur obligations and make payments must be an authorization and appropriation act of the Congress. The appropriation or funding authority of Congress may take several forms.

Revenue Appropriations

Few agencies are authorized to collect significant revenues on behalf of the federal government. The more significant receipt appropriations relate to the Internal Revenue Service and the Bureau of Customs. These collections are considered to be *general fund receipts* collected pursuant to the sovereign taxing and regulatory authority of the federal government. Considerable revenues also are collected by the United States Postal Service.

Unless specific authorization and appropriation legislation is enacted by Congress, these collecting agencies may not use the collected receipts for agency operations.

Several agencies are permitted by the Congress to assess and collect *proprietary receipts.* Such receipts generally result from fees charged the public for rendering of services. Depending upon Congressional action, the receipts could be used to supplement the agency's appropriation or may have to be deposited in the general fund receipts account of the Treasury Department.

Expenditure Appropriations and Other Authorizations

The operations or activities of an agency may be financed by funding received from a variety of sources. In addition to a direct appropriation, an agency may have authority to obtain operating funds by appropriation transfers, allocations or reimbursements, or under a form of contract authority.

Direct Expenditure Appropriation

A direct expenditure appropriation is the more common source of funding for a federal agency's operations. An account is established with the Treasury Department that is available to the agency for incurring and paying obligations. Often the direct appropriation is the only funding source for paying obligations for employees' salaries, expenses, grants, contracts and other authorized activities.

Appropriation Transfers

When authorized by the Congress, an agency will establish an account to receive and later disburse transfers of appropriations from other agencies. The appropriation transfer is treated as a non-expenditure transaction at the time of transfer, and the account will carry the appropriation symbol of the original appropriation. A non-expenditure transaction withdraws amounts available for obligation and expenditure from one appropriation and credits the amounts to another appropriation. (Payments made for goods and services received are not transfers, but are expenditure transactions of the paying agency.)

Allocations of Appropriations

An allocation of an appropriation is an amount set aside by one agency in a separate appropriation or fund account for use by another agency, which has been given a role in carrying out the purposes of the original appropriation. The term "allocation" refers to the amounts set aside in an appropriation transfer account.

Reimbursement of an Appropriation

A reimbursement of an appropriation consists of an amount collected for services or work performed or to be furnished to another appropriation or fund account. The amount may be collected for items as accounts receivable, reimbursements earned, but not billed, and interagency orders. The appropriation reimbursement is distinct from a refund to an agency's appropriation. A refund would represent a recovery of an advance or amount disbursed by the agency in error. Refunds are not included as a reimbursement, but rather as a reduction of the earlier disbursement. Refunds also may include accounting adjustments, where permitted by law.

Contract Authority

The Congress has elected to finance certain government programs under contract authority. With such authority, the agency is authorized to incur obligations by the issuance of contracts or other obligating documents prior to the enactment of an appropriation by the Congress to pay for such obligations. With the exception of the recording of the appropriation, the accounting process of the agency under such authority is similar to other agencies.

Budgetary Accounting in an Agency

Incorporated into the federal appropriation accounting process is a series of budgetary control requirements. The budgetary or fund controls are required by law (the Anti-Deficiency Act) to (1) prevent incurring obligations or making disbursements that would create deficiencies in appropriations or other funding authority, (2) fix responsibility within an agency for excess obligations or disbursements, and (3) assist in more effective and economical use of the appropriated funds. The primary budgetary controls relate to the apportionment procedures of the Office of Management and Budget and the allocation and obligation procedures within the agency.

Apportionments by Office of Management and Budget

Section 3679 of the revised federal statutes provides for the financial apportionment of appropriations, funds and contract authorizations to be made by the Office of Management and Budget. Obligations and expenditures by individual agencies may not be made in excess of such apportionments.

An "apportionment," as defined by the Office of Management and Budget, is a distribution by OMB of the amounts made available by the Congress for obligation and expenditure in an appropriation or fund by (1) amounts, (2) time periods or (3) activities, functions, projects, objects or combinations thereof. Amounts apportioned limit the obligations that may be incurred or the expenditures that may be accrued by the agency.

The apportionments are transmitted in writing by the OMB to the agency. Controls must be established to insure that apportionment ceilings are not violated.

Allotment of Apportioned Funds

To insure that violations of apportionments do not occur, federal agencies have instituted a system of allotting apportioned funds to the programs and activities for which they are responsible.

An "allotment, as defined by the Office of Management and Budget, is an authorization, generally by the head of an agency, to another authorized employee in the agency to incur obligations within a specified amount pursuant to the appropriation or other statutory provisions. Within the agency, this authorization is generally transmitted by forms known as "advices of allotments," which could be formal documents, memoranda or letters. Typically the advices of allotments are issued at the beginning of the fiscal year to program officials.

In some agencies, the allotments are further subdivided into allowances. Allowances are reservations of allotted funds, establishing monetary limits that can not be exceeded without prior approval of higher authority in the agency.

Obligating Alloted Funds

An obligation of alloted funds restricts the appropriated funds from being otherwise committed. The obligation of funds must be consistent with the agency appropriation act, made within the appropriate time periods, and be for an authorized purpose. An obligating action is required in advance of receipt of assets, liabilities incurred, or payments made for expenses.

An "obligation," as defined by the Office of Management and Budget, is an amount for orders placed, contracts awarded, grants issued, services received and similar transactions during a given period that require the disbursement of money. Such amounts include disbursements not preceded by the recording of obligations, and reflect adjustments for differences between obligations and actual disbursements.

The federal Supplemental Appropriation Act of 1955 (Section 1311) sets forth several specific criteria that must be considered before an action of an agency official will constitute a valid obligation of the government. In summary, the required obligating documents would include:

A binding agreement in writing;

A valid loan agreement;

An order placed with a government agency;

An order by an agency, necessitated by public exigency or for perishables;

A grant or subsidy;

A liability that may result from pending litigation;

Employment or services of persons and expenses of travel and public utilities services; and

Other legal liabilities of the United States.

Within an agency, internal control procedures have been established that generally require the formal authorization of a commitment prior to the execution of the supporting or binding document. An accounting entry often is made for each obligation incurred by the agency.

Liquidating Obligations

An obligation is liquidated by the receipt of the goods or services for which the obligation originally was established or by an adjustment or reversal of the earlier obligating entry. If the liquidation relates to the receipt of goods or services, a definite liability is created for which payment must be made by the agency. Some examples of actions that would liquidate or reduce the unliquidated obligation balance include:

Receipt of goods or services;

Receipt of an expenditure report under long-term grants or contracts;

Receipt of an invoice for services or goods rendered;

Completion of a receiving report;

Transfers or assistance performed by other agencies; and

Recording of payroll and other employee expenses.

The accounting system must provide for a segregation between capital expenditures and operating expenses. When expenditures are capitalized, costs or operating expenses are recognized as the capitalized items are consumed, used or applied to support the activities or programs of the agency.

Accruing of Expenditures

Concurrent with the entry to liquidate the earlier established obligation, an entry will be made to record the accrual of the appropriation expenditure. The formal amount of the debt is recognized at this time.

An "accrued expenditure," as defined by the Office of Management and Budget, is the liability incurred for goods and services received, other assets acquired, performance accepted and other liabilities not involving the furnishing of goods and services.

Expenditures may be accrued for either capital or current expenditures. Capitalized expenditures would involve the receipt of a fixed asset or other assets that will benefit future accounting periods. Current expenditures are recorded as costs of the period during which they were incurred. Examples of the latter type of expenditures would be payroll and other employee-related expenses. Additionally, a current expenditure may include the application or consumption of a previously capitalized amount.

Payments by Federal Agencies

For many years, the federal government defined expenditures as cash disbursements or on a "checks issued" basis. As mentioned above, expenditures now refer to receipt of services or goods and the recognition of the liability. *Payments or disbursements* refer to "checks issued." While reference is made to an agency "paying its bills," technically only the Treasury Department issues checks for the government. Individual agencies submit to the Treasury Department schedules containing lists of payees for whom checks must be drawn. Once the check is issued and mailed by the Treasury Department, the annotated schedule of voucher payments is returned to the agency.

The Treasury Department is the financial center for the federal government, maintaining the undisbursed or credit balances of each appropriation and fund. The reciprocal asset or debit balance of the appropriation on the agency books constitutes the remaining withdrawal authority.

Pro Forma Accounting Entries

The transactions required to account for an appropriation may be grouped into three classifications of accounting entries: the appropriation or authorizing entries, the budgetary entries, and the proprietary entries. Exhibit, 3-5 illustrates the summary account titles in general usage within the federal government and the timing or event generating the accounting entry.

Exhibit 3-5

Illustrative Pro Forma Accounting Entries for Federal Appropriation Transactions

Nature of Entry	Initiating Action	Pro Forma Entry		
		Account	Debit	Credit
Appropriation or Authorization	• Legislation by Congress			
	• Warrant by Treasury Department	Balance with Treasury-Cash	X	
		Unapportioned Appropriation		X
	• Apportionment by OMB	Unapportioned Appropriation	X	
		Unallotted Apportionment		X
	• Allotment by Agency Head	Unallotted Apportionment	X	
		Unobligated Allotment		X
Budgetary	• Obligation of funds by Federal program officials	Unobligated Allotments	X	
		Unliquidated Obligations		X
	• Receipt of goods, services, other performance (1)	Unliquidated Obligations	X	
		Expended Appropriation		X
Proprietary				
Capital Expenditures	• Acquisition of capital assets or re-sources for future use (1)	Assets	X	
		Inventory	X	
		Accounts Payable		X
Current Expenditures	• Receipt of goods, services, other performance, (1) (or application of previously capitalized costs)	Expenses	X	
		Asset or inventory account	X	
		Accounts Payable		X
Disbursement	• Payment of liability	Accounts Payable	X	
		Balance with Treasury-Cash		X

(1) Concurrent entries made to reflect adjustment to budgetary accounts and record proprietary transaction in accounting records.

As mentioned earlier, the receipts, obligations, expenditures, refunds, reimbursements and other changes must be continually related to the authorizing appropriation. The illustrated accounting entries are required for each appropriation or fund balance for which an agency is responsible. It is permissible to record balances in total, for fixed periods of time, or by other labor-saving or cost-effective practices. Regardless of the practices adopted, the accounting must provide for the continual monitoring of the appropriation or fund status.

Classification of General Ledger Accounts

Exhibit 3-6 illustrates a chart of accounts that could be applicable to an agency accountable for appropriations, revenue or income collection, and revolving and trust fund activities. This account structure, by the General Accounting Office, is merely an example of the accounts that might be adopted by an agency. Each agency has the discretion and the responsibility to adopt that account structure which best provides complete accountability for the resources under its control.

Exhibit 3-6

Illustrative Chart of General Ledger Accounts

Assets	Accounts Applicable to			
	General and Special Funds	Revolving Funds [1]	Trust Funds	Deposit Funds [2]
Current Assets:				
Fund Balances with U. S. Treasury	X	X	X	X
Cash in Banks		X	X	
Deposits in Transit	X	X	X	X
Undeposited Collections	X	X	X	X
Imprest Funds	X	X	X	
Agent-Cashier Funds	X	X	X	
Investments	X	X	X	
Accounts Receivable—Repayments to Appropriations	X		X	
Accounts Receivable from Government Agencies		X		
Accounts Receivable—Other	X	X	X	
Allowance for Uncollectible Accounts	X	X	X	
Loans Receivable	X	X	X	
Allowance for Uncollectible Loans	X	X	X	
Accrued Interest Receivable	X	X	X	
Allowance for Uncollectible Interest Receivable	X	X	X	
Work in Process for Others	X	X	X	
Inventories	X	X	X	
Advances to Government Agencies	X	X	X	
Advances to Others	X	X	X	
Travel Advances	X	X	X	
Prepaid Expenses	X	X	X	

[1] Includes Trust Revolving Funds, although some accounts in the Trust Funds column are applicable to Trust Revolving Funds.

[2] The accounts listed in the Deposit Funds column may be recorded in the books and reported in the financial statements as part of the general, special, revolving, and trust funds, unless otherwise classified by the United States Treasury.

	Accounts Applicable to			
	General and Special Funds	Revolving Funds [1]	Trust Funds	Deposit Funds [2]
Fixed Assets:				
Land	X	X	X	
Buildings	X	X	X	
Allowance for Depreciation—Buildings	X	X	X	
Other Structures and Facilities	X	X	X	
Allowance for Depreciation—Other Structures and Facilities	X	X	X	
Equipment	X	X	X	
Allowance for Depreciation—Equipment	X	X	X	
Leasehold Improvements	X	X	X	
Allowance for Amortization—Leasehold Improvements	X	X	X	
Construction Work in Progress	X	X	X	
Other Assets:				
Undistributed Stores Expenses	X	X	X	
Undistributed Equipment Expenses	X	X	X	
Undistributed General Overhead Expenses	X	X	X	
Other Undistributed Charges	X	X	X	
Estimated Appropriation Receipts	X [3]		X	
Estimated Appropriation Reimbursements	X		X	
Securities on Deposit			X	
Special Fund Receipts on Deposit	X			
Trust Fund Receipts on Deposit			X	
Reciprocal Account—Civil Service Commission	X	X	X	
Retirement Deductions — Prior Periods (Credit)	X	X	X	
Retirement Deductions—Current Calendar Year (Credit)	X	X	X	
Liabilities				
Current Liabilities:				
Disbursements in Transit	X	X	X	
Accounts Payable to Government Agencies	X	X	X	

[3] This account does not apply to the general fund.

	Accounts Applicable to			
	General and Special Funds	Revolving Funds [1]	Trust Funds	Deposit Funds [2]
Current Liabilities—Con.				
Accounts Payable to Others..............	X	X	X	
Advances from Government Agencies......	X	X	X	
Accrued Liabilities	X	X	X	
Accrued Interest Payable	X	X	X	
Liability for Accrued Leave..............	X	X	X	
Employees' Bond Deductions		X		X
Employees' Tax Deductions		X		X
Employees' FICA Deductions		X		X
Employer's Share of FICA		X		X
Liability under Lease—Purchase Agreements	X	X	X	
Contract Holdbacks				X
Other Deposits				X
Other Liabilities:				
Bonds, Debentures, and Notes Payable....	X	X		
Liability for Imprest Fund Advances......	X	X	X	
Liability for Agent—Cashier Fund Advances	X	X	X	
Liability for Securities on Deposit.........			X	
Deferred Credits	X	X	X	
Investment of the United States Government and Trust Fund Investment				
Unappropriated Funds	X [3]		X	
Unapportioned Appropriations	X		X	
Appropriations Allocated to Other Agencies	X		X	
Appropriations Allocated by Other Agencies [4]	X		X	
Unallotted Apportionments	X		X	
Unobligated Allotments	X		X	
Unliquidated Obligations	X		X	
Expended Appropriations	X		X	

	Accounts Applicable to			
	General and Special Funds	Revolving Funds [1]	Trust Funds	Deposit Funds [2]
Reimbursements to Appropriations [a]	X		X	
Special Fund Receipts Deposited [a]	X [b]			
Trust Fund Receipts Deposited [a]			X	
Transfers of Costs or Property to and from Government Agencies	X	X	X	
Funds Returned to U. S. Treasury [a]	X			
Trust Fund Payments to U. S. Treasury [a]			X	
Invested Capital	X			
Appropriated Capital		X		
Trust Capital			X	
Borrowings from U. S. Treasury	X	X	X	
Donations	X	X	X	
Profit and Loss		X	X	
Retained Income		X	X	

Income and Expense Accounts

Income	X	X	X	
Expenses	X	X	X	

[a] These accounts usually have debit balances.
[b] These accounts apply only to special funds.

Source: *Accounting Principles and Standards and Internal Auditing Guidelines, pp. 2-237 to 2-241.*

Chapter 4
The State and Local Government
Accounting Process

Like the accounting concept of the federal government, the accounting concept at the state and local government levels is fund accounting. However, the definition and the implemented practices of state and local governments vary from those used by the federal government. No single legal requirement exists to insure uniformity of financial management among the several states and the thousands of local governments. The generally accepted principles and procedures of accounting for governmental units, except federal agencies, are set forth in *Governmental Accounting, Auditing and Financial Reporting* (GAAFR), published by the National Committee on Governmental Accounting. Additional guidance has been provided by the American Institute of Certified Public Accountants in its industry audit guide, *Audits of State and Local Governmental Units.* Subsequent to the issuance of the industry audit guide, the National Council on Governmental Accounting issued

Interpretation No. 1, which reconciled the positions appearing in GAAFR and the AICPA's audit guide.

GAAFR establishes the basis for accounting principles for state and local governmental units and forms the conceptual framework for fund accounting as it is practiced by non-federal governmental units.

Governmental Accounting Principles and Practices

The GAAFR accounting prescriptions are a codification of accounting practices generally practiced by state and local governmental entities. In summary, GAAFR contains 12 basic principles or requirements.

Fund Defined

Possibly because of the overriding concern with legal compliance and the necessity for greater fiscal control when expending public resources, a state or local government's accounting system will appear fragmented to an auditor familiar with the single accounting system of a commercial organization. In comparison to federal appropriation accounting, the fund accounting of state and local governments will appear detailed and will demand more bookkeeping.

Generally, no single, unified set of accounts is maintained to permit the overall assessment of fiscal condition of a state or local government entity. The accounts of these governments are maintained on the basis of funds or groups of accounts, each of which is segregated in the records as a separate accounting entity.

For governmental accounting purposes, GAAFR has defined a "fund" as:

> ... an independent fiscal and accounting entity with a self-balancing set of accounts recording cash and/or other resources together with all related liabilities, obligations, reserves, and equities which are segregated for the purpose of carrying on specific activities or attaining certain objectives in accordance with special regulations, restrictions, or limitations.

Care must be exercised by the auditor to insure that the above definition is intended when reference is made to "funds." In practice, the term may be used to refer to budget accounts or reservations of appropriations that represent an administrative segregation of transactions in the accounting records. These budget or reservation accounts may be several hundred in number and do not fall within the GAAFR definition of a fund.

Generally Accepted Governmental Accounting Procedures

The AICPA's industry audit guide summarizes the authority of GAAFR as follows:

> GAAFR's principles do not represent a complete and separate body of accounting principles, but rather are a part of the whole body of generally accepted accounting principles which deal specifically with governmental units. Except as modified in this guide, they constitute generally accepted accounting principles.

The National Council on Governmental Accounting, in its Interpretation No. 1, (titled, *GAAFR and the AICPA Audit Guide)*, on April 1, 1976 stated that:

> The provisions of the AICPA Audit Guide are effective for periods beginning on or after January 1, 1974. State or local governmental agencies desiring to receive independent auditor opinions on financial statements which do not contain qualifications or exceptions *must conform in all material respects to the generally accepted accounting principles contained in GAAFR as modified by the Audit Guide.* [Emphasis by NCGA in its Interpretation.]

Governmental Principles and Practices

The 12 generally accepted principles and practices set forth in *GAAFR Restatement Principles* (draft dated September 1978) are:

(1) *Accounting and reporting capabilities.* A governmental accounting system must make it possible:

To present fairly and with full disclosure the financial position and results of financial operations of the constituent funds and account groups of the governmental unit; and

To determine and demonstrate compliance with relevant legal provisions.

(2) *Fund accounting systems.* Governmental accounting systems should be organized and operated on a fund basis.

(3) *Types of funds.* The following types of funds should be used in accounting for governmental financial operations:

Governmental funds

The *general fund* to account for all financial transactions not properly accounted for in another fund;

Special revenue funds to account for the proceeds of specific revenue sources (other than special assessments, expendable trusts or major capital projects) that are legally restricted to expenditure for specified purposes;

Capital projects funds to account for financial resources to be used for the acquisition of major capital facilities (other than those financed by special assessment and other enterprise funds);

Debt service funds to account for the accumulation of resources for the payment of interest and principal on general long-term debt (other than special assessment and revenue bonds); and

Special assessment funds to account for the financing of public improvements deemed to benefit the properties against which special assessments are levied.

Proprietary funds

Enterprise funds to account for operations that are financed and operated in a manner similar to private business enterprises—where the intent of the governing body is that the costs (expenses, including depreciation) of providing goods or services to the general public on a continuing basis be financed or recovered primarily through user charges—or where the governing body has decided that periodic determination of revenues earned, expenses incurred, and/or net income is appropriate for capital maintenance, public policy, management control, accountability, or other purposes;

Internal service funds to account for the financing of goods or services provided by one department or agency to other departments or agencies of the governmental unit, or to other governmental units, on a cost-reimbursement basis.

Fiduciary funds

Trust and agency funds to account for assets held by a governmental unit in a trustee capacity for individuals, private organizations, other governmental units and/or other funds. These include (a) expendable trust funds, (b) non-expendable trust funds, (c) pension trust funds and (d) agency funds.

(4) *Number of funds.* Governmental units should establish and maintain those funds required by law and sound financial administration.

(5) *Accounting for fixed assets and long-term liabilities.* A clear distinction should be made between (a) fund fixed assets and general fixed assets and (b) fund long-term liabilities and general long-term debt.

Fixed assets related to specific proprietary funds or non-expendable trust funds should be accounted for through those funds. All other fixed assets should be accounted for through the general fixed assets account group.

Non-current liabilities of proprietary funds, special assessment funds and trust funds should be accounted for through those funds. All other unmatured general obligations and long-term liabilities should be accounted for through the general long-term debt account group.

(6) *Valuation of fixed assets.* Fixed assets should be accounted for at cost or, if the cost is not practicably determinable, at estimated cost. Donated fixed assets should be recorded at their estimated fair value at the time received.

(7) *Depreciation of fixed assets.*

Depreciation of general fixed assets should not be recorded in the accounts of governmental funds. Depreciation of general fixed assets may be recorded in cost accounting systems or calculated for cost finding analyses; and accumulated depreciation may be recorded in the general fixed assets account group.

Depreciation of fixed assets accounted for in a proprietary fund should be recorded in the amounts of that fund. Depreciation is also recognized in those trust funds where expenses, net income and/or capital maintenance are measured.

(8) *Accrual basis in governmental accounting.* The modified accrual basis of accounting, as appropriate, should be utilized in measuring financial position and operating results.

Governmental fund revenues and expenditures should be recognized on the modified accrual basis. Revenues should be recognized in the accounting period in which they become available and measurable. Expenditures should be recognized in the accounting period in which they are incurred, if measurable, except for unmatured interest on general long-term debt and on special assessment indebtedness secured by interest-bearing special assessment levies, which should be recognized when due.

Proprietary fund revenues and expenses should be recognized on the accrual basis. Revenues should be recognized in the accounting period in which they are earned and become objectively measurable; expenses should be recognized in the period incurred, if objectively measurable.

Fiduciary fund revenues and expenses or expenditures (as appropriate) should be recognized on the basis consistent with the fund's accounting measurement objective. Non-expendable trust and pension trust funds should be accounted for on the accrual basis; expendable trust funds should be accounted for on the modified accrual basis.

Transfers should be recognized in the accounting period in which the interfund receivable and payable arise.

(9) *Budgeting, budgetary control and budgetary reporting.* Annual budget(s) should be adopted by every governmental unit. The accounting system should provide the basis for appropriate budgetary control. Budgetary comparisons should be included in the financial statements of each governmental fund for which an annual budget has been adopted.

(10) *Transfer, revenue, expenditure and expense classification.*

Interfund transfers and *proceeds of general long-term debt issues* should be classified separately from fund revenues and expenditures or expenses.

Governmental fund revenues should be classified by fund and source. Expenditures should be classified by fund, function (or program), organization unit, activity, character and principal classes of objects.

Proprietary fund revenues and expenses should be classified in essentially the same manner as those of similar business organizations, functions or activities.

(11) *Common terminology and classification.* A common terminology and classification should be used consistently throughout the budget, the accounts and the financial reports of each fund.

(12) *Interim and annual financial reports.*

Appropriate interim financial statements and reports of financial position, operating results and other pertinent information should be prepared to facilitate management control of financial operations, legislative oversight and, where necessary or desired, for external reporting purposes.

A comprehensive annual financial report covering all funds and account groups of the governmental unit, including appropriate combined, combining and separate fund statements, schedules, and statistical tables, should be prepared and published.

General purpose financial statements may be issued separately from the comprehensive annual financial report. Such statements should include (as a minimum) the basic financial statements and notes to the financial statements that are essential to fair presentation of financial position and operating results (and changes in financial position of proprietary funds).

Two references, which provide background on the evolution of governmental accounting principles are:

GAAFR Restatement Working Draft, March 31, 1977, published by the National Council on Governmental Accounting

GAAFR Restatement Exposure Draft, February, 1978, published by the National Council on Governmental Accounting.

The objective of the above documents is to provide a revision or update of the GAAFR, published in 1968. Additionally, pertinent aspects of the AICPA's guide for *Audits of State and Local Governmental Units* (1974) are related to GAAFR.

Guidelines of the AICPA

The conduct of a financial audit of a governmental unit requires a detailed knowledge of the position of the AICPA. A complete discussion of the application of generally accepted accounting principles to governmental units appears in the AICPA's *Industry Audit Guide*. In summary, the AICPA has taken the following positions, in the Guide, with respect to certain of the GAAFR principles:

A governmental accounting system should incorporate such accounting information in its records as necessary to make it possible to both: (a) show compliance with all applicable legal provisions; and (b) present fairly the financial position and results of operations of the respective funds, and the financial position of the self-balancing account groups of the governmental unit, in conformity with generally accepted accounting principles. Where these two objectives are in conflict, generally accepted accounting principles take precedence in financial reporting.

With respect to the modified accrual basis of accounting, the basis of accounting for a fund depends upon the purpose of the fund:

Revenues are to be recorded as received in cash, except for revenues susceptible to accrual and revenues of a material amount that have not been received at the normal time of receipts. "Susceptible to accrual" implies that the revenues are both measurable and available. "Available" is defined as a resource that can be used for governmental operations during the fiscal year.

Expenditures are to be recorded on the accrual basis, except that disbursements for inventory items may be considered as expended at the time of purchase or at the time of use. Additionally, expenditures are not to be divided between years by recording prepaid expenses. Interest due on long-term debt should be recorded as an expenditure on its due date, as set forth in GAAFR.

The *encumbrance* method of accounting represents an additional modification to the accrual method of accounting and may be used. An outstanding encumbrance is recognized as an expenditure; and the related obligation is carried until liquidated, either by the realization of the actual liability or cancellation of the encumbrance. (Note: GAAFR would account for an encumbrance as part of the budgetary accounting system, representing a commitment or reservation of the unencumbered appropriation. The 1978 *GAAFR Restatement Exposure Draft* states that encumbrances outstanding at year's end do not constitute expenditures or estimated liabilities.)

For some fixed assets, recording for stewardship purposes is not as significant, as it is in other categories. Such assets (improvements other than buildings, roads, bridges, curbs, streets, etc.) are normally immovable and of value only to the government. Thus, cumulative accountability is not critical.

An allowance for depreciation may be deducted from the related assets in the general fixed assets group of accounts, with a contra reduction in the investment in the general fixed assets account.

Since the independent auditor is concerned primarily with financial reporting in accordance with generally accepted accounting principles, the AICPA takes no objection to other reporting requirements placed upon governmental units to comply with GAAFR. The Industry Audit Guide recognizes the supplemental schedules may be desirable and, in some cases, necessary to provide full disclosure.

Nature of State and Local Government Accounting

Fund Descriptions

The accounting treatment of appropriated funds, the multiple fund structure and the accrual and encumbrance accounting method vary from the fund accounting used by federal agencies in discharging responsibilities to the Congress. However, the fund accounting practices of states, in some instances, closely parallel the practices of federal agencies.

As defined at state and local government levels, a "fund" is a fiscal and accounting entity having a self-balancing set of accounts, generally utilizing double-entry bookkeeping procedures. The multiple fund structure is viewed by proponents as necessary to permit the full and accurate reporting of the sources and purposes for which public moneys are received, controlled and disbursed. Opponents or critics believe that the GAAFR approach to fund structuring fractures the single governmental entity and unnecessarily complicates the accounting for public moneys and activities of state and local governments.

The selection of the appropriate fund for accounting purposes could be dictated by law, generally accepted principles or financial management and control considerations. However, the number of funds should be held to the absolute minimum to avoid undue rigidity, complexity and costly administrative efforts.

The governmental fund and non-fund account groupings suggested by GAAFR may be described in several ways:

By type of *organizational entity*—government or business entity;

By the *nature of the source of funding*—unrestricted, restricted, specific purposes;

By the *purpose for which the funds are authorized*—operations of the fiscal period or capital projects or debt issues; or

By the *permanency of the assets of the fund*—expendable or non-expendable.

Exhibit 4-1 illustrates the multiple classifications that may be used in describing the types of funds used in state and local governmental accounting. These descriptions should not be construed as being all-inclusive or mutually exclusive of other fund structures.

Accrual Accounting

As cited earlier, the recommended basis for accounting by state and local governmental agencies is the accrual basis. The accrual method has been accepted, in practice, to include both full accrual and the modified accrual basis. At times, though, the cash basis of accounting may be more appropriate for specific transactions.

With respect to the budgetary funds—the general fund, special revenue funds and debt service funds—the AICPA's Industry Audit Guide recommends the following modifications from the full accrual method of accounting:

Revenues are recorded as received in cash, except for:

Revenues susceptible to accrual; and

Material revenues not received at the normal time of receipt.

Expenditures are recorded on an accrual basis, except for:

Disbursements for inventory type items, which can be considered as expended at time of purchase or when used;

Prepaid expenses, which are not normally recorded; and

Interest on long-term debt, which should be recorded when due.

The encumbrance method of accounting may be adopted as a modification of the accrual method.

Exhibit 4-1

Overview of Governmental Funds and Non-Funds Account Groups

Fund & Nonfund Types

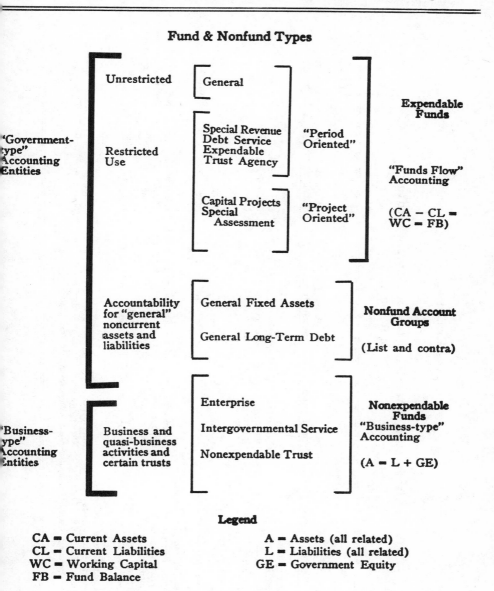

Legend

CA = Current Assets	A = Assets (all related)
CL = Current Liabilities	L = Liabilities (all related)
WC = Working Capital	GE = Government Equity
FB = Fund Balance	

Source: Robert J. Freeman, Ph.D, Professor of Accounting, University of Alabama, Tuscaloosa, Alabama.

Exhibit 4-2 divides the recommended funds between operating and non-operating and illustrates the basis of accounting generally applied to the several types of funds.

Exhibit 4-2

Classification of Accounting Characteristics of Funds and Groups of Accounts

Funds	Type of Fund	Basis of Accounting	Treatment of	
			Capital Expenditures	Long-Term Liabilities
Budgetary Funds:				
General	Operating*	Modified Accrual	Expenditures	Not recorded
Special Revenue	Operating*	Modified Accrual	Expenditures	Not recorded
Debt Service	Operating*	Modified Accrual	None	Not recorded
Commercial-Type Funds:				
Enterprise	Operating*	Accrual	Capitalize	Recorded
Intergovernmental Service	Operating*	Accrual	Capitalize	Recorded
Other Governmental Funds:				
Capital Projects	Nonoperating	Accrual (with exceptions)	Expenditures	Not recorded
Special Assessment	Nonoperating	Accrual (with exceptions)	Expenditures	Not recorded
Expendable Trust	Nonoperating	Accrual	None (generally)	None (generally)
Nonexpendable Trust	Operating*	Accrual	Capitalize	Recorded
Agency	Nonoperating	Accrual	None	None
Nonfund Account Groups:				
General Fixed Assets	Not applicable	Not applicable	Capitalize	Not Applicable
General Long-Term Debt	Not applicable	Not applicable	Not applicable	Recorded

* "Operating" funds have repetitive revenues and expenditures (expenses).

Source: Fred M. Oliver, Partner, Haskins & Sells, Salt Lake City, Utah.

Revenue and Expenditure Accounts

Classification of Accounts

GAAFR provides that governmental revenues be classified by fund and source. Additionally, revenues might be grouped by organizational units. Expenditures should be classified by fund, function, organization unit, activity, character and class of object. Following are several examples.

Accounts	Classification	Examples, Illustrations
Revenues		
	Fund	One of the several funds recommended by GAAFR
	Source	General property taxes, penalties, interest, rents, fees
	Organization unit	Department, bureau, division, or other organizational unit
Expenditures		
	Fund	One of the several funds recommended by GAAFR
	Function	A group of governmental activities or programs
	Organization unit	Department, bureau, division, or other organizational unit
	Activity	A line of work performed by one or more organizational units
	Character	Grouping of expenditures by time period benefitted—the past, present, and possibly the future—current operating, capital outlay, debt service, intragovernmental expenditures
	Classes of object	Article or service purchased (materials, contracts, travel, etc.)

While the descriptors vary, a comparison would show that the revenue and expenditure classifications of state and local governments are similar to those used at the federal level.

Sources of Agency Funding

With few exceptions, individual state and local government agencies do not collect funds to support their expenditures. The expenditure authority is provided by legislative enactment, usually in the form of an approved budget or appropriation. The revenues, or fund raising authority, also must be enacted by the legislature. The resultant collections generally are made by a central department or office.

The revenues of governments generally are obtained pursuant to legal enactments or other tax statutes passed by the legislature. Legislation is required for the assessment of property taxes. Other revenues, such as sales taxes, income taxes, licenses, fees, etc., often are continuing in nature and will change if the tax is rescinded or modified. Laws relating to the raising of revenues should be specific as to the purpose of the levy, the basis and time period of assessment and the amount or rate of the tax. The subsequent accounting and reporting then must conform to the legislation.

Expenditure Appropriations and Other Authorizations

Expenditure appropriation legislation represents the legal authorization or formal approval of the budget. These acts or ordinances represent the maximum expenditure levels permitted by the legislature for the fiscal period or designated purpose. Depending upon the legislation, the unexpended or unencumbered portion of the appropriation may lapse or continue beyond the end of the fiscal year.

Like the revenue legislation, expenditure appropriations are usually definite with respect to the authorized purpose for which expenditures can be made, the time period for which the expenditure authority exists and the dollar amount of the spending authority.

In addition to a direct appropriation, a governmental agency could receive expenditure authority from such other sources as transfers, reimbursements and allocations.

Direct appropriations. The direct appropriation by the legislature or governing body is the most common source of agency resources. This method of authorizing expenditures is used to support the expenditures of the general fund activities and may be used with several other funds. The direct appropriation is often the only funding source for payment of governmental salaries, expenses, grants, contracts and other authorized activities.

Appropriation transfer. When permitted, an agency or activity may receive expenditure authority by the transfer of part of an appropriation from another fund or agency. The appropriation transfer has the effect of increasing the budget authority of the recipient agency or fund, and is available for expenditure subject to any legal restraints.

Reimbursement of appropriations. A reimbursement of an appropriation will be required when one agency performs work or furnishes services to another appropriation, agency or fund. Often, a working capital fund or service fund may be established to provide a common service to all agencies on a cost-reimbursement basis. The servicing activity then must replenish its expended funds by collecting payments from agencies utilizing its services. The term revolving fund is another designation used for an activity that receives reimbursement of its appropriation for the cost of services rendered to other benefiting agencies.

Allocation of appropriations. At times, authority may exist to permit the distribution of a single appropriation to several agencies or activities. The allocation of an appropriation is the division of an appropriation into parts designated for expenditure by specific units or for special purposes. The allocated appropriation has the effect of raising the expenditure authority of the receiving organization.

State and Local Government Financial Process

As with commercial and federal accounting, the nature of the entity dictates the accounting. At state and local government levels, governmental operations similar to business operations are accounted for as separate entities, reflecting assets, liabilities, net worth, income and expenses. These are typically the activities accounted for in the proprietary funds (enterprise, internal service, non-expendable trust funds). The greater segment of governmental operations require an accounting that is different and designed to reflect compliance with legal and contractual requirements. Accounting for the activities of these entities is done in governmental funds (general, special revenue, capital projects, debt service, special assessment, expendable trust and agency funds). Additionally, two non-fund account groups are used to record general fixed assets and long-term debt accounts. Income determination is of no relevance in an accounting for activities of governmental-type funds. Of importance, though, is an accounting for the sources, uses and balances of the funds resources.

While variations exist, the accounting for activities of state and local government operations is generally similar and consistent with the prescriptions of GAAFR, as revised. Exhibit 4-3 illustrates, in summary form, the financial process for state and local governmental funds. The following paragraphs provide an overview of the accounting that often exists.

Accounting Period

While the budget period for governmental units is often an annual or biennial period, an accounting usually is required of revenues and expenditures on a fiscal year basis. In some instances, the accounting period is not related solely to a fiscal period. An appropriation may be made and will remain available for expenditure until the accomplishment of the purpose for which the funds were appropriated. In this instance, the reporting is more aligned with the progress being made. Additionally, the governing body may provide an appropriation for a specific period of time, which differs from the general fiscal period. Funds not expended within the specified time period cannot be expended unless new appropriation authority is obtained.

Exhibit 4-3

Generalized Financial Process for Governmental Funds

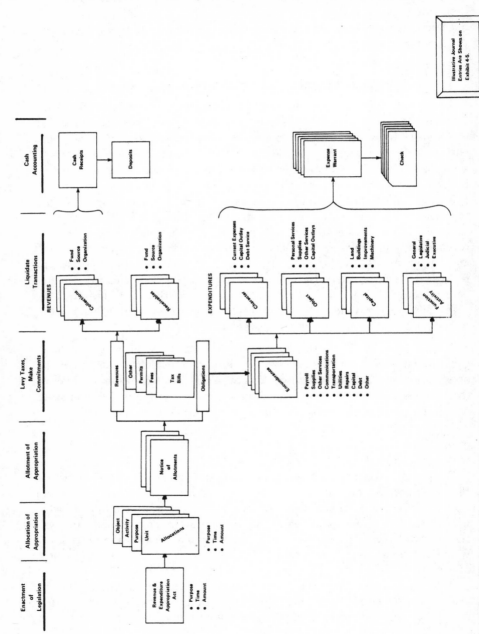

Budgetary Accounting

Within governmental financial management, budgetary accounting is a common control technique for providing a continual comparison of the budget to actual encumbrances and expenditures. Because the budget embodies legal compliance requirements, budgetary accounting is employed and is integrated into the accounting process for transactions of the general, special and other similar governmental funds.

Allotments. Budgetary accounting might include the formal recording of allotments of appropriations and encumbrances. An "allotment," pursuant to GAAFR, is a part of an appropriation that may be encumbered or expended during the allotment period. The allotment period is for less than a fiscal year, often bi-monthly or quarterly. Notices of allotments should be specific as to the purpose, time period and dollar amount.

Encumbrances. The "encumbrance" would be the commitment of the allotted funds. Unless later liquidated or cancelled, these same funds cannot be authorized or reserved for another expenditure.

Encumbered amounts should be evidenced by formal documentation such as:

salary commitments properly authorized as a charge against an appropriation;

properly executed purchase orders and contracts;

grants or subsidy agreements between the government and a third party; or

other agreements or contingent liabilities of the government.

Governmental accounting provides for the integration of these budgetary entries into the formal accounting process of the entity. In governmental accounting, encumbrances are not treated as expenditures, but as merely a reservation of money to meet a future expenditure.

Funds are reserved at year-end for payment of outstanding commitments or encumbrances. The carry-over of encumbrances often forms a part of the appropriation authority for the next fiscal year.

At the close of the fiscal year, the outstanding encumbrance balance may be shown as a reservation of the fund balance available for expenditure in the later year. As noted earlier, the AICPA's Industry Audit Guide suggests a different accounting. That is, the outstanding encumbrance balance would be treated as an expenditure and shown on the balance sheet on a separate line between liabilities and fund balance.

The AICPA views the encumbrance method as a modification of the accrual method of accounting. However, in its Industry Audit Guide, the AICPA recognizes the outstanding encumbrance as an expenditure and the related obligation is reflected on the accounting records until liquidated, whether by the realization of a liability or by replacement or cancellation.

Liquidated encumbrances. An encumbrance is usually *liquidated,* or reduced, by the receipt of services or work performed or the completion of the conditions of an agreement. An encumbrance ceases to exist when the payment is made to satisfy the commitment or liability or when the liability is established for the work performed or services received, even though not paid immediately.

Concurrent with the entry to liquidate the encumbrance, an entry will be made to record the accrual of an appropriation expenditure. According to GAAFR, an *expenditure* designates the cost of goods delivered or services rendered, whether paid or unpaid, and includes expenses, provision for debt retirement and capital outlays. If the accounts are kept on a cash basis, the term expenditures then would be synonymous with disbursements.

Note that expenditures may include charges that benefit future periods; but these expenditures will be recorded in total against the appropriation of the year in which incurred and classified as expenses of that year, even though the benefits extend to other periods.

Payments by government. In the governmental sector, the term "expenditure disbursement" occasionally will be used to refer to cash disbursements or checks issued. The more widely used term for payments, though, is checks issued, or disbursements. The term expenditure has, in recent years, been used to refer to the liquidation of an earlier encumbrance and the determination of the actual liability of the government. Payment may or may not be made at that time.

Pro Forma Entries

Unlike in private sector accounting, the assets, liabilities and equity of a governmental agency may not be accumulated in a single accounting entity. The generally accepted accounting entities for state and local governments include proprietary funds (commercial-like operations—enterprise, internal service and nonexpendable trust funds in government), governmental funds (the general, special revenue, capital projects, debt service, special assessment, expendable trust, and agency funds) and account groups (general fixed assets and long-term debt account groups).

Exhibit 4-4 provides an overview of the types of general ledger accounts that might be included in the accounting for entries affecting various funds. Illustrative journal entries appear in Exhibit 4-5. These entries are required, where appropriate, for each fund and for recording the activities of departments and agencies operating within the fund.

Exhibit 4-4

Summary of General Ledger Accounts and Types of Funds

Type of Funds	Assets Other Than Fixed	Fixed Assets	Other Debits	Liabilities Other Than Long-Term	Long-Term Liabilities	Other Credits	Fund Balance/Retained Earnings
Governmental							
General	Yes	No	Yes	Yes	No	Yes	Yes
Special revenue	Yes	No	Yes	Yes	No	Yes	Yes
Debt service	Yes	No	No	Yes	Yes	No	Yes
Special assessment	Yes	No	Yes	Yes	Yes	Yes	Yes
Capital project	Yes	No	Yes	Yes	No	Yes	Yes
Proprietary							
Enterprise	Yes	Yes	No	Yes	Yes	Yes	Yes
Trust and agency	Yes	No	No	Yes	Yes	Yes	Yes
Intragovernment service	Yes	Yes	No	No	Yes	Yes	Yes
Other Groups of Accounts							
General fixed asset group	No	Yes	No	No	No	No	Yes*
General long-term debt group	No	No	Yes	No	Yes	No	No

* Investment in General Fixed Assets.

Source: *Governmental Accounting, Auditing and Financial Reporting,* National Committee on Governmental Accounting, 1968, Municipal Finance Officers Association, pp. 179—181.

Exhibit 4-5

Illustrative Pro Forma Accounting Entries for State and Local Governmental Appropriations

Nature of Entry	Initiating Action	Possible Account Title	Debit	Credit
Adoption of Budget	Enactment of appropriation legislation	Estimated Revenues	X	
		Appropriations		X
Budgetary	Incur obligations, commit unencumbered appropriations	Encumbrances	X	
		Reserve for Encumbrances		X
	Receipt of services, cancel encumbrance	Reserve for Encumbrances	X	
		Encumbrances		X
Revenues	Levy taxes	Taxes Receivable-Current	X	
		Estimated Uncollectible Taxes		X
		Revenues		X
	Collect taxes	Cash	X	
		Taxes Receivable-Current		X
	Record delinquent taxes	Taxes Receivable-Delinquent	X	
		Estimated Uncollectible Taxes	X	
		Taxes Receivable-Current		X
		Estimated Uncollectible Delinquent Taxes		X
	Grants due from other governments	Due from State Government	X	
		Due from Federal Government	X	
		Revenues		X
	Collections from other governments	Cash	X	
		Revenues		X
Current Expenditures	Receipt of goods, services	Expenditures	X	
		Inventory of Supplies	X	
		Accounts Payable		X
	Cost of inventoried supplies used	Expenditures	X	
		Inventory of Supplies		X
Capital Outlays	Purchased fixed assets	Advanced to Fixed Asset Account Group	X	
		Cash		X
	Recorded in Fixed Asset Group of Accounts	Assets	X	
		Investment in Fixed Assets		X

Part II
Governmental Audit
Standards, Criteria and Guides

Governmental Audits and the Nature of Audit Responsibilities

Governmental Auditing Standards and Guides

Cost Principles Applicable to Federal Contracts and Grants to State and Local Governments

Chapter 5
Governmental Audits and the Nature of Audit Responsibilities

In the public sector, governmental audits are made by many organizations. Some of these organizations are headed by appointed government officials. Other officials are elected to office, and still other auditors are retained under contract. Other audits are made through some form of working agreement with non-governmental organizations. One level of government might undertake to audit activities of another level of government, with the observations of the audit being made available to both levels. It is important in governmental auditing to know the varied audit organizations and their differing responsibilities.

The objective of this chapter is to outline the types of federal, state and local governmental audit organizations and to discuss the nature of the contractual arrangements under which governmental entities have retained public accountants for audits.

Federal Government Audit Organizations

At the federal level, a clear distinction should be made between the auditing activities of the General Accounting Office, which is in the legislative branch,

72

and the audit organizations of the executive agencies. Additionally, a relatively recent audit concept has been mandated by the Congress—that of Inspector Generals, who have a legal reporting responsibility to both the legislative as well as the executive. Also, while not uniform throughout the government, several executive agencies have organized their audit function into an internal and an external audit staff.

General Accounting Office

Organization

The General Accounting Office, established in 1921, is an independent audit organization in the legislative branch under the control and direction of the Comptroller General of the United States. Both the Comptroller General and the Deputy Comptroller General are appointed by the President, with the advice and consent of the Senate. They serve for a 15-year term, subject to removal only by a joint resolution of Congress for specified causes or impeachment, and neither is eligible for reappointment. By law, the GAO is required to investigate all matters relating to the receipt, disbursement and application of federal funds and to make reports to the Congress.

Scope of Audits and Investigations

The scope of the audits and investigations made by the GAO cover the broadest definition of accountability and auditing. As a result of many laws, the authority and responsibility of the GAO for audit has been defined as including:

Fiscal accountability—including fiscal integrity, disclosure and compliance with applicable laws and regulations;

Managerial accountability—directed towards the efficient and economical use of personnel, funds and other resources of government; and

Program results—concerned with the effectiveness of governmental programs or the benefits being attained.

With a few exceptions, GAO's authority to audit extends to all activities, financial transactions and accounts of the federal government, including those of organizations that have received funds, support or other assistance from a federal agency. In the execution of its responsibilities, the GAO will have access to and may conduct on-site reviews of federal agencies, non-federal agencies, grantees, contractors and organizations who have received other assistance from the federal government. The purpose of such examinations is to make, for the Congress, independent examinations of the manner in which agencies of the federal government are discharging their responsibilities under the applicable laws.

Responsibility for Audit

As part of its review of agency management and controls, the GAO will pay particular attention to the quality and nature of the agency's auditor. Where warranted, the GAO may place reliance upon, or make appropriate use of, the agency auditor's work in the GAO examination. GAO reviews audits by public accountants and other governmental auditors to assess the adequacy of audit coverage and to evaluate whether there is sufficient breadth and scope of audit coverage to minimize any duplicate audit coverage by the GAO.

The primary responsibility of the GAO is to provide an independent view to the Congress as to how the executive branch and its fund recipients are discharging the mandates of various laws. While considerable assistance and benefits may accrue as a result of a GAO audit, a GAO audit is not done for benefit of a governmental agency, nor is a GAO audit to be seen as a substitute or supplement to an agency's own audit staff.

Offices of Inspector General

Organization

Historically, some federal agencies have long had an office of inspector general, whose responsibilities, while including audit, were much broader, addressing all types of reviews and investigations required by the agency. In October, 1978, Congress, by Public Law 95-452, attempted to reorganize the executive branch of the government and increase its economy and efficiency by establishing offices of inspector general in many of the larger agencies and departments. The law required that an inspector general be established in the following organizations:

The departments of Agriculture, Commerce, Housing and Urban Development, Interior, Labor, and Transportation;

The Community Services Administration;

The Energy Research and Development Administration;

The Environmental Protection Agency;

The General Services Administration;

The National Aeronautics and Space Administration;

The Small Business Administration; and

The Veterans Administration.

The stated purpose of these offices would be to create independent and objective units (1) to conduct and supervise audits and investigations of programs and operations of the named agencies and departments; (2) to provide leadership and coordination and recommend policies for activities designed to promote economy and efficiency in administration of, and to prevent and detect fraud and abuse in, such programs and operations; and (3) to provide a means for keeping the head of the agency and the Congress fully and currently informed of problems and deficiencies relating to administration and the necessity for, or progress of, corrective actions.

Each Inspector General is appointed by the President, with the advice and consent of the Senate, on the basis of integrity and demonstrated ability and without regard to political affiliation.

Responsibility for Audit

Each Inspector General is required to have an assistant Inspector General for Auditing. The duties and responsibilities of the Inspector General include:

To provide policy direction for, and conduct, supervise and coordinate, audits and investigations relating to programs and operations;

To review existing and proposed legislation and regulations and to make recommendations semi-annually concerning the impact of such legislation or regulations on the economy and efficiency of programs and operations or the prevention and detection of fraud and abuse;

To recommend policies for and conduct, supervise or coordinate, other activities carried out or financed by their establishment for the purpose of promoting economy and efficiency in the administration of, or preventing and detecting fraud and abuse in, programs and operations;

To recommend policies for, and conduct, supervise or coordinate, relationships between their establishments and other federal agencies, state and local governmental agencies, and nongovernmental entities with respect to matters relating to the promotion of economy and efficiency, the prevention and detection of fraud and abuse in programs or operations, or the identification and prosecution of participants in such fraud or abuse; and

To keep the head of their establishment and the Congress fully and currently informed concerning fraud and other serious problems, abuses and deficiencies relating to the administration of programs and operations and to recommend corrective action and report on the progress made in implementing corrective action.

To carry out these responsibilities, Inspector Generals are authorized to approve the use of nonfederal auditors.

Reporting Responsibilities

Specific reporting responsibilities were established by Congress, including a unique reporting mandate to both the head of the agency or department and the Congress. Each Inspector General was directed to:

Make semiannual reports to the head of the agency and to Congress (for periods ending March 31 and September 30) on significant problems, abuses and deficiencies of programs and operations, including recommendations for corrective action, an evaluation of progress in implementing recommendations, a summary of matters referred to prosecutive authorities and a summary of all instances where requested information has been unreasonably refused; and

Report immediately to the head of the agency particularly serious or flagrant problems, abuses or deficiencies relating to the program and operations, such reports being transmitted by the head of the agency to Congress within seven calendar days, with any comments deemed appropriate.

The law further provides that the required reports shall be transmitted to the head of the agency or department and to the Congress without further clearance or approval, except that the monthly and quarterly report should be delivered to the head of the agency or department sufficiently in advance of the due date to permit comments to be appended to the reports prior to delivery to Congress.

Federal Agency and Departmental Audit Staffs

Legal Requirements

The "Inspector Generals" law notwithstanding, the head of each federal agency is required by law to provide for an audit function. The provisions of the Budget and Accounting Procedures Act of 1950 state, in part:

The head of each executive agency shall establish and maintain systems of accounting and internal control designed to provide effective control over and accountability over all funds, property, and other assets for which the agency is responsible, including appropriate internal audit.

In addition to the requirement to audit the activities and programs operated by federal employees, the head of the agency is required to conduct an audit program of those organizations to which funds or assistance have been provided under grants, contracts, loans, guarantee programs or other forms of assistance. In recent years, considerable effort has been made to attempt to coordinate the audits of nonfederal agencies receiving federal assistance through the cooperative, non-duplicative audits by federal, state and local government auditors and by public accounting firms.

Organization of Federal Audit Function

In agencies and departments that have not adopted the Inspector General structure for conducting investigations and inspections, an audit division may be established to conduct both internal and external audits of the federal organizations and its programs.

Internal audits are examinations made by federal employees of an agency's programs, operations or activities. The scope of individual audits will vary, consistent with management desires, laws, regulations, program complexity, and the purposes or objectives of the internal audit function. There is no legal prohibition against an agency using public accountants to conduct internal audits of governmental agencies, but more often such audits are made by agency personnel.

External audits are examinations of the programs, operations and activities of organizations that are not part of the federal agency. Typically external audits are made of grantees, contractors, borrowers and recipients of other forms of federal assistance. These audits may be made by federal, state and local governmental auditors or by public accountants.

Scope of Audits

The scope of audits that might be made by a federal audit organization could include the broad, full-scope audit described by the GAO in its *Standards for Audit,* which would be:

An examination of financial transactions, accounts and reports, including an evaluation of compliance with applicable laws and regulations;

A *review of efficiency and economy* in use of resources by a governmental program, function, activity or organization; and

A *review of effectiveness* to determine whether desired program results are being achieved.

Generally, though, few agency audits are this broad in scope. For example, the recurring internal audits of a federal agency often will include audits of payroll, imprest funds, grant administration, contract administration, accounts and financial statements, travel and transportation, year-end balances and property management. The external audits generally are directed to an audit of costs incurred and to a review of the manner in which the agency's grantees, contractors or borrowers (depending upon the nature of the program) are complying with the administrative and financial provisions of the specific agreements under which federal assistance is being provided to these recipients.

Coordination of Governmental Audits

Cross-Servicing of Audits Between Federal Agencies

With respect to agency audits, the Office of Management and Budget has directed each federal agency to give full consideration to establishing cross-servicing between two federal agencies to minimize the impact of duplicate audits on a single audited organization. This program, initiated under the FMC Circular 73-2, *Audit of Federal Operations and Programs by Executive Branch Agencies* later superseded by OMB Circular No. A-73, March 15, 1978, *Audit of Federal Operations and Programs,* has been rather successfully implemented, particularly with respect to federal grant and contract programs or operations. In these instances, a single cognizant federal audit agency has been appointed, often based on which agency has the most funds involved.

Coordination With Other Levels of Government

Additionally, the Office of Management and Budget, by OMB A-73, has directed federal agencies to consider the audit program of partnership organizations and to coordinate the audits of these organizations to the maximum extent possible. This reliance on nonfederal audits is specifically required for those agencies that administer federal grant-in-aid programs and that are subject to OMB Circular A-102 (the uniform administrative requirements for grants-in-aid to state and local governments). Pursuant to OMB A-73, the scope of the federal audits must give full recognition to the nonfederal auditing effort. When the following conditions exist, reports of nonfederal auditors will be used in lieu of federal audits:

If the reports and supporting workpapers are available for review by the federal agencies;

If tests by federal agencies indicate that the audits were performed in accordance with generally accepted auditing standards, including those issued by the GAO; and

If the audits otherwise meet the requirements of the federal agencies.

State and Local Government Audit Organizations

The authorizing legislation and other legal bases for audit organizations vary between states and among the local governmental units. Additionally, the requirements or perceived audit need among state and local governments differ considerably.

Structure of State and Local Governmental Audit Organizations

The structure of the state and local governmental audit organizations is dependent upon the method of appointment and the role for audit, as outlined in authorizing legislation or as established by historical practices. The title of the audit organization seldom provides clear information as to the nature of the audit agency.

Method of Appointment

The "method of appointment" is the process by which the senior audit official or director of the audit organization holds office. The methods vary, but generally may be described as falling into two groups:

Appointed auditors—The auditor is appointed by the executive or the legislative branch and may serve for a fixed or specified time period or for an unspecified period at the pleasure of the appointing officer or body.

Elected auditors—The auditor assumes office as a result of a general election, serves for the time period specified in law and is, generally, independent of the executive and legislative.

In the instance of appointed auditors, incumbents may or may not be required to be appointed on a merit basis or be subject to existing civil service rules or regulations.

General Audit Structure

There is no typical or common structure by which audit services are provided by state and local governmental units. As mentioned, the name of the audit office is not a clear guide to the type of audit performed or to the reporting responsibility of the audit organization.

State-wide auditors—Often this audit official has the broadest authority to perform audits. The head of the audit function might have the title of state auditor, auditor general or legislative auditor. This auditor could have the responsibility for conducting audit of other levels of the government and of state commissions, corporations, departments and agencies, grantees, contractors and other organizations. These types of audits might be viewed as independent or external in relation to audits conducted by the auditor of a specific agency of the state government.

The official may be appointed or elected. If appointed, the official could be in either the legislative or executive branch. In some jurisdictions, the legislature will have its own auditor, while another official performs audits for the executive agencies.

City, municipal and other local governmental auditors—While many of the auditors of local governmental units are appointed, other auditors at these levels of government have obtained their positions by election or by merit programs of civil service. These auditors could report to the legislative or governing body, the chief executive officer (elected or appointed) or to both types of officials.

Often, these auditors will not perform full financial statement audits in accordance with generally accepted auditing standards, but may concentrate on voucher audits, procedural or compliance reviews, fiscal post audits and other evaluations of importance to the local government.

Agency auditors—Agency auditors may be viewed as the auditors for specific departments, agencies and other governmental organizations. For the most part, these audit officials are appointed pursuant to the existing merit or civil service rules or regulations. An agency auditor's responsibility extends to making audits of his own agency and of programs for which his agency is responsible. If such an official is employed by a state agency, the audit responsibility may include the examination of certain programs operated by other levels of government throughout the state.

Independent Public Accountants—Both state and local governmental units retain public accountants to perform independent audits of financial statements of governmental units. These firms also have been employed to make audits of governmental organizations and programs.

Type of Audits Performed

At the state and local government level, the scope of audits is, in many instances, similar to that of audits performed at the federal level. At the federal level, the larger dollar magnitude might permit more functional-type, special-emphasis audits (e.g. travel, payroll, imprest funds, property, year-end obligations), although these areas are also reviewed as part of other governmental audit programs. The several types of audits performed are discussed in the following sections.

Voucher Preaudits

Voucher preaudits consist of examinations of vouchers and supporting documentation prior to approval for disbursement. The scope of such an examination will, often, include: a review of the purpose of the contemplated expenditure for appropriateness and consistency with legislation; the amount of funds required to insure sufficiency of approved funding; supporting documentation to determine the correctness of accounting; and authorization from a proper approving official.

Fiscal Postaudits

Fiscal postaudits generally consist of reviews of the accounts and records, and the adequacy of supporting documentation, for the disbursements made. In some jurisdictions, all or a large sample of expenditures must be audited on a specified cycle basis. This audit function could be performed at a central location, with the necessary supporting documentation being transferred to the audit site. Alternatively, the audit could be made at dispersed agency sites.

Compliance Audits

Compliance audits are directed toward assessing the degree of compliance that exists between the practices and activities of the audited organization and the applicable laws, regulations or other requirements. The items being examined may include both financial and other areas, such as programs and legislative, for which compliance is required.

Financial Statement Audits

The objective of financial statement audits is to determine whether the financial operations and procedures have been properly performed and whether the amounts appearing in the accounting records and related financial statements fairly reflect the financial positions and operations of the audited organizations, pursuant to generally accepted accounting principles.

Performance or Operational Audits

The scope of performance or operational audits may be both financial and non-financial in emphasis. Within this general category would be the audits made for economy, efficiency and program results.

Contracting with Public Accountants

As indicated above, all levels of government have retained public accountants to assist in the audit of governmental programs and activities. In the case of federal programs, financial audits may be made only by qualified auditors.

Qualifications of Governmental Accountants

With respect to the audit of governmental programs and activities fully or partially supported or assisted with federal monies, the Comptroller General of the United States has established qualifying criteria for auditors.

According to the Comptroller General, when outside auditors are employed for assignments requiring the expression of an opinion on financial statements of governmental organizations and programs, only fully qualified public accountants should be employed. In a letter of September 15, 1970, to the heads of federal departments and agencies, the Comptroller General stated that:

> Such audits shall be * * * conducted by independent certified public accountants or by independent licensed public accountants licensed on or before December 31, 1970, who are certified or licensed by a regulatory authority of a State or other political subdivision of the United States. . . .

This position was reaffirmed by the Comptroller General on May 28, 1975, in a letter to the chairman of the Senate Government Operations Committee.

Method of Contracting

As indicated above, all levels of governments have retained public accountants to assist in the audit of governmental programs and activities. The method of contracting differs if the audit is being made of a federally assisted program operated by a state or local government.

The federal government has contracted with public accountants to conduct audits of governmental programs in two ways:

Directly, by entering into a contract with the accounting firm. The contract requires that the audit be made pursuant to the governmental agency's requirements. Under this type of contractual arrangement, the agency makes direct payment to the firm.

Indirectly, by having a governmental grantee or other organization retain the public accounting firm, with the condition that the firm be acceptable to the grantor agency. The audit must be conducted in a manner that meets both the requirements of the grantee and the sponsoring agency. The audit firm will be paid by the grantee organization.

In the latter instance, the public accounting firm should accept the engagement with caution and only after determining the scope of audit desired by the sponsoring federal organization. Generally, the only source of funding for the audit fee will be the governmental agency, which often will require a scope of work that may not be fully understood by the retaining grantee organization. In other words, the performance of an audit pursuant to the grantee's direction may not be adequate for the governmental agency. Unless the requirements of both organizations are met, payment for services rendered could be delayed.

Types of Contracts Used with Audit Firms

A variety of contracts are used by governmental organizations for procuring audit services from accounting firms. It is important to have an understanding of each, since the risks, liability for performing the scope of work and the method of payment differ considerably.

There are two general types of contracts used by government in retaining public accounting firms: cost type and fixed price type contracts.

With *cost type contracts,* the scope of the contract cannot be defined with specificity. Thus, the firm is required to provide its best efforts to perform the identified work for an estimated cost. Should the cost estimate be insufficient to complete all of the outlined work, the government agency must provide additional funds or the firm is under no obligation to continue to render the services. In contrast, a *fixed price contract* requires that the contracted scope of work be performed for the specified fixed price regardless of the costs incurred by the audit firm.

Under a cost type contract (which has been defined at the federal government level as including cost-plus-fixed fee, labor-hour and time and materials contracts), the firm has minimal risk and is primarily responsible for providing its best effort. Payment for services, under these types of contracts, is made frequently, often monthly, as work is performed.

The fixed price type contract places the maximum risk on the firm. There is no relief to the firm if its estimate of cost to perform the scope of work is not adequate. Additionally, payment for services rendered under fixed price contracts are often made only upon completion of the scope of work. In some instances, when the contract is for a long duration, a method of partial or interim payment may be negotiated. Where this is possible, the government agency often will withhold a significant portion of the contract price until the contracted effort has been completed.

Exhibit 5-1 summarizes the types of contracts, nature of risks and certain implications of the various contracts that may be used by governmental organizations in procuring audit services.

Responsibility to Perform Government Audits

Practitioner's Responsibility

There is no obligation for public accountants to accept governmental audit engagements. However, once accepted, the practitioner has the obligation to comply with the contract conditions.

The responsibility for independence, professionalism and due care in the performance of the audit with respect to governmental audits is no less than that which exists with respect to private clients. Historically, fees charged governmental clients have been discounted for many reasons; it does not follow, however, that discount or less than professional work is acceptable.

The auditor is liable to perform the scope of work accepted pursuant to the contract conditions. Adherence to generally accepted auditing standards may not be sufficient, if the scope of work contains other criteria.

For example, most agencies require audits to be made in accordance with the agency audit guides. If the practitioner has agreed to follow the requirements of the audit guide, he is bound by such requirements as well as by generally accepted auditing standards. Where such standards are not followed, this fact must be disclosed in the report and the reasons stated.

Procedure for Substandard Audit Reports

The AICPA has established a program with governmental agencies whereby allegedly substandard audit reports may be submitted to the Ethics Division of the AICPA for investigation. Upon review, the Ethics Division can decide to:

Dismiss the case with no further action on the part of the AICPA;

Recommend that the auditor be required to attend an educational program;

Recommend that the auditor be admonished by the AICPA; or

Find a prima facie case against the auditor, with a recommendation that the case be referred to the Trial Board.

Should the latter position be sustained, the decision of the Trial Board could be published to the profession, with possible disclosure of the practitioner.

AICPA's Position on Governmental Audits

At the time of the issuance of the GAO *Standards for Audit,* the AICPA was concerned that the profession would not take notice of the significant difference in the scope of the contemplated audits in relation to the audits

Exhibit 5-1

Types of Government Contracts

Type of Contract	Burden of Risk	Implications of Contract and Price
Cost plus fixed fee	Risk is on government; auditor liable for best effort within contract price	Scope of work not specific or agency has not sufficiently defined; usually has provisional * fringe and overhead expense rates that must later be adjusted to actual rates
Labor-hour	Risk on government; auditor liable for providing qualified staff	Hourly labor rate negotiated, includes recovery of labor, fringe, overhead, other costs, plus profit. Government can audit only hour charged to engagements; rate is firm
Time and materials	Same as labor-hour contract	Hourly rate negotiated, but agency agrees to reimburse auditor for materials and other expenses separately from hourly rate, which includes same elements as for labor-hour contract
Firm fixed price	Risk on auditor to perform full scope of contract within total contract price	Both auditor and government are certain of product to be delivered. Auditor entitled to all savings due to under-runs; but liable to perform regardless of actual costs incurred. Minimal or no audit requirements
Purchase order	Risk on auditor to perform services within amount	Firm fixed price, but for small purchases. Recently increased from $2,500 to $10,000 at federal government level

* Provisional rates are used to permit the interim recovery of expenses incurred in rendering services to the government. These rates are adjusted by the government, up or down, depending upon actual expense levels. Generally, recovery of actual expenses in excess of provisional rates can be made only if the total costs are within the contract price.

historically made pursuant to generally accepted auditing standards. This concern was well founded.

After several years, the profession still has not fully recognized that the GAO *Standards for Audit* outline the requirements for a considerably broader and more far-reaching scope of audit. Many years after the issuance of these *Standards,* some public accountants still are accepting governmental audit contracts that do not specify a definite scope of review, but merely incorporate by reference the entire audit contemplated by the GAO *Standards.* This latter practice was not contemplated by the GAO and it is likely that none of the public accountants are performing the full-scope audit (i.e. financial and compliance audits and a review for economy and efficiency, and an evaluation for effectiveness and program results).

In anticipation of possible implementation problems, the AICPA's Committee on Relations with the General Accounting Office in 1973 set forth conclusions and recommendations (in the publication titled, *Auditing Standards Established by GAO—Their Meaning and Significance for CPA's*) with respect to these *Standards* and governmental audits. In part, the Committee's position stated:

> While the GAO *Standards* are intended to be identical to the profession's for financial audits, the *Standards* may also be concerned with efficiency and economy of operations, compliance with financial and non-financial laws and regulations and program effectiveness.

This broader definition of an audit will require that agreement be reached as to the criteria for evaluation of economy, efficiency and effectiveness.

> Independent accountants must define carefully, in the engagement agreement, the scope of each engagement and the method of reporting.

It is erroneous to assume that the *Standards* contain sufficient detail to define or limit the scope of work to be performed. In fact, in many instances, the full-scope audit, outlined in the *Standards,* might be impossible to perform. Reporting, pursuant to the *Standards,* varies considerably from the profession's reporting and should be carefully reviewed with the governmental client.

> When non-accounting expertise is needed, the independent accountant should determine in advance its availability and costs and how his use of the work of the non-accountant experts will be made known in the report.

For many of the audits, the independent accountant will not usually have the required skills to meet the second standard for governmental auditing, that the auditor ". . . collectively possess adequate professional proficiency for the task required." Care must be taken before the audit contract is executed to determine how this standard can be met.

> Audits concerned with economy, efficiency, and program effectiveness will presumably require more time than those covering only financial presentations. Care should be taken to provide for sufficient time to complete the engagement.

Reviews by the GAO of audits made by public accountants have repeatedly disclosed that these cautions are frequently ignored. It was found that public accountants did not understand the implications of the terms of the governmental audit contract and, in fact, did not perform many parts of the required audit scope.

Chapter 6
Governmental Auditing Standards and Guides

To a degree, the standards and guides used in governmental auditing are similar to auditing requirements in the corporate sector. Federal, state and local governments have, to the extent possible, placed reliance on the substantial body of applicable audit knowledge represented by:

AICPA's *Statement on Auditing Standards;*

AICPA's *Industry Audit Guide—Audits of State and Local Governmental Units;*

National Council on Governmental Accounting's *Governmental Accounting, Auditing and Financial Reporting;*

General Accounting Office's *Accounting Principles and Standards and Internal Auditing Guidelines for the Guidance of Federal Agencies;*

Comptroller General's *Standards for Audit of Governmental Organizations, Programs, Activities & Functions;* and

Federal Audit Guides (presently these guides number in excess of 100, issued by over 20 different federal agencies—available on a subscription basis, titled *Federal Audit Guides,* from Commerce Clearing House, Inc., Chicago, Illinois).

Within governmental auditing, the above standards and guidelines would be considered the body of appropriate auditing procedures. Departure from, or an application of auditing procedures inconsistent with, these standards or guidelines must be justified by the practitioner. The standards to be applied may vary due to the nature of the governmental organization being audited.

Generally Accepted Auditing Standards

The Statement on Auditing Standards No. 1, issued by the American Institute of Certified Public Accountants, codified and superseded earlier Statements on Auditing Procedures. In the conduct of financial statement examinations, the auditor must state whether his examination was made in accordance with generally accepted auditing standards. It is also these standards that require the auditor to express an opinion as to whether the financial statements accompanying his opinion conform to generally accepted accounting principles and the consistency with which these principles have been applied between the current and preceding reporting periods. These auditing standards govern the quality of the procedures and acts performed by the auditor in the conduct of his examination. The standards also are concerned with the judgment exercised by the auditor during his review and the expression of his opinion in his report on financial statements.

The generally accepted auditing standards, as approved and adopted by the membership of the AICPA, relate to the general standards, standards of field work and standards of reporting. The 10 basic standards appear in Exhibit 6-1 and in Statement No. 1 as continuing indices of acceptable practices of the auditing profession.

While the basic 10 generally accepted auditing standards have endured through the years, the interpretations and definitions have been refined, and acceptable practices have been established. Exhibit 6-2 lists the several additional statements on auditing standards issued since 1973.

For many years, the generally accepted auditing standards of the public accounting profession were adopted by federal, state and local government audit personnel as the criteria for performance. In 1972, the Comptroller General of the United States (who is the chief executive of the U.S. General Accounting Office) published standards, which were to be applied to governmental audits. These standards, while similar to generally accepted auditing standards in many respects, were broader in scope and related to audits other than financial statements, e.g., to compliance and program reviews and examinations.

Exhibit 6-1

Generally Accepted Auditing Standards

(American Institute of Certified Public Accountants)

General Standards

1. The examination is to be performed by a person or persons having adequate technical training and proficiency as an auditor.

2. In all matters relating to the assignment, an independence in mental attitude is to be maintained by the auditor or auditors.

3. Due professional care is to be exercised in the performance of the examination and the preparation of the report.

Standards of Field Work

1. The work is to be adequately planned and assistants, if any, are to be properly supervised.

2. There is to be a proper study and evaluation of the existing internal control as a basis for reliance thereon and for the determination of the resultant extent of the tests to which auditing procedures are to be restricted.

3. Sufficient competent evidential matter is to be obtained through inspection, observation, inquiries, and confirmations to afford a reasonable basis for an opinion regarding the financial statements under examination.

Standards of Reporting

1. The report shall state whether the financial statements are presented in accordance with generally accepted accounting principles.

2. The report shall state whether such principles have been consistently observed in the current period in relation to the preceding period.

3. Informative disclosures in the financial statements are to be regarded as reasonably adequate unless otherwise stated in the report.

4. The report shall either contain an expression of opinion regarding the financial statements, taken as whole, or an assertion to the effect that an opinion cannot be expressed. When an overall opinion cannot be expressed, the reasons therefor should be stated. In all cases where an auditor's name is associated with financial statements, the report should contain a clear-cut indication of the character of the auditor's examination, if any, and the degree of responsibility he is taking.

Source: *Codification of Auditing Standards and Procedures,* Statement on Auditing Standards, No. 1, 1973, p. 5.

Exhibit 6-2

Statement on Auditing Standards

(American Institute of Certified Public Accountants)

Statement Number	Statement Title
1	Codification of Auditing Standards and Procedures (Nos. 33 through 54, previously issued by the Committee on Auditing Procedures)
2	Reports on Audited Financial Statements
3	The Effects of EDP on the Auditor's Study and Evaluation of Internal Control
4	Quality Control Considerations for a Firm of Independent Auditors
5	The Meaning of "Presents Fairly in Conformity with Generally Accepted Accounting Principles" in the Independent Auditor's Report
6	Related Party Transactions
7	Communications Between Predecessor and Successor Auditors
8	Other Information in Documents Containing Audited Financial Statements
9	The Effect of an Internal Audit Function on the Scope of the Independent Auditor's Examination
10	Limited Review of Interim Financial Information
11	Using the Work of a Specialist
12	Inquiry of a Client's Lawyer Concerning Litigation, Claims, and Assessments
13	Reports on a Limited Review of Interim Financial Information
14	Special Reports
15	Reports on Comparative Financial Statements
16	The Independent Auditor's Responsibility for the Detection of Errors or Irregularities
17	Illegal Acts by Clients
18	Unaudited Replacement Cost Information
19	Client Representations
20	Required Communications of Material Weaknesses in Internal Accounting Control
21	Segment Information
22	Planning and Supervision
23	Analytical Review Procedures
24	Review of Interim Financial Information

AICPA's Industry Audit Guide

Originally published in 1974, and reissued with a statement of position by the Accounting Standards Division of the AICPA, the *Industry Audit Guide—Audits of State and Local Government Units* was intended to assist the independent auditor in examining and reporting on financial statements of government entities other than federal organizations.

The industry guide provides comparative explanations and illustrations of generally accepted accounting principles and of accounting requirements outlined for state and local governments in *Governmental Accounting, Auditing and Financial Reporting* (GAAFR). Basic distinctions between accounting for government and commercial enterprises are discussed. This guide also outlines several audit procedures that are unique to governmental organizations.

In response to the AICPA's Industry Audit Guide, the Municipal Finance Officers Association issued the NCGA Interpretation No. 1, the purpose of which was to present an analysis of the differences between the practices contained in *Governmental Accounting, Auditing and Financial Reporting* and the audit guide. Thus, additional guidance was provided in the use of GAAFR and the pronouncements of the AICPA.

The Industry Audit Guide discusses several aspects of governmental audits and the importance of certain auditing and accounting procedures that are uniquely applicable to public sector audits. In summary, several important areas of governmental auditing are covered in the guide:

Generally accepted accounting principles applicable to state and local governmental units are discussed, and distinctions between public sector accounting and private sector accounting are highlighted;

The importance of budgeting, auditing and reporting operations of governmental units is summarized;

Concepts of auditing that are unique to state and local governmental units are illustrated, including both general and specific audit procedures that would be appropriate to such audits; and

The presentation of financial information and reporting of audit opinions in governmental financial statements are illustrated, using as examples the several unique governmental issues that will arise during public sector audits.

Illustrative forms of selected financial statements and supplemental schedules of governmental units also have been included in the Guide.

State and Local Governmental Standards

For many years, state and local government audits required the application of the generally accepted auditing standards of the public accounting profession. The authoritative accounting and auditing principles for non-federal government operations and activities were set forth in the publication titled, *Governmental Accounting, Auditing and Financial Reporting.* With respect to auditing, this publication reiterates the standards of the profession and provides guidance to assist the auditor and the governmental unit in defining the minimal requirements for a governmental audit scope and specific requirements for the annual report. Audit procedures, applicable to the post-review of governmental units, that might vary from the audit of commercial organizations are also delineated in GAAFR.

No separate standards for governmental audits, however, are identified in addition to the generally accepted standards of the profession.

GAO Governmental Audit Standards

In the late 1960s, the General Accounting Office perceived a need for information concerning governmental operations considerably broader than could be met by the public accounting profession's auditing standards for financial reporting. It was believed that responsible governmental auditing also must consider whether publicly funded programs achieved the purposes for which the programs were established and whether the operations of governmental programs were efficient and effective. Compliance with authorizing legislation was also of concern.

The standards to meet the full range of governmental audits were titled *Standards for Audit of Governmental Organizations, Programs, Activities & Functions,* issued in 1972. These standards were applicable to all audits of governmental operations, whether such audits were performed by auditors employed by federal, state or local governments, independent public accountants or others qualified to make audits under the standards. Similarly, these standards were to be applied to internal audits of government agencies and audits or grantees, contractors and other organizations external to governmental entities.

While the *Standards for Audit* incorporate the essence of the generally accepted auditing standards outlined earlier, the scope is broader and responsibilities are different. Care, therefore, must be taken to insure that audits of governmental agencies are performed in accordance with the considerably enlarged definition of auditing.

The governmental standards are founded on the premise that governmental accountability should identify not only the objects for which funds have been spent, but also the manner and effectiveness of the expenditures. The standards, therefore, provide for a scope of audit that includes not only financial and compliance auditing, but also auditing for economy, efficiency and achievement or effectiveness of program results. The *Standards for Audit* specifically state that the outlined scope of audit is not intended to apply to all audits of government or that this broadened or enlarged scope is always desirable. The elements of this type of audit have been defined by the GAO *Standards for Audit* as:

Financial and compliance—determines whether financial operations are properly conducted, whether the financial reports of an audited entity are presented fairly and whether the entity has complied with applicable laws and regulations;

Economy and efficiency—determines whether the entity is managing or utilizing its resources (personnel, property, space and so forth) in an economical and efficient manner and the causes of inefficiencies or uneconomical practices, including inadequacies in management information systems, administrative procedures or organizational structure; and

Program results—determines whether the desired results or benefits are being achieved, whether the objectives established by the legislature or other authorizing body are being met and whether the agency has considered alternatives that might yield desired results at a lower cost.

Exhibit 6-3 contains the several standards for governmental audits. It is important to note that there exist distinctive requirements, which differ materially from the similarly titled generally accepted auditing standards.

Exhibit 6-3

Standards for Audit of Governmental Organizations, Programs, Activities & Functions

(Comptroller General of the United States)

NOTE: boxed sections differ materially from the generally accepted auditing standards appearing in Exhibit 6-1.

General Standards

1. The full scope of an audit of a governmental program, function, activity, or organization should encompass:

   a. An examination of financial transaction, accounts, and reports, including an evaluation of compliance with applicable laws and regulations.

   b. A review of efficiency and economy in the use of resources.

   c. A review to determine whether desired results are effectively achieved.

In determining the scope for a particular audit, responsible officials should give consideration to the needs of the potential users of the results of that audit.

2. The auditors assigned to perform the audit must collectively possess adequate professional proficiency for the tasks required.

3. In all matters relating to the audit work, the audit organization and the individual auditors shall maintain an independent attitude.

4. Due professional care is to be used in conducting the audit and in preparing related reports.

Examination and Evaluation Standards

1. Work is to be adequately planned.

2. Assistants are to be properly supervised.

3. A review is to be made of compliance with legal and regulatory requirements.

4. An evaluation is to be made of the system of internal control to assess the extent it can be relied upon to ensure accurate information, to

ensure compliance with laws and regulations, and to provide for efficiency and effective operations.

5. Sufficient, competent, and relevant evidence is to be obtained to afford a reasonable basis for the auditor's opinions, judgments, conclusions, and recommendations.

Reporting Standards

1. Written audit reports are to be submitted to the appropriate officials of the organizations requiring or arranging for the audits. Copies of the reports should be sent to other officials who may be responsible for taking action on the audit findings and recommendations and to others responsible or authorized to receive such reports. Unless restricted by law or regulation, copies should also be made available for public inspection.

2. Reports are to be issued on or before the dates specified by law, regulation, or other arrangements and, in any event, as promptly as possible so as to make the information available for timely use by management and by legislative officials.

3. Each report shall:

a. Be as concise as possible but, at the same time, clear and complete enough to be understood by the users.

b. Present factual matter accurately, completely, and fairly.

c. Present findings and conclusions objectively and in language as clear and simple as the subject matter permits.

d. Include only factual information, findings, and conclusions that are adequately supported by enough evidence in the auditor's working papers to demonstrate or prove, when called upon, the bases for the matters reported and their correctness and reasonableness. Detailed supporting information should be included in the report to the extent necessary to make a convincing presentation.

make improvements in operations. Information on underlying causes of problems reported should be included to assist in implementing or devising corrective actions.

f. Place primary emphasis on improvements rather than on criticism of the past; critical comments should be presented in balanced perspective, recognizing any unusual difficulties or circumstances faced by the operating officials concerned.

g. Identify and explain issues and questions needing further study and consideration by the auditor and others.

h. Include recognition of noteworthy accomplishments, particularly when management improvements in one program or activity may be applicable elsewhere.

i. Include recognition of the views of responsible officials of the organization, program, function, or activity audited on the auditor's findings, conclusions, and recommendations. Except where the possibility of fraud or other compelling reason may require different treatment, the auditor's tentative findings and conclusions should be reviewed with such officials. When possible, without undue delay, their views should be obtained in writing and objectively considered and presented in preparing the final report.

j. Clearly explain the scope and objectives of the audit.

k. State whether any significant pertinent information has been omitted because it is deemed privileged or confidential. The nature of such information should be described, and the law or other basis under which it is withheld should be stated.

4. Each audit report containing financial reports shall:

a. Contain an expression of the auditor's opinion as to whether the information in the financial report is presented fairly in accordance with generally accepted accounting principles (or with other specified accounting principles applicable to the organization, program, function, or activity audited), applied on a basis consistent with that of the preceding reporting period. If the auditor cannot express an opinion, the reasons therefor should be stated in the audit report.

b. Contain appropriate supplementary explanatory information about the contents of the financial reports as may be necessary for full and informative disclosure about the financial operations of the organization, program, function, or activity audited. Violations of the legal or other regulatory requirements, including instances of non-compliance, and material changes in accounting policies and procedures, along with their effect on the financial reports, shall be explained in the audit report.

Because all audits may not require, nor be suited to, application of the full scope contemplated by the governmental standards, specific agreements of understanding should be established at the outset of each audit between the governmental entity and the independent accountant and other audit organizations. These agreements should clearly identify whether a part or all of the elements of a full scope governmental audit are to be conducted. The scope to be undertaken must be clearly understood by all parties concerned.

These concerns have been explored, and the auditing profession's viewpoint on governmental standards has been published, by the AICPA in *Auditing Standards Established by the GAO—Their Meaning and Significance for*

CPAs. While the AICPA concluded that the auditing profession should be encouraged to participate in the broader-scoped governmental audits, the profession was cautioned about the importance of careful scope definition, the criteria for assessing compliance and performance, and the method of reporting.

Federal Agency Audit Guides

Where an audit is to be made of an organization that has been the recipient of some form of federal assistance, such audits often must be made in accordance with a specific audit guide issued by a federal agency. When such audits are undertaken, particular care must be given by the public accountant to insure that the client has included all of the audit requirements in the contemplated audit contract. A federally assisted program may solicit an audit that does not meet the need of the federal sponsor, who, in many instances, provides the funds for audit.

At the date of this publication, over 20 different federal agencies have issued over 100 different audit guides. The audit guide for each program to be audited must be closely reviewed, since each program will have specific requirements that must be examined.

As a general rule, a governmental audit guide should be viewed as the minimum scope of tests that should be performed to satisfactorily complete the audit engagement. Typically, the audit guide will incorporate the profession's generally accepted auditing standards as well as the GAO *Standards for Audit.* It is important for the auditor to discern which of the standards are appropriate for the desired audit and to have the audit contract modified accordingly.

While the AICPA has attempted over the years to insure, through its audit guide review process, that the content of governmental audit guides is consistent, variances do exist. In a report to the Office of Management and Budget and to directors of audit of other federal agencies, the AICPA suggested that audit guides contain a certain structure and content. All governmental audit guides should contain certain minimal information, such as:

A *discussion of the background* of the governmental program to provide an understanding of the objectives and operational characteristics, citing important instructions, manuals and program documents that should be available to the client and the auditor;

A *definition of unique terms,* titles, designations and other words having significance to the governmental program, and, possibly, references to other explanatory materials;

An *identification of objectives of the audit,* including such items of primary interest to the agency as internal control, government assets in custody of the audited organization, compliance requirements and financial reporting;

An outline of specific guidelines to be applied in the audit, defining the technical matters to be covered and specifically addressing the criteria for performing financial and compliance audits and other studies and evaluations that might be required to be performed by the auditor;

An identification of reporting responsibilities, describing the format of the desired reporting, the nature of any opinions required, the distribution that is to be made of the report and who will make the distribution; and

A reference to exit conferences. Some agencies prefer that the auditors hold such meetings at the conclusion of the audit; other agencies specifically direct that such meetings shall not be held. Still other agencies prescribe the format and nature of the matters that may be discussed at exit conferences.

There is limited uniformity of audit criteria or audit scopes among the several federal agencies. Special preparation is required prior to accepting audit engagements from different agencies. The audit guide must be closely examined, since this document, unless modified by the client, becomes the legally binding scope of work that must be performed by the auditor.

Other Audit Considerations

Other considerations important to governmental audits relate to:

The competence of governmental auditors;

The independence of audit staff;

The scope of governmental audits;

The materiality of reportable items;

The responsibility for fraud detection; and

The application of government audit standards.

Each of these subjects is discussed further in the following paragraphs.

Professional Competence of Governmental Auditors

In the governmental sector, the required standard of qualification relates not only to the individual auditor, but also to the audit team collectively.

An important initial distinction to recognize is that the term "auditor" may not be applicable only to individuals having a background and training in accounting and audit. Such skills are necessarily required for the audit of financial statements, but different, and possibly more diverse, skills might be required for the conduct of compliance and program results audits. For the audit team to be viewed as professionally proficient, members of the audit team may be required to collectively possess academic training and experience in such other fields as medicine, law, mathematics, economics or computer sciences, depending upon the governmental program or activity under audit.

The audit must be conducted by personnel who individually are competent and possess professional training and knowledge in their specialty, and who, collectively, possess the professional proficiency for the type of audit to be made.

It has been determined by GAO that only certified public accountants and public accountants licensed before December 31, 1970, possess the qualifications to perform financial audits of governmental organizations that would lead to the expression of an opinion on financial statements. This decision was published initially in 1970, and reaffirmed in 1975, by the Comptroller General of the United States and is applicable to all levels of government including state and local agencies. In a separate decision, the Comptroller General earlier concluded that governmental entities provide some of the most diverse and challenging work in the accounting and auditing field and that, accordingly, government departments and agencies needed the best audit skills obtainable. It was concluded that authorizing auditors without these skills to render opinions on financial statements would not provide the public with the protection it needs.

Independence of Audit Staff

Governmental audits require that the auditor be independent in fact and appearance. Like a public accountant, an auditor, to be independent, must be intellectually honest. To be recognized as independent, the auditor must be free of any obligation or interest in the audited organization. In public accounting, apparent independence has been interpreted as being free of familial, organizational, and financial conflicts of interests.

The same standard is applicable in government. To insure that the work of the auditor is not later compromised, members of the audit team must be selected so as to insure independence and objectivity. The team members, individually and collectively, must be free of real and apparent conflicts of interest, either personal, financial, occupational or organizational. The injudicious selection of staff can be harmful to the audit team and possibly damaging to the professionalism and acceptance of the audit report. Conditions or circumstances that would be viewed as impairments to this independence as outlined in the governmental Standards for Audit, include:

Personal impairments—official, professional or personal relationships, preconceived ideas about the audit operations, prior involvement in a decision-making or management capacity, biases or prejudices resulting from employment or loyalty to a group, entity or level of government or any financial interests;

External impairments—interference improperly influencing the scope or character of audit, interference with the audit procedures to be applied, denial of access to records and other sources of information, interference with assignment of personnel, or other restrictions or actions that tend to impair the performance of the audit; and

Organizational impairments—organizational structures and reporting relationships that require the auditor to be subject to policy direction from superiors who are involved in policy affecting the audit staff or who are undergoing the audit.

Independence and objectivity, as well as competence, are attained in government audit from time to time by having the audit team comprised of staff:

Borrowed from other departments within the government;

Obtained from other levels of government;

Obtained under interchange programs with other levels of government or from industrial organizations; or

Hired from outside government.

In March, 1978, the Board of Directors of the AICPA approved a policy statement providing specific guidance on the independence of governmental auditors conducting financial audits. At that time, the AICPA stated that the third general standard of the GAO *Standards for Audit* established the goals for achieving independence in fact and appearance and that the requirements of the Office of Revenue Sharing provided explicit criteria for evaluating independence of governmental auditors making financial audits. The Revenue Sharing Act considered two groups of governmental auditors to be independent:

State auditors when:

auditing local governments; or

auditing their state's accounts if elected by the citizens of the state, elected or appointed by and reporting to the state legislature or a committee thereof, or appointed by a governor and confirmed by and reporting to the state legislature.

Local government auditors auditing their government's accounts if:

elected by the citizens of the local government,

elected or appointed by and reporting to the governing body of the local government or a committee thereof, or appointed by the chief executive officer and confirmed by and reporting to the governing body.

When expressing an opinion on the fair presentation of financial statements in conformity with generally accepted accounting principles, a governmental auditor should disclose the position he holds in the governmental organization;

if certified, it would be appropriate for him to include the designation CPA. According to the AICPA, if the independence tests are met, the auditor may state that his report has been made in accordance with generally accepted auditing standards, but where personal, external or organizational impairments to his independence exists, the audit cannot be made in accordance with generally accepted auditing standards.

Scope of Governmental Audits

Statement on Auditing Standards, No. 1, states that the objective of the ordinary examination of financial statements is the expression of an opinion on the fairness of financial position, results of operations and changes in financial position.

The standards for the full scope governmental audit include a similar financial examination, but also may require a compliance review and an examination for economy, efficiency and achievement of program results. Not all audits will require the full scope examination; but, to the extent that some element is not performed, there will be government users whose needs for information will not be satisfied.

The general objectives for these differing types of audit elements have been identified in the governmental *Standards for Audit:*

A *financial and compliance examination* should include sufficient auditing to determine that the audited entity is controlling resources, properly accounting for the assets and operations of the agency, reporting accurately and fairly, and complying with applicable laws and regulations;

A *review of efficiency and economy* should include inquiry as to whether the audited entity is giving consideration to conserving its resources and minimizing expenditures; and

A *review of program results* should include an examination of the results or benefits achieved and a determination whether the program is meeting the established goals and objectives.

GAO recognizes that the terms "efficiency and economy" are relative and that it is not possible to express an opinion on whether the maximum has been obtained. No such opinion is contemplated, therefore, under the government standards. With respect to the review of program results, there is no standard opinion that can be rendered. Such reporting must be in detail, explaining the established objective of the review, the work performed and the audit observations.

Materiality of Reportable Items

A basic premise of reporting and financial statement presentation is that the information is useful to the readers—management, public, stockholders, legislatures, electorate. Usefulness, however, does not require total disclosure to the point of reporting minutiae, making the report unnecessarily complex or incomprehensible. The reported information must be relevant and important.

The concept of materiality is relevant in the governmental sector in much the same manner as in the private sector. Size, magnitude and relative importance are the general criteria of materiality. Although no precise definition for materiality exists in the auditing profession, the GAO *Standards for Audit* contains six specific indicators of materiality, which are to be applied individually or in combination:

Absolute dollar amount of an item;

Ratio of amount of the item to an appropriate base figure;

Useful asset life of the item;

Importance of the item to accomplishment of the mission;

Importance of the item to the maintenance of adequate controls, such as a pattern of small discrepancies; and

Characteristic of the item, such as indication of malfeasance or misfeasance.

Often materiality must be defined in terms of reporting the extent of compliance with an established criterion, law or regulation. In such instances, noncompliance, although not quantifiable, with a basic tenet or operating premise of an entity must be reported.

Responsibility for Fraud Detection

In neither the private nor the public sector is the auditor responsible for the detection or uncovering of fraudulent practices. While it is true that, on occasion, the application of generally accepted auditing standards might disclose conditions or circumstances warranting further investigation or maybe even evidence of fraudulent actions, such detection cannot be guaranteed.

Statement on Auditing Standards, No. 16 states that, under generally accepted auditing standards, the independent auditor has the responsibility, within the inherent limitations of the auditing process, to plan the examination to search for errors or irregularities that would have a material effect on the financial statements and to exercise due skill and care in conducting the examination. The existence of effective internal and external controls reduces the probability, but does not eliminate the possibility, that such errors or irregularities will occur. The failure to detect such conditions does not, in itself, indicate inadequate audit performance. Under generally accepted auditing standards, the auditor is not to be viewed as an insurer or guarantor; the same premise is valid in governmental auditing.

In governmental audits, increased reliance must be placed on the existence and adherence to sound internal controls and procedures. The lack of personnel continuity in elected and appointed responsible positions results in the absence of a control element that is generally inherent in a corporate audit. The GAO *Standards for Audit* states that the standard requiring due professional care does not impose upon the auditor a requirement to give an absolute assurance that no material impropriety or fraud exists, nor does it require that a detailed audit of all transactions normally be undertaken.

Generally accepted audit standards outline the procedure for reporting errors or irregularities or possible evidence of fraudulent actions. Pursuant to Statement on Auditing Standards No. 16, "The Independent Auditor's Responsibility for the Detection of Errors or Irregularities," the auditor should discuss such observations with the appropriate level of management that is at least one level above those involved. Should the auditor continue to believe that material errors or irregularities exist, the auditor should determine that the board of directors or the audit committee is aware of the circumstances. In some instances, the auditor may elect to consult with the client's legal counsel; and, in some instances, particularly when considering withdrawal from the audit, the auditor may wish to consult with his own legal counsel.

The Comptroller General of the United States, in an interpretative document relating to the governmental *Standards for Audit,* has stated that, if evidence of fraud related to federal funds is noted, it should be reported to the head of the agency involved and to the Federal Bureau of Investigation. State and local violations should be reported with supporting documentation to the head of the agency involved and to the proper state and local authorities.

Application of Government Audit Standards

The application of governmental audit standards differs considerably from that of generally accepted auditing standards. The latter standards, including interpretations and refinements, are applicable in total to all audits made for the purpose of expressing an opinion concerning the reasonableness and fairness of information presented in financial statements. In contrast, the government audit standards apply to each element and are applicable to audits of less than full coverage. A governmental audit will not always require that all three elements of the total government audit be performed, nor will there necessarily be a requirement or a desire by the client organization to have all of the governmental audit standards adhered to.

In the way of example, the auditor may not be required or permitted to perform the full scope audit defined by the first governmental general audit standard. That standard makes reference to a full scope audit, which would include three elements: a financial and compliance review, a review of efficiency and economy, and a review to determine whether the desired program results are effectively achieved. Similarly, the government auditor may be directed to not adhere to the several reporting standards. For various reasons, the audited organization or other government officials may desire not to have the full reporting as contemplated by the first governmental reporting standard.

With respect to the auditor's opinion or discussion in Auditing Standard No. 2, "Reports on Audited Financial Statements," the auditor may issue an unqualified opinion only if the audit is conducted in accordance with generally accepted auditing standards. Any restriction on the scope of the audit, whether imposed by the client or by conditions or circumstances, may require that the auditor qualify the opinion or, possibly, disclaim an opinion.

This same application does not exist with respect to the governmental audit standards. If an audit does not cover all three elements of a full scope audit, it is not necessary for the auditor to qualify the report. The report alternatively, should clearly identify the scope of the audit that was performed.

Chapter 7
Cost Principles Applicable to Federal Contracts and Grants to State and Local Governments

Government-Wide Requirements
Contract and Grant Costs
Definition of Costs
Indirect Cost Plans
Methods of Reimbursing Indirect Cost
Unallowable Costs
Matching Share and In-Kind Contributions
Other Federal Allowability Criteria
Applicability of Criteria Affecting Allowability of Costs

Government-Wide Requirements

Billions of dollars are transferred annually under contracts and grants from the federal government to state and local governments to support programs administered by these governments. While the contracts and grants are issued for some 1,000 programs by some 50 different federal departments, agencies, commissions and offices, the cost principles governing the allowability and collectability of expenses under these contracts and grants are set forth in a uniform guide, *Principles for Determining Costs Applicable to Grants and Contracts with State and Local Governments.* This document often is referred

104

to as the Office of Management and Budget Circular A-87 (or Financial Management Circular 74-4).

The conduct of governmental audits requires a knowledge of these costs principles to permit conclusions to be reached on the validity of the receivables and payables balances at the end of the accounting period and on entitlement to receipts collected during the period. Tests must be made of expenses incurred and charged to governmental contracts and grants during the accounting period to ascertain that these expenses, for which reimbursement has been claimed from the federal government, are allocable and allowable under the federal cost criteria.

The cost principles are to be used in cost determinations and are not intended to set forth circumstances or establish the extent of governmental participation in the financing of a grant or contract. The overall purpose is to insure that federally assisted programs bear the fair share of costs recognized under the principles.

Caution is required in the application of the general principles of Circular A-87. These principles may be superseded by the specific conditions of the contract or grant executed between the recipient of federal funds and the federal agency. Where this circumstance exists, the more specific conditions prevail and will be enforced by the federal agency in any subsequent dispute or audit.

Contract and Grant Costs

Allowable and Allocable Costs

Costs charged to contracts and grants by state and local governments that later will be claimed for reimbursement by the federal government must be (1) allowable, (2) allocable and (3) reasonable. The following paragraphs outline the definition of these criteria, as set forth in Circular A-87.

Allowable Costs

To be allowable, costs must:

Be necessary and reasonable for proper administration of the program, be allocable to the program under Circular A-87 principles and not be a general expense of state or local governments;

Be authorized or not prohibited under state or local laws or regulations;

Conform to limitations or exclusions set forth in Circular A-87 principles, federal laws or other governing limitation as to types and amounts of costs;

Be consistent with policies, regulations and procedures that apply uniformly to both federally assisted and other activities of the governmental unit;

Be accorded consistent treatment through application of generally accepted accounting principles;

Not be allocable to or included as a cost of any other federally financed program; and

Be net of all applicable credits (discounts, rebates, scrap sales, adjustments for overpayments or erroneous charges).

Allocability of Costs

A cost must be allocable to a particular cost objective to the extent of benefits received by such objective. Such allocable cost may not be shifted to other federal programs to overcome fund deficiencies, avoid restrictions imposed by law or grant agreements, or for other reasons.

Where an allocation of joint cost ultimately will result in charges to a federally supported program, an indirect cost allocation plan must be prepared.

Reasonableness of Costs

A cost is reasonable if, in its nature and amount, it does not exceed the cost that would be incurred by an ordinarily prudent person in the conduct of competitive business.

Definition of Costs

Under Circular A-87 and other federal procurement regulations, the total program costs include both allowable direct costs and the allocable portion of indirect costs, less any applicable credits. There is no universal rule for classifying costs as direct or indirect. It is possible for a cost to be direct with respect to a function or service, but indirect with respect to a program or ultimate cost objective. Of importance is the consistency of accounting treatment.

Direct Costs

Direct costs are those costs that can be identified with a particular contract or grant or other cost objective. Direct costs also may be charged to an indirect cost objective used for the accumulation and later allocation to contracts, grants or other cost objectives. With minor variance, the following object classes or categories of direct costs are applicable to federal contracts and grants:

Compensation for personal services—compensation for personal services of employees for time and effort devoted specifically to the execution of the program, including all remuneration, paid or accrued;

Employees' fringe benefits—costs related to authorized absences and benefits in the form of employers' contributions or expenses, provided such costs are consistent with an approved plan, and that the total compensation for employees is reasonable and distributed equitably to all programs and activities;

Travel—cost for transportation, lodging, subsistence and related items incurred by employees in travel status on business incident to the program;

Contracts, consultants—payments made to specialists or experts and for organizations, external to the program, that are rendering services to the program;

Materials and supplies—cost of purchases made specifically for the program, net of all allowances, discounts and refunds;

Equipment—cost of purchasing, leasing or renting non-expendable, high value assets necessary for meeting program objectives;

Space—cost of obtaining, by lease, purchase or donation, facilities necessary to carry on the program;

Other direct costs—costs specifically identified in the contract or grant budget, not considered within the above categories.

Indirect Costs

Circular A-87 defines indirect costs as those costs:

(1) incurred for a common or joint purpose benefiting more than one cost objective, and

(2) not readily assignable to the cost objective specifically benefited without effort disproportionate to the results achieved.

By this definition, the term "indirect costs" would apply to:

Costs allocable to several programs or activities of the governmental contractor or grantee;

Costs originating in the governmental contractor's or grantee's department;

Costs incurred by other departments in supplying goods, services and facilities to the contractor or grantee department; and

Minor direct cost items for reasons of practicality.

Indirect Cost Plans

For governmental contractors or grantees to recover, as part of the total cost of a federally assisted program, allocable indirect costs, two plans must be developed: (1) a government-wide (e.g., for the state or the local governmental unit) *consolidated cost allocation plan;* and (2) an *indirect cost plan* for the specific governmental unit. The indirect cost plan for each state agency operating a federally sponsored program had to be submitted to the federal government annually. The cost allocation plan and the indirect cost proposal constituted the agreements by which the federal government would reimburse the state and local governments for indirect costs.

Cost Allocation Plan

The cost allocation plan covers the distribution of costs of support services provided on a government-wide basis to the contractor or grantee agency by other agencies of the governmental unit. Costs of these supporting agencies' services are treated as indirect costs and added to the indirect costs of the contractor or grantee agency. A cost allocation plan must contain or explain:

The nature and amount of the services provided and the relevance to federal government projects and programs;

The items of expense included in the indirect cost;

The methods used to distribute the indirect cost;

The identification of the government agency rendering the services and the agency receiving the services; and

The government-wide organizational chart, showing both government-wide organizations rendering services and all non-central departments, whether or not these departments are reflected as benefiting from central services in the government-wide allocation plan.

In summary, preparation of the government-wide cost allocation plan includes the following steps:

Identification of the costs of each type of service to be claimed;

Determination of the method of allocation for each type of service to user agencies;

Mathematical allocation of the cost of services to user agencies; and

Summarization of the amounts allocated into a single, formal comprehensive government-wide plan.

Indirect Cost Plan or Proposal

The second plan covers distribution of indirect costs within the individual contractor or grantee agency to all work performed by the agency. The costs distributed would include costs of services allocated to the contractor or grantee agency under the government-wide consolidated cost allocation plan. This second plan is referred to as an indirect cost proposal.

The total costs of a contractor or grantee agency include both direct project or program costs and indirect costs that jointly benefit two or more activities. As mentioned, indirect costs will be comprised of two factors: the indirect costs of the individual agency, plus a proportionate share of government-wide indirect costs, as reflected in the government-wide cost allocation plan.

Care must be taken to insure that the indirect cost plan or proposal has assured that:

All activities of the contractor or grantee agency are included;

The distribution of indirect costs is based on a method(s) that is reasonably indicative of the amount of services provided;

The services provided are necessary to the success of the federally assisted program or project;

The level of costs incurred are reasonable;

The costs for central government-wide services are charged in conformance with the government-wide consolidated cost allocation plan; and

All costs claimed under the proposal are allowable in accordance with OMB Circular A-87.

In cooperation with the Office of Management and Budget, the Department of Health, Education and Welfare has, for some years, published government-wide guidelines for establishing both consolidated cost allocation plans and indirect cost plans for contractors and grantees of the federal government. The guides include a detailed explanation of OMB Circular A-87, specific instructions relating to the preparation of the indirect cost plans and sample illustrations of cost allocation and indirect cost plans.

The most current series of these guidelines should be obtained and examined prior to undertaking an audit of any governmental unit receiving assistance from the federal government.

Statutory Limitations on Indirect Costs

As mentioned, costs may not be recovered as part of a cost allocation plan or indirect cost plan if such costs cannot be recovered by law or other statutory limitation. Further, when the maximum allowable costs are less than the amounts that otherwise would be recoverable under the plans, the excess is not recoverable and may not be shifted to another federally supported program.

For example, the Department of Health, Education and Welfare (in its Departmental Staff Manual—*Grants Administration*) outlines indirect costs reimbursements for several programs that will be limited or prohibited:

Fellowships and similar awards under which federal financing is exclusively in the form of fixed amounts or the normal published tuition rates of an institution;

Construction grants;

Grants to individuals;

Grants to organizations located outside the territorial limits of the United States; and

Programs with legal prohibitions or limitations against the reimbursement of indirect costs.

Knowledge of these types of cost prohibitions can be determined only by examining the laws and regulations of the specific federally assisted program under which the indirect costs are being claimed.

Importance of Cost Allocation Plans and Indirect Cost Proposals

The failure of a contractor or grantee agency to comply with OMB Circular A-87 could place the agency's claim for reimbursement of indirect costs in jeopardy. A federal contracting and grantor department may disallow indirect costs previously awarded and approved on a provisional basis. Further, in the absence of an approved provisional indirect costs rate, the new contract or grant amounts will not include an amount for indirect costs. Thus, the retention of amounts received and the realization of any end of period receivables is not certain.

If an indirect cost rate is later established, based on a late submission or delinquent preparation of an indirect cost plan, the indirect costs may be allowed as a claim under the contract or grant only for the period after the date the plan existed.

Thus, if extenuating circumstances prevent on-time submission or current preparation of these plans, it is important that the federal agency be requested to formally extend the due date for plans and that the extension be made a part of any special condition of the contract or grant.

Methods of Reimbursing Indirect Cost

Governmental contractors and grantees may be reimbursed for allowable indirect costs by one of several methods. The methods are often identified by the following descriptors.

Provisional Indirect Cost Rate

A provisional indirect cost rate is an estimated, interim, negotiated indirect cost rate, used to reimburse the governmental contractor or grantee for indirect expenses or costs incurred during the contract or grant period. The adjustment to actual indirect expenses or costs incurred will be negotiated or determined by government audit after the close of the fiscal period during which performance was rendered.

Fixed Indirect Cost Rate

A fixed indirect cost rate is a predetermined, negotiated indirect cost rate used when the governmental contractor or grantee is sufficiently experienced to calculate the probable level of indirect expenses or cost that will be incurred during the period of performance. The fixed rate limits the extent to which indirect expenses will be reimbursed.

Lump-Sum Indirect Cost Amount

A lump-sum indirect cost amount is a predetermined, negotiated, fixed amount that will be reimbursed for indirect cost. The lump-sum amount is considered appropriate when the benefits from an indirect service cannot be determined precisely. The lump-sum amount must be deducted from the other costs being allocated to other activities of the governmental contractor or grantee.

Negotiated Indirect Cost Rate

The negotiated indirect cost rate is the most common form of rate determination, whereby a contractor or grantee submits an indirect cost plan or budget that is used as the basis for establishing a provisional overhead rate for the period of performance. The actual rate will be calculated after the close of the fiscal period. Once the actual rate is known, the federal agency and the contractor or grantee will negotiate a final rate to be accepted for the contracts or grants.

Audited Indirect Cost Rate

An audited indirect cost rate is an indirect cost rate that is determined by government audit. The auditor is the final determinant of the nature and level of costs that will be allowed or accepted for reimbursement under the contract or grant. No negotiations are conducted with the agency when indirect cost rates are determined by audit.

Fixed Rate with Carry-Forward

A fixed rate with carry-forward provision is an indirect provisional rate, permitted by the Department of Health, Education and Welfare, having the characteristics of both. An indirect cost rate is computed and fixed for a future fiscal period based upon an estimated level of activity. As the actual indirect costs become known, the difference between the provisional rate and the actual rate is "carried forward" or "rolled forward" as an adjustment of the indirect cost rate of a subsequent accounting period.

The audit of a governmental contractor or grantee requires that general and special conditions of all agreements relating to indirect costs be carefully examined. Costs not chargeable under one agreement may not be allocated, directly or indirectly, to another program for recoverable purposes. Particular attention must be given to compliance with any conditions precedent to recovery of indirect costs that must be met by a governmental contractor or grantee.

Unallowable Costs

As a matter of public policy, several types of expenses or costs may not be charged to federal contracts or grants. The following costs, cited in the OMB Circular A-87 and other federal cost principles guides, are the most common unallowable expenses:

Advertising—includes cost of advertisements in newspapers, magazines, radio and television, direct mailings, trade papers and the like, unless such advertising is done solely for contract or grant purposes;

Budgeting—includes cost for services of a central budget office since such costs are cost of general government, unless cost is related to services identifiable or related to the contract or grant;

Legal—includes cost for legal services furnished by the chief legal officer of a state or local government solely for the purpose of discharging his general responsibilities as legal officer and legal expenses for prosecution of claims against the federal government;

Travel—includes cost for transportation and travel, lodging and subsistence in excess of less-than-first-class accommodation (except when such accommodations are not reasonably available) and cost in excess of prescribed federal governmental travel and per diem travel regulations;

Bad debts—includes cost for any losses arising from uncollectible accounts, other claims, related costs and reserves or allowances established for similar costs;

Contingencies—includes cost for contributions to a contingency reserve or other similar provision for unforeseen events;

Contributions and donations—includes cost of gifts, contributions or donations of any kind;

Entertainment—includes cost of amusement, social activities and incidental costs relating thereto, such as meals, beverages, lodgings, rentals, transportation and gratuities;

Fines and penalties—includes cost resulting from violations of or failure to comply with federal, state and local laws and regulations;

Government officials' expenses—includes cost of the office of governor of a state or the chief executive of a political subdivision that are considered as a general cost of the government;

Interest or other financial expense—includes cost of interest or borrowings (however represented), bond discount cost of financing and refinancing operations and legal and professional fees paid in connection therewith, except where authorized by federal legislation;

Legislative expenses—includes cost of salaries and other expenses of the state legislature or similar local governmental bodies, such as county supervisors, city councils, school boards, etc., whether incurred for purposes of legislation or executive direction; and

Underrecovery of costs under contract or grant agreements—any cost in excess of the federal contribution under another contract or grant, regardless of whether such costs were charged or recovered as a direct or an indirect cost.

In addition to the above listing of unallowable costs, the special or general conditions of the contract or grant, or the regulations of a federal agency, may, for some reason, establish other expenses or costs that will not be accepted as allowable charges, or claims under a contract or grant with that agency.

Matching Share and In-Kind Contributions

Many federal government contracts and grants require that benefit recipients provide a specified ratio or matching share of funds, resources, other assets or services as a condition of the award. These matching or in-kind contributions are subject to federal audit and will be evaluated for allowability, allocability and reasonableness in the same manner as the direct and indirect costs described earlier. Supporting records and documentation must be maintained for the matching share or in-kind contributions with the same care and for the same time period as is applied to other project costs.

Definition of Related Terms

The obligation to provide an agreed-to matching share or in-kind contribution constitutes a legal liability. A deficiency in this share may have to be met by providing a cash payment or reducing the amount of an earlier claim to the federal government. For this reason, an understanding of certain government-wide terms is essential. OMB Circular, A-102, which sets forth the administrative requirements for contracts and grants with state and local governments, has prescribed the following terminology relating to matching share or in-kind contributions:

Project costs—all necessary charges by a contractor or grantee in accomplishing the objectives of the program, with such costs being limited to the allowable types of costs set forth in the OMB Circular A-87.

Matching share—that portion of project costs not borne by the federal government, usually a minimum percentage for matching share prescribed by federal legislation and included in the formal agreement. The matching share may consist of:

Project costs not requiring cash outlay, but including charges such as depreciation, and use charges for buildings and equipment;

Services and real or personal property, or use thereof, donated by other public agencies, institutions, private organizations or individuals; or

Cash contributed or donated by other public agencies, institutions, private organizations or individuals.

Cash contributions—cash outlay, including outlays of money contributed to the contractor or grantee by other public agencies and institutions, private organizations and individuals, and, when authorized by federal legislation, funds received from other federal contracts, grants or entitlements.

In-kind contributions—the value of noncash contributions that may consist of charges for real property and equipment, value of goods and services directly benefitting and specifically identifiable with the federally assisted program and, where authorized by federal legislation, property purchased with federal funds. To be allowable, all in-kind contributions must meet several criteria:

The contributions must be identifiable from the records of the recipient organization;

The contributions may not be included as contributions for any other federally assisted program;

The contributions must be necessary and reasonable for the accomplishment of the program or project objectives.

Valuation of Matching Share and In-kind Contributions

Questions relating to the valuation of amounts claimed for matching share or in-kind contributions may arise during an audit of a governmental contractor or grantee. The following government-wide criteria, established by OMB Circular A-102, may be used as a guide in assessing the reasonableness of the valuations claimed.

Rates for Volunteer Services

The rates for volunteers should be consistent with the rates regularly paid for similar work in the state or local government or in the labor market in which the governmental contractor or grantee competes for the kind of services involved.

Volunteers of Other Organizations

When another employer furnishes services of an employee, the services shall be valued at the employee's regular rate of pay, exclusive of any fringe benefits and overhead costs, provided the services require the same skill as that for which the employee normally is paid.

Valuation of Materials

Contributed materials may include office supplies, maintenance supplies or workshop and classroom supplies. The valuation placed on the donated materials should be reasonable and not in excess of the cost of the materials to the donor or the current market price, whichever is less, at the time the materials are charged to the project.

Valuation of Equipment, Buildings, Land, Space

The valuation of donated equipment, buildings and land could differ, depending upon the purpose of the program. Under a federally assisted program, if the purpose is to provide a facility or space, the total value of the donated property may be claimed as the matching share. Where the purpose is to support activities requiring the use of equipment, buildings or land on a temporary or part-time basis, depreciation or use charges for equipment and buildings may be claimed and fair rental charges for land, provided the federal agency has approved the charges.

The value of donated equipment or buildings should be based on the donor's cost, less depreciation or the current market price of similar property, whichever is less. The value of donated land or its usage charge should be established by an independent appraiser.

Required Supporting Documentation

For federally assisted projects or programs, the documentation requirements for matching share or in-kind contributions are the same as for other direct and indirect costs claimed under the contract or grant. For example, the hours of volunteers must be supported by the same methods used by the governmental contractor or grantee for its own employees. The basis for charges for personal services, materials, equipment, buildings and land must be documented. Audit exceptions may be taken to unsupported claims for matching share or in-kind contributions in the same manner as for other claimed costs.

Other Federal Allowability Criteria

Earlier in this chapter, the general federal criteria for determining the acceptability of costs charged to a governmental contract or grant were cited as (1) allowability under law or statute or general federal government-wide cost principles, and (2) allocability directly or indirectly pursuant to cost allocation and indirect cost plans.

Costs claimed or charged to federal programs also must be examined from the standpoint of supportability and reasonableness. A cost may be questioned and disallowed in a subsequent government audit of a contract or grant for either of these two reasons.

Supportability of Costs

Costs, direct or indirect, that have been claimed or charged to a federal contract or grant must be supported by acceptable documentary evidence describing the type or classification of the expenditure, the purpose for which the expenditure was incurred, and the amount of the expenditure.

Both the GAO *Standards for Audit* and the AICPA's Statement on Auditing Standards contain similar requirements that sufficient competent evidence must be obtained through inspection, observation, inquiry or other confirmation methods to afford a basis for the conclusions reached by the auditor. The AICPA has defined evidential matter as the underlying accounting data and all corroborating information available to the auditor, which would include:

Records of original entry, such as journals, general and subsidiary ledgers, related accounting manuals, informal and such memorandum records as worksheets, supporting cost allocations, computations and reconciliations. Alone, this accounting data is not sufficient support for financial statements.

Corroborating evidence, such as checks, invoices, contracts, minutes of meetings, confirmations and other written statements by knowledgable people, information obtained by inquiry, observation, inspection and personal examination, and other information developed by or available to the auditor.

Independent tests of data and other records, including analysis and review, retracing procedural steps of the financial process, recalculating and reconciling data in work sheets relating to allocations.

In the public sector, auditors typically would question and, often, be required to disallow costs charged to contracts and grants when such costs are not supported by the above type of evidence and when the auditor is unable to satisfy himself by other evidential means as to the propriety of the costs.

Reasonableness of Costs

Most federal audit criteria require the application of a test of reasonableness in reaching a judgement as to the allowability of a specific cost. Reasonableness requires consideration of whether the cost was ordinary, necessary, prudent and within established practices. For example, the Environmental Protection Agency, in its audit guide for the construction grant program, stated that in determining reasonableness, consideration must be given to:

Whether the cost is of a type generally recognized as ordinary and necessary for the conduct of the contractor's or grantee's business and the performance of the contract or grant;

The restraints or requirements imposed by such factors as generally accepted sound business practices, arm's length bargaining, federal and state laws and regulations, and contract or grant terms and specifications;

The action that a prudent businessman would take in the circumstances, considering his responsibilities to the owners of the business, his employees, his customers, the government and the public at large; and

Significant deviations from the established practices of a contractor or grantee that may unjustifiably increase the contract or grant costs.

Exhibit 7-1 lists examples of costs and charges found to be unacceptable under the contracts or grants of the EPA. The illustrations are similar in nature to the exceptions taken by other federal agencies with respect to costs charged or claimed under governmental contracts and grants.

Exhibit 7-1

Examples of Costs Questioned Because of Audits of EPA Grant Programs

Examples of Unallowable Costs
- Interest on bonds or other financing
- Fines and penalties resulting from violation of Federal, State, and local laws
- Personal injury compensation or damages as a direct result of construction on the project

Examples of Unreasonable Costs
- Purchase of a six month's supply of materials during the last month of the grant except under EPA program grants where Federal assistance is obtained on a continuing basis
- Purchase of expensive equipment needed only for a short period when a lease would have been more economical
- Costs for which appropriate evidence is not available that the grantee employed those controls necessary to assure that the price was reasonable

Examples of Improperly Allocated Costs
- Costs already matched to another Federal program
- Inequitable allocation of indirect costs to the grant
- Costs allocated in total to the grant, which also benefited other grant programs

Examples of Improper Documentation of Costs
- Lack of time and attendance records, invoices, etc.
- Lack of written contracts with consultants and/or subcontractors
- Non-Federal contributions recorded but not documented

Examples of Costs Not Properly Approved by EPA
- Hire of consultants and/or subcontractors
- Purchase of capital equipment

Source: *Audit Guide for Construction Grant Program,* 1976, Environmental Protection Agency, Washington, D.C.

Applicability of Criteria Affecting Allowability of Costs

While often not clearly stated, there is a hierarchy of criteria affecting the allowability of costs charged or claimed under governmental programs. Typically, the most specific statements concerning the allowability or unallowability of costs prevail. For example, if a governmental unit accepts a federal contract or grant with specific conditions related to the allocation of costs, these conditions would prevail, provided compliance still was achieved with other broader conditions. If a cost is generally allowable, but is identified in the grant agreement as unallowable, that cost may not be later claimed under the grant.

At the federal government level, the broader cost principles established by higher level organizations relate to the subject of cost determination. These principles do not identify the circumstances or dictate the extent to which a grantor must participate in the financing of a particular grant. The broader principles, however, may clearly establish that certain types of costs are not allowable under any conditions; and these prohibitions cannot be overturned or rescinded by the negotiation of specific grant conditions to the contrary. Generally, the hierarchy of cost principles would be as described in the following sections.

Public Law or Statute

On occasion, laws or statutes will declare certain costs to be allowable or unallowable as part of the claim for expenditure reimbursement under a contract or grant. Where the legal provisions contain such specificity, other organizations may not overturn or waive such restrictions or prohibitions.

Government-Wide Regulations

In carrying out its legally mandated responsibilities on a government-wide basis, an agency, like OMB, may properly issue rules or regulations that prohibit or restrict the actions of individual agencies of that government. Without some form of formal exception or waiver, these government-wide criteria may not be ignored by the individual agency.

Departmental Regulations

Individual departments and agencies customarily will issue administrative and operational regulations to their constituent organizations setting forth terms and conditions for the guidance of these organizations. The subordinate organizations are required to comply with these regulations.

Agency Criteria

Program guidelines issued by individual agencies must be in compliance with all the criteria issued by the foregoing organizations. Additionally, however, the agency may impose further restrictions or prohibitions on its recipients through the issuance of program guidelines and other criteria that would tend to govern or control the conduct of recipients.

Contract or Grants

Care must be taken by the auditor to examine the specific contract or grant held by a governmental unit. Reliance should not be placed upon one's general knowledge of governmental regulations. The specific contract or grant conditions may contain limitations, exclusions, prohibitions and other restrictions that have been deemed necessary prerequisites to assisting the particular governmental unit under audit. Violations of the specific terms and conditions will render charges and claims unallowable, regardless of the overall acceptability of the expenditure.

Part III
Planning and Conducting Governmental Audits

Planning and Conducting a Government Audit

Examples of Special Scope Governmental Audits

Audits of Federally Assisted Programs

Performance Audits

Audit Test Methodoloy

Chapter 8
Planning and Conducting a Government Audit

Nature of Government Audits
Developing the Audit Approach
Developing the Audit Plan
Conducting the Audit Survey
Studying and Evaluating Controls, Systems, Practices
Conducting the Detailed Audit
Developing the Audit Budget

Unlike the literature on commercial auditing, the literature on planning and conducting governmental audits is limited. Much has been written concerning the accepted approaches to undertaking financial audit of a corporation. These audits, generally, have a singular objective (the issuance of a certificate as to the reasonableness of the financial statements) for a single entity (the corporation) and may not require the original planning effort that is necessary to undertake a governmental audit.

In contrast, a governmental organization, a federal agency or a municipality, will have several entities that must be audited. These entities are referred to as appropriations at the federal level and as funds on the municipal or local government level. These entities often must be examined from several aspects—the agency as an organization, legal and statutory requirements, budgetary conformance, alternative accounting practices. In addition, limited scope or special scope audits often may be required to satisfy the total audit requirement.

To assume that a governmental audit is similar to a corporate financial audit, or to undertake the government audit without the benefit of a planned audit approach, will most assuredly result in duplication of audit effort, delays in performance of the reviews, and possibly the omission of critical examination steps. Careful planning of each government audit will avoid many problems and minimize risks.

Nature of Government Audits

Elements of a Government Audit

For each government audit, it is important that all parties have an understanding of the scope of audit. The scope of commercial financial statement audits is clearly documented in the Statement on Auditing Standards of the AICPA. Such audits must be made in accordance with generally accepted auditing standards, which presume the conduct of a specific audit scope. Presently, the applicable audit criteria for governmental audits set forth in the GAO *Standards for Audit* (Chapter 6) include three elements:

Financial and compliance audits, to assess the propriety of financial operations and financial reports, as well as to assess compliance with laws and regulations;

Economy and efficiency audits, to determine whether governmental managers are adhering to efficient and economical practices; and

Program results audits, to assess whether the goals, objectives, benefits or results are being achieved as contemplated in authorizing legislation.

The completion of all elements would be required only when undertaking a full-scope government audit. Elements also may be interchanged. It is important to note that compliance auditing is not only involved in financial audits, but also in economy and efficiency and program results audits. Additionally, the reporting may vary. Separate reports may be required, although, in a full scope audit, a single report is preferred.

Establishing Audit Objectives

The objectives or goals of government audits may be established by legislative units, chief executives of the government, heads of agencies or the direct governmental client. If the audit is to be performed by government auditors, the audit unit determines which of the elements of a full scope audit would be applicable and establishes the scope of audit necessary to meet the goals and objectives. In instances where the audit is to be made by an independent public accountant, the government organization typically will describe the goals and objectives, as well as specific elements or other types of the audits that will be required. The scope of the audit generally will be set forth in a formal agreement or contract, which may be later modified, but only through formal amendment to the engagement agreement, which may entail a change in price.

Developing the Audit Approach

An appropriate investment in planning a government audit will mitigate the need for retracing audit steps, changing audit direction and modifying testing and sampling approaches once the audit has begun. There is no uniform, "best" way to undertake a government audit. Even the best planned audit must be modified when the observed circumstances vary from the contemplated conditions.

There are several steps required to develop an audit approach. Each succeeding step involves detailed testing and examination, evaluating earlier planning and continually assessing risks and benefits in relation to audit cost being incurred. The steps include:

Develop audit plan;

Conduct audit survey;

Make tests and reviews of controls, systems and practices pursuant to an audit guide;

Conduct detailed audit, pursuant to an audit program.

Exhibit 8-1 illustrates the breadth of planning that might be required to undertake an audit of financial, compliance, economy and efficiency. (The program results or performance audit is described in Chapter 11.)

Exhibit 8-1
Generalized Audit Approach—Financial, Compliance, Economy, Efficiency Reviews

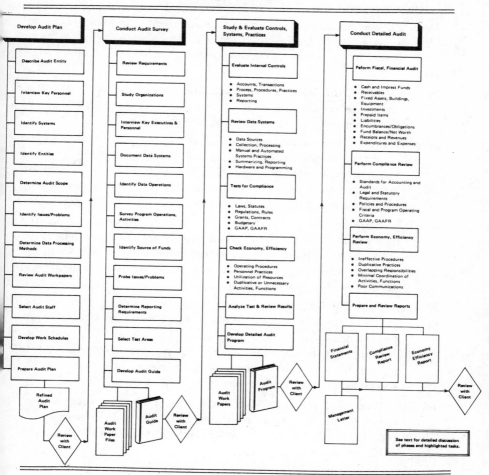

Developing the Audit Plan

An audit must be developed to insure that the most efficient and effective steps, tests and reviews will be made in arriving at the conclusions set forth in the reports issued at the completion of the audit. A sound plan requires that a series of inquiries, interviews and limited testing be done to obtain an orientation concerning the scope, possible difficulties, special circumstances and other conditions that might limit or affect the performance of the audit. The efforts required to develop the audit plan also will permit a clearer definition of the staff skills, experience and academic training required to perform the audit.

To develop an audit plan, several general areas should be explored. While these areas will vary according to the nature of the audit, audits of financial statements and compliance as well as of economy and efficiency could require that information be gathered on the following subjects:

Define the audit entity—Is a particular government appropriation or fund to be audited? Are all funds under control of a single agency to be audited? Are all organizations operating within a single fund to be audited?

Interview key client personnel—Are line and staff management aware of the audit? Is the legislative as well as executive branch of the responsible governmental unit aware of the audit?

Identify the systems to be reviewed—Is the audit to be limited to the accounting system or will other financial systems be involved? Must tests be made of management information systems not directly integrated into fiscal or accounting systems? Will reviews be required of other systems (communications, statistical, reporting)?

Identify entities to be included in audit—Is management of the audited entity centralized or decentralized? Are geographical locations of the entity known? Have areas of activity, function and responsibility been identified and related to specific organizational units and personnel?

Determine the scope of audit—Is the audit limited to financial statements? What is the extent of required compliance examinations? Must compliance with federal, state or local laws and statutory requirements be determined? Should the audit be extended to include tests to assess economy and efficiency of operations? Are special examinations and reports expected?

Identify issues and problems—Are there special or other conditions or circumstances that could affect the audit? Have there been recent reports or evidence of questionable practices or weaknesses published on such subjects as:

accounting,

auditing,

reporting,

systems performance,

management practices,

staff practices, or

other matters?

Determine method of processing data—Are any portions of the financial and data systems automated? Which portions of systems are performed manually? Is there an inventory of the automated data processing equipment, peripheral accessories and operating languages? Does a formal library of computer programs exist? What is the method of data input? How is data stored—in file or data base structure?

Review audit workpapers—Do audit workpapers exist from prior years or from audits by other activities? Have audit reports for past audits been obtained and examined? Are prior audit deficiencies and concerns clearly inventoried for follow-up during the current audit? Do written EDP procedures and application control procedures exist?

Select the audit staff—Will a team of professional auditors possess adequate professional proficiency for the tasks required? Are other disciplines and skills required? Will the proposed audit team be perceived as experts, qualified to conduct the full required scope of audits?

Develop work schedules—When will the survey be conducted? What tests will be made during any interim and final audit periods? When will receivables be confirmed, inventories observed, computer systems and processes examined, and other systems verified? What level of staffing will be required for the survey, the testing and reviews, and the detailed audits? Can the audited organization's staff assist? Do audit procedures permit use of internal audit workpapers or staff? Must the audit effort be coordinated with other existing examinations or other audits? What locations are involved?

The development of a plan will assist in setting overall direction of the audit. Written plans can serve as orientation aids for briefing audit staff and management and for providing an assurance that goals and objectives will be achieved.

Conducting the Audit Survey

The codification of auditing standards and procedures, Statement on Auditing Standards, No. 1, requires a study of the internal controls, including accounting controls. The study should be in two phases: (1) a survey to obtain knowledge and understanding of the organization and of prescribed procedures; and (2) tests for compliance and a determination that procedures and controls have been applied in practice.

This section of the audit approach is designed to meet the survey phase of the study. Information and facts on subject areas highlighted in the preceding paragraphs would be obtained by discussion, interviews and reference to such documentation as procedure manuals, organization manuals, flow charts, decision tables, authorizing legislation, regulations, reports, etc.

The plan should be prepared to permit the conduct of an audit survey. Interrelated legal, accounting and performance criteria of government audits also make it prudent to conduct a preliminary survey in advance of conducting detailed tests and reviews of transactions, controls, systems and accounts. The product of the survey should be an audit guide, sufficiently detailed to permit efficient execution of all tests and reviews of controls and systems with minimum duplication and maximum economy.

During the survey, inquiries should be made into several areas that will affect the extent of later testing and reviews. Some of the more general survey areas include:

Examine governing or applicable legislative or other requirements:

   Study laws and statutes affecting or governing the audited entity;

   Study records of legislative, council, public or other hearings;

   Read promulgated rules and regulations prescribing operating requirements;

   Obtain policies and procedures published by management of the audited entity; and

   Identify requirements of federal, state, other governmental grants or contracts.

Study organizations involved:

   Determine the structure of organizations involved in the audit;

   Confirm which operations are centralized, which decentralized, note locations, activities, functions, programs;

   Obtain a description of responsibility and authority of various organizations, levels within organizations, activities, programs;

   Visit locations, activities, functions, programs to be audited; and

   Interview key line, financial and staff executives and personnel.

Review financial and other information:

   Obtain and review financial and other information reports management relies upon;

   Assess importance, frequency, timeliness, usefulness of reported information;

   Obtain and review charts of accounts, financial procedures, data dictionaries; and

   Examine samples of forms, documents, reports and other output generated by systems.

Document the various data systems:

   Inventory the several systems that could affect the audit;

Execute a flow chart of systems, e.g. accounting, fiscal, information, statistical planning, budgeting, reporting;

Analyze systems relating to audit; and

Examine manuals and forms.

Identify data operations:

Identify and study manual systems;

Examine automated systems and consult experts;

Identify computer hardware, programs and security; and

Create a flow chart for the processes showing the flow of information.

Survey program operations and activities:

Identify the classifications of employees involved;

Determine whether grantees and contractors are involved; and

Decide whether independent authorities and business-type enterprises are in existence and whether trust funds are involved.

Identify the sources of funds:

Determine whether funds are to come from general taxes (property, income), fees or assessments, grants and contracts from other levels of government and private organizations, or reimbursements to working capital funds

Probe into issues and problems that might affect the audit:

Catalog the cited effects and causes;

Assess, on a preliminary basis, the impacted organizations, operations, activities, etc.;

Review earlier reports, studies, other documentation; and

Interview knowledgeable officials.

Determine reporting requirements:

Define the nature of reporting desired;

Decide on the format of reporting;

Determine the distribution of reports; and

Isolate special reporting requirements.

Select test and review areas:

Establish criteria for conducting tests and reviews of systems and controls (e.g. applicable auditing standards, newness of program, dollar magnitude, duration of program period, legal requirements, sensitivity and public concerns, past practices, observed or known weaknesses, results of other evaluations, types of expenses, sources of funding, sample of organizations and, grant and contract requirements).

The resultant audit guide should specifically address several aspects of tests and reviews to be made of internal controls and systems. Additionally, the guide should contain a detailed inventory of compliance requirements for auditing the entities affected. Efficiency and economy considerations must be identified, and the nature of the examination to be made must be clearly described.

The U. S. General Accounting Office, in its publication, *The Audit Survey—A Key Step in Auditing Government Programs,* defines a survey as the first step in an audit, the main purposes of which are to identify problem areas warranting additional review and to obtain information for use in planning and performing detailed review work. Exhibit 8-2 summarizes four broad groups of information often required during the conduct of an audit survey.

Exhibit 8-2

The Audit Survey—Information or Data Required

Categories	Specific Information Required
• General background information	Organization—divisions, duties, responsibilities, location and characteristics of field offices, grantee organizations, number and location of employees
	Financing—appropriations, budget requests, budget data submitted to legislators, comparative fiscal information, borrowing authority, type, cost and location of assets, operations costs
	Operating methods—established policies, operating methods, goal setting and performance monitoring process, problems and areas of special interest
• Authority	Legal and judicially interpreted authority, administrative regulations, management directives, resolutions
• Goals and objectives	Statements of goals and objectives, criteria or standard and performance indicators
	Implicit goals of economy and efficiency audits
	Intended accomplishments of activities
	Creating goals not job of auditor
• Extent desired goals are achieved	Evidence of weaknesses in controls, inefficient operations, impairment of program results
	Identify problem, examine controls and procedures, confirm existence of deficiencies, suggest corrective actions

Source: *The Audit Survey—A Key Step in Auditing Government Programs,* undated (issued 1978), U.S. General Accounting Office, Washington, D.C.

Studying and Evaluating Controls, Systems, Practices

A study and evaluation is required of the controls, systems and practices of the audited entity for the purposes of placing reliance thereon in determining the nature, extent and timing of audit tests to be made during detailed examination.

Applicable Standards

Of concern here would be systems, internal control, including accounting controls defined in the Statement on Auditing Standards, No. 1, as:

Accounting controls comprise the plan of organization and procedures and records concerned with safeguarding assets, and reliability of financial records.

Of additional concern would be the economy and efficiency of procedures. In governmental audits, these terms are used in a relative sense and do not relate to the total organization. The General Accounting Office believes that the observations, findings and conclusions should be related to specific processes, methods or activities that can be made more economical or efficient. The reporting is viewed as being similar to the established commercial auditing practice of advising management of needed operational improvements. The AICPA industry audit guide has taken the position that Statement on Auditing Standards, No. 1, Section 320 and subsection 320a and 320b, relating to the review of internal controls, are applicable in their entirety to the audits of governmental units.

General Scope of Tests and Reviews

As indicated, the overall purpose of the tests and reviews of controls, systems and practices is to determine the degree to which the auditor can place reliance on adherence to these requirements by management and staff of the audited organization. The auditor's degree of reliance will be demonstrated by the detailed auditing deemed necessary to assess the reasonableness of the financial and performance aspects of the audited entity.

The audit guide should, minimally, require:

Evaluation of internal controls—including tests of financial transactions, subsystems, accounts, and the process and application of procedures and practices by management and employees;

Review of data systems—including checks of data sources, tests of processing controls and procedures, and evaluation of manual and automated processes for originating, collecting, processing, summarizing and reporting information;

Tests for compliance—including not only adherence to policies and procedures prescribed by management, but also adherence to laws, regulations, grant requirements, contract requirements, budgetary limitations as well as generally accepted accounting procedures applicable to the audited entity;

Checks for economy and efficiency—including an evaluation of the appropriateness of operating procedures, personnel practices, utilization of assets and equipment, procurement procedures, and activities that would contribute to minimizing costs and promoting operating efficiency; and

Analysis of tests and review results—preferably in the form of narrative or flow chart descriptions of controls, evaluation of controls— weaknesses, strengths, relative effectiveness—and conclusions as to whether certain aspects of the system controls can be relied upon and where more detailed tests must be made.

The above work will yield the information necessary to develop an audit program to be used for conducting the detailed audit. Multiple concerns and criteria that must be considered generally require that a written audit program be prepared. Such a document will minimize duplication of detailed audit steps, permit a variety of accountability concerns to be addressed and provide assurance that audit steps are applied uniformly to all aspects of the audited entity.

The audit program will contain those detailed audit steps required to permit final conclusions to be reached with regard to financial statements, records, accounts and systems, execution of organizational responsibilities, impact of known issues and problems, and compliance with legal and other criteria imposed or applicable to the audited entity.

Testing Methodology

As indicated, the AICPA, in Statement on Auditing Standards, No. 1, requires a study and evaluation of internal controls in two phases. The first phase is the earlier survey discussed above. The second phase includes tests for compliance and a determination that controls are being applied in practice.

A general methodology for conducting the application analysis phase would require that the several following steps be performed:

Determination, by analysis and inquiry, of the controls that have been established. Workpapers, consisting of preliminary organization charts, flow charts and narrative descriptions of procedures should be prepared.

Creation of "walkthroughs" of the systems for selected transactions to confirm that the systems are functioning as described and that the controls prescribed for classes of transactions are being applied.

Complete documentation of the final organization, including flow charts of systems, document routing and information, and preparation of narrative procedural memos for the workpapers.

Determination, through tentative assessment of the systems of internal control, of the degree of reliance that may be placed on the system in selecting the nature and extent of audit procedures to test internal controls and applying audit procedure to account balances.

Testing, as documented in the workpapers, to confirm, modify or reject earlier tentative assessment of the system of internal controls.

Preparation, on the basis of the study and tests, of an audit program for selecting samples and procedures to audit account balances, transactions, activities, functions and practices.

Exhibit 8-3 illustrates a general methodology for the conduct of the study and evaluation of an organization's controls, systems and practices. The applications should be construed as examples and not as the total requirements necessary for complete testing of controls. Also, the nature of the governmental organization or particular scope of the audit may require consolidation of several applications and, possibly, may not require the completion of other applications.

Conducting the Detailed Audit

The primary purpose of making detailed audits of the account balances is to enable the auditor to assure himself that the balances of these accounts at the end of the reporting period are stated in conformity with the generally accepted accounting principles applicable in the circumstances, that such principles have been applied on a basis consistent with those of the preceding periods, and that the practices of personnel, activities and functions are in compliance with required laws, statutes, regulations and other criteria.

To conclude that financial statements of the organization fairly reflect the position of the audited organization, asset, liability, fund balance, revenue and expenditure accounts must be audited. Similarly, the detailed audit will examine and verify adherence to economical and efficient practices.

A formal audit program should be developed to assure uniform application of audit tests to the various accounts and activities and functions of the audited entity. Proper planning at the outset of the detailed audit phase will minimize duplicate examination of transactions and provide a basis for systematic application of audit tests. Additionally, proper structuring to conduct tests simultaneously will provide the basis for arriving at conclusions on the myriad compliance requirements that exist within an audit of a governmental organization, fund or appropriation.

Scope of the Detailed Audit

As mentioned, the scope of a governmental audit can be considerably broader than corporate audits, particularly if such an audit is made in accordance with the full scope audit outlined in the GAO *Standards for Audit.* As indicated in Exhibit 8-1, the detailed audit could require the performance of a fiscal, financial audit, a compliance review, and an examination of the

Exhibit 8-3

Illustration of Process to Study & Evaluate Controls, Systems and Practices

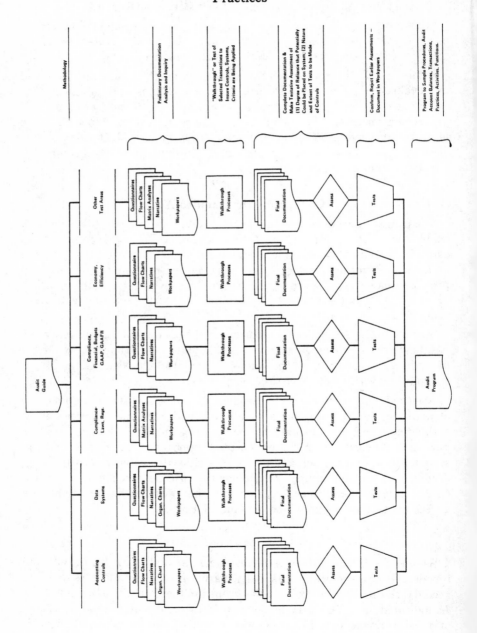

economy and efficiency of the practices of the audited entity. Many specific tests and factors that must be considered to conduct such audits include:

For the fiscal or financial audit:

Tests of various types of transactions;

Examination of account balances, trial balance totals and amounts on financial statements;

Possession of letters from counsel, management and third parties;

Verification and confirmation of cash and receivables;

Review and confirmation of receivables, encumbrances, obligations and payables;

Inspection of fixed assets;

Confirmation, verification, inspection and valuation of investments;

Observation and valuation of inventories, supplies and materials;

Determination of prepaids and accruals;

Verification of revenues and of estimates of uncollectibles; and

Verification of costs, expenses, obligations and encumbrances.

For the compliance review:

Ascertainment of consistency of policies and procedures to practices;

Determination of consistency of activities with laws, statutes, regulations and other requirements;

Assessment of compliance with applicable grant and contracting rules and regulations; and

Determination of consistency in application of governmental regulations, requirements and practices among the activities and functions of the audited entity.

For the economy and efficiency review:

Examination of observed ineffective procedures and practices of organizations, activities and functions; and

Review and documentation of any noted weaknesses, duplications, wasteful practices or other evidence of uneconomical or ineffective operations or use of personnel efforts, investments or other activities supported by governmental resources.

Exhibit 8-4 illustrates the various considerations that should be planned in undertaking the detailed audit of a governmental entity to avoid or minimize redundant auditing. The sample selection must be made with care to insure that sufficient evidence has been examined to give a basis for conclusions and opinions relating to specific compliance, economy and efficiency requirements.

Governmental Auditing

Exhibit 8-4

Sampling Considerations for Governmental Audit Entries

Audit Applications	Governmental Audit Entity				
	General Fund	Special Fund	Fixed Asset Fund	Grant Program	Contract Activity
Compliance Tests					
Verify Accounts	Fund Account Balances	Fund Account Balances	Fund Account Balances	Fund Account Balances	Fund Account Balances
Review Economy & Efficiency					
Compliance Tests					
Tests of Revenues	Revenue Transactions	Revenue Transactions	Revenue Transactions	Revenue Transactions	Revenue Transactions
Review Economy & Efficiency					
Compliance Tests					
Review Economy & Efficiency					
Tests of:					
Personnel	Obligation, Encumbrance, Expenditure Transactions	Obligation, Encumbrance, Expenditure Transactions	Obligation, Encumbrance, Expenditure Transactions	Obligation, Encumbrance, Expenditure Transactions	Obligation, Encumbrance, Expenditure Transactions
Travel					
Grants					
Procurement					
Equipment, Etc.					

Detailed audit requirements for various account balances and governmental revenue and expenditure transactions are described in other chapters. Additionally, guidance on detailed governmental audit procedures is provided in several authoritative publications such as:

Industry Audit Guide—Audits of State and Local Governmental Units, AICPA's Committee on Governmental Accounting and Auditing, 1973,—particularly the section titled, "Audit Procedures for Specific Accounts," pages 50 to 69.

Governmental Accounting, Auditing, and Financial Reporting, Municipal Finance Officers Association (National Commission on Governmental Accounting), 1977,—particularly the section titled "Auditing Procedure", pages 131 to 146.

Audit Guidelines for Audits of Financial Operations of Federally Assisted Programs, United States General Accounting Office, October, 1978, particularly the section titled, "Tests of Account Balances and Other Audit Procedures," pages 30 to 37.

Developing the Audit Budget

Concurrent with development of the audit approach, planning should be done with respect to the audit budget. To insure that both the financial and the time budgets are met, an analysis and estimate should be made of the calendar time required to complete each phase of the outlined audit approach. Additionally, an estimate should be made of the level, number and skill or discipline of personnel or staff necessary to conduct the required audit.

To avoid omissions or minimize the risks of underestimates of requirements, audit organizations have made effective use of modified GANNT charts to display the time and staffing budgets required. Exhibit 8-5, illustrates one version of a time and staff budget for an audit.

It is important to recognize that the greater the detail of planning, the greater the likelihood that estimates will be met. It is possible, particularly on repeat audits, to prepare estimates of time and staffing required for each of the subphases of an audit. Uncertainty of problems that may be encountered or unanticipated difficulties should not be viewed as reasons for not constructing an audit budget. The allocation of audit resources and identification of skills and disciplines required to perform the audit, no matter how uninformed, will provide a benchmark from which deviations or variances can be assessed and adjustments made.

The audit budget should clearly identify the critical milestones of the audit and the times that audit phases must be completed.

Exhibit 8-5

Illustration of Time and Staff Budget

PHASES OF AUDIT	CALENDAR DAYS					ENGAGEMENT STAFF BUDGET					
	PERIOD 1	PERIOD 2	PERIOD 3	PERIOD 4		Director	Managers	Seniors	Specialists	Staff	Support
DEVELOP AUDIT PLAN					TOTAL	4	12	5	3		1
Describe Audit Entity							1		1		
Interview Key Personnel							1		1		
Identify Systems							1	1	1		
Identify Entities							1				
Determine Audit Scope						1	1	1			
Identify Issues/Problems						1	1	1			
Determine Data Processing							1				
Review Audit Workpapers							1				
Select Audit Staff						1	1				
Develop Work Schedules							2	1			
Prepare Audit Plan						1	2	1			1
CONDUCT AUDIT SURVEY					TOTAL	4	8	10	11	21	3
Review Requirements						1			1		
Study Organizations							1	1	1		
Interview Key Executive							1	1	1		
Document Data Systems							1	2	2	4	
Identify Data Operations							1	1	1	4	
Survey Program Operations							1	2	2	4	
Identify Sources of Funds								1		4	
Probe Issues/Problems						1	1	1	1	5	
Determine Reporting Requirements								1			
Select Test Areas						1	1		1		
Develop Audit Guides						1	1		1		3
MAKE TESTS AND REVIEWS					TOTAL	4	6	5	3	16	3
Evaluate Internal Controls						1	1	1	1	4	
Review Data Systems						1	1	1	1	4	
Tests for Compliance							1	1		4	
Check Economy, Efficiency							1	1		4	
Analyze Tests and Review Results						1	1	1			
Develop Detailed Audit Program						1	1		1		3
CONDUCT DETAILED AUDIT					TOTAL	4	5	10	6	40	10
Perform Fiscal, Financial Audit						1	2	4	1	20	
Perform Compliance Review						1	1	2	2	10	
Perform Economy, Efficiency Review						1	1	2	2	10	
Prepare and Review Reports						1	1	2	1		10
PROGRESS REPORTS											
					TOTAL FOR AUDIT	16	31	25	23	77	17

LEGEND:

△ Refined Audit Plan
◇ Recommended Discussion with Audited Organization
②△ Audit Program
△ Audit Guide

Reports:
① Financial Statements
② Management Letter
③ Compliance Review
④ Economy, Efficiency

Chapter 9
Examples of Special Scope Governmental Audits

Audits of Accounting Systems and Controls
Audits of Financial Statements and Reports
Economy and Efficiency Audits
Compliance Audits of Expenditures
Obligation and Encumbrance Audits
Settlement Audits
Procurement and Contract Audits
Grantor and Grant Audits
Efforts to Consolidate Governmental Audits

In governmental auditing, a variety of special scope audits are performed. While aspects may be duplicative of parts of other broader scope audits, agency management and legislatures often require these in-depth examinations to provide assurance that specific operations and activities are being conducted in compliance with legal and other requirements and that there is a reasonable level of efficiency and economy practiced. The expansion of inter-agency cross servicing audit agreements and increased reliance on the audits of other levels of government may permit the performance of some of these special scope audits as a part of another scheduled audit, thus conserving audit resources and simultaneously minimizing disruptions caused by audits.

A generalized methodology for planning and conducting a full scope governmental audit is presented in greater detail in Chapter 8. Performance audits, or examinations of agency or program effectiveness, are discussed in Chapter 11. The several special scope audits and reviews discussed in this chapter include:

Audits of accounting systems and controls;

Audits of financial statements and reports;

Audits for efficiency and economy;

Audits for expenditure compliance, including audits of

Personnel and payroll,

Travel and transportation,

Property, and

Petty cash and imprest funds;

Audits of obligation and encumbrance;

Audits of accountable or certifying officers;

Audits of procurement or contract; and

Audits of grantor and grants.

Audits of Accounting Systems and Controls

Periodically, audits are made of a government's financial and information systems and internal controls. While one objective of these audits is to provide an indication of the reasonableness of the information reported to management, another important objective is to determine the extent to which policy and procedures are implemented and adhered to.

Internal controls will be observed and test-checked to assess their observance in practice. Accounting policy statements and procedures will be reviewed and related to the current practices. Reviews will be made of conditions, controls and individual accounts to assure:

The segregation of employee activity dealing with fiscal and financial data and currency;

The existence of prescribed authorization and approval procedures and of any delegation thereof;

The degree of compliance with policies and procedures;

The adequacy of forms, adherence to control procedures and the appropriateness of other controls;

The adherence to sound practices for coding, recording, summarizing and reporting financial transactions; and

The adequacy of documentation to support representations reflected in the accounts.

Many of the audit steps will be similar to those performed in conducting an audit pursuant to generally accepted auditing standards. However, special audit steps generally will be required to provide detailed audit coverage of specific financial and statistical accounts and controls. The resultant report is often made to agency management in narrative form and outlines the specific scope, audit observations, effect of observed conditions, conclusions and recommendations for improvement.

The General Accounting Office, in providing guidance to internal auditing staffs of the federal government, suggested in *Internal Auditing in Federal Agencies—Basic Principles, Standards, and Concepts* (1974) that the following audit inquiries might be made in examining the financial systems and controls of government agencies:

Do effective controls exist over revenues, expenditures, assets, liabilities?

Does proper accounting for resources, liabilities and operations exist?

Are financial reports accurate, reliable, useful and fairly presented?

Is there compliance with laws and regulations?

Are the policies, procedures, internal controls related to financial operations, accounting and financial reporting adequate?

Are revenues collected and accounted for?

Were expenditures made for approved purposes and properly authorized?

Do agency procedures result in prices, rates or fees that conform to laws and regulations?

Are prescribed procedures for expenditures being followed?

Are the data used by management for internal and external reporting reliable?

Do internal reports serve a purpose? Are they useful?

Are assets accounted for and protected from loss, misuse or deterioration?

Is there any possibility of fraud, dishonesty or practices that could lead to fraud, dishonesty, or loss?

Audits of Financial Statements and Reports

Governmental auditors are concerned with both the financial statements issued to external users and the reports, financial and statistical, used internally by management.

Financial Statements

Many governmental units issue annual financial statements for use by the government executive and by users external to government. Generally, these statements include a balance sheet, a statement of operations and a statement of changes in fund balances. In many instances, these statements have been audited by an independent auditor—either a state auditor or an independent public accountant. In numerous other instances, no independent audit is made of the published statements.

Depending upon the governmental entity's activities, the auditor's report might state that the financial statements were prepared in conformity with generally accepted accounting principles or with a comprehensive basis of accounting other than generally accepted accounting principles as prescribed by the government regulatory authority or agency. The report often takes the form of an opinion-type report that is related to the accompanying statements.

Financial and Statistical Reports

Periodically, generally on some cyclical basis, audits are made of the financial and statistical reports used in the management of the agency. Some of the objectives of such an audit will be:

To determine the currency, accuracy and completeness of the reported data;

To assess the continued usefulness and timeliness of the information that is being accumulated and reported;

To assure the consistency of the data being reported from one period to another; and

To determine the uniformity of definition of recorded cost and other data between the several organizations in the agency.

The scope of the audit will include a review of agency financial and information-reporting policies. A comparison of implementing procedures might be made to insure consistency with policy. Basic documentation will be examined to verify that practices are consistent with procedures. Observations will be made of recording, coding, processing and reporting practices. Examinations and tests may be made of prescribed controls to insure the continued integrity of the reported information. Tests will be made to determine the uniformity of the data reported by the several constituent organizations and the consistency of practices between accounting periods. Visits often will be made to geographically dispersed offices to assess the quality of the data input from these sources.

These audits typically are made by governmental auditors, although public accountants have been requested to perform such reviews. The report of such audits is narrative in form and describes the scope of work, audit observations, conclusions and recommendations.

Economy and Efficiency Audits

Auditors increasingly are performing audits with the objective of assessing the economy and efficiency of activities. In practice, it generally is recognized that these terms are relative and that there is no criteria to truly assess when or how any organization could attain the ultimate level of economy and efficiency. With the publication of the GAO *Standards for Audit,* a formal set of objectives was established for practitioners. The *Standards* describe the objectives of an audit for economy and efficiency as one to determine:

> ... whether the entity is managing or utilizing its resources (personnel, property, space and so forth) in an economical and efficient manner and the causes of any inefficiencies or uneconomical practices, including inadequacies in management information systems, administrative procedures or organizational structure.

GAO provided several examples of uneconomical or inefficient practices, in its publication titled *Internal Auditing:*

Procedures that are ineffective, wasteful or more costly than necessary;

Procedures that duplicate the efforts of employees or organizational units;

Work serving little or no useful purpose;

Procedures that use equipment inefficiently or uneconomically;

Overstaffing, in relation to work to be done;

Faulty buying practices and accumulation of excess property, materials and supplies; and

Wasteful use of property.

These audits are made pursuant to specially developed audit guides directed towards selected areas that the auditor has identified for review. Typically, the selected audit areas are determined after the performance of a preliminary survey or review. In other instances, the audit may have been directed by management. The audit findings and observations are set forth in a narrative-type report that should contain a full description of the work performed and all observations, conclusions and recommendations. The scope of work should be detailed, including the nature and number of interviews, tests, independent confirmations and other examinations made in the development of the reported conditions. Where clarity would be promoted, graphs, charts, tables and other data arrays are used. Wherever possible, attempts should be made to present the cost/benefit data of recommended alternatives to present practices.

In June, 1978, the U.S. General Accounting Office issued an exposure draft of a publication titled "Guidelines for Economy and Efficiency Audits of Federally Assisted Programs." This guide provides a uniform approach and uniform documentation procedures for economy and efficiency audits of governmental organizations, primarily state and local governmental units. Specific procedures are illustrated for several audit areas, such as: procurement, property management, personnel, fiscal administration and management information.

Compliance Audits of Expenditures

Governmental agencies have a particular concern with the disbursement of public funds for certain classifications or objects of expenditures. This concern is directed towards those expenditures offering an opportunity for abuse or personal gain. The controls and review processes relating to these types of expenditures are detailed, and strict compliance is required by agency officials. For this reason, governmental auditors generally perform annual audits of such expenditure areas as personnel and payroll activities, travel and transportation costs, property, and petty cash or imprest fund disbursements.

The following audit descriptions should not be considered as all-inclusive, but merely as illustrative. Other types of compliance audits might include audits of taxes and receipts, donations, royalties, communications and utility costs, investments and portfolio maintenance, printing and reproduction activities, computer acquisition and utilization, etc.

Personnel and Payroll Audits

Expenditures related to personnel often are the largest expenditures of governmental agencies. The rules and regulations relating to personnel, payment for services and fringe benefits are voluminous and detailed. The objective of a personnel or payroll audit is to determine the extent of compliance with the appropriate rules and regulations of the civil service or of labor union agreement, or with other criteria affecting the conditions of employment, compensation and related benefits.

The scope of such an audit will include a review of policies and procedures and an examination of practices relating to:

Application procedures for governmental employment;

Methods and types of appointments;

Decisions related to positions, qualifications and salary;

Changes in pay status relating to promotions, performance or discharge; and

Publication of vacancies, transfers and retirements.

The payroll audit may include:

Examining timekeeping procedures;

Reviewing costing and labor distribution practices;

Testing recording, accounting and reporting of personnel costs;

Observing payroll distributions;

Recomputing withholding and examining support for deductions; and

Performing other verification steps to assure that payments were authorized, appropriate and made to eligible persons.

Travel and Transportation Audits

Next to personnel, possibly the most closely monitored area is the cost incurred for travel and transportation. Government agencies typically will require an approval by a key official in advance of any trip. Additionally, a certification must usually be obtained that funds exist and that rather high levels of management have passed on the appropriateness of the proposed travel. Next, the employee or official must perform the travel in strict accordance with the applicable travel regulations. After the trip, a voucher detailing specifics surrounding all cost must be submitted and certified. Next, with few exceptions, this voucher is subjected to a close pre-payment audit.

The objective of an audit of travel and transportation costs is to determine that there is a system of control requiring compliance with the rules and regulations. The scope of such audits could vary, but often will include an assessment of the extent of compliance with applicable regulations and procedures relating to local travel costs (mileage, taxis, public transportation), per diem costs (lodging, meals and other costs incidental to travel), relocation costs (common carrier rates, permitted tonnage, distances moved, elapsed time periods, etc.), public transportation (common carrier, less-than-first-class accommodations, direct routing etc.), travel advances (procedures for requesting, liquidating and settling), and accounting procedures and practices (recording, accounting and reporting of costs).

Property Audits

Government agencies hold title to considerable inventories of property, including supplies, goods, equipment, buildings, furniture and fixtures. Additionally, there will be instances where the government has furnished property, equipment or other assets to grantees and contractors. In other cases, funds may have been advanced to grantees and contractors to acquire property, title to which vests in the government. Requirements must exist to procure, protect, preserve and properly dispose of these assets.

The objective of a property audit, regardless of who possesses the government's asset, is to assess the adequacy of policies, procedures, practices and controls relating to purchasing, storing, using, maintaining, disposing and accounting for the property of the government. Accordingly, the scope of governmental property audits are, in many respects, similar to the scope of those conducted in the corporate sector. Tests are made to assess the adequacy of accounting and internal controls over the property:

Records are examined;

Location, condition and existence of assets are verified;

Inventories are taken;

Counting and recording practices are observed;

Subsidiary property records, ledger accounts and asset reports are reviewed; and

Depreciation policies and procedures are assessed.

Where property is in the possession of grantees or contractors, the audit often is extended to include a review of the procedures and controls related to these assets as well.

Petty Cash or Imprest Fund Audits

With few exceptions, governmental agencies maintain petty cash or imprest funds for the purposes of making payment or advancing funds for relatively minor expenditures. The existence of such funds expedites payments and minimizes administrative costs of minor disbursements.

Periodically, the fund custodian and any alternate cashiers must undergo audit to determine that fund disbursements were proper, that no unreported losses exist and that the fund has not been used for other than authorized purposes. Petty cash and imprest funds usually are subjected to surprise audits, no less than annually. The scope of the audit will cover, among other areas:

A review and verification of the authority of the cashier and any alternate cashiers;

A count of cash;

Reconciliation of receipts and other expenditure documents;

A review of the type, amount and purpose of disbursements; and

Tests of controls to assess their adequacy to safeguard the fund.

Additionally, the auditor will be concerned with the volume or frequency of turnover of the fund balance. (Funds with rather nominal balances can be the conduit for extremely large volumes of disbursements, depending upon the rate of turnover, and might be used as a vehicle to circumvent a more formal method of disbursement.)

Audit Guides

Audits of the above expenditures generally are made pursuant to specially designed audit guides, prepared to insure that compliance is examined with respect to agency or government policies, procedures, agency-wide requirements and other criteria. While the scope of the annual compliance audits might be limited, an attempt often is made to review all aspects of compliance for specific expenditures within a given time period. These audits might be made for a single agency, for an entire department or for the entire government.

Additional suggestions and guidance appears in the General Accounting Office publication titled "Guidelines for Financial and Compliance Audits of Federally Assisted Programs" (October 1978). This document provides a uniform audit approach and uniform documentation procedures for financial and compliance audits of governmental organizations receiving federal funds.

Audit Reports

The reports resulting from the above audits are considered to be special reports, generally narrative in format. The report content should describe the scope of audit, audit findings, the effect of the observed conditions, comments of the audited organization, conclusions and recommendations. As with other audit reports, graphs, charts, tables, and other data arrays may be used. The cost or benefits of audit recommendations or suggested alternatives to existing conditions or practices should be included, wherever practicable.

Obligation and Encumbrance Audits

At all levels of government, the incurrence of obligations or encumbrances in excess of legislative appropriations is a legal violation. Accounting and internal controls must be directed towards insuring that financial and budget limitations are observed. If the rate of obligations or encumbrances is controlled, and no prospective or contingent liabilities are permitted in excess of the appropriation, generally no violations will result.

An audit or review of obligations or encumbrances takes on special significance at year-end. The government executive should know, with a high level of accuracy, the balances of these future liabilities. At the federal level, precise criteria are set forth in law, and claims or other alleged liabilities have no legal standing unless specific documentation or agreements have been executed pursuant to the appropriate legislation. At year's end, the unliquidated obligations constitute claims against an appropriation for which the federal government may later make payments. At the state and local government level, legal encumbrances must be considered as a claim that must be paid from the balance of the current, or from the next, fiscal year's appropriation. The misstatement of year-end obligations or encumbrances precludes an accurate accounting of either current or next year's appropriation.

The objective of the audit of obligation and encumbrance balances at year end is to provide management with an opinion as to the reasonableness of the balances reported by the operating agencies. If not properly controlled in the current year, prospective claims or liabilities could be incurred in excess of the legislatively approved appropriation. Unless the amounts for such transactions are properly reflected at year's end, unplanned liabilities could arise in the subsequent fiscal year, thus becoming a claim for which no appropriated funds exist.

The scope of this type of audit is directed towards confirming that the transactions comprising the reported balance of unliquidated obligations or encumbrances represent valid estimates or claims against the government.

Typically, each transaction should have documentation that meets certain criteria. (Examples of acceptable documentation are illustrated in Chapter 15.)

The observations of such an audit are set forth in a narrative report, which contains explanations of any exceptions that might be taken to the reported balance of the unliquidated obligations (in the case of the federal government) or the reserve for encumbrances (in the case of state and local governments).

Settlement Audits

There exist within government organizations certain key officials whose duties place them in positions of accountability. Generally, these officials are responsible for the collection or disbursement of money or for certifying the appropriateness of a prospective commitment or disbursement. At the federal level these officials' records of transactions relating to the fund balance, receipts, disbursements, and certifications or representations are referred to as their "account." Periodically, these "accounts" are settled or audited. Settlement audits may be made during the tenure of an accountable officer, but a settlement audit must be made of the account as of the date of termination of an accountable officer's tenure. Exceptions or variances of the records and the factual conditions, as determined by audit, must be settled by the departing official. Personal liability may, in some cases, result from exceptions made during a settlement audit.

The objective of a settlement audit is to provide an accounting of the stewardship of an accountable officer. A determination is required as to the reasonableness of the balances that are to be transferred from one accountable officer to his successor. The scope of audit is fiscally oriented, with transactions being traced back to such supporting documentation as vouchers and other records relating to the changes in the fund balances.

Within the federal government, the General Accounting Office is responsible for the formal settlement of an accountable officer's account. At the state level, an official may be legally designated to conduct such audits at the time an accountable officer's responsibilities are transferred. Local officials also may have the responsibility for making such reviews of officials in their governments.

The resulting report should contain a positive opinion that no exceptions were noted during the audit or a description of the facts relating to identified exceptions that must be resolved.

Procurement and Contract Audits

Audits of government procurement activities may be viewed from two general perspectives. An audit might be made of the procurement function, including an assessment of the contract negotiation, award, administration and settlement activities; or audits may be made of contractors and include such efforts as examining pricing reviews, preaward surveys and cost audits.

Procurement Audits

An audit of the procurement function is viewed by a government agency as an examination of government personnel and the degree to which the procurement practices are consistent with the policies and procedures of agency management. These audits are principally compliance in nature. An assessment often is made of the procedures by which agency personnel determine needs and prepare internal estimates of costs, methods by which qualified sources of supply are contracted and proposals requested, contract negotiation and award practices, degree to which contractors are monitored and detailed contract provisions administered, adequacy of property management procedures, and timeliness and appropriateness of contract closeout procedures and practices.

Contract Audits

Audits of contractors are primarily financially oriented, although many tests must be made to assure that there is compliance with non-financial conditions of the contracts. The examinations of government contractors may be categorized as pricing reviews, pre-award surveys, or cost audits.

Pricing or Cost Reviews

A pricing or cost review is an examination of the contractor's proposal, as submitted to the government in anticipation of a contract award. The scope of the review includes an assessment of the factual bases and underlying documents and circumstances from which the contractor developed its estimate of proposed direct costs. An examination also is made of the level of proposed indirect costs and the reasonableness of allocations in relation to past and projected sales, cost bases, and volume and nature of business. Any estimates for subcontractors and other costs, such as costs for travel and transportation, also will be reviewed to determine the reasonableness of the estimates in relation to the scope of work to be performed under the contract.

Pre-Award Survey

A pre-award survey may be required by a government agency, particularly in those instances where the agency has not previously issued a contract to the contractor organization. The objective of the survey is to determine the adequacy of the accounting and internal controls and of the system for contract management. The agency also might request performance information about the prospective contractor from other organizations.

Cost Audit

A cost audit could be made by an agency during or at the completion of a contract. The scope of such an audit includes an examination of the costs incurred and charged to the contract, including comparison of actual costs to the contract budget. Tests are made of the accounting and controls systems. Supporting documentation is examined for the various costs charged to the contract. A determination is made as to whether the costs charged to the contract are allowable, allocable, supportable and reasonable under the applicable procurement regulations and the terms of the specific contract.

The report for procurement and contract audits seldom has a prescribed format. The findings and observations are described in narrative form, and the report will include the auditor's conclusions and recommendations.

Grantor and Grant Audits

Within government, there is a need to monitor the grant management function of an agency as well as that of the grantee to whom funds are awarded. In the last decade, in many agencies, the amount of money distributed through grant awards has exceeded the dollar value of contracts. Today, it is difficult to distinguish between grants and contracts. Both may require the performance of services and the two instruments are viewed as binding legal agreements, with specified periods of performance. In many government agencies, the management of grant programs is a major activity of the agency, requiring top management dedication, considerable staff and large sums of public money. Additionally, assessments must be made of the organizations to which grants are awarded.

Grantor Audits

The objective of audits made of the grant or program management of an agency is to determine the degree to which practices comply with agency and government-wide policy and procedures. There often is a concern over whether sound administrative and financial management principles are being employed to protect the government's interests. Audits of grant management activities often are concerned with the grant application and award process, administration and monitoring of grantees, procedures for controlling the level of government funds in grantees' possession and the accuracy and timeliness of reporting, practices for controlling government property furnished to grantees, and the timeliness and appropriateness of grant closeout procedures and practices.

Grantee Audits

Grantee organizations, in order to do business with government agencies, must be fiscally responsible organizations, must possess management expertise, and must be capable of controlling, properly expending and accurately reporting the funds of a governmental grant. To provide some assurance to the grantor that the prospective grantee has the management competence to accept and perform, grantees may be required to undergo such examinations as pre-award surveys, post-award surveys and periodic audits.

The periodic audits could be examinations of both the financial management and the compliance aspects of the grant.

Pre-Award Survey

The objective of a pre-award survey is to determine the adequacy of the prospective grantee's systems of accounting, administration and internal controls. It is part of the process for determining if the organization is or can be a financially responsive grantee of the government. In some instances, systems and controls are non-existent and must be designed and implemented as a condition precedent to the full funding of the grant.

Post-Award Survey

The post-award survey may be made by some grantors between 60 to 90 days after the award of the grant. The objective of this examination is to determine, early in the grant period, whether the grantee has, or is in process of installing, effective management and financial controls. Tests also are made to assess compliance with grant conditions prior to full funding or maximum program operations.

Periodic Audits

Periodically, financial audits and compliance examinations are made of grantees. The financial audit is made to determine the allocability, allowability and reasonableness of costs charged to the grant. The scope of such an audit will include tests of transactions, observations of practices and controls, and a review of supporting documentation. The charged costs will be compared to the grant budget, and any ceilings or other restrictions will be examined for compliance. Local matching or other cost-sharing or contributed amounts will be audited to determine their appropriateness and value. The compliance aspects of the audit will be directed towards evaluating adherence by the grantee to the special and general conditions of the formal grant agreement. These conditions may often relate to non-financial matters, which are of significance to the grantor.

The report for audits of the grantor's management of the grant program or of grantees generally will be in narrative form. The findings and observations will be set forth, along with any conclusions, effects of the observed conditions and recommendations. Audits of grantees often will require the preparation of financial exhibits comparing the costs charged to the grant to the approved financial budget. Any exceptions are highlighted in the report, generally with comments from the management of the audited organization and a description of the condition or circumstances relating to the exception.

Efforts to Consolidate Governmental Audits

For years, the policy of the federal government has been to minimize repetitive audits of governmental programs in order to conserve audit resources, promote greater efficiency in the utilization of audit staffs and minimize the disruptive impact of audits on the operations of organizations subjected to audits. The publication of the GAO *Standards for Audit* contributed significantly to the adoption of uniform standards for the conduct of governmental audits. Earlier, OMB Circular A-102 (discussed in more detail in Chapter 17), provided standards for financial management systems for grant-supported activities of state and local governments. This Circular (Attachment G) required that, as a minimum, financial compliance audits be made at least once every two years. In December, 1978, in Attachment P to Circular A-102, OMB informed federal agencies that financial and compliance audits will be conducted with reasonable frequency on a continuing basis or at scheduled intervals. OMB stated that the audits usually will be made annually, but not less frequently than every two years. Additionally, in OMB Circular A-73, which sets forth the policies to be followed in the audit of federal operations and programs, federal agencies were directed to coordinate their audit requirements and approaches with those of state and local governments to the maximum extent possible. The scope of the individual federal audits must give full recognition to the non-federal audit effort. The same Circular requires that non-federal audit reports will be used in lieu of federal audits if the reports and supporting workpapers are available for review by the federal agency, if testing by the federal government indicates the audits were performed in accordance with generally accepted auditing standards (including those standards issued by the GAO) and if the audits otherwise meet the requirements of the federal agency.

Adherence to these federal policies will contribute significantly to the reduction of duplicative audits. The economy and efficiency in the application of audit resources will dictate that, in the future, even greater reliance will be placed on cross-servicing audit agreements and on the performance of audits by other levels of government.

Chapter 10
Audits of Federally Assisted Programs

Due to the limited numbers of government auditors and the increasing requirements of federal legislation for periodic audits, federal agencies regularly retain public accountants to conduct audits. During the 1970s, numerous federal agencies published audit guides for use by independent public accountants and other government auditors. These guides (available on a subscription basis from Commerce Clearing House, Inc., Chicago, Illinois) now exist for over 100 programs.

As the government placed increased reliance on audits by independent accountants, problems arose with respect to the scope and quality of the audits performed. The problems, related to audits of federally assisted activities, were sufficiently significant to warrant the AICPA developing a program to handle allegedly substandard accountants' reports submitted by federal agencies to the AICPA's professional ethics committee. Additionally, the Comptroller General of the United States, during the years 1976 to 1978, conducted reviews of the practices of several agencies that made extensive use of public accountants in the auditing of governmental programs. Generally, the conclusion of the General Accounting Office's reviews was that many practitioners did not fully understand the scope or nature of the program for which the audit was attempted.

This chapter describes several areas and subjects of significance to accountants accepting engagements to audit federally assisted governmental programs. The following list cites several federal agencies whose programs generally are referred to as federally assisted programs:

ACTION

Agency for International Development

Department of Commerce

Community Services Administration

Environmental Protection Agency

Federal Energy Administration

Department of Energy

Department of Health, Education & Welfare

Department of Housing and Urban Development

Department of the Interior

Department of Labor

Law Enforcement Assistance Administration

Office of Revenue Sharing

Small Business Administration

Department of Transportation

Department of Treasury

Authority for Audits

Legal and Other Federal Authority

Historically, the authority for auditing federally assisted programs was implicit in the general responsibilities of a federal agency to manage and account for the funds appropriated to it by the Congress of the United States. The head of each federal agency was charged, under various laws, to establish and maintain a system of internal controls and accounting to properly discharge the stewardship responsibilities assigned to the agency by law. A program for audits was an integral part of the system of internal controls. As federal expenditures increased and partnerships were formed with state and local governments for the support of numerous types of governmental programs, federal laws became more specific with respect to requirements for audit. Today, many laws specifically require that audits be made and dictate the frequency and general scope of the audits.

Contracts for Governmental Audits

Independent accountants have been retained under formal contract to conduct audits of federally assisted programs. These contracts might require the audit of contract-operated, grant-type, loan-guaranty or other types of assistance programs. Of importance to the auditor is both the type of audit contract negotiated and the unique client relationship that might exist when auditing particular federally assisted activities.

Types of Audit Contracts

Because the federal government requires the audit, the nature of the contractual arrangements by which the audit firm is retained closely relate to the federal procurement regulations. The contract for audit services might be one of the following types of contracts permitted by these regulations.

Cost-plus-fixed-fee contracts, often referred to as *CPFF* contracts, may be issued by the governmental agency when the scope of work cannot be sufficiently defined. The terms of CPFF contracts provide for direct cost reimbursement, fringe benefits, indirect expenses and a profit factor. Usually, the firm is reimbursed for fringe and indirect expenses on the basis of provisional expense rates, often monthly, that are adjusted to actual experienced rates at the end of the firm's fiscal period. Under a CPFF contract, the audit firm is liable for a best-efforts performance, within the contract price. Because the financial risk is assumed by the governmental agency, the profit factor generally is minimal. This type of contract imposes a considerable burden on the audit firm to maintain its own accounting records in a detailed manner to facilitate a post-audit by government auditors.

Labor-hour contracts and *time and material contracts* are viewed by the federal government as cost-reimbursement-type contracts. These types of contracts minimize the audit firm's accounting and other contractual compliance requirements. In both instances, an hourly rate is negotiated by the government. The rate provides for the recovery of labor, fringe, overhead and profit. The time and material contract will provide for separate identification and reimbursement of non-labor related costs, while the hourly rate for a labor-hour type contract will be used when the government cannot precisely define the scope of work to be performed. The financial risk, as with the CPFF contract, is assumed by the government. The audit firm is liable for providing qualified staff and for making its best effort to perform the desired scope of audit.

A *firm-fixed-price contract* places the maximum risk on the audit firm. By accepting such a contract, the audit firm enters into a legal contract to perform the scope of audit regardless of the cost required to complete the audit. The firm is entitled to all savings resulting from cost underruns, but, conversely, must assume all costs in excess of the contract price that might be required to complete the engagement. With such contracts, there are minimal accounting or audit requirements imposed on the audit firm. In many instances, fixed price contracts provide for payment at the completion of the scope of work. Often, though, interim partial payments may be negotiated by the firm for engagements of long duration. A fixed price contract places the financial risk on the audit firm to perform the full scope of the services sold and limits the firm's fee recovery to the amount of the contract price. It is imperative, with such contracts, that the auditor be certain of the scope, nature, and other particulars of the services to be delivered to the governmental client.

On occasion, a purchase order might be issued for audit services. Purchase orders are fixed-price-type contracts, requiring the auditor to perform the full scope of services for which the governmental client will pay the amount of the purchase order. Some years ago, the dollar amount of purchase orders was increased from $2,500 to $10,000 at the federal government level.

The *contractual relationships* for retaining firms to make audits of federally assisted-type programs are unique and can, at times, be the source of considerable legal and financial disagreement. There is no uniform manner by which audit contracts are issued by the governmental client, although two types of arrangements seem to prevail.

Retention by federal agency—The audits for many federally assisted programs are performed pursuant to a contract between the federal governmental agency, which provided the assistance to a governmental unit, and the audit firm. While these contracts might be issued by either the central or the regional office of the agency, there is no dispute over the fact that the federal governmental agency is the client. The performance of the audit must be in compliance with the agency's audit guides.

Retention by other units—For many federally assisted programs, the federal agency requires that the benefiting governmental unit (which could be a contractor, grantee, loan beneficiary, etc.) retain the accountant to make the independent audit. Under these circumstances, the benefiting governmental unit pays the audit firm, but the audit must be conducted in accordance with the federal agency's guidelines. When the benefiting governmental unit is permitted to select the independent auditor, the federal agency often has the final right of approval of the firm. Frequently, the contract or grant agreement for the federally assisted program provides a budgeted amount for the audit.

Federal Audit Guides

Format and Content

For several years, the audit guides of federal agencies generally have conformed to a uniform format and have attempted to outline several subjects of importance to the auditor. The audit guide formats often follow the structure suggested in the AICPA's publication, *Suggested Guidelines for the Structure and Content of Audit Guides Prepared by Federal Agencies for Use by CPA's* (1972), which identified the following subjects as being pertinent to the auditor:

Program background;
Definition of terms;
Audit objectives;
Audit program;
Auditor's report;
Exit conference;
Applicable references; and
Listing of regional offices.

Referenced Audit Standards and Guides

The governmental audit guides require compliance with several sets of audit standards and guides, which may be incorporated in the audit contract only by reference. Unless careful study is made by the auditor of these standards and guides, the auditor may be contractually liable for a more extensive audit than was contemplated. For example, it is not uncommon for a governmental audit guide to require that an audit be made in accordance with all or part of the following documents:

Standards for Audit of Governmental Organizations, Programs, Activities & Functions, published by the Comptroller General of the United States;

Generally accepted auditing standards, as set forth in the *Statement on Auditing Standards,* by the American Institute of Certified Public Accountants;

Those portions of the AICPA's industry audit guides considered applicable; and

The specific procedures and tests outlined in the audit guide designed by the governmental agency as being applicable to the program.

A close examination of these and any other cited guides is important, since the scope of audit in these guides may not be consistent with the scope of audit negotiated with the governmental client. For example, in very few circumstances would a governmental grantee desire to have a full scope governmental audit performed, similar to the type of audit outlined in the GAO *Standards for Audit.* Similarly, the activities and accounting of a federally assisted program may not be conducive to an audit performed in total compliance with generally accepted auditing standards.

As mentioned in other chapters, the General Accounting Office recently issued several guides to assist in the review of federally assisted programs:

Guidelines for Financial and Compliance Audits of Federally Assisted Programs, October 1978—particularly the section titled "Tests of Account Balances and Other Audit Procedures";

Guidelines for Economy and Efficiency Audits of Federally Assisted Programs, June 1978, Exposure Draft; and

Comprehensive Approach for Planning and Conducting a Program Results Review, June 1978, Exposure Draft.

At this time, adherence to these guides is not mandatory among the federal grantors. Each of the agencies continues to require compliance with its own guides.

Often, the government will include qualifications as to the completeness of the audit guide and will insert the caveat that the guide is not intended to supplant the auditor's judgment of the work required. Thus, unless the contract for the audit engagement clearly sets forth the scope, questions may arise concerning the performance of significantly greater audit work than was contemplated by the client or, worse, the audit work performed could be far less than that necessary to satisfy the audit criteria.

Nature of Audits of Federally Assisted Programs

A full scope governmental audit of a federally assisted program often is not desired. In some instances, the audit guide will specifically state that an audit or expression of an opinion with respect to efficiency or economy or an evaluation of the operations of a governmental unit is not required. In other audit guides, no limitation is set forth. Unless qualified or restricted by the audit firm in the engagement contract, the legal expectation is that the audit firm is undertaking to perform the full range of services contemplated in the contract, including all of the work implicit in any referenced documents.

The federally assisted audit program often consists of conducting financial examinations and compliance reviews. Additionally, these audit guides usually provide for a review of the governmental unit's systems of internal controls and accounting. The specific audit phases and detailed audit tasks require that a close examination be made of the governmental audit guide before commencing an audit. A considerable research and orientation period often is necessary to insure the development of a comprehensive audit approach and to avoid redundant audit testing. The illustration, in Exhibit 10-1, outlines to the type of audit required by the Environmental Protection Agency for its construction grant program. The scope of these audits are not too different from audits required of other federally assisted programs.

Financial or Fiscal Audit

Audit guides for federally assisted programs generally require that a limited scope or special financial or fiscal examination be made of the expenditures incurred and claimed by the governmental unit under the program. This examination requires the auditor to test program expenditures from several views, such as:

Allocability—Is the expenditure allocable to the federally assisted activity, either directly or as part of a properly allocable overhead?

Allowability—Is the claimed expenditure allowable under the general cost principles relating to federal contracts and grants or under the specific contract or grant conditions?

Reasonableness—Is the expenditure reasonable in amount in relation to the level of program activity and the duration of the program and consistent with the practices of economy that might be expected of a reasonable prudent businessperson?

Supportability—Is the expenditure supported by documented evidence that identifies the claim as being a proper charge to the program?

Many times, the scope of the examination outlined in the audit guide does not permit the full application of either the GAO *Standards for Audit* or the profession's generally accepted auditing standards. Probably as often, the AICPA's industry audit guides would not be applicable. In such instances, the auditor should attempt to eliminate from the terms of the audit contract the requirement for complying with these guides. A formal change should be made to the audit contract, rather than having the burden placed on the audit team to use its own judgment, which later may be disputed by the governmental unit or the federal agency.

Two opinions often are required of the auditor. One opinion will be required for the financial exhibit or special financial statement that is to be made a part of the audit report. A second opinion will relate to expenditures that the auditor may question or challenge as not being an applicable or an appropriate charge or claim to the program.

Compliance Examinations

With few exceptions, the audit guides for federally assisted programs will contain a requirement to make an examination to determine that the governmental unit has complied with various aspects of the program agreement. The examination may be required to assess nonfinancial, as well as financial, compliance.

For example, the Congress or the federal agency may have stated that expenditures cannot be made for certain items; or dollar ceilings may have been placed on the amounts that might be charged to the program for various

Exhibit

Summary of Financial and Compliance Audit

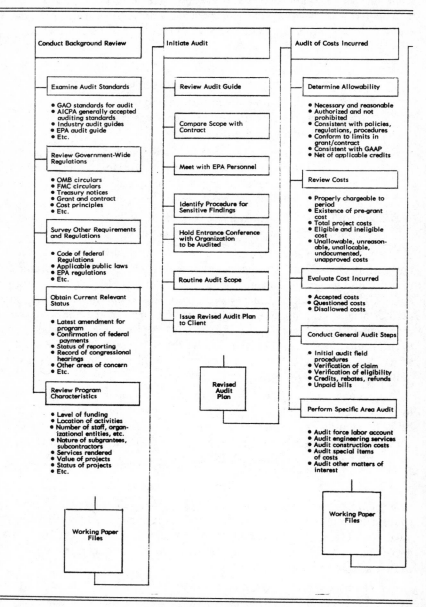

Conduct Background Review

Examine Audit Standards

- GAO standards for audit
- AICPA generally accepted auditing standards
- Industry audit guides
- EPA audit guide
- Etc.

Review Government-Wide Regulations

- OMB circulars
- FMC circulars
- Treasury notices
- Grant and contract
- Cost principles
- Etc.

Survey Other Requirements and Regulations

- Code of federal Regulations
- Applicable public laws
- EPA regulations
- Etc.

Obtain Current Relevant Status

- Latest amendment for program
- Confirmation of federal payments
- Status of reporting
- Record of congressional hearings
- Other areas of concern
- Etc.

Review Program Characteristics

- Level of funding
- Location of activities
- Number of staff, organizational entities, etc.
- Nature of subgrantees, subcontractors
- Services rendered
- Value of projects
- Status of projects
- Etc.

Working Paper Files

Initiate Audit

Review Audit Guide

Compare Scope with Contract

Meet with EPA Personnel

Identify Procedure for Sensitive Findings

Hold Entrance Conference with Organization to be Audited

Routine Audit Scope

Issue Revised Audit Plan to Client

Revised Audit Plan

Audit of Costs Incurred

Determine Allowability

- Necessary and reasonable
- Authorized and not prohibited
- Consistent with policies, regulations, procedures
- Conform to limits in grant/contract
- Consistent with GAAP
- Net of applicable credits

Review Costs

- Properly chargeable to period
- Existence of pre-grant cost
- Total project costs
- Eligible and ineligible cost
- Unallowable, unreasonable, unallocable, undocumented, unapproved costs

Evaluate Cost Incurred

- Accepted costs
- Questioned costs
- Disallowed costs

Conduct General Audit Steps

- Initial audit field procedures
- Verification of claim
- Verification of eligibility
- Credits, rebates, refunds
- Unpaid bills

Perform Specific Area Audit

- Audit force labor account
- Audit engineering services
- Audit construction costs
- Audit special items of costs
- Audit other matters of interest

Working Paper Files

10-1

Required for Federally Assisted Program

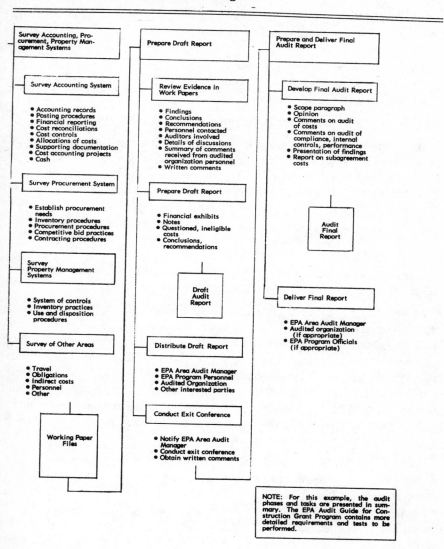

Survey Accounting, Procurement, Property Management Systems

Survey Accounting System
- Accounting records
- Posting procedures
- Financial reporting
- Cost reconciliations
- Cost controls
- Allocations of costs
- Supporting documentation
- Cost accounting projects
- Cash

Survey Procurement System
- Establish procurement needs
- Inventory procedures
- Procurement procedures
- Competitive bid practices
- Contracting procedures

Survey Property Management Systems
- System of controls
- Inventory practices
- Use and disposition procedures

Survey of Other Areas
- Travel
- Obligations
- Indirect costs
- Personnel
- Other

Working Paper Files

Prepare Draft Report

Review Evidence in Work Papers
- Findings
- Conclusions
- Recommendations
- Personnel contacted
- Auditors involved
- Details of discussions
- Summary of comments received from audited organization personnel
- Written comments

Prepare Draft Report
- Financial exhibits
- Notes
- Questioned, ineligible costs
- Conclusions, recommendations

Draft Audit Report

Distribute Draft Report
- EPA Area Audit Manager
- EPA Program Personnel
- Audited Organization
- Other interested parties

Conduct Exit Conference
- Notify EPA Area Audit Manager
- Conduct exit conference
- Obtain written comments

Prepare and Deliver Final Audit Report

Develop Final Audit Report
- Scope paragraph
- Opinion
- Comments on audit of costs
- Comments on audit of compliance, internal controls, performance
- Presentation of findings
- Report on subagreement costs

Audit Final Report

Deliver Final Report
- EPA Area Audit Manager
- Audited organization (if appropriate)
- EPA Program Officials (if appropriate)

NOTE: For this example, the audit phases and tasks are presented in summary. The EPA Audit Guide for Construction Grant Program contains more detailed requirements and tests to be performed.

supplies, services, equipment, buildings, indirect costs and other items. Also, the auditor may be required to make tests to assess the degree of compliance with various labor standards (such as the Davis-Bacon Act), nondiscrimination requirements (such as the Civil Rights Act), protection and preservation of property needs, environmental conditions and citizens' participation.

Where a compliance examination is required, it is anticipated that the auditor will express a formal opinion, identifying any instances of noncompliance in the audit report.

Review of Internal Control and Accounting Systems

In the past, confusion sometimes has arisen between practitioners and governmental audit clients over the nature of the review that is required of the systems of internal controls and accounting. The profession's generally accepted auditing standards require, as a part of the second standard of field work that there be:

> . . . a proper study and evaluation of the existing internal control as a basis for reliance thereon and for the determination of the resultant extent of the tests to which auditing procedures are to be restricted.

Under these standards, no separate opinion usually is issued concerning adequacy or reasonableness of the systems of control or accounting.

Guides for the audits of federally assisted programs often require that a detailed review be made of many aspects of an organization's controls and accounting and may extend the review to systems of personnel, property control, procurement and other management areas. It is important to note that this type of review is considerably broader than the study and evaluation required as a basis for establishing the level of tests to be conducted during the financial audit. A separate opinion and, at times, a separate report often will be required concerning the adequacy of the internal controls, accounting system and other management practices.

Key to the performance of this aspect of a federal audit guide is the recognition that observations concerning the adequacy of the organization's controls are not a by-product of the work required for the financial audit. The normal survey and tests of controls may not be adequate for the purposes of expressing an opinion on the controls. A considerably enlarged scope of work is contemplated by the government, along with the expression of separate comments on the adequacy of internal controls.

Audit Report

Nature of the Report

The audit report is another area where misunderstandings arise between the auditor and the governmental client.

The AICPA, in its Statement on Auditing Standards, has outlined other types of reports, in addition to the short-form opinion report, that might be required of an auditor in the private sector. These other reports have been referred to as long-form reports and, in some cases, as management letters. Typically these reports include details, statistical data and comments, some of which may be of a non-accounting nature.

It is important to note how the Management Advisory Services Executive Committee of the AICPA (in its publication, *Guidelines for CPA Participation in Government Audit Engagements to Evaluate Economy, Efficiency and Program Results)* describes the nature of the greater detailed evaluations that are required by the GAO *Standards for Audits.* The Committee stated:

> Some government entities and practitioners who are familiar with the management letters often accompanying financial audits equate the level of work in an expanded-scope audit to that required to prepare management letters. This is not correct. Such letters are almost totally a by-product of the work required for the financial audit. The GAO has made it clear that its standards do not refer to such a by-product.

The same general approach should be considered when undertaking an audit of a federally assisted program. The audit report should contain observations concerning the auditor's findings, conclusions and recommendations. This report is to be based on an expanded scope audit or examination that may exceed the scope of work required for a financial audit.

Content of the Report

While most reports relating to audits of federally assisted programs will contain the standard short-form opinion paragraph, the governmental client often requires substantially more information in the report. While the format may vary by client, some guides will require an audit report to include several subjects, such as:

A description of the scope of the financial audit, compliance examination and review of internal controls and accounting systems;

The expression of an opinion with respect to:

the results of operations as represented in the financial statements,

the allowability of costs charged to the audited program,

the adequacy of the systems of internal controls, accounting and other management practices, and

The extent of compliance with financial and nonfinancial criteria and requirements;

A full discussion of all material or sensitive audit observations, complete with the auditor's own conclusions and recommendations;

The views of the audited organization, whether in agreement or disagreement; and

An identification of the key governmental unit personnel with whom the auditor had contact.

Report Distribution

No uniform procedures exist among federal agencies concerning the distribution of the audit report. Particular care should be taken to identify the parties to whom the auditor should provide a copy of the report. This is another area where full compliance with the referenced standards may not be desired by the governmental client. For example, the first reporting standard of the GAO *Standards for Audit* states, among other requirements, that:

> Written reports are to be submitted to the appropriate officials of the organizations requiring or arranging for the audits. Copies of the reports should be sent to other officials who may be responsible for taking action on audit findings and recommendations and to others responsible or authorized to receive such reports. Copies should also be made available for public inspection.

While the governmental client may have incorporated the GAO *Standards for Audit,* without qualification, into the audit guide, this may be an example of where the client does not intend that the full scope of these standards be applied. Clarification should be obtained and any deviations from the referenced standards formally noted.

There may be valid reasons for the governmental client not to permit the auditor to distribute the audit report to the audited organization or the public. As an example, the observations of the auditor are tentative and, therefore, preliminary until examined and approved by the governmental client. Additionally, guidance for revising procedures or practices or taking corrective action should come formally from the responsible governmental executive, not from the auditor.

Special reporting procedures often are identified in the audit guide for instances of suspected fraud, collusion or other irregularities. Generally, the auditor should suspend the engagement until such matters have been discussed with the governmental client and a revised audit approach has formally been adopted.

The auditor should not independently pursue these areas without specific instruction. This approach will avoid inadvertently impairing any future legal action. Almost as important, the pursuit of such matters often is beyond the scope of most audit engagements, and the auditor may find himself in the position of having performed considerable audit work that is later determined to be out of the scope of the engagement contract for which no audit fee will be paid.

Working Papers

The ownership and custody of the audit working papers should be clarified by the auditor at the outset of the engagement. In most instances, it is assumed that the working papers are the property of the auditor; however, absent specific reference in the audit guide or the contract, the governmental client may have assumed that the working papers, reports and other records related to the audit would be delivered to it at the conclusion of the audit. An agency might believe that it is necessary for it to retain possession of working papers to provide a permanent record of the audit. This is particularly so if it is possible that another firm might be selected for subsequent periods' audits.

The more common condition of a governmental audit contract is that the firm will retain ownership and custody, but both the governmental client and the Comptroller General of the United States (the head of the General Accounting Office) will have access to the working papers. The following condition relating to the retention of working papers appears in the audit guide for the revenue sharing program and is typical of the requirement relating to retention of working papers:

> Section 52.83
>
> Audit workpapers and related audit reports shall be retained for three years after the issuance of the audit report, and shall be available upon request to the Director [of the Office of Revenue Sharing, in this instance] and the Comptroller General or to their representatives.

The Comptroller General has, with increasing frequency, exercised this right; and his representatives have examined the working papers of many accounting firms. For several years, working papers have been examined by the GAO for federally assisted programs of, among others, the Departments of Commerce, Housing and Urban Development, Labor and Health, Education and Welfare, the Environmental Protection Agency and the Community Services Administration. The objective of these reviews is to assess the quality of audits being procured by governmental agencies. In its review, the GAO will closely examine papers and audit reports for evidence of:

The quality and care with which the auditor performed the engagement;

The extent to which due professional care was exercised and the full scope of the intended audit performed; and

The nature of the evidence supporting the opinions, conclusions and recommendations appearing in the report.

Often, in its review, GAO will "re-audit" transactions initially selected by the auditor, thus verifying that the audit work was performed and that reported audit observations are reasonable. Additionally, GAO may conduct its own survey to assess the adequacy of the judgments made by the auditor in conducting the audit. In some intances, GAO representatives have held interviews with members of a firm's audit team.

In 1976, the GAO published a report on its review of audits provided to the federally assisted programs managed by the Department of Housing and Urban Development. This report cited some instances of audit work not being performed or being performed poorly, of audit work in support of report opinions not always meeting the AICPA's generally accepted auditing standards, and of audits otherwise being below the profession's standards. The GAO attributed the conditions to several factors: inadequacies in the audit guide, limitation on third party-type information available in a timely manner to the auditor, and the unfamiliarity of auditors themselves with the audit requirements, which differed considerably from the requirements of an audit of a commercial organization.

Chapter 11
Performance Audits

Chapter 9 provided an overview of several examples of special scope audits performed in the governmental sector. In Chapter 10, the considerations for planning and conducting governmental audits were outlined. This latter chapter also provided illustrations of the scopes of fiscal and financial audits, compliance reviews and economy and efficiency reviews. The assumption should not be made, however, that these types of audits are necessarily the most significant or most informative audits performed of governmental units.

Many recipients of fiscal, financial, compliance or economy and efficiency audit reports often conclude that their questions about the audited activity remain unanswered. In recent years, increased emphasis has been given to audits of program results, often referred to as management or performance audits. The concern or interest shown by governmental executives in performance audits does not, of course, obviate the need for or value of other types of audits.

167

Nature of Performance Audits

In the 1950s, increased attention was given in the governmental sector to reviews or evaluations referred to as "performance audits." While not audits within the profession's formal definition of the term "audit," these types of reviews or evaluations do require the application of skills, disciplines, ethical restraints, independence and professional competence to the same degree as required by other types of audits. Since the scope of performance audits generally is considerably broader than that of other audits, particular attention must be devoted by the auditor to defining the area of audit, insuring acceptable and quantifiable performance criteria and identifying the nature of the skills required to conduct a performance audit.

A distinguishing feature of performance audits is the dearth of precedence. To date, the accounting profession has had limited experience with these types of evaluations in the governmental sector. The required expertise also is difficult to define, since each audit typically is for a unique or specific governmental agency, program, activity or function.

The AICPA, in addressing the meaning and significance of the GAO's *Standards for Audits,* described the nature of performance audits by contrasting these audits with audits for compliance, economy and efficiency. For these latter types of audits, the AICPA stated that the things an entity has chosen to do are evaluated or measured as ends or criteria. In contrast to audits of financial statements, a performance audit would require that these things be evaluated differently: the question now becomes whether the entity or its major activities are achieving established goals, objectives or other criteria.

Definition of Performance Audits

While many authors have selected or preferred a particular phrase, there is a degree of acceptance that the terms performance audits, management audits, effectiveness audits, program audits and operational audits are synonymous. Performance audits are evaluations or assessments of what has been achieved for the expenditure or consumption of labor, material, money or other resources. Typically, performance audits require the use of a team possessing a variety of academic backgrounds, technical skills and experience.

The General Accounting Office, in its *Standards for Audit,* defines a program results or effectiveness review (or performance audit) as an audit to determine:

> ... whether the desired results or benefits are being achieved, whether the objectives established by the legislature or other authorizing body are being met, and whether the agency has considered alternatives which might yield desired results at a lower cost.

By this definition, it can be seen that performance audits entail a scope of review considerably broader than financial statement and compliance audits.

The Scope of Performance Audits

In the government, the legislation that established the agency or program may include specific goals, objectives or conditions that can be used to develop criteria for purposes of measuring or assessing performance. Agency management may have been organized and may have established policies and procedures consistent with that legislation. Financial management information and statistical systems may have been designed to allow management to monitor and measure its progress or achievement in relation to the goals and objectives.

Under these conditions, the performance audit can be made with little difficulty. In this instance, the auditor would be concerned with assessing the appropriateness of the legal or other criteria, testing the validity of the financial and other information collected and comparing the achievement data to the established criteria.

The above description is ideal. In many cases, legislation will contain no statement of goals, objectives or other criteria of expected performance or achievement. Policies and procedures may not be directly related to programs. Possibly, basic specific financial information will not be recorded for the program activities. In short, there could be little or no historical or other data upon which to assess performance. It can be seen that an audit of an agency or activity under these conditions will require considerably more effort. Indeed, a survey should be made by the auditor before he accepts the performance audit to ascertain the extent to which the lack of sufficient legal criteria and financial and operating data will limit or affect the desired scope.

The Management Advisory Services Executive Committee of the AICPA developed (in the publication *Guidelines for Participation in Government Audit Engagements to Evaluate Economy, Efficiency and Program Results, 1977*) the following key questions to permit the auditor more clearly to understand the nature or objective of performance audits and to assist in structuring an audit plan:

Have agency, program, activity or functional goals and objectives been well-defined?

Have specific timetables or dates been established for meeting the goals and objectives?

Have criteria — in terms of performance levels or costs—been established to permit the evaluation of results or achievement?

Have the criteria been quantified to permit objective measurement of results or achievements?

Have arrangements been made to insure that this data will be available to the auditor?

Has management or someone else prepared a current assessment of the program's results or achievements?

Have any previous external evaluations been made of the agency, program or activities?

Have actions been taken by management as a result of these previous evaluations?

Requests for performance audits may be vague, may require definition or may call for a scope different than that interpreted by the auditor. A careful review of the above list should permit a clearer definition of the desired scope of audit and avoid the acceptance of engagements that are difficult or impossible to perform within finite time and cost budgets.

There will be instances where an initial phase of the audit may require that the audits identify the goals, objectives and performance criteria. In this case, no audit work should be commenced until management officials have examined and commented upon the performance or achievement factors. In other cases, no data will exist concerning performance. Here the auditor may be responsible for developing the data base and other information to assess performance. When placed in this position, the auditor should test the general acceptance of the developed criteria and the relevance of the information to be analyzed. Later disagreements over either may otherwise be used to invalidate the results of the performance audit.

Staffing of Performance Audit Teams

The staffing of performance audit teams is, in itself, different from the procedure used in staffing other audit teams. Performance audit teams must possess the collective professional proficiency to competently undertake the audit. In its Statement on Auditing Standards, No. 1, the AICPA established the first general standard of a financial audit as:

> The examination is to be performed by a person or persons having adequate technical training and proficiency as an auditor.

This standard is interpreted to mean that, regardless of one's competence in other fields, one still must have the proper education and experience in the field of auditing. However, the application of such a standard to governmental performance audits might not be adequate. Accounting and auditing training often are only two of several skills that must be blended into a multidisciplined performance audit team. The need for a broader standard of proficiency was recognized by GAO in its *Standards for Audit.* The GAO's second general standard for governmental auditing is:

> The auditors assigned to perform the audit must collectively possess adequate professional proficiency for the tasks required.

The General Accounting Office defined the phrase, "collectively possess adequate professional proficiency," to mean that, if an organization possesses personnel or consultants with acceptable skills in, for example, accounting, statistics, law, engineering, actuarial science and related skills, each individual member of the organization need not himself possess all of these skills. The *Standards for Audit* require staff performing governmental audits to have:

A basic knowledge of auditing theory and procedures and the education, ability and experience to apply such knowledge to the type of auditing work required for the task at hand;

A basic knowledge of governmental organization and operation; and

The skills appropriate for the work required in the audit.

Collectively, auditors must possess the skills to conduct the audit. In governmental auditing, the audit team must minimally possess:

Diversity of academic background necessary to examine or review the functional areas under audit. This may require persons skilled in finance, computer science, medicine, law or social science as well as in accounting and auditing.

Experience with the governmental program or activity under audit. The required experience could be in such specialized areas as transportation, health, public assistance, crime, education, etc.

Knowledge of the specific government agency to be audited. This might require team members to possess prior knowledge of the transit authority, public hospitals, welfare, police departments, school department, etc, as the case may be.

It is important that personnel of audited organizations should view the audit team as their professional and technical peers. The perceived competency of the audit team is critical to the conduct of a successful performance audit.

Identifying Agency or Program Goals, Objectives, Criteria

The absence of existing or predefined goals, objectives or other evaluative criteria is often a limiting factor in commencing performance audits. Often, as mentioned above, the legislature will not clearly identify the goals and objectives of the governmental program in the founding law. Legislatures even less frequently will set forth the performance criteria or levels of achievement expected from the expenditure of program money. On occasion, the law may make reference to the maintenance of performance data or may contain the requirement that periodic evaluations be made and reports be submitted to the legislature. Even in these instances, the nature, form and frequency in which program financial and statistical information is collected is often left to the discretion of program officials. At times, the adequacy of the information systems is not evaluated until the requirements for making the evaluation become imminent.

In the absence of defined goals, objectives and evaluative criteria, the audit team may be charged with the responsibility for describing these factors in qualitative and quantitiative terms. There is a general methodology that may be applied in this effort. The same methodology also might be used to independently assess the usefulness of earlier established performance or achievement criteria.

Methodology for Performance Audits

In summary, a methodology for performance audits proceeds from general goals and objectives to the specific information that must be analyzed in reaching conclusions on the relative effectiveness of a program or activity. For example:

General goals and objectives may be obtained from initiating legislation, records of legislative hearings, policies and procedures issued by the agency management for the particular program, and the nature of the information and data that is collected on operations;

Inquiries concerning programs and activities can be made to identify and quantify the types of services rendered, constituencies served and frequency of services that would provide evidence of meeting goals and objectives;

Indicators of performance can be obtained by postulating questions to obtain data that would indicate levels of performance or activities, such as increases or decreases of service levels, costs, decreased backlogs or errors, financial and other resources budgets, comparative costs and other performance statistics, activity trends and volume indicators; and

Methods by which data can be obtained may involve a variety of data collecting techniques and evaluative approaches, including systems reviews, document reviews, statistical sampling, questionnaires, interviewing, data analysis, personal observations, confirmations, etc.

An Illustration

This methodology can be applied to the evaluation of any activity or function. It does, however, require the careful assessment of skills and disciplines to competently perform the evaluation and render a professional opinion on the effectiveness of operations.

In applying the methodology to the evaluation of a local transit system, for example, the initial effort must be devoted to identifying or postulating, if they are not already stated, the goals and objectives of the transit operations. To achieve the goals and objectives, the transit service must perform certain services, which can be evaluated as to economy, efficiency or effectiveness.

Inquiries or questions to be examined in assessing the overall effectiveness of the transit system might, initially, include:

What types of services are offered?

To whom are the services offered?

When or with what frequency is the service provided?

At what price are the services sold?

Are the costs of activities and operations known and periodically reviewed?

To resolve or address these types of inquiries, financial and performance statistics must be accumulated, studied and analyzed, and conclusions made. In the case of governmental services, it is often necessary to conduct a survey or census of the user population as well as of non-users to obtain third-party opinions as to the real and perceived effectiveness of the public service offered. Not infrequently, analytical data do not exist, or exist only in part. Often, a data base must be established for obtaining the appropriate information. The required information may take several forms: statistical, financial, operational or judgmental. Even opinions should be considered, particularly if the opinions are obtained from responsible officials and from those public constituencies intended to be served by the public system.

Exhibit 11-1 illustrates, in a general manner, the application of the methodology to the development of initial inquiries that might be made in undertaking an assessment of the effectiveness of a local transit system. The listing of inquiries and sources of data, as well as the data collection methods and suggested analyses should not be construed as exhaustive, but merely as representative of the way in which the performance audit approach would proceed.

Performance Audit Process

The specific inquiries made, data examined and techniques applied necessarily will vary, depending upon the organization undergoing the performance audit. Nevertheless, there is a process that must be applied to insure that the audit is properly planned, the work is professionally and objectively performed and the reporting is fair, complete and reflective of the audited conditions. Typically, the phases of this process would include:

Completing certain initial audit activities;

Conducting a preliminary survey;

Completing a preliminary review;

Conducting the detailed audit or examination;

Developing and reviewing audit findings; and

Preparing draft and final reports.

The titles of various phases of the audit might differ, or an auditor may merge phases of the audit. There is a general scope of review or work, however,

Exhibit 11-1

Methodology for Planning Performance Audit of Local Transport System

Goals or Objectives	Inquiries to Test Achievement of Goals	Data to Indicate Performance or Achievement	Data Analyses and Collection Methods
To provide an integrated transit system to serve the population of the county	• Are all areas of county served	• Comparison of route structure to business and residential areas, rural versus urban centers	• Document reviews
	• Frequency of service in peak and non-peak periods		• Interviews
		• Traffic logs, passenger counts, surveys of attitudes	• Questionnaires
	• Reasonableness of fares—peak, non-peak, group rates, older citizens, school children		• Comparisons to other governments and services
	• Programs for serving commuters, shoppers, aged, school children, urban, rural constituencies	• Records of pre- and post-program initiation; comparison to alternative transportation modes; coverage of operating costs	• Trend and comparative analyses
			• Statistical sampling
	• Adequacy of route structure; length of runs; need for transfers	• Scheduling of equipment; special parking lots; express buses; curb-to-curb service; dial-a-ride; shuttle buses	• Personal observations
			• Independent confirmations
	• Age or condition of transit equipment, stations, rights-of-way	• Origin and destination studies; analysis of transfer usage	• Survey and polls of public, customers, legislatures
	• Financial Performance—revenues, operating, capital and administrative costs, projects	• Acquisition, maintenance and repair records	• Accounting and information systems
		• Other data reflective of levels or volume of service, comparative costs and statistical data; surveys, complaints, legislative concerns, voter preferences, etc.	

that must be performed. There is a methodology or process that should be executed. The major phases of a performance audit are illustrated in Exhibit 11-2, and discussed generally in the several following sections.

Initial Audit Activities

For maximum benefits, a performance audit should not necessarily be viewed by the audited organization as a critical or negative review. Such audits have been beneficial to many governmental operations. The initial meeting of the auditor and agency management will do much to set the tone for relations between them for the duration of the audit.

An initial, pre-audit meeting with agency management and staff should be held for purposes of introduction and discussion. The auditor should make a full presentation of the contemplated audit scope, review protocols that will be adhered to throughout the audit and provide a written outline of the audit. Typical of the subjects that should be discussed with staff and management are:

The audit staff and their qualifications and expertise—from the viewpoint of their education as well as from that of their governmental agency and program expertise;

The scope of the and details concerning their involvement;

The guides that might be developed for conducting interviews, making surveys, handling questionnaires, visiting sites, making observations and completing other audit steps; and

The procedures by which any findings will be relayed to the staff and management of the audited organization and the details for coordination and treatment of agency comments.

To insure that there is a clear understanding of the audit process and the protocol procedures that must be adhered to, the auditor should consider providing agency management with a written outline of the audit operating procedures that will be used.

Preliminary Survey

A preliminary survey should be made at the outset of any audit. In the case of performance audits in the governmental sector, this phase of the audit is extremely critical. During this phase, the auditor is concerned with researching the history of the program. Legislative and management guidelines for the direction of the audit must be determined. An understanding must be acquired of the operating characteristics, issues, problems, accomplishments and services of the program. Information must be obtained concerning financial and statistical data, agency plans and budgets, and other measurement and reporting systems relied upon by management for monitoring program performance.

Exhibit

Overview - Process for Performance Audits

Summary of Audit Phases

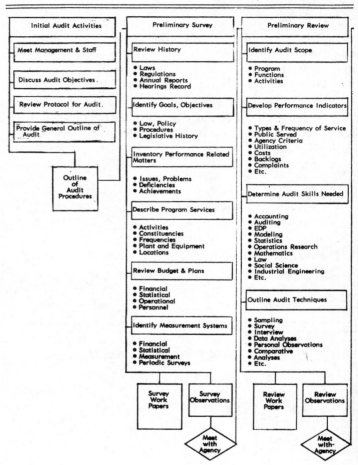

Initial Audit Activities	Preliminary Survey	Preliminary Review
Meet Management & Staff	Review History	Identify Audit Scope
Discuss Audit Objectives.	• Laws • Regulations • Annual Reports • Hearings Record	• Program • Functions • Activities
Review Protocol for Audit.	Identify Goals, Objectives	Develop Performance Indicators
Provide General Outline of Audit	• Law, Policy • Procedures • Legislative History	• Types & Frequency of Service • Public Served • Agency Criteria • Utilization • Costs • Backlogs • Complaints • Etc.
	Inventory Performance Related Matters	
Outline of Audit Procedures	• Issues, Problems • Deficiencies • Achievements	Determine Audit Skills Needed
	Describe Program Services	• Accounting • Auditing • EDP • Modeling • Statistics • Operations Research • Mathematics • Law • Social Science • Industrial Engineering • Etc.
	• Activities • Constituencies • Frequencies • Plant and Equipment • Locations	
	Review Budget & Plans	Outline Audit Techniques
	• Financial • Statistical • Operational • Personnel	• Sampling • Survey • Interview • Data Analyses • Personal Observations • Comparative • Analyses • Etc.
	Identify Measurement Systems	
	• Financial • Statistical • Measurement • Periodic Surveys	
	Survey Work Papers / Survey Observations	Review Work Papers / Review Observations
	Meet with Agency	Meet with Agency

11-2

for Government Program

and Other Tasks

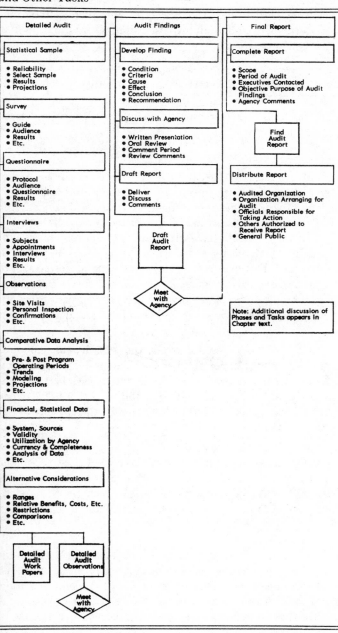

Detailed Audit	Audit Findings	Final Report

Statistical Sample

- Reliability
- Select Sample
- Results
- Projections

Survey

- Guide
- Audience
- Results
- Etc.

Questionnaire

- Protocol
- Audience
- Questionnaire
- Results
- Etc.

Interviews

- Subjects
- Appointments
- Interviews
- Results
- Etc.

Observations

- Site Visits
- Personal Inspection
- Confirmations
- Etc.

Comparative Data Analysis

- Pre- & Post Program Operating Periods
- Trends
- Modeling
- Projections
- Etc.

Financial, Statistical Data

- System, Sources
- Validity
- Utilization by Agency
- Currency & Completeness
- Analysis of Data
- Etc.

Alternative Considerations

- Ranges
- Relative Benefits, Costs, Etc.
- Restrictions
- Comparisons
- Etc.

Detailed Audit Work Papers

Detailed Audit Observations

Meet with Agency

Develop Finding

- Condition
- Criteria
- Cause
- Effect
- Conclusion
- Recommendation

Discuss with Agency

- Written Presentation
- Oral Review
- Comment Period
- Review Comments

Draft Report

- Deliver
- Discuss
- Comments

Draft Audit Report

Meet with Agency

Complete Report

- Scope
- Period of Audit
- Executives Contacted
- Objective Purpose of Audit Findings
- Agency Comments

Find Audit Report

Distribute Report

- Audited Organization
- Organization Arranging for Audit
- Officials Responsible for Taking Action
- Others Authorized to Receive Report
- General Public

Note: Additional discussion of Phases and Tasks appears in Chapter text.

The duration of this phase and the extent of work to be performed will vary considerably from audit to audit. In some instances, the agency staff and management will possess an inventory of preliminary research materials. In other audits, the auditor will be responsible for identifying background sources, defining agency goals and objectives, establishing criteria for measurement and performance, and obtaining cost and other information that might be used for assessment purposes.

Generally, in this phase, no real assessment is attempted with respect to validating evidence. The primary objective at this time is to obtain an overview of the agency to be audited and some indication of the specific activities and functions that might require a more detailed review later during the audit.

Preliminary Review

The preliminary review phase of the audit is contrasted with the earlier survey phase by the greater depth and specificity of the inquiries to be made. During this phase, the program, activity or function areas for detailed audit will be identified. The criteria against which performance will be assessed must be established and discussed with agency management for appropriateness. Usually, work performed during this phase will permit a more complete definition of the types of staff skills and experiences needed to make a competent and technical assessment of management performance. Specific auditing techniques (sampling plans, interview programs, data analyses, site observations, survey questionnaires, comparative analyses, etc.) will be outlined.

In this phase, tests will be made to assess the validity of views or impressions obtained during the earlier audit phase. The systems utilized by management will be examined. At the conclusion of this phase, the program, activity or functional areas to be reviewed in detail are identified. Work programs should be defined for each of the skills to be utilized during the detailed audit or verification phase.

There will be instances where the audit team will have a restricted scope. In some instances, agency management already may have conducted the major portion of the tasks outlined in the review and survey phase. The audit team's role will be to assess the extent of performance or lack thereof. In other words, the audit team will be charged with conduct of the detailed audit phase.

Detailed Audit

The detailed audit phase is the confirmation part of the performance audit or review. The currency, completeness and accuracy of data must be determined. Factual and independent assessments must be made by the audit team. The overall objective of this phase of the audit is to identify those areas of agency performance that warrant management attention. In this phase of the audit, evidence should be obtained on the effectiveness or achievement of management. According to GAO (as outlined in *Internal Auditing in Federal Agencies—Basic Principles, Standards, and Concepts,* 1974), the detailed audit tests should be directed towards such concerns as:

Program effectiveness—Is the program accomplishing the results intended by the legislature?

Cost effectiveness—Are goals and objectives being attained within the authorized budgets?

Adequacy of information systems—Is essential and reliable information available to management on a timely basis, and is the information being used?

Cost benefits relationships—Are program costs reasonably commensurate with the benefits achieved?

Consideration of alternatives—Has management made assessments of alternative program structures and activities for achieving program objectives with increased economic efficiency?

Need for the program—Is there a continuing need for the program, or has the need passed and the legislature failed to provide for program termination?

Appropriateness of program—Does the program continue to meet the target need for which it was established?

Clarity and consistency of objectives—Are program objectives sufficiently clear to permit agency management to accomplish desired program results? Are the program activities and sub-components structured in a manner consistent with the overall program objectives?

Data to permit such evaluations may be derived from a variety of sources and through a number of techniques. Some of these techniques may include: statistical sampling, conducting personal surveys, mailing questionnaires, conducting interviews with management and key staff, making on-site observations, performing comparative analyses, assessing and analyzing financial and statistical information, obtaining confirmations from third parties, etc. Certain audit considerations, suggested by the GAO for internal auditors appraising performance include:

Review, appraise and report on the extent and nature of internal compliance with policies, plans and procedures;

Review, appraise and report on extent of compliance with legal and external regulatory requirements;

Review operation of system of management controls over operations and resources to assess effective functioning;

Make comparative examinations of similar functions in other organizational components of the agency;

Identify possibilities for improving operations, identifying opportunities for more efficiency and economy; and

Assess adequacy and effectiveness of plans, policies, intra-agency relationships and procedures in relation to top management objectives.

Audit Findings

The audit finding phase primarily is related to the evaluation and analysis of the facts and other evidence gathered during the earlier phases of the audit. Careful analysis of the identified conditions and circumstances is required. A technique to insure that a reportable and significant condition exists is to critically review the evidence in support of all elements of the finding:

Condition—the situation, circumstance or practice which has been identified as contributing to less than the desired results;

Criteria—the goal, objective, standard, rule, regulation or other guideline that is not being achieved;

Cause—the contributory circumstances or practices that have resulted in the less than desired results;

Effect—the materiality, damage or cost or impairment resulting from the existence or perpetuation of the less than desired performance;

Conclusion—the auditor's opinion or assessment of situation, circumstance or practice; and

Recommendation—the suggested corrective actions or alternatives that will promote more effective performance.

The development of findings must be done with caution. The auditor is responsible for the accurate assessment of the data acquired and examined during the course of the audit. Issues and problems must be examined critically to determine whether the condition is an isolated example or if the condition permeates the audited entity.

Because an audit should result in more effective performance, the development of audit findings should be done with the full knowledge of the audited organization. Agency staff and management must be convinced that the recommended alternative conduct or practice will be an improvement, will be beneficial, and will be in their interests. Minor or insignificant issues, problems or findings should not be reported. Once all elements of the finding have been evaluated, the finding should be presented to agency staff and management for discussion, comment and possible suggestions of other information that might be researched to examine the condition more closely.

Further, considerable rapport is generated when the auditor provides sufficient time for the audited organization to respond to the findings. Complete findings will contain the comments and, possibly, the corrective efforts taken by the audited organization.

Audit Report

With performance audits, there is no standard scope and opinion paragraph in the audit report. Further such audits generally are not made in accordance with certain previously established standards. It is not sufficient to submit a brief summary report to the audited organization, with the facts and other evidence residing in the working papers.

Alternatively, the number and nature of interviews, observations, tests, independent confirmations and other audit efforts should be disclosed in the body of the report. The fiscal or operating period covered, and the financial or other statistical records examined, should be clearly identified. All facts and other information of relevance to the reported finding must be included in the report in narrative, chart, table or graphic form. The reader of the report should have sufficient information to permit an "audit" of the auditor. For each reported finding, all elements of that finding should be clearly and objectively described.

The distribution of governmental audit reports should be clarified at the outset of the audit. It may not be sufficient for the auditor to complete the audit by making delivery of the report to the organization that arranged for the audit. For example, an audit performed in accordance with the GAO *Standards for Audit,* unless qualified in the audit engagement letter, requires written audit reports to be submitted to:

Appropriate officials of the organizations requiring or arranging for the audits;

Other officials responsible for taking actions on the audit observations;

Others responsible or authorized to receive such reports; or

Public inspection.

The distribution of governmental audit reports continues to be a matter of disagreement. For the protection of the auditor, the addressee and all other recipients of the audit report should be identified specifically at the outset of the audit. State and local government organizations often must agree to a broad release of the audit report as a condition of receiving federal funds, and any later restrictions by the audited organization would be a violation of the funding conditions.

Effectiveness or Program Results Audits

In 1978, the General Accounting Office published its views concerning the conduct of program effectiveness or program results audits. In its guideline,

"Comprehensive Approach for Planning and Conducting a Program Results Review," the GAO proposed a universal approach to be used to govern the quality and consistency of program results reviews. The guide noted that program results reviews are conducted in an uncertain environment. Numerous variables cause an uncertainty that precludes the design of a step-by-step guideline format. Nonetheless, a process should govern the conduct of such examinations. An example of the flow, interrelationship and purpose of the several activities comprising a program results review have been summarized by the GAO (see Exhibit 11-3).

Exhibit 11-3

Program Results Review Process

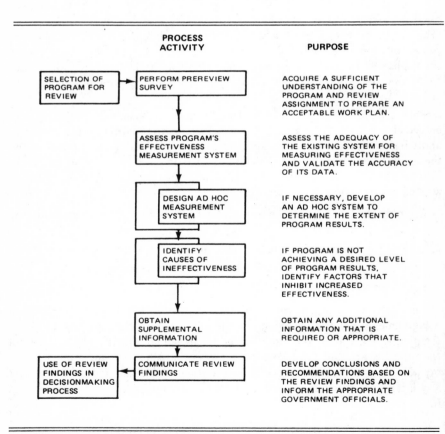

Source: *Comprehensive Approach for Planning and Conducting a Program Results Review* (Exposure Draft, June, 1978), U.S. General Accounting Office, Washington, D.C.

Publications Relating to Performance Audits

As mentioned earlier, published information concerning the conduct of performance audits is limited. Publications that will provide some guidance to the conduct of such audits, however, include:

"Performance Auditing—An Untraditional Concept in a Very Traditional Environment," *Governmental Finance,* November 1976, Municipal Finance Officers Association, Chicago, Illinois.

"Guidelines for Participation in Government Audit Engagements to Evaluate Economy, Efficiency, and Program Results," 1977, AICPA's Management Advisory Services Executive Committee.

Comprehensive Approach for Planning and Conducting a Program Results Review (Exposure Draft, June, 1978), U.S. General Accounting Office, Washington, D.C.

Chapter 12
Audit Test Methodology

The transaction test concept is as applicable to public sector audits as it is to audits of private organizations. This chapter will present an example of the testing methodology applied to the audit of governmental appropriated funds. The illustrated methodology is acceptable for and applicable to audits of other types of financial transactions.

For the purposes of the example, it is presumed that a review has been made of the internal and accounting controls and that these controls and checks have been found to be adequate. Thus, the auditor may proceed with selecting a representative sample of transactions and accounts for detailed testing and examination.

Acceptance of Transaction Test Concept

It is not the function of an auditor to verify all postings and trace all transactions to assure that, in all instances, the appropriate accounts were charged. For many years, the practice of auditing has relied on a sampling or testing methodology in the examination of transactions. The acceptance of this approach is based on the established principle that an auditor's opinion

184

attests to the reasonableness and not the absolute correctness of the balances reflected in the financial statements of the audited organization. The auditor is not a guarantor of the financial presentations, nor is the detection of fraudulent actions an objective of financial statement audit. Further, the costs to examine and trace the accounting for all transactions would be prohibitive.

This acceptance of test methodology has been formally expressed in the AICPA's Statement on Auditing Standards, No. 16, titled *The Independent Auditor's Responsibility for the Detection of Errors or Irregularities.* This SAS states in part that:

> ... the concept of selective testing of the data being examined, which involves judgement both as to the number of transactions to be examined and as to the areas to be tested, has been generally accepted as a valid and sufficient basis for an auditor to express an opinion on financial statements.

This SAS provides guidance for detecting errors or irregularities and discusses procedures to be performed when these types of deficiencies may exist. The Statement on Auditing Standards, No. 1, titled "Codification of Auditing Standards and Procedures," discusses many other aspects of testing, including the extent, timing, sample size and selection of the test population, and relationship of the tested items to other auditing procedures.

Pyramidal Audit Testing Concept

A Description

To provide a perspective on the nature of audit testing, it may be helpful to visualize the structure of information as an inverted pyramid, illustrated in Exhibit 12-1. Top management is concerned, initially, with the general financial position of the organization—that is, with the overall financial statements and trial balance. Operating managers require additional details for monitoring performance and assessing compliance, relying more on account balances, comparative analyses, trends, variances and other indicators of change or achievement. The detail of the individual transactions comprise the most specific information, which once recorded and accumulated into an account, often may not be re-examined unless a specific inquiry requires analysis at this level.

Relationship to Government Audits

The pyramidal concept also applies to the conduct of an audit. The auditor's opinion relates to the reasonableness and fairness of the overall financial statements of the organization. However, tests must be conducted of the underlying accounts, groupings of receipts and expenditures, and individual transactions. Additionally, analyses for comparative purposes and for evaluation of changes, trends and compliance with laws, regulations and other requirements also should be made during the course of the audit.

Exhibit 12-1

Pyramidal Audit Testing Concept

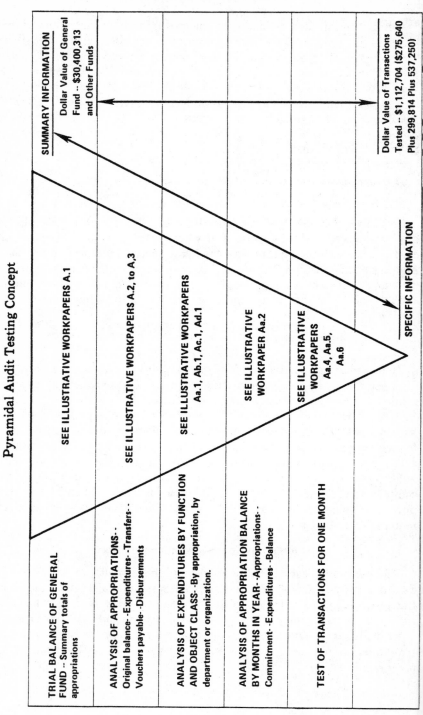

Reviews must also be made of the expenditure of the appropriations, changes in fund balance and unexpended appropriations. The testing methodology, in practice, causes the auditor to proceed from the overall balance of a fund or an appropriation towards the accounting for specific transactions — moving from the summary information towards more specific details. In governmental accounting, this process generally will include the following hierarchy or flow:

General or other fund financial statements;

Agency or departmental financial reports;

Appropriations accountability;

Apportionment or allocation of appropriated funds;

Commitment or reservation of funds for specific contemplated expenditures;

Obligation or encumbrance of funds to meet contemplated liabilities;

Recording of expenditures and confirmed liabilities;

Accounting by object classifications; and

Disbursement of funds.

Selected Glossary of Governmental Financial Terms

Other chapters contain definitions of some unique terms of governmental accounting. For convenience, to permit a review of the audit test methodology, an abbreviated glossary of terms is included in the following paragraphs.

Allocation—an administrative breakdown or division of the full appropriation passed by the legislature.

Allotment—a further subdivision of the allocated appropriation, intended to provide more detailed control of expenditures by operating offices.

Appropriation—the specific authorization of funds by the legislature to provide financial resources for the support of governmental activities.

Budget—the plan for financing government operations and meeting obligations for the fiscal year. Compiled by the executive, the budget requires the consent of the legislature and constitutes a legal requirement for compliance.

Commitment—an early reservation of appropriated funds for a specific purpose, which may or may not be recorded formally in the financial records of the governmental unit.

Deficiency appropriation—an additional or supplemental appropriation approved by the legislature to provide additional expenditure authority in those instances where an earlier appropriation is not sufficient to cover program operations or the cost of legislated activities.

Disbursements—cash disbursed or "checks issued" by the government.

Encumbrance—a reservation of appropriated funds to meet a formal obligation of the government, which should precede the recording of the expenditure and the actual disbursement of funds.

Expenditures—the recognition of the definite liability of the government to pay for goods received or services rendered, resulting in the identification of an asset or recording of an expense.

Fiscal year—the 12-month period constituting the accounting period for the governmental unit, varying among and between levels of government. (The federal fiscal year is the period from October 1 to September 30; numerous states and local governmental units prefer a fiscal year from July 1 to June 30.)

Fund—the fiscal or accounting entity, which may be comprised of one or more appropriations at the state and local government levels; at the federal level, the term is synonymous with appropriation.

General fund—comprised of the general revenues and the general expenses of the governmental entity.

Object class of expenditures—the classification or accounting for expenditures by such categories as personnel, equipment, contracts, grants, capital expenditures, etc.

Requisition—an order placed for supplies, services, equipment, etc. to another governmental entity, accounted for by the requesting entity in a manner similar to a commitment or order placed with a non-governmental organization.

Surplus—a fiscal condition whereby cash intake or revenue of a government is more than the incurred expenditures and encumbrances.

Voucher schedule—a listing of payees submitted to the treasury agent for the purpose of having a check issued.

The above glossary of terms should not be construed as all-inclusive. Knowledge of these terms, though, will aid in understanding the audit program and the related audit work papers discussed in succeeding sections of the chapter.

Use of the Audit Program

Purposes of Audit Program

It is necessary that an audit be made pursuant to a formal audit program, which should be constructed or modified after sufficient review and survey. The review and survey will provide an assurance that the required tests and steps are relevant to the organization being audited. Some of the more important purposes served by requiring adherence to a formal audit program include:

The program provides a measure of uniform quality and consistency in performing the audit;

The program provides detailed guidance to subordinates and is an important aspect in properly supervising work of assistants;

The program, properly modified to the specific circumstances, permits evaluation and assessment of controls and systems to determine the detailed tests that must be performed; and

The program permits advance planning of the audit, determining skill requirements, constructing budgets, time-phasing staff, scheduling client meetings and estimating additional costs or services needed (e.g. statistical sampling plan, computer programming skills, computer availability, etc.).

The audit program represents the scope of work, in the judgement of the auditor, required to render an opinion as to the reasonableness of the financial statements of the audited organization.

Development or Modification of Audit Program

Numerous examples exist of audit programs that would apply to the audit of governmental units generally. Earlier chapters outlined the process for developing the detailed tasks that should appear in an audit program or that should be considered in modifying an existing audit program to the specific circumstances of the entity under audit. A comprehensive example of one such audit program is included in Appendix A. This program was prepared by the Pennsylvania Institute of Certified Public Accountants for the review of internal controls and detailed audit of governmental entities in that state. The audit requirements discussed, though, are equally applicable to most municipalities.

Completion of the Audit Program

For illustrative purposes, selected excerpts from an audit program have been highlighted in workpapers A 1/7 to A 7/7 in the appendix to this chapter. This abbreviated audit program provides guidance for the detailed examination of expenditures of a governmental appropriation. Upon completion of the steps appearing in the audit program, the program should be permanently filed with the audit workpapers. Completion of the audit program requires that the performing auditor personally attest, by initialling the audit program, to the completion of the required audit steps. The date that the audit work was performed also must be noted in the audit program. Steps in the audit program must be cross-referenced to specific workpapers containing evidence and to details of audit work performed to satisfy the program requirements.The steps of the audit program could further be cross-referenced to weaknesses identified in the survey and review of internal controls.

The Detailed Audit

Requirement for Evidential Matter

The AICPA's third standard of field work requires that:

> Sufficient competent evidential matter is to be obtained through inspection, observation, inquiries, and confirmations, to afford a reasonable basis for an opinion regarding the financial statements under examination.

The GAO *Standards for Audit* are somewhat broader, but no less stringent. These *Standards* apply equally to the examination of financial statements as well as to the other types of governmental audits to which these *Standards* are applicable. The GAO *standard* relating to evidence states:

> Sufficient, competent, and relevant evidence is to be obtained to afford a reasonable basis for the auditor's opinions, judgements, conclusions, and recommendations.

The AICPA's Statement on Auditing Standards, No. 1, states that evidential matter supporting financial statements consists of both underlying accounting data and corroborating information. *The underlying accounting data,* in support of the financial statements would include

> ... the books of original entry, the general and subsidiary ledgers, related accounting manuals, informal and memorandum records as work sheets supporting cost allocations, computations, and reconciliations. . . .
>
> *Corroborating evidential matter* includes documentary materials such as checks, invoices, contracts, and minutes of meetings; confirmations and other written representations by knowledgeable people; information obtained by the auditor from inquiry, observations, inspection, and physical examination; and other information developed by, or available to, the auditor. . . .

A record of the work performed and of the evidential matter upon which the auditor based his conclusions and recommendations must be recorded in the audit workpapers. These requirements are applicable to governmental audits in the same manner as to audits of private organizations.

Conducting the Audit

While specific audit steps and scope of coverage must be determined for each audit, audits of governmental entities will be concerned with the existence of funds appropriated by legislatures and the encumbrance and expenditure of these funds by operating agencies and departments. In a similar manner, audit steps must be performed to assure that revenues have been properly assessed and received in a manner and for purposes contemplated by the legislature.

Audits of appropriated funds often, in summary, will include:

The confirmation of an appropriation and a determination of the key characteristics of the appropriation legislation, such as the dollars appropriated, the time period or availability of the appropriation for expenditure, and the purposes for which the appropriation may be spent.

A determination of the status of the fund balance, including the expended, encumbered, committed, and uncommitted amounts of the appropriation.

A comparison of actual expenditures to the budget, often including comparisions between years, months in the year, organizations, program activities, types of expenditures, etc.

Analyses of changes in the appropriations, including additions, deletions, transfers in and out, supplemental appropriations or augmentations, lapsed balances, deficiencies and surpluses, etc.

A detailed audit of a sample of transactions which might include, among other tests or steps:

Footing and comparing financial records, journals and summaries to determine consistency of these accounting documents;

Validating the propriety and existence of evidence showing the authority and approval to obligate and disburse governmental funds;

Confirming the appropriation number, limitations, expenditure criteria and other requirements of the legislation;

Examining supporting documents and obtaining evidence to demonstrate compliance with law, policy, procedures, contractual and other agreements affecting the receipt or disbursement of funds;

Reviewing the accuracy of the accounting for all transactions in the test sample, including the accuracy or authenticity of authorization, account coding, recording, processing, posting, accumulating and reporting.

Examining individual transactions and control procedures to insure that the governmental funds have been committed, encumbered, expended or disbursed within any time period, and were utilized for the purpose set forth in the governing legislation, and that expended amounts are reasonable for the product or services acquired and do not exceed any total or other budgetary restriction.

Some of these tests or steps are identified in the sample audit program appearing in the appendix to this chapter.

Purpose of Audit Workpapers

There are no specific guides established for audit workpapers relating to either format or content. The design, substance, quantity and coverage of audit workpapers are left to the judgment of the auditor. It should be remembered, however, that adequate workpapers form the best defense in support of the audit opinion. A general working guideline is that the workpapers should be sufficient to permit an independent reviewer to perform an "audit of the auditor," with a minimum of assistance or explanation by the auditor.

The AICPA's Statement on Auditing Standards, No. 1, suggests that workpapers are kept by an independent auditor as a record of the audit procedures followed, tests performed, information obtained, and conclusions reached. This Standard states that the workpapers generally would include:

Sufficient data to demonstrate that the financial statements or other information on which the auditor is reporting is in agreement with the audited organization's records;

Evidence that the engagement was planned (possibly by the use of work plans), that assistants were supervised and their work reviewed;

A record indicating that the system of internal control was reviewed and evaluated to determine the extent of the audit tests performed;

Various forms and other documentary evidence, such as memoranda, check lists, work programs, schedules and other records to permit reasonable identification of the audit procedures followed and tests performed by the auditor;

A record indicating how exceptions and unusual matters were disclosed, resolved or treated by the auditor;

Appropriate comments by the auditor setting forth his conclusions and his recommendations relating to significant aspects of the audit.

Preparing Audit Workpapers

Workpapers often are divided into two general categories—the *permanent workpapers,* which are more historical and general in nature and applicable to audits of two or more years, and *current workpapers,* which evidence the procedures followed, tests performed and conclusions reached for the current audit.

Often firms will utilize a standard set of symbols to indicate the work performed and method of cross-referencing various workpapers. In many financial audits, the overall financial statements or the detailed trial balance of the accounts is used as a summary or control workpaper with each account balance or line item being referenced to other more detailed workpapers that contain evidence of the work performed. For nonfinancial audits, the specific steps or tasks in a detailed audit program or work plan should be cross-referenced to supporting workpapers that contain the evidence of the audit work.

The appendix to this chapter illustrates a method of workpaper compilation that might be used in support of the work performed in testing selected appropriation records of a governmental entity. The audit program is referenced to related audit workpapers containing evidence of audit procedures followed and tests performed. Workpapers containing more detailed evidence relating to the fund or appropriation balances are cross-referenced, with the overall trial balance of accounts being used as the summary record. Workpapers exist for each appropriation examined.

These papers have been arranged in a manner that permits a reviewer to examine the work performed, proceeding from the summary, or general, level to the specific, or detailed, level. For example:

Workpapers A 1/7 through A 7/7 illustrate portions of an audit program providing guidance for the detailed examination of expenditures of a government department. Selected steps have been cross-referenced to evidence in other supporting workpapers.

Workpaper A.1. 1/2 and 2/2 display the trial balance of general and special funds, showing the totals of the several appropriations comprising the funds. Each appropriation has been cross-referenced to more detailed analyses.

Workpaper A.2 is an analysis of allocations of appropriations by the quarters of the fiscal year, including a summary reconciliation of the total amount available for expenditure by the department.

Workpaper A.3 is an analysis of expenditure by the different funds and the amounts ultimately disbursed by the Treasury during the fiscal year.

Workpaper A.4 provides an explanation of the several audit notations and symbols used in the audit workpapers to avoid repetitive and time-consuming detailed explanations on each of the individual workpapers.

Workpapers Aa.1 through Aa.6 include details relating to the selection and examination of detailed transactions.

Workpapers Ab.1 through Ad.1 illustrate other specific analyses and audit steps performed for individual appropriations and augmentations to appropriations.

These workpapers should be viewed as only illustrative of an audit testing methodology and of workpaper techniques that might be utilized during an audit. The noted verification, scope of tests, and workpaper format and content are not intended to be all-inclusive.

Appendix to Chapter 12

Illustrative Workpapers

Relating to Audit of Appropriated

Funds for an Executive Branch

Government Agency

Table of Contents

EXECUTIVE BRANCH DEPARTMENT

AUDIT PROGRAM

FOR THE YEAR ENDED JUNE 30, 1978

GENERAL PROCEDURES	INITIAL DATE	WORKPAPER REFERENCE

1. Visit Department, conduct entrance conference with Departmental Secretary, Comptroller and financial management personnel.

   Not Illustrated

2. Obtain review and discuss the Department's operating and capital budgets, operating plans and financial statements including the status of appropriations.

3. Review prior reports and internal management information to identify significant activities.

4. Discuss the systems of internal control, the safety of automation of those systems and arrange for preliminary evaluations.

5. Obtain current organization and operating manuals policy statements, memorandum and correspondence pertaining to the financial management and accounting function and the financial statements.

6. Discuss major operating systems with appropriate personnel. Prepare a preliminary plan for systems documentation, review and analysis.

7. Arrange for preparation of trial balances account analysis and schedules, and other working papers by auditor personnel where it is feasible for them to do so.

Prepared by GW Date 10-15

Index No. A 1/7

EXECUTIVE BRANCH DEPARTMENT

AND PROGRAM

FOR THE YEAR ENDED JUNE 30, 1978

GENERAL PROCEDURES	INITIAL DATE	WORKPAPER REFERENCE
8. Prepare a memorandum detailing the nature and expected complexity of financial statements supplementing information internal control and compliance commentary, and programmatic data which must be presented along with the audit report.	Not Illustrated	
9. Obtain and review, along with prior periods reports for this Department, similar reports prepared for other like agencies. Identify usual reporting problems.		
10. Maintain an ongoing analysis of accounting and auditing problems for supervisory evaluating and identify ultimate dispositions.		
11. Accumulate summaries of material and significant internal control weaknesses and instances of failure of compliance with financial and accounting requirements (see synopsis of financial compliance requirements prepared by Departmental personnel.		
12. Prepare the initial audit time budget and obtain code for audit time accumulation.		
13. Initial and index each workpaper and cross-reference workpaper containing related analysis.		

Prepared by C W

Date 10-15

Index No. A 2/7

EXECUTIVE BRANCH DEPARTMENT

AND PROGRAM

FOR THE YEAR ENDED JUNE 30, 1978

INTERNAL CONTROL	INITIAL DATE	WORKPAPER REFERENCE
1. Obtain an understanding of the following systems and document that understanding from interviews, manuals and observations.	Not Illustrated	

- Cash receipts
- Purchases/accounts payable
- Payroll
- Fixed assets
- Investments
- Other major systems identified

Place emphasis on control points.

2. Perform a "walkthrough" of those systems documented in (1) above to confirm that they are operating as described. Detail material exceptions.

3. Perform transaction tests for those system selected for detailed testing. This will involve tracing a sample of transactions (judgemental or statistical) from the time they enter the system until completion with emphasis on tests of controls to determine their expectiveness.

4. In connection with the review of internal controls to determine the nature, timing, and extent of substantive procedures, prepare comments for management letter purposes on any observed material weaknesses.

Prepared by	Index No.
C W	*A* 3/7
Date 10-15	

EXECUTIVE BRANCH DEPARTMENT

AND PROGRAM

FOR THE YEAR ENDED JUNE 30, 1978

SURVEY PROCEDURES - EXPENDITURES	INITIAL	DATE	WORKPAPER REFERENCE
1. Prepare or obtain a summary trial balance for all appropriations payable from all funds administered by the Department.	CW	10-20	A.1
2. Prepare a schedule of allocations of current period appropriations and trace to authorizing documentation.	CW	10-21	A.2
3. Prepare a detailed analysis of each appropriation including: . Beginning balance . Addition and deductions . Ending balances . Reconciliations with appropriations acts and Treasury Balances.	CW CW	10-20 10-21	A.1 A.3
4. Prepare for each appropriation a schedule of expenditures by common object, detailed by program, function, and organization.	JB AH	10-23/24 10-23/27	Aa.1 Ab.1 Ac.1 Ad.1
5. Develop a comparative analysis with the prior year for major appropriations at common object level. Identify material variances.	JB/AH	10-23 10/23	Aa.1 Ac.1
6. Perform remaining steps for those appropriations where material inconsistencies or variance have been observed resulting from (3) through (5) above. Additional substantive testing should be done to the degree considered necessary based on your previous review of internal controls and the extent to which they are in place and operating effectively.			

Prepared by   *CW*

Date   *10·15*

Index No.   *A*   4/7

EXECUTIVE BRANCH DEPARTMENT

AND PROGRAM

FOR THE YEAR ENDED JUNE 30, 1978

SUBSTANTIVE TESTS - EXPENDITURES	INITIAL	DATE	WORKPAPER REFERENCE
Note The following procedures are to be performed for appropriations meeting criteria set forth in step #6 above.			
1. Prepare a monthly analysis of expenditures chargable against allocations. Detail each element of increase or decrease.	CW	10-28	Aa.2
2. Verify that encumbrances and expenditures do not exceed allocations (quarterly) or total appropriations (annually).	CW	10-28	Aa.2
3. Scan trend of monthly expenditures for any exceptional periods and consider result in designing your detail testing plan.	CW	10-28	Aa.2
4. Obtain computer audit assistance to survey all voucher schedules prepared during the year. The survey should include: . number of voucher schedules processed . numerical sequence of schedules . cost categorization of schedule . percentage relationship of cost categories to total schedules amount.	PT	10-29	Aa.3
5. Based on information obtained from the computer survey in (4) above, determine the range of schedule categories and both the dollar and percentage of total amounts for further testing.	PT	10-29	Aa.3

Prepared by CW	Index No. A 5/7
Date 10-15	

EXECUTIVE BRANCH DEPARTMENT

AUDIT PROGRAM

FOR THE YEAR ENDED JUNE 30, 1978

			WORKPAPER
SUBSTANTIVE TESTS - EXPENDITURES	INTIAL	DATE	REFERENCE

6. Obtain those schedules selected
   in (5) above from the comptroller's
   office and:

   . account for the total and type
     of vouchers
   . reconcile quantity of vouchers
     to voucher number range per
     schedule.
   . compare appropriations title
     and account codes on selected
     vouchers (including list of
     vouchers and grouping sheets)
     to voucher schedules
   . survey for completeness
   . re-add schedules   JB   10-30   Aa.4

7. For those vouchers selected for
   detail testing perform the
   following analyses:

   . trace authorized signers to
     signature codes on file
     with comptroller
   . determine that vouchers are
     properly signed by:

     1. sellers
     2. receiving officer

   . trace vendor code number to
     master vendor file with the
     comptroller
   . re-extend, recompute discounts,
     foot and crossfoot
   . trace content descriptions to
     supporting documentation   JB & AH 10-31   Aa.5

8. For selected vouchers examine
   supporting documentation to determine:

   . Properly prepared and authorized
     purchase orders.

Prepared by
CW
Date *10-15*

Index No.
A 6/7

EXECUTIVE BRANCH DEPARTMENT

AUDIT PROGRAM

FOR THE YEAR ENDED JUNE 30, 1978

SUBSTANTIVE TESTS - EXPENDITURES	INITIAL DATE	WORKPAPER REFERENCE

- Evidence of receipt of goods.
- Evidence of verifications of prices, quantities, etc.
- Correctness of account charged.
- Propriety of material or service purchased.
- Evidence of legal compliance in regard to advertising for or soliciting quotations for prices, where applicable.
- Approval for payment.
- Effectively cancelled or mutilated
- Account distributions are reasonable (charged to the correct appropriations and sub-object classification
- Agree with contract provisions, where applicable.   JB & AH   10-31   Aa.6

Prepared by CW
Date 10-15

Index No. A 6/7

EXECUTIVE BRANCH DEPARTMENT

TRIAL BALANCE - ALL FUNDS

FOR THE YEAR ENDED JUNE 30, 1978

APPROPRIATIONS CODE				APPROPRIATIONS/ACTIVITY BY FUND CATEGORY	APPROPRIATIONS TYPE	WORKPAPER REFERENCE
FUND	DIVISION AGENCY	APPRO. TYPE	FISCAL YEAR			
100	12,200	-	-	General Purpose Funds		
101	12,201	00	77	General Government Operation	Current	*Aa*
101	12,201	76	76	General Government Operation	Re-appropriation	*Aa*
109	12,210	07	74	Emergency & Disaster Relief	Continuing/Aug- menting	*Ab*
200	12,200	-	-	Special Revenue Funds		
206	12,200	-	-	Beautification Fund:		
206	12,220	00	77	Landscaping & Develop- ment	Current	*Ac*
700	12,200	-	-	Federal Revenue Sharing:		
701	12,230	99	77	Aid to the elderly	Augmenting Appropriation - Transfer	*Ad*

BALANCE JULY 1, 1977		APPROP- RIATIONS	AUGMENTING APPRO- PRIATIONS AND RECEIPTS		TRANSFERS IN FROM OTHER FUNDS	AVAILABLE FOR DISPOSITION	
ENCUMBERED	AVAILABLE		FEDERAL	RESTRICTED		ENCUMBERED	AVAILABLE
$ ---	---	15,500,000 ✗ (A.2)	---	---			15,500,000
273,550	32,470	---	---	---		273,550	32,470
67,420	26,593	8,000,000 ✗ (A.2)	4,155,750 (A.2)	---		67,420	12,182,343
---	---	1,500,000 ✗ (A.2)		75,000			1,575,000
---	110,500	---	---	---	1,000,000		1,110,500
$340,970	169,563	25,000,000	4,155,750	75,000	1,000,000	340,970	30,400,313

EXECUTIVE BRANCH DEPARTMENT

TRAIL BALANCE - ALL FUNDS

FOR THE YEAR ENDED JUNE 30, 1978

FUND	AGENCY	DIVISION	APPRO TYPE	FISCAL YEAR	APPROPRIATION/ACTIVITY BY FUND CATEGORY	APPROPRIATION TYPE	ENCUMBERED	AVAILABLE FO DISPOSITION AVAILABLE
	APPROPRIATION CODE							
100	122	00	--	--	General Purpose Funds			
101	122	01	00	77	General Government Operations	Current	$ ---	15,500,00
101	122	01	76	76	General Government Operations	Reappropriation	273,550	32,47
109	122	10	07	74	Emergency & Disaster Relief	Contingency/ Augmenting	67,420	12,182,34
200	122	00	--	00	Special Revenues Funds			
215	122	20	--	--	Beautification Fund			
215	122	20	00	77	Landscaping & Development	Current		1,575,000
700	122	00	--	--	Federal Revenue Sharing	Augmenting		
701	122	30	99	77	Aid to elderly	Appropriation/ Transfer		1,110,500

$340,970   30,400,313

EXPENDITURES	REFUNDS OF EXPENDITURES	TRANSFERS OUT	BALANCE JUNE 30, 1978		VOUCHERS SCHEDULES IN TRANSIT	LAPSES IN TRIAL	BALANCE WITH TREASURY
15,324,697 *(Aa.1)*	(63,260)	25,000	175,303 *(Aa.2)*	38,260	25,275		238,838 X
157,470	---	50,000	23,550	---		75,000	98,550 X
12,133,830 *(Ab.1)*	(91,549)		42,046	165,436	21,753		229,235 X
1,535,960 *(Ac.1)*	(10,784)		24,824	---	5,000	25,000	54,824 X
1,110,500 *(Ad.1)*	---	---	---	---			---
30,262,457	(165,593)	75,000	265,723	203,696	52,028	100,000	621,447

Prepared by *CW*
Date *10.20*

Index No. *A.1 ½*

EXECUTIVE BRANCH DEPARTMENT
ANALYSIS OF CURRENT PERIOD ALLOCATIONS
FOR THE YEAR ENDED JUNE 30, 1978

| CODE | FUND CATEGORY AND APPROPRIATION TITLE | QUARTERS | | | | |
		FIRST	SECOND	THIRD	FOURTH	TOTAL
101-1H01-0077	General - General Govt. Grants	$3,875,000	3,875,000	3,875,000	3,875,000	$15,500,000
		⅄	X	X	X	*(A.1)*
109-2201-07-74	General - Emergency & Disaster Relief	2,000,000	1,000,000	4,000,000	1,000,000	8,000,000
		X	X	X	X	
				4,155,750		4,155,750
				∮		12,155,750
						(A.1)
206-12220-00-77	Spec. Rev. - Beautification	375,000	375,000	375,000	375,000	1,500,000
		X	X	X	X	*(A.1)*
701-12230-99-77	Spec. Rev. Revenue Sharing	250,000	250,000	250,000	250,000	1,000,000
		⅄	⅄	⅄	⅄	*(A.1)*

Summary and Reconciliation

Allocations	25,000,000
Augmenting Allocations	4,155,750
Augmenting Allocations - transferred in	1,000,000
	$30,155,750

Prepared by C W
Date 10-21

Index No. A.2

EXECUTIVE BRANCH DEPARTMENT
ANALYSIS, OF DISBURSEMENT
APPROPRIATED FUNDS
FOR THE YEAR ENDED JUNE 30, 1978

	GENERAL FUND			BEAUTIFICATION FUND	REVENUE SHARING
	CURRENT OPERATIONS	PRIOR YEAR OPERATIONS	EMERGENCY AND DISASTER RELIEF	LANDSCAPING AND DEVELOPMENT	AID TO THE ELDERLY
Departmental Expenditures	$15,324,697	154,470	12,133,830	1,535,960	1,110,500
Less:					
Vouchers Payable	25,275	-	21,753	5,000	-
Not Disbursements per Treasury	15,299,422 ✗	157,470 ✗	12,112,077 ✗	1,530,960 ✗	1,110,500 ✗
Add:					
Refunds of Expenditures	63,260	-	86,585	10,784	-
Petty Cash Advance Balance	2,500	1,000	1,500	2,500	-
Gross Disbursements per Treasury	$15,365,182 ✗	158,470 ✗	12,200,162 ✗	1,544,244 ✗	1,110,500 ✗

Prepared by C W Date 10.21 Index No. A.3

Executive Branch Department
Legends Supporting A Workpapers
For the Year Ended June 30, 1978

✓ Traced to Certified copy of the Appropriation Act

✗ Traced to appropriation listing prepared by the Bureau of the Budget

X̲ Traced to allocation schedule released quarterly by the Bureau of the Budget.

Ⴍ Traced to the allocation schedule of entitlements released quarterly by the Bureau of the Budget

\ Traced to the schedule of Federal Grants-in-aid and contracts prepared by the Office of Management and Finance

/ Traced to the Treasury Department Report of Activity

X Confirmed with Treasury Department

∅ Examined Lapsing Schedule released by Office of Management and Finance

- Totals for workpapers A1, and A3 were taken from reconciliations prepared by Central Accounting

- Totals for object code detail schedules were taken from Central Accounting Summary Report of Expenditures by Object Code.

Prepared by C⍟ Date 10.21	Index No. A.4

EXECUTIVE BRANCH DEPARTMENT
ANALYSIS OF APPROPRIATIONS BY FUNCTION
AND COMMON OBJECT

FOR THE YEAR ENDED JUNE 30, 1978

GENERAL PURPOSE FUND
GENERAL GOVERNMENTAL OPERATIONS - CURRENT (101-12201-00-77)

COMMON OBJECT CODE	COMMON OBJECT CATEGORY	PERSONNEL	CONTROL ACCOUNTING	WEIGHTS AND MEASURES	ADMINISTRATIVE SERVICES	PROGRAM A	ORGANIZATION A	SPECIAL PROJECTS	TOTAL	PRIOR YEARS TOTAL	DIFFERENCE INCREASE (DECREASE)	NOTES
1000	Personnel Service	$1,210,671	1,317,560	1,529,710	1,438,210	2,851,970	2,765,919	1,071,650	12,185,690	10,996,650	1,189,040	(A)
1100	Contractual Services	35,450	27,945	62,750	15,000	157,250	167,415	77,910	543,720	553,125	(9,405)	(B)
1200	Consumable Supplies	38,193	55,260	48,622	77,240	96,438	124,690	51,321	491,764	447,125	44,639	(C)
1300	Equipment	8,519	36,129	25,851	154,260	22,615	48,516	21,495	317,385	284,120	33,265	(D)
1500	Electronic Data Processing	18,661	32,495	43,276	21,640	75,265	84,120	56,428	331,885	245,192	86,693	(E)
1600	Telecommunications	5,419	3,257	6,212	5,497	16,684	13,769	3,082	53,920	47,580	6,340	(F)
1700	Operation of Automotive Equipment	5,196	5,864	5,412	8,924	27,186	17,492	8,047	78,121	69,186	8,935	(G)
1800	Awards & Grants	-	-	-	-	1,275,000	-	-	1,275,000	1,167,500	107,500	(H)
2000	Furnishings	3,876	3,729	4,086	7,619	12,919	8,468	6,515	47,212	53,129	(5,917)	(I)
		$1,325,985	1,482,239	1,725,919	1,728,390	4,535,327	3,230,389	1,296,448	15,324,697	13,863,607	1,461,090	

(A.1) (A.1)

Prepared JB 10-24
Date
Index No. Aa.1

NOTES:

VARIANCE ANALYSIS

(A) Mandated increment of 6% in September plus net staff additions in Program A (26) - numerical step increase.
(B) Contract terminations totaling $75,000 (effect $53,000) offset by special projects increases.
(C) Normal increase with heavy additions in Program A and Special Projects.
(D) No explanation.
(E) Expendable equipment set up costs ($56,000) plus normal increases due to inflationary impact.
(F) No explanation.
(G) Increase principally due to fuel cost increases.
(H) Reflects Program A sub-grant increases consistent with budget.
(I) Reduction due to austerity and budget cuts for this line item.

Executive Branch Department
Monthly Analysis of Appropriations Expenditures
For the Year Ended June 30, 1978

Federal Government Operations - Current (101-12201-00-77)

	Appropriation	Cumulative Allocation	Commitments	Expenditures	Cumulative Balance
July	15,500,000	3,875,000	$196,240	1,240,100	2,438,660
August			23,910	1,221,530	1,193,220
September			(83,720)	1,276,940	-
October		7,750,000	57,423	1,210,463	2,607,114
November			46,122	1,364,132	1,196,860
December			(86,352)	1,283,212	-
January	11,625,000		21,619	1,255,367	2,598,014
February			11,018	1,298,652	1,288,344
March			51,770	1,236,574	-
April		15,500,000	49,573	1,293,216	2,532,211
May			(89,536)	1,267,532	1,354,215
June			(22,764)	1,376,979	-
			$175,303	15,324,697	

Transfers out　　　　　　　　(A.l)　　(Aa.l)　　<25,000>
Refunds of Exenditures　　　　　　　　　　　　63,260
Available Balance　　　　　　　　　　　　　　38,260 (A.l)

Prepared by　C W　Date 10-28　　Index No. Aa.2

Executive Branch Department
Summary of Computer Survey of Voucher
Schedule by Relative Life General Govt. Appropriation
(#101-12201-00-77)
For the Year Ended June 30, 1978

Dollar Value Range	Category No.	Number of Schedules	Total Amount	Percentage of Total Amount	
Zero -$ 50,000	1	35	$1,489,180	9.7%	
$50,000 - 150,000	2	41	3,964,286	25.9%	
150,000 - 300,000	3	36	8,236,512	53.7% }	64.4%
300,000 - above	4	4	1,634,719	10.7% }	
		116 ᴹ	$15,324,697 ᴧ	100.0%	

(Aa. 2)

Note   An election to test voucher schedules in the two highest ranges
(3&4) will result in coverage of approximately 65% of the expenditure universe printing detail for 40 out of 116 possible
voucher schedules.

ᴹ Source   for these figures in the total expenditure survey analysis
for the appropriation prepared with computer audit programming assistance. The source schedule accounts for all
voucher schedules by numerical sequence in addition to the
above detailed information.

Prepared by ρⅡ	Index No.
Date 10.29	Aa.3

EXECUTIVE BRANCH DEPARTMENT
LISTING OF VOUCHER SCHEDULES
SELECTED FOR TESTING
FOR THE YEAR ENDED JUNE 30, 1978

VOUCHERS SCHEDULE NUMBERS		NUMBER OF VOUCHERS ON EACH SCHEDULE		TOTAL AMOUNT OF EACH VOUCHER SCHEDULE		CORRECT NO. OF VOUCHERS ATTACHED	
#3	#4	#3	#4	#3	#4	#3	#4
1,568	1,575	9	12	$ 229,238	429,360	✓	✓
1,571ʌ		12ʌ		275,640ʌ		✓	
1,576	1,606	10	17	219,333	318,046	✓	✓
1,580		7		184,619		✓	
1,585	1,654ʌ	16	21ʌ	293,413	537,250ʌ	✓	✓
1,588		6		153,531		✓	
1,591	1,673	12	16	246,198	350,063	✓	✓
1,594		11		213,836		✓	
1,599		11		216,563		✓	
1,601		13		238,512		✓	
1,607		12		232,196		✓	
1,608		15		247,317		✓	
1,612		8		198,004		✓	
1,613		11		203,912		✓	
1,616		13		228,413		✓	
1,620		14		236,367		✓	
1,626		11		226,519		✓	
1,628		9		213,416		✓	
1,631		10		186,912		✓	
1,635		10		199,364		✓	
1,637		12		229,819		✓	
1,640		11		217,765		✓	
1,644		12		236,594		✓	
1,648		8		164,487		✓	
1,651ʌ		9ʌ		299,814ʌ		✓	
1,652		13		246,012		✓	
1,657		11		213,014		✓	
1,662		12		219,921		✓	
1,665		14		256,043		✓	
1,668		17		260,136		✓	
1,670		12		239,005		✓	
1,677		13		241,091		✓	
1,679		11		236,512		✓	
1,680		15		264,312		✓	
1,681		14		213,056		✓	
1,682		14		255,419		✓	
		448	66	$ 8,236,512	1,643,719		
			448		8,236,512		
			514		$ 9,871,231		

ʌ Selected for detail testing

PROCEDURES USED IN
TEST OF VOUCHER SCHEDULES LISTED

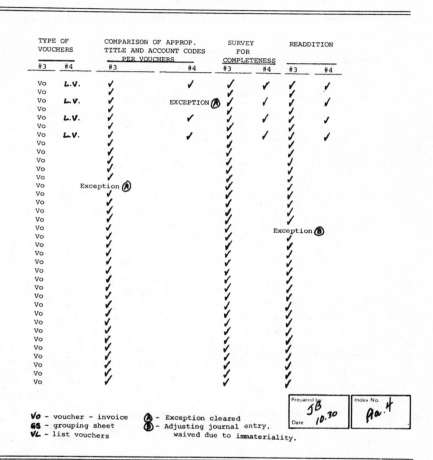

TYPE OF VOUCHERS		COMPARISON OF APPROP. TITLE AND ACCOUNT CODES PER VOUCHERS		SURVEY FOR COMPLETENESS		READDITION	
#3	#4	#3	#4	#3	#4	#3	#4
Vo	L.V.	✓	✓	✓	✓	✓	✓
Vo		✓		✓			
Vo	L.V.	✓	EXCEPTION Ⓐ	✓	✓	✓	✓
Vo		✓		✓		✓	
Vo	L.V.	✓	✓	✓	✓	✓	✓
Vo		✓		✓		✓	
Vo	L.V.	✓	✓	✓	✓	✓	✓
Vo		✓		✓		✓	
Vo		✓		✓		✓	
Vo		✓		✓		✓	
Vo		✓		✓		✓	
Vo		Exception Ⓐ		✓		✓	
Vo		✓		✓		✓	
Vo		✓		✓		✓	
Vo		✓		✓		✓	
Vo		✓		✓		✓	
Vo		✓		✓		Exception Ⓑ	
Vo		✓		✓		✓	
Vo		✓		✓		✓	
Vo		✓		✓		✓	
Vo		✓		✓		✓	
Vo		✓		✓		✓	
Vo		✓		✓		✓	
Vo		✓		✓		✓	
Vo		✓		✓		✓	
Vo		✓		✓		✓	
Vo		✓		✓		✓	
Vo		✓		✓		✓	
Vo		✓		✓		✓	
Vo		✓		✓			

Vo - voucher - invoice
GS - grouping sheet
VL - list vouchers

Ⓐ - Exception cleared
Ⓑ - Adjusting journal entry,
    waived due to immateriality.

Prepared by	JB 10.30	Index No. Aa.4
Date		

Executive Branch Department
Schedule and Analysis of Vouchers
Selected for Detail Testing
For the Year Ended June 30, 1978

Voucher Schedule Number	Voucher Number	Voucher Amount	Content Description Correct	Authorized Signatures	Vendor Code Number	Extended Cross Foot
					Testing Procedures	
1571	13212	$ 15631	✓	Exception	③ ✓	✓
		22914	✓	✓	✓	✓
		26817	✓	✓	✓	✓
		20413	✓ ✓	Exception	② ✓	✓
		14919	✓	✓	✓	✓
		26014	✓	✓	✓	✓
		28100	✓	✓	✓	✓
		20473	✓	Exception	②② ✓	✓
		35013	✓ ✓	Exception	✓	✓
		20216	✓	✓	✓	✓
		21518	✓	✓	✓	✓
	13223	23612	✓	✓	Exception ③	✓
		$275640				
1651	13904	30153	✓	✓	✓	✓
		42015	✓	Exception	② ✓	✓
		39318	✓	✓	✓	✓
		37214	✓	✓	✓	✓
		41004	Exception ①	✓	✓	✓
		15318	✓ ✓	Exception	② ✓	✓
		37612	✓	✓	✓	✓
		30419	✓	✓	✓	✓
	13912	26761	✓	Exception	② ✓	✓
		$299814				
1654	13310	$537250	✓ ✓	✓	N/A ④	✓
		(Aa.4)				

✓ Selected for detail invoice examination

Exception Summary

① Reclassified form repairs and maintenance to capital improvements - building
AJE - 23

② Significant number of exceptions due to vouchers unsigned by vendors.

Prepared by JB AH
Date 10.31
Index No. Aa.5 1/2

Exception Summary Cont'd.

3 Incorrect - notified Asst. Controller for update in vendor listing.

4 Bi-weekly payroll - traced to detailed
   Payroll register (See clerical payroll and reasonableness tests)

Governmental Auditing

Executive Branch Department
Examination of Invoices and Contracts
Supporting Vouchers
For the Year Ended June 30, 1978

Voucher Number	Voucher Amount	Compliance with Purchasing Act	Purchase Order or Service Purchase Contract	Receiving Report	Pricing & Quarterly Checks
13215	$ 20,413	✓	✓	N/A	✓
13226	35,013	✓	✓	N/A	✓
13909	15,318	✓	✓	✓	✓
13310	537,250	✓	N/A	N/A	N/A

(Aa.5)

Approved in Correct Amount	Proper and Valid Purchase	Cancelled and Mutilated	Proper Account Distri-bution	Description of Item
✓	✓	✓	✓	Telephone charges - September 1977.
✓	✓	✓	✓	Contractual Services - organizations and management study.
✓	✓	✓	✓	Materials and supplies Program A.
✓	✓	N/A	✓	Bi-weekly Departmental payroll. See clerical payroll and reasonable-ness tests.

Prepared by JB AH
Date 10-31

Index No. AR.6

Executive Branch Department
Analysis of Augmenting Appropriation
For the Year Ended June 30, 1978

Federal Revenue Sharing (701-12230-99-)

Unexpended appropriation balance carried
forward from prior years $ 110,500

Transferred in from Federal Revenue
Sharing Trust Fund   1,000,000

    Funds to be accounted for $ 1,110,500

Disposition

    All revenue sharing funds have been
    expended for contratual service (#1100)
    in providing aid to the elderly through
    third party service providing organi-
    zations. Providers are detailed as
    follows:

      Cork - DeKalb Congregate Feeding   450,000 ✓ᴎ ᴎ

      Southeastern Community Resources
        Council, Inc.   375,500 ✓ᴎ ᴎ

      Western Regional Cooperational for
        the Aged, Inc.   285,000 ✓ᴎ ᴎ

        Total Expenditures $ 1,110,500
                               (A.1)

✓ Regional budget and proposal to provide services
ᴎ Traced to authorized and executed contract.
ᴎ Received final independent audit of contract and dismissed minor
    questioned costs as immaterial.

Prepared by AH Date 10-27 | Index No. Ad.1

Governmental Auditing

EXECUTIVE BRANCH DEPARTMENT
ANALYSES OF APPROPRIATIONS BY FUNCTION
AND COMMON OBJECT
FOR THE YEAR ENDED JUNE 30, 1978

COMMON OBJECT CODE	COMMON OBJECT CATEGORY	GENERAL PURPOSE FUND EMERGENCY DISASTER RELIEF PROGRAMS (109-12210-07-74)		DISASTER RELIEF GRANTS
		SHORT TERM LOANS		
		INDUSTRIAL	PERSONAL	
1000	Personal Services	$ 75,750	157,290	575,200
1100	Contractual Services	25,000	25,000	320,500
1200	Consumable Supplies	9,578	33,816	22,001
1300	Equipment	-	-	-
1500	Electronic Data Processing	7,491	6,249	11,156
1600	Telecommunications	1,075	1,764	26,047
1700	Operation of Automotive Equipment	5,026	4,069	63,114
1800	Awards and Grants	-	-	3,500,000
2000	Furnishings	4,023	3,711	11,692
2200	Short Term Loans	2,500,000	500,000	-
		$2,627,943	731,899	4,529,710

Note: Detail testing and confirmation of major loans, grants and awards, and leases, on a regional, county, and individual basis has been performed in connection with the ongoing special audit of the Emergency and Disaster Relief appropriation. We have selectively reviewed major contracts and agreements and financial workpapers prepared by the Special audits division. No further procedures are considered to be required in view of the excellent evaluation of the overall system of internal and appropriation control.

PUBLIC FACILITIES REHABILITATION	TEMPORARY HOUSING	GENERAL ADMINISTRATION	TOTAL
132,600	48,980	67,500	1,057,320
815,913	944,772	10,000	2,141,185
36,520	22,551	52,454	176,920
95,600	9,190	5,750	110,540
8,315	5,019	8,302	46,532
13,918	15,460	15,027	73,291
56,093	49,251	36,819	214,372
1,734,910	–	–	5,234,910
2,015	10,836	46,483	78,760
–	–	–	3,000,000
2,895,884	1,106,059	242,335	12,133,830

(A.1)

Prepared by JB
Date 10.24

Index No.
Ab:1

Executive Branch Department
Analysis of Appropriation By Functions and
Common Object
For the Year Ended June 30, 1978

Labeling & Development - Current (215-11220-00-77)

Common Object Code	Common Object Category	Current Period	Prior Period	Increase (Decrease)
1000	Personal Services	$ 1,172,150	$ 1,046,563	125,587
1100	Contractual Services	7,500	10,000	(2,500)
1200	Consumable Services	37,004	30,620	6.384
1300	Equipment	116,452	84,105	32,347
1500	Electronic Data Processing	64,210	59,817	4,393
1600	Telecommunications	36,818	34,159	2,659
1700	Operating Automotive Equipment	97,451	91,550	5,901
1800	Awards & Grants	-	-	
2000	Furnishings	4,375	5,152	(777)
		$ 1,535,960	1,361,966	173,994

(A.1)

Variance Analysis

- Mandated increase of 6% in September plus staff step
  increases and turnover determined to be within a
  normal range.

- Decrease due to contract terminations, responsibility
  assumed by force accounts.

- Attributable to equipment modernization program –
  major items – mechanical sporadic – $25,000"⋏

Note: Remaining untested accounts have been determined
       to be within normal ranges of increase (decrease).
       No further procedures are recommended based on
       comparative analysis.

⋏ Traced to purchase order, invoice voucher, and
  requisite authorization.

Prepared by A H	Index No.
Date 10·23	Ac. 1

Governmental Auditing

EXECUTIVE BRANCH DEPARTMENT

TRIAL BALANCE - ALL FUNDS

FOR THE YEAR ENDED JUNE 30, 1978

FUND	DIVISION AGENCY	APPRO. TYPE	FISCAL YEAR	APPROPRIATIONS/ACTIVITY BY FUND CATEGORY	APPROPRIATIONS TYPE	WORKPAPER REFERENCE
100	12,200	-	-	General Purpose Funds		
101	12,201	00	77	General Government Operation	Current	Aa
101	12,201	76	76	General Government Operation	Re-appropriation	Aa
109	12,210	07	74	Emergency & Disaster Relief	Continuing/Augmenting	Ab
200	12,200	-	-	Special Revenue Funds		
206	12,200	-	-	Beautification Fund:		
206	12,220	00	77	Landscaping & Development	Current	Ac
700	12,200	-	-	Federal Revenue Sharing:		
701	12,230	99	77	Aid to the elderly	Augmenting Appropriation - Transfer	Ad

The column headers under APPROPRIATIONS CODE are: FUND, DIVISION AGENCY, APPRO. TYPE, FISCAL YEAR.

| BALANCE JULY 1, 1977 | | APPROPRIATIONS | AUGMENTING APPROPRIATIONS AND RECEIPTS | | TRANSFERS IN FROM OTHER FUNDS | AVAILABLE FOR DISPOSITION | |
ENCUMBERED	AVAILABLE		FEDERAL	RESTRICTED		ENCUMBERED	AVAILABLE
$ ---	---	15,500,000 ✗ (A.2)	---	---			15,500,000
273,550	32,470	---	---	---		273,550	32,470
67,420	26,593	8,000,000 ✗ (A.2)	4,155,750 (A.2)	---		67,420	12,182,343
---	---	1,500,000 ✗ (A.2)		75,000			1,575,000
---	110,500	---	---	---	1,000,000		1,110,500
$340,970	169,563	25,000,000	4,155,750	75,000	1,000,000	340,970	30,400,313

Prepared by C.W. Date 10-30   Index No. A.1 ⁴/₇

Part IV
Account Balances and
Accounting Transactions

Assets, Liabilities and Fund Balances/Net Worth

Revenues and Receipts

Expenditures and Expenses (Part I—An Overview)

Expenditures and Expenses (Part II—Personnel, Travel and Transportation)

Expenditures and Expenses (Part III—Contracts, Grants, Inter-Agency or Intra-Governmental Transactions)

Chapter 13
Assets, Liabilities and Fund Balances/Net Worth

Introduction

All levels of government are required to provide an accounting for assets, liabilities and fund balances/ net worth. These are subject to verification and should be controlled by safeguards similar to those in existence at commercial organizations. The unique requirement of governmental accounting is maintenance of a fund as an accounting entity, with a separate reporting required for each fund. Compliance with the legal, administrative or other requirements relating to the receipt and disbursement of monies is another essential aspect of reporting fiscal integrity of governmental fund balances.

Requirements for Independent Audit

Variances exist between federal, state and local governmental units with respect to independent audits. The assets, liabilities and fund balances or investments of the federal government are not subjected to independent audits. On the other hand, annual independent audits are made of the accounts of many state and local governments.

Federal Government Audits

At the federal government level, there is, with limited exceptions, no legal requirement to have audits made of the assets, liabilities and fund balances of governmental agencies. (The exceptions generally would be the quasi-governmental corporations such as the Federal Deposit Insurance Corporation, the Federal Reserve Board and other similar organizations.) While the General Accounting Office, under the direction of the Comptroller General, is responsible for conducting independent audits of the executive branch agencies, such audits generally do not include audits of an agency's financial statements. Some agencies have internal audit staffs who may make an examination of the financial statements on a cyclical basis, but this may not be annually.

State and Local Governmental Unit Audits

Many state and local governments are required by law to have annual independent audits made of the financial statements of the government. The auditing organizations vary. In some instances, the auditor may be an elected official, a permanent agency of the government or a selected public accountant.

Definitions

The terms "assets," "liabilities" and "fund balances or net worth" have the same general meaning at all levels of the government, although some differences do exist.

Assets generally can be defined as things or items of value owned by the government. At the federal level, the assets presented on a financial statement would include current, fixed and long-term investments, and prepaid and deferred assets. State and local governmental units, in compliance with accepted governmental accounting, would provide an accounting for these same assets, although the assets would be distributed among several types of funds and account groupings.

Liabilities represent amounts owed by the government, whether or not due for payment. Generally, liabilities are shown in financial statements as current and other liabilities. State and local governmental units would account for long-term liabilities and general long-term debt in the accounts of specific funds and the general long-term debt account group.

Fund balances and net worth represent the excess of the asset balances over the liabilities and reserve balances, depending upon whether references are being made to a governmental or a proprietary fund. At the federal level, the fund balance accounts are referred to as the investment of the government and represent the unexpended balances of any appropriated funds.

The preferred account structure for a federal agency incorporates the accounts for all sources of funds used to finance the agency programs into a single, integrated accounting system. Depending upon the authorizing and appropriation legislation, an agency may be accounted for as a single appropriation or fund. In other instances, the agency may be responsible for the expenditure of monies from several appropriations, each of which is a separate fund that requires separate accountability.

State and local governmental units, in compliance with *Governmental Accounting, Auditing and Financial Reporting,* account for activities by classification among several funds and account groupings (for general fixed assets and long-term debt). These funds are further explained in Chapters 3 and 4.

Internal Controls

Internal Control Review Guides

As in the audit of commercial organizations, the adequacy of internal controls is an important factor in the design of an audit program and in determining the extent of testing that might be required. Numerous checklists exist for examining and evaluating the adequacy of the internal controls for safeguarding assets, controlling and accounting for liabilities and properly reflecting the residual fund balance or net worth or investment of the government. These checklists will contain many elements or requirements that are equally applicable to the review of controls in a governmental entity.

The AICPA's Statement on Auditing Standards, No. 1, relating to the evaluation of internal controls is applicable to the audits of governmental units, specifically, the following sections:

Section 320—"The Auditor's Study and Evaluation of Internal Control";

Section 320-A—Appendix A, "Relationship of Statistical Sampling to Generally Accepted Auditing Standards"; and

Section 320-B—Appendix B "Precision and Reliability for Statistical Sampling in Auditing."

Assets

Governmental units may have other procedures, mandated by law or statutes, that require assessment or examination for compliance. In many instances, these procedures have significance only to audits of governmental entities and normally would not be considered significant or material items in the audit of a commercial organization.

Cash

With respect to cash transactions, the private and public sector concerns over controls are similar. For example:

There should be an adequate segregation of responsibilities among employees handling collections, reconciling bank statements, maintaining the records, disbursing cash and handling the mail;

Receipts should be recorded on prenumbered forms, deposits made immediately, accounts reconciled frequently and an identification maintained by types, sources, dates and amounts of all receipts;

Disbursements should be made by prenumbered checks, properly authorized, with supporting evidence, for approved expenditures, with the checks and applicable bank accounts being reconciled on a frequent basis;

Rebates, adjustments, corrections and miscellaneous entries should be approved in advance of posting by an authorized official;

Petty cash and imprest funds should be in the hands of a bonded custodian, with procedures requiring receipts for all disbursements and prohibiting the deposit of checks payable to the government.

With respect to governmental units, there are other concerns. For example:

Separate deposit accounts may be required for various receipts, or funds may be commingled. (In either event, sound control procedures should exist and be practiced.)

Depositaries may have written instructions concerning the cashing of checks payable to government officials.

Bank accounts and depositaries may be authorized by the governing officials.

Multiple depositaries may exist, with the accounting being maintained at other than the central administration location.

Inter-bank and inter-fund transfers may be permitted, but only with prior approval by an authorized official and under adequate accounting control.

Designated officials at differing locations may be responsible for collecting certain types of funds, with settlement being required at certain intervals.

A system of issuing warrants (an order to pay drawn by a legislative body or a designated official upon the treasury may exist, necessitating maintenance of the specified supporting records.

On occasion, depositaries may be required to pledge security or collateral for governmental balances on deposit.

Officials and employees handling or accounting for cash may be bonded for amounts that are insufficient to protect the governmental unit against losses.

The authorization for disbursement may be separated from the actual treasury function.

By law, a prepayment voucher audit may be required prior to approval for disbursement or issuance of a warrant for payment of a governmental obligation.

Receivables

Generally, the controls deemed adequate for a commercial entity would suffice for a governmental unit, although the concern over fiscal compliance might be the basis for imposing more detailed control procedures. The internal control considerations related to tax collections are discussed in Chapter 14, which outlines certain aspects of revenue and receipts. Other governmental receivables warrant the existence of differing internal controls and procedures. For example:

Receivables from other levels of government should be consistent with the conditions of grants, contracts or other agreements;

Travel advances and other advances of funds to officials and employees should be accounted for separately from other receivables of the government;

Interfund receivables should be established consistent with approved procedures, be aged in a manner similar to external receivables and be periodically reconciled with payables of other funds; and

Unrecorded receivables should be controlled, formally identified and periodically aged.

Inventories

The internal controls normally required or considered adequate for commercial organizations typically are sufficient for governmental entities. For example, written procedures should exist and be adhered to relating to ordering, receiving, storing, controlling, issuing and inventorying inventories.

It is common, though, for governmental entities not to record inventories. Therefore, the controls inherent in a formal inventory control system would not be present, and the value of inventories might not be readily identifiable.

Fixed Assets

The controls required of a commercial organization to preserve and protect fixed assets would be equally applicable to governmental entities. Financial and quantitative records should be maintained and periodic inventories made of all properties. Unless the entity is self-insured, adequate insurance should be carried on all properties. With respect to governmental entities, unique conditions may exist that warrant specific attention. For example:

The procurement of fixed assets often require advance approval by the legislative or governing body, and procedures often require that acquisitions be made by competitive bid procedures;

Depreciation accounting may or may not be applicable or consistently applied among the various types of assets or from one accounting period to another;

Non-expendable property, acquired under contracts and from grants received from ther levels of government, generally require adherence to specific conditions relating to acquisition, control, preservation, inventory and disposal:

A separate accounting should be made of all assets furnished to a government unit by other governmental entities, and

Donated or contributed assets should be controlled and accounted for in a manner similar to that for purchased assets;

Fixed or capital assets may not be accounted for in the operating accounts of the governmental entity, but rather (1) as capital expenditures, (2) in the long-term fixed assets group of accounts or (3) in an enterprise or working capital type fund;

Controls should exist to insure that fixed assets are recorded as capital expenditures and not as operating expenditures.

Securities and Investments

The controls relating to securities and investments of a governmental entity should be similar to those required of a commercial organization. For example:

The purchase of securities and investments should be made only with appropriate authorization;

The securities and investments should be adequately safeguarded, periodically inventoried, properly accounted for and accessible only to authorized individuals;

Disposals of securities and investments should be made only with prior appropriate approval, in the manner prescribed, with prompt depositing of all proceeds; and

Income should be promptly collected and deposited.

However, there are other controls that are applicable to governmental entities. For example:

Securities and investments should be in the name of the governmental entity;

Law or statute may permit the purchase of only specific securities and investments;

The purchase of securities and investments with monies of several funds often will require separate accounting for each fund's allocation of principal and interest; and

Separate records should be maintained for securities and investments owned by the governmental unit and negotiable securities that may have been received by the government as a deposit or collateral.

Other Assets

Unlike the generally accepted accounting principles applicable to commercial organizations, other assets, such as prepaid expenses and deferred charges, may not be recorded by governmental units. Disbursements for such items might be recorded as current operating expenditures, with no attempt to prorate the financial impact to the appropriate accounting period. Where significant, these accounting procedures and controls must be examined.

Where prepaid expenses and deferred charges are recorded, the controls of a governmental entity should be the same as those used by a commercial organization.

Liabilities

As was the case with assets, the internal controls used by governmental entities with respect to liabilities should be similar to those employed by commercial organizations. The controls exercised over corporate or institutional accounts payable, notes payable, payroll accruals and long-term debt generally are applicable to similar liabilities of governmental entities.

Other controls might be mandated by law or implicit in the application of GAAFR to the governmental unit:

Procedures may be required for the appropriate application of collected property taxes to the retirement of specific general obligation bonds or tax anticipation warrants or for the utilization of enterprise fund revenues in the retirement of revenue bonds;

The governing body may have imposed a sinking fund requirement to insure the retirement of specific types of debt;

Where governmental entities adhere to a practice of not recording salaries and wages payable, accruals of vacation and sick leave, purchases and contracts, other accounts payable and liabilities, controls must exist to insure that appropriate fiscal period accounting is achieved;

A periodic reporting should be made by the governmental attorney to the governing body concerning any judgments against the government;

A practice may exist whereby the governmental unit has received "good faith" deposits from contractors or citizens which are held for a specified time period and should be segregated and separately accounted for as a liability of the government;

General obligation bonds are recorded in the general long-term debt group of accounts and not reflected as a liability of the general fund, but such debt might, alternatively, be reflected as an obligation of another fund; and

Long-term liabilities may be recorded as a liability of specific proprietary-type funds and not of the general fund.

Fund Balances/Net Worth

The terms "fund balance" and "net worth" are similar in that they refer to the excess of asset balances over liabilities balances. In the absence of reserves to the fund balance, the residual fund balance represents the unobligated or uncommitted portion of the appropriated fund balance. The term "fund balance" generally is used in reference to the general fund, or similar governmental-type funds, a trust or deposit fund or a special revenue fund. "Net worth" represents the equity or investment of the government in a business-type operation and generally is used in reference to an enterprise fund or inter-agency service fund of a state or local government unit or a working-capital or revolving fund of the federal government.

Controls should exist to permit periodic determination of the amount of the fund balance or net worth account balance that should be reserved and withheld from further obligation. Reserves to fund balances are often established for such items as encumbrances, advances to other funds, imprest or petty cash and change funds, and inventory of material and supplies.

Note that impairments or consumption of assets are not recorded as reserves, but rather are shown as allowances for uncollectibles (in the case of receivables such as taxes) or for depreciation (where appropriate in the case of fixed assets).

Federal agencies will refer to the excess of asset balances over liabilities as the investment of the United States government, which consists of the unexpended appropriation balance. Typically, internal agency procedures and controls exist to insure the appropriate reservation of the unexpended appropriation. For example, the unexpended appropriation might be subjected to reservations or commitments for unapportioned appropriations, unallotted apportionments, unobligated allotments and unliquidated obligations.

Generally, the unexpended appropriations would represent the portion of the appropriation fund balance that is free of any commitments, contingencies or reserves.

Auditing Requirements

The audit of the assets, liabilities and fund balances/net worth of governmental funds will require the application of the same verification tests as made of the accounts of a commercial organization. More emphasis must be given, however, to accounting restraints and legal restrictions inherent in fund accounting. Each fund is viewed as an accounting entity, with separable asset, liability, fund balance/net worth, revenue and expense transactions. Detailed tests for compliance with fiscal-type restrictions are required to insure that monies are expended from the appropriate funds only for authorized purposes, in authorized amounts and within appropriate time periods, and that the fiscal integrity of the fund is maintained.

The conduct of an audit of a governmental organization requires that the auditor be familiar with the criteria set forth in:

AICPA's *Statement on Auditing Standards;*

AICPA's *Industry Audit Guide—Audits of State and Local Governmental Units;*

National Council on Governmental Accounting's *Governmental Accounting, Auditing and Financial Reporting* (GAAFR);

U.S. General Accounting Office's *Manual for Guidance of Federal Agencies* (particularly Title 2—Accounting Principles and Standards and Internal Auditing Guidelines);

U.S. General Accounting Office's publication, *Accounting—Principles and Standards for Federal Agencies,* 1978;

U.S. General Accounting Office's *Standards for Audit of Governmental Organizations, Programs, Activities & Functions;* and

Specific audit guides and requirements published by governmental agencies related to the acceptance and receipt of government funds or other assistance.

Each of these documents outlines general and specific internal control, accounting and auditing requirements applicable to the governmental financial statements and other aspects of governmental financial management. Since this information is comprehensive and widely available, only selected references have been made to these requirements.

Audit Considerations for Assets, Liabilities, Fund Balance/Net Worth Accounts

Assets

The assets of a governmental organization are subject to the same tests for verification as would be performed in the audit of a commercial organization. Of particular importance, though, is the requirement to determine that transactions of a fund are related to the fund and to the purposes for which the fund was established. Particular vigilance is required to protect against the funds of one appropriation being used to support activities of another appropriation, thus violating the authorizations of legislative bodies or other administrative procedures.

Cash

In government, where requirements often exist for the maintenance of separate cash accounts, depositaries often are designated by law or statute; and not all cash balances are recorded on the central accounting records of the governmental agency. Therefore, diligence must be exercised in inventorying cash accounts that might not be maintained in the name of the governmental unit or that might be maintained in remote or removed locations.

Certain audit steps must be performed in the same manner as would be used in the audit of cash for a commercial organization:

Balances must be confirmed with all depositaries as of balance sheet date;

Cash receipts and disbursement cut-offs should be established and transactions after cut-off date examined;

Transfers between bank accounts and funds should be examined and documents supporting both sides of the transaction examined;

Reconciliations of bank accounts should be checked or prepared;

The arithmetic accuracy and correctness of postings should be checked and verified to supporting documentation and to the books of account;

Petty cash, imprest and change funds should be counted, support documentation examined and postings to the accounting records tested; and

Undeposited receipts and outstanding checks should be examined later for proper disposition.

In addition to the above, legal and other requirements dictate that additional steps be performed to determine the reasonableness of the cash balances shown by a governmental entity. For example:

Laws may require that the money for each fund be kept in a separate bank account, and an inventory of the numerous depositaries that might exist thus must be made;

Certain officers and employees may be authorized to collect and periodically remit funds to the central treasury, and the number and conditions of such collection authority and the amounts of any undeposited amounts thus must be determined;

Some municipalities require that depositaries pledge securities or other collateral for the governmental accounts maintained with the institutions, and tests thus must be made to determine the appropriateness of the type and amount of the collateral pledged;

Often officers and employees of governmental organizations handling money, securities and other valuables are required to be bonded, and tests thus must be made for compliance;

The disbursing or treasurer's function may be separate from the governmental unit requesting disbursement, and reconciliations thus must be made of the records of both organizations;

Inter-fund transfers and reimbursements to funds must be examined to insure that the utilization or availability of these resources is permitted under the authorizing legislation of the governmental unit;

Reimbursement checks included in cash balances must be simultaneously confirmed as disbursements and cash on deposit and must be verified to approved supporting documentation; and

Balances with all depositaries must be confirmed.

Receivables

The audit program for receivables should be similar to the program used in a review of a commercial organization's accounts. Notes receivables and accounts receivables should be aged, confirmed and verified to supporting documentation; estimates should be made of any uncollectible amounts, and allowances should be provided.

Governmental receivables might require some additional testing. For example:

When the receivable cannot easily be confirmed, as is the case with property taxes, or assessments, other steps—such as making a review of collections after the balance sheet date or comparing past collection efforts and trends in delinquencies—must be performed;

The entitlement to amounts claimed as due from other government agencies must be verified and, possibly, confirmed;

Receivables due from government officials and employees must be examined to determine currency and status of these amounts;

Receivables from contractors and grantees of the government unit must be tested for appropriateness and collectibility;

Cancellations of amounts due, statements of taxes and other reductions of amounts owed to the government must be examined for proper approval and propriety; and

Inter-fund and inter-agency receivables and payables must be carefully examined for propriety and for the possibility that such transactions might be a method for violating an appropriation ceiling imposed by the legislative or administrative body.

Inventories

Where inventories of supplies and materials are maintained or periodically taken, the procedures for audit should be the same as those applied to inventories of a commercial organization. Typically, inventories would be maintained for enterprise and, possibly, inter-agency service, working capital or revolving funds.

For many governmental organizations, the purchase of supplies and materials will be accounted for as current expenditures. In this instance, the auditor should witness or take an inventory for purposes of determining the appropriate cost to apply to the fiscal period under audit and the amount of inventory value benefiting the future fiscal periods. If the amount of inventories is capitalized as an asset, a reserve to the fund balance must be established in the same amount.

Fixed Assets

Fixed assets, such as property, plant and equipment, should be audited in the same manner as is done for commercial organizations. Physical inspections should be made, title verified, valuations confirmed, utility of the assets checked, and insurance and other indemnity contracts relating to the assets examined. Where applicable, depreciation charges should be examined and tested.

Legal and other restrictions may exist relating to the acquisition, maintenance, inventory, control, disposal and accounting of capital assets.

Additionally, audit procedures may have to be extended to include consideration of other aspects of capital asset accounting, such as:

Laws or statutes may require that capital assets be procured only by competitive bid procedures, after formal approval has been received from the legislature or the governing body;

Disposal of capital assets should be made only in a manner consistent with established procedures, which typically require sale at public auction or retirement, after approval by certain officials;

Fixed assets owned by the governmental organization should be segregated from other capital assets provided or loaned to the governmental organization by other levels of government, which generally require adherence to specific control procedures;

Fixed assets transactions should be accounted for as capital expenditures, not as operating expenditure, and should be reflected in the accounting by only one fund or account group; and

Tests should be made of title, physical possession, contracts, income or costs due to or owed by the governmental organization for property and equipment leased by or to the governmental organization.

Investments and Securities

As in the audit of investments and securities held by a commercial organization, a complete listing of all investments and securities on hand at the beginning of the audit period should be prepared. This listing then should be used as a check on additions, disposals and balances on hand at the balance sheet date. Additionally, the securities should be inspected, counted and tested for title and proper recordation, examined for market value in relation to purchase prices, convenants or other restrictions, and inspected for accrued income, amortization of bond premium and accrual of bond discount, and maturity dates.

Audits of governmental organizations holding investments and securities also should include tests to:

Determine that the possession of investments and securities is consistent with any legal restrictions concerning investments of government funds and permissible risks;

Determine that there is proper control over and separate custody of negotiable deposits in possession of the government that belong to contractors, licensees, citizens, etc.;

Because securities may be held by both treasurer's offices and individual government agencies and because of the possible fungible nature of deposit securities with governmental investments, consider simultaneous inventory counts and verifications of instruments at the several physical locations;

Determine that there has been a proper allocation of principal and income among the various funds, consistent with guidance provided by the legislative or governing body;

Review the accounting and allocation of investments and securities, principal amounts, and related income and expenses made to the various funds and account groups for propriety as well as consistency with legal or other requirements; and

Confirm all investments and securities held by other than the treasurer or central fiscal officer.

Prepaid Expenses and Deferred Charges

When recorded by governmental organizations, prepaid expenses and deferred charges should be verified in the same manner as would be done in the audit of a commercial organization. Prior-period balances should be examined to determine the amount of write-off required and the allocations of cost to funds verified.

Generally, though, governmental organizations will not record disbursements benefitting future fiscal periods as prepaid expenses or deferred charges. Usually such disbursements will be accounted for as current expenditures. Where such expenditures are material in amount, the auditor may have to consider commenting upon the expenditure in the audit report.

Liabilities

For the most part, liabilities of a governmental organization are similar to those of a commercial organization. While terminology will differ in some instances, the audit program used in commercial audits is equally applicable to the government audit. Of particular note is the practice of some governments to not account for purchases or other obligations until payment is made. Care also must be taken to insure that unrecorded liabilities are properly considered in the preparation of the financial statements.

Accrued Payroll and Withholdings

Some governmental organizations will record payrolls on a cash basis: no end of period accrual is computed or reflected in the accounting records.

Where no accrual has been made, a determination of amounts owed should be made and shown in the financial statement as a liability or as a footnote to cash-basis financial statements. The propriety of withheld amounts should be checked, and tests made to ascertain that withheld amounts are disbursed to designated depositaries at the appropriate times.

Additional audit considerations related to payroll and personal services expenses are discussed in Chapter 16.

Accounts and Vouchers Payable

Often a governmental organization may not record the liability related to purchases until the invoice or bill has been received. In such instances, there is minimal control over accounts and vouchers payable, and a careful review must be made to determine the amount of the outstanding liability of the government at statement date for accounts and vouchers payable.

Some audit tests that should be made of accounts and vouchers payable of governmental organizations may include:

An aging and validation of purchase orders, obligations and encumbrances to ascertain those that have been liquidated, eliminated, revised or partially completed;

A test to verify the accuracy of the accounting entries and charges to the several funds and account groups;

An examination of entries in journals, voucher registers, cash disbursement records and supporting documentation subsequent to balance sheet date to assess the accuracy of cut-off procedures;

A possible confirmation of accounts and vouchers payable with creditors who normally do business with the government; and

A test for propriety of inter-fund and inter-agency payables and receivables and the possibility that such transactions might violate an appropriation ceiling imposed by the legislature or the governing body.

Additional audit considerations related to expenditures are discussed in Chapters 15, 16 and 17.

Notes, Tax Anticipation Loans

Governmental units commonly have a category of short-term indebtedness, possibly in the form of notes, and of tax anticipation loans. As with similar liabilities of a commercial corporation, tests should include checks to ascertain that the correct amounts were received from the issuance, repayments were properly made and the transactions were authorized by the governing body. In the case of a governmental audit, the following additional efforts should be considered:

Tests to determine that the incurrence of the debt, including both the amount and purpose, was permissible under applicable laws or statute;

Confirmation of the liability from the creditor;

Determination that the debt is recorded in the proper fund or funds;

Determination that resources are available to meet the debt and, where required, that cash exists or has been placed in special accounts to meet the debt at maturity; and

Determination that the cash from collections was applied to the liabilities in the prescribed order and amounts.

Deposits, Contracts Payable and Other Liabilities

Certain liabilities include amounts required from citizens or persons doing business with the government. For example, monies will be collected from "good faith" deposits, which typically are refundable in full. In other instances, monies will be withheld from amounts otherwise payable to contractors doing business with the government. The withheld amounts are payable at a certain date or upon the completion of an event. Other liabilities could include monies from assessments and taxes that are held in escrow.

For these types of liabilities, the following tests, as a minimum, should be made to evaluate the appropriateness and accuracy of the reported amounts:

Confirmation of the amounts, if material, with the depositor or other individuals or organizations;

Review of authorizations to substantiate the appropriateness of the retained monies and to determine that repayments are being properly made; and

Determination, where the monies are required to be segregated and controlled in a specific manner, of compliance with such directions.

Taxes Collected in Advance

Taxes collected in advance are not a liability of the government. Such monies should be accounted for as a deferred credit until it is appropriate to recognize the revenues. If material, these amounts should be confirmed and, where feasible, a review made of the regulations relating to the control of these monies to determine the extent of compliance.

Judgments

Written representations should be received from the government's counsel regarding the existence of debts or amounts due under any judgments rendered against the government. Additionally, a review should be made to insure that the determinable amounts of all judgments due are properly reflected in the accounts. Contingent liabilities, the probability of occurrence and the estimable amount should be disclosed by footnote in the financial statement.

Long-Term Debt

The long-term debt of a government may include notes, contracts, general obligations bonds and other obligations having a maturity date beyond the end of the fiscal year or current operating cycle. (For example, tax anticipation warrants payable in the next fiscal year often are carried as a current liability. Tests normally applied to similar liabilities of commercial corporations—including the development of a detailed inventory schedule showing principal amounts, purchase and cancellation or maturity dates, interest expense, premiums or discounts, sinking fund requirements or payment schedules—would be appropriate to governmental organizations. Additionally, the auditor must

Review the terms and conditions of law, statutes, bond ordinances and indentures to insure that there has been compliance with all governing regulations;

Inspect the elections records approving the bond issue or resolutions of the body authorizing the bond issue to assess the appropriateness of the issuance;

Check to determine that redeemed bonds and coupons have been properly controlled and disposed of;

Check to determine that the obligations are accounted for in the correct fund or group of accounts; and

Determine that the designated revenues have been set aside and that collections have been applied to the maturing debt in the appropriate sequence.

Other Aspects of Governmental Liabilities

Because of materiality, considerable audit effort must be expended to audit certain obligations and liabilities of governmental units that are not required to be recorded in the financial records. The omission of these amounts will, in many instances, materially affect the reported financial position of the governmental unit. Varying opinions and reasons have been offered in the profession's literature for not formally recording and accounting for these debts. It is becoming increasingly necessary, however, to determine the impact that these amounts would have on the governmental unit and the claim that such obligations and liabilities have on the current taxing powers of a government.

Pensions

Probably most significant of the amounts frequently omitted from the financial statement are the costs related to the potential liability of pensions for governmental employees. Many governmental units reflect a "cash basis" or "pay as they go basis" accounting, which substantially undercharges current budgets for the cost of pensions. Such accounting is contrary to the AICPA's Accounting Principles Board Opinion No. 8, "Accounting for Cost of Pension Plans," which contains a discussion of the issues relating to pension costing applicable to corporate accounting and the opinion that:

> [I]n the absence of convincing evidence that the company will reduce or discontinue the benefits called for in a pension plan, the cost of the plan should be accounted for on the assumption that the company will continue to provide such benefits. This assumption implies a long-term undertaking, the cost of which should be recognized annually whether or not funded. Therefore the accounting for pension cost should not be discretionary.

A discussion of the accounting and disclosure aspects of pension plans and pension funds appears in the AICPA's Industry Audit Guide, "Audits of State and Local Governmental Units," which sets forth a recommended disclosure for financial statements.

Vacation and Sick Pay

Governmental units often will not currently accrue the liability to employees for earned, but unused vacation and sick pay. These costs, if vested in employees and allowed to accumulate, also can become significant. This "cash basis" accounting is consistent with the AICPA's Accounting Standards Division's Statement of Position No. 75-3, "Accrual of Revenues and Expenditures by State and Local Governmental Units." For the reasons stated in 75-3, the AICPA concluded:

> Considering these factors and the nature of accumulated unused vacation and sick leave, it is appropriate to disclose the estimated amount of such commitments in a footnote, if material, and not record the costs as expenditures at the time the leave is accumulated.

The federal government's accounting is not unlike that of states and local governmental units. Governmental employees incur the liability for unused vacation and sick pay by rendering services for one or more employing agencies; however, the lump-sum settlement (because of death, disability, retirement or other reasons) often becomes the liability of another government agency or the last employing agency.

Fund Balances/Net Worth

The key to the audit of the equity accounts of governmental organizations—which are reflected as fund balance or net worth amounts, depending upon the nature of the fund—would be an accurate determination of that equity amount that is free of all contingencies, reserve requirements or other limitations. Such limitations might include:

Encumbrances or obligations outstanding at the end of the period;

Advances to other funds, which are not available for disbursement by the reporting fund;

Imprest, petty cash and change funds, for which an accounting generally is made at the time the funds are replenished; and

Inventories of supplies, materials and equipment that will benefit future periods, but are not a portion of the appropriation or fund balance available for obligation or encumbrance.

In connection with the unliquidated obligations (in the case of a federal agency) or encumbrances (in the case of a state or local governmental unit), balances at year's end might be reflected in a variety of ways, depending upon the governing legislation. The governing legislation may:

Require that all outstanding or unliquidated obligations or encumbrances lapse at the end of the fiscal year;

Permit the liquidation of the earlier obligations or encumbrances in the later fiscal period, with the requirement that such amounts be accounted for separately from the succeeding year's appropriation; or

Provide authorization that permits the unliquidated balance of obligated or encumbered amounts to be "rolled-forward" as a part of the balance of the next year's appropriation.

Where specific legislation does not exist to indicate the desired accounting, the auditor should consider disclosing the past practices and should report the basis of accounting used in the audit report.

Depending upon the specific authorizing or appropriation legislation, all of the above presentations could be used by one or several federal governmental agencies.

GAAFR recommends that encumbrances be treated as a reservation or commitment of the unexpended appropriation balance that would be available for the payment of outstanding commitments. At year's end, funds are reserved to meet unliquidated commitments; any later adjustments are made to the fund balance account. Carryover encumbrances are permitted to be shown as part of the appropriation balances of the next fiscal period.

In contrast, the AICPA's *Industry Audit Guide for State and Local Governmental Units* states that an outstanding encumbrance is to be recognized as an expenditure, and the related obligation is carried until liquidated, whether by replacement with a liability or by cancellation. Differences between an actual expenditure and the earlier commitment or encumbrance are adjusted, at the time the expenditure is recognized, by adjusting the account originally charged with the commitment. If the difference is known only in a later period, an adjustment should be made to a sundry expenditure account in a non-departmental category of the related fund.

Factually, obligations or encumbrances are neither expenditures nor liabilities of the governmental entity. In many respects, obligations or encumbrances are analogous to contingencies for which reservations of fund balances and net worth accounts are required.

Reporting of Assets, Liabilities and Fund Balances/Net Worth

Illustrative financial statements and accompanying explanations relating to governmental assets, liabilities and fund balances/net worth appear in Chapters 18 and 19.

Chapter 14
Revenues and Receipts

Introduction

At all levels of government, budgets are established for revenues and receipts, classified by sources. Federal, state and local governments consider receipts as synonymous with cash collections; revenues generally refer to the accrual of funds.

The broad classes of revenues and receipts vary by governmental levels, although the process for assessing, levying and collecting taxes is somewhat similar.

Federal Revenues and Receipts

Definitions

Receipts

The federal government, in the Office of Management and Budget's Circular A-11 *(Preparation and Submission of Budget Estimates)*, defines

247

receipts as amounts deposited in agency receipt accounts, classified by three main categories:

Governmental receipts—arising from the sovereign and regulatory powers unique to government and the net increase or decrease in clearing accounts for undistributed collections of the agencies;

Proprietary receipts—arising from the public that are market-oriented or derived from activities operated as business-type enterprises; and

Intragovernmental transactions—derived from off-budget agencies or from within the budget agencies (deposits in receipt accounts that are payments from other appropriations or funds, intra-fund transactions, inter-fund transactions).

Revenues

At the federal level, the General Accounting Office has defined revenues as representing the increase in assets or decrease in liabilities that results from operations. By GAO's definition (in its publication, *Accounting—Principles and Standards for Federal Agencies,* 1978), revenues could be generated by or could result from:

Services performed by the government;

Goods and other tangible property delivered to purchasers; or

Amounts owed for which no current performance is required.

Classes of Receipts

Within the federal government, the collection of receipts is principally the responsibility of the Treasury Department. The budget receipts, according to source, include:

Individual income taxes;

Corporation income taxes;

Social insurance taxes and contributions;

Excise taxes;

Estate and gift taxes;

Custom duties; and

Miscellaneous receipts.

The Internal Revenue Service and the Bureau of Customs, both in the Treasury Department, are the two organizations responsible for the collection of the preponderance of federal receipts. However, agencies often may collect significant fees and other receipts for services rendered pursuant to a legal authority.

State and Local Revenues and Receipts

Definitions

Revenues and Receipts

The terms "revenues" and "receipts" have a slightly different connotation at other levels of government. Except for the national government and agencies, the following definitions (as set forth in *Governmental Accounting, Auditing, and Financial Reporting*), have had wide acceptance:

Revenues—designates additions to assets that:

do not increase any liability;

do not represent the recovery of an expenditure;

do not represent the cancellation of certain liabilities or a decrease in assets; and

do not represent contributions of fund capital in Enterprise and Intragovernmental Service Funds.

Receipts—designates, unless otherwise qualified, cash received.

The above definition of revenues would apply to those instances where revenues are recorded on the accrual, modified accrual or cash basis, with the exception that the addition to assets would be partially or entirely in cash. The term "revenue receipts" is used by some governments and refers to the accounting for revenues on a cash basis.

Classes of Revenues and Receipts

For classification purposes, the National Council on Governmental Accounting, in GAAFR, recommends that revenues and receipts be classified by fund, source and organization. State and local governmental units generally adhere to the following general classes of revenue or receipt groupings:

General property or real estate taxes;

Sales tax or gross receipt taxes;

Income taxes;

Licenses, fees, and permits;

Grants and subsidies;

Rentals and leases;

Sales of commodities and services;

Franchise income;

Interest on bank accounts and investments;

Other receipts, such as

sale of investments,

sale of bonds or notes,

sale of fixed assets,

issuance of notes payable or tax anticipation notes, and

receipts from other governments; and

Enterprise revenues.

The GAAFR also outlines numerous more detailed and subsidiary groupings of revenues and receipts.

The responsibility for collecting revenues may be decentralized or centralized among state and local governmental units. This diversity of collection agents, at times, presents some difficulty to the auditor particularly in his attempts to examine the total receipts and cash accounts of the governmental unit.

Requirements for Independent Audit

The requirement for independent audit varies considerably. At the federal level, there is no statutory requirement to conduct an independent audit of the receipts of the government. While the U.S. General Accounting Office under the direction of the Comptroller General, is responsible for conducting independent audits of the executive agencies of the government, no such reviews are made of the individual or corporation income tax collection process of the Internal Revenue Service. Periodic or intermittent examinations are made by the GAO of the collection process of the Bureau of Customs.

No audit is made of the financial condition of the United States government as a whole. Until 1976, when the Treasury Department issued prototype consolidated financial statements, there was no reporting on the financial condition of the federal government. The prototype statements attempted to apply accounting principles of business to the business of government.

In contrast, many state and local governments, by law, require annual audits of their units' financial condition. Certified financial statements are then published for inspection by the public and others. The auditing organization may, however, vary. In some governments, the auditor may be an elected or appointed official, a permanent agency of the government staffed by governmental employees in either the executive or legislative, or a selected firm of independent certified public accountants.

Transaction Analysis

Documentation

The right to tax and assess other financial burdens on citizens is established by governing legislators.

The form of a levy varies from the issuance of a definite billing upon a segment of the population or citizens to a self-assessment by the taxpayer, where the determination of amounts due for income and sales taxes, in the form of a completed tax form, often are initially made by the taxpayer. Real estate and property taxes generally are collected as a result of a billing made by the government to the taxpayer. Amounts collected for licenses, fees, permits and franchises are previously established and are assessed immediately upon application by parties desiring or seeking certain rights or privileges. Rental and lease income is collected pursuant to executed agreements for compensation for services or facilities. Interest on bank accounts and investments is collected pursuant to a financial agreement with the financial institution involved. Proceeds from the sale of investments, bonds, notes or fixed assets are recognized in accordance with a formal agreement or statute.

Exhibit 14-1 provides an overview of the general receipts process. While the collection agencies may be decentralized or varied, collectors generally are required to receive and provide for frequent, if not immediate, deposits to a depository designated by the governing unit. A record of the assessment or collection often is made simultaneous with the deposit, in the financial records.

Internal Controls

The AICPA's Statement on Auditing Standards, No. 1, relating to evaluation of internal controls, is applicable to the audits of governmental units. Specifically, the following sections are applicable in their entirety:

Section 320—"The Auditor's Study and Evaluation of Internal Control";

Section 320-A—"Appendix A—Relationship of Statistical Sampling to Generally Accepted Auditing Standards"; and

Section 320-B—"Appendix B—Precision and Reliability for Statistical Sampling in Auditing."

In government, as in the private sector, the adequacy of internal controls is an important factor in the design of an audit program. Numerous checklists exist for evaluating the internal controls of governmental organizations and programs. In most instances, the internal control evaluations are the same as those made to assess the adequacy of controls in a corporate organization. For example:

There must be an adequate segregation of responsibilities among employees in handling collections, reconciling accounts, maintaining the financial records and handling mail;

Collections must be deposited intact to a designated depository upon receipt or pursuant to established procedures;

Receipt forms must be prenumbered, properly executed, controlled and reconciled frequently;

Receipt records must provide an idéntification of types, sources, dates and amounts of all receipts;

Checks or other payments must not be disbursed from cash receipts unless specifically authorized; and

Balance maintained at all depositaries must be regularly reconciled to the official records of the government by persons independent of the collection and accounting processes.

Additionally, though, governmental units may have other procedures, derived from the legal or legislative mandates imposed upon the units, that require assessment. For example:

Multiple designated depositories might exist, each of which should be adhering to sound internal control procedures;

All receipts might not be credited to the general fund, but might be legally required to reside in other funds and to be available for specified purposes;

Receipts from grants, subsidies or donations might require the establishment of separate deposit accounts, not routinely incorporated in the financial statements of the governmental unit being audited;

Procedures should exist and require compliance to insure that the legally or administratively mandated integrity of the funds is maintained; and

Rebates, adjustments and abatements, in the case of taxes, should be supported by specific approving authority.

Accounting Principles

Federal Accrual Criteria

The General Accounting Office requires that federal agency accounts be maintained on an accrual basis. If an agency uses the cash or obligation basis of accounting and periodically converts to the accrual basis, the conversions should be made not less than monthly.

In its guide to federal agencies *(Accounting Principles and Standards for Federal Agencies),* the General Accounting Office requires that agency accounting systems provide for recording revenues transactions in accounting records when earned. The agency is to establish the point when revenues become realizable, with reasonable practicable certainty, in terms of valid claims against the persons or organizations receiving goods and services.

Where amounts are received in advance, such amounts shall be accounted for as liabilities until the revenues are earned by the government or the

Exhibit 14-1

Overview of Selected Receipt Transactions and Documentation

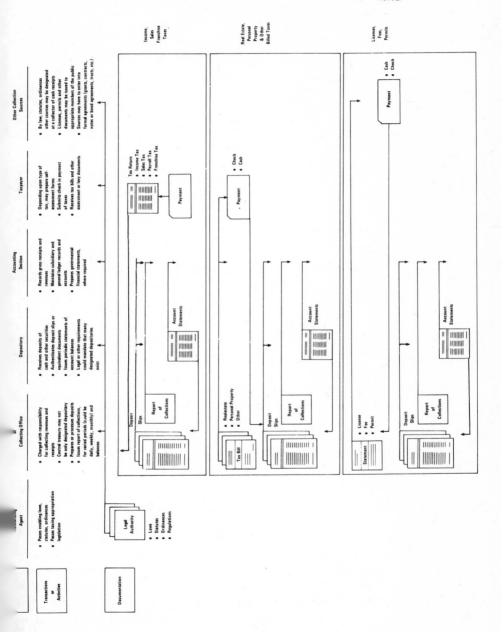

Exhibit 14-1—continued

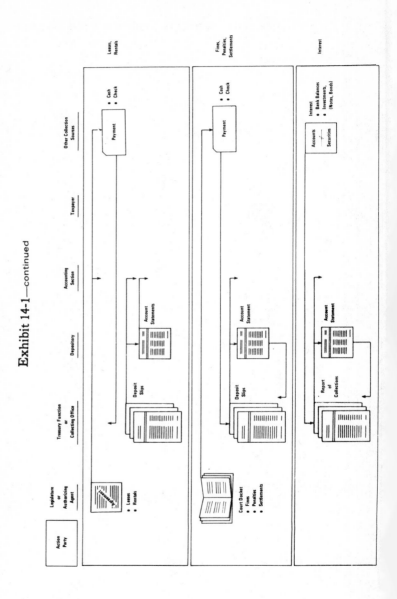

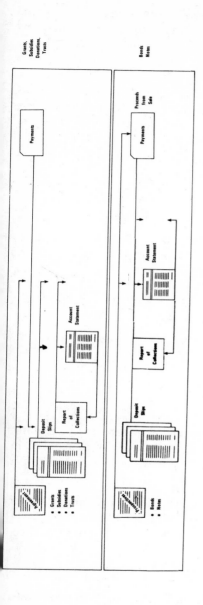

amounts become owed to the government. For business-type activities, the financial statements must disclose revenues and cost, comparing or matching revenues to the applicable costs.

State and Local Accrual Criteria

The basis for accounting for revenues and receipts of governmental units varies and is related to the fund that the transactions affect and the purpose for which the fund was established. Generally, the accounting bases are accrual or modified accrual.

For state and local governments GAAFR identifies these bases with the following funds:

Funds utilizing accrual basis:

> Enterprise funds;
>
> Intragovernmental service funds; and
>
> Non-expendable trust and pension funds.

Funds utilizing modified accrual basis:

> General fund;
>
> Special revenue funds;
>
> Expendable trust and agency funds;
>
> Debt service funds;
>
> Capital projects funds; and
>
> Special assessment funds.

Modified Accrual Basis

The AICPA's industry audit guide for state and local governments requires that revenues, under the modified accrual basis, be recorded as received in cash except for (a) revenues susceptible to accrual and (b) revenues of a material amount that have not been received at the normal time of receipt.

The "modified accrual basis" of accounting is defined as the method of accounting under which revenues are recorded when received in cash, except for material or available revenues, which should be accrued to properly reflect taxes levied and revenues earned.

Revenues Susceptible to Accrual

The AICPA's industry guide requires generally that revenues be recorded on the accrual basis only if they are susceptible to accrual. "Being susceptible" has been defined as meaning both measurable and available. "Available" means that the revenue is a resource that can be used to finance the governmental operations of that year.

Revenues not generally considered susceptible to accrual include those generated on a self-assessment basis, such as income taxes, gross receipts taxes and sales taxes. These taxes would be recorded when received.

Revenues that may be accrued are those that are billable by the government or levied by law, those with amounts determinable in advance, and those resulting from a legally enforceable claim that attaches to tangible property or rights. Property taxes are an example of a major revenue that may be accrued.

Revenues of a Material Amount

According to the AICPA's industry guide, some revenues, though not susceptible to accrual in accordance with the above discussion, should be recorded prior to actual receipt. Generally, material revenues that would not otherwise be accrued should be accrued if receipt is delayed beyond the normal time of receipt. Conversely, material revenues received in advance of the due date should be recorded as deferred revenue.

Other Bases of Accounting

An auditor may find federal as well as state and local governmental units maintaining financial accounts on a cash or hybrid accrual reporting basis. Some units may account for transactions throughout the reporting period on a cash basis. Other units may use a cash basis during the accounting period, but may make adjusting entries at the end of the period to permit the accounts and financial statements to reflect a financial position on an accrual basis.

Auditing Requirements

The audit of governmental revenues and receipts is subject to the same verifications as is an audit of the revenues and receipts of a private enterprise or institution. Characteristics unique to governmental audits, though, are the accounting restraints and legal restrictions inherent in fund accounting. Each fund is an entity, with separable asset, liability, fund balances, and receipt and expense transactions. Unique accounting and compliance testing is required to insure that monies are received in the amounts and manner authorized and that the fiscal integrity of the funds is maintained in the accounting for the receipts.

Published Guidelines

Proper preparation for an audit of revenues and receipts of a governmental unit requires that the auditor be thoroughly conversant with the auditing standards and guides applicable to the public sector. The auditing criteria are set forth in several publications, *e.g.*:

AICPA's *Statement on Auditing Standards;*

AICPA's *Industry Audit Guide—Audits of State and Local Governmental Units;*

National Council on Governmental Accounting's *Governmental Accounting, Auditing and Financial Reporting* (GAAFR);

U.S. General Accounting Office's *Manual for Guidance of Federal Agencies;*

U.S. General Accounting Office's *Accounting—Principles and Standards for Federal Agencies,* 1978;

U.S. General Accounting Office's *Standards for Audit of Governmental Organizations, Programs, Activities & Functions;* and

Specific audit guides and requirements related to the acceptance and receipt of funds from other governments and entities.

Each of these documents outlines general and specific internal control, accounting and auditing requirements that apply to the profession as a whole and to the audit of governmental units in particular. Since this information is comprehensive and generally available, only selected references have been made to these sources.

General Revenue and Receipt Audit Considerations

At the different levels of government, revenues and receipts can come from a variety of sources; but all receipts have a basis in some form of legislation, statute or ordinance. At the federal government level, the primary source of receipts is income taxes—personal and corporate. The predominant source of local government revenues is property taxes. But all levels of government collect receipts in the form of fees, penalties, rents, interests and proceeds from the sale of investments or from enterprise-type operations.

Because of the absence of uniform administrative structures and the abundance of legal restraints and conditions, certain governmental audit procedures have an importance that they do not have when applied in a corporate audit. Some general audit procedures of import in the governmental sector include tests to insure that:

Reviews are made of the responsibility for collecting and controlling monies and for determining that an accounting was established at the outset of the audit. The collector often will not be the designated depository, and both may differ from the entity responsible for providing an accounting.

Collected monies are examined to determine that deposits have been made immediately to designated depositories and that the monies have been credited to the proper fund.

The legal provisions surrounding all receipts are examined, and appropriate tests made of the procedures and practices governing receipts and reporting to insure that the balances are maintained pursuant to specific legislation.

Diligent searches and inquiries are made for deposit accounts that are not reported as a part of the governmental unit as a whole.

Interfund, interagency, and intergovernmental cash transactions and transfers are identified and closely examined for propriety, timing, authorization and possible duplicate accounting.

The appropriateness of any exonerations, remissions, adjustments, rebates and abatements of revenues and receipts is examined.

Verifications are made and reconciliations are prepared for documentation representing billings or claims of the government, receipts of cash, journal entries, subsidiary ledgers and general ledger account balances.

Positive confirmations are made of both paid and unpaid taxes or other amounts due or received from the public, organizations and other governments.

All payments from receipts are examined for underlying legal authority to apply receipts for certain purposes.

Audit Considerations for Specific Receipts

Self-Assessed Taxes

A large portion of governmental revenues are generated in the form of self-assessed taxes. That is, the initial determination of the tax due to the governmental unit is calculated by the taxpayer. Income taxes (corporate and personal), sales taxes, franchise taxes, and payroll taxes are some examples of self-assessed taxes. The audit of such taxes should include steps to:

Assure that the tax program was applied to all persons subject to the tax, pursuant to the law;

Test procedures for determining the accuracy of filed tax returns, or any adjustments thereto, and assuring compliance with the law;

Reconcile the value of the tax returns, less adjustments, to receipts records;

Confirm receivables for taxes owed, but not paid by the taxpayers;

Confirm the reasonableness of the tax collector's records by comparison to such external and other independently prepared evidence as voter registration rolls, assessment rolls, student and other census data, telephone directory listings, utility customer accounts, etc.;

Verify amounts paid by the taxpayers;

Confirm in writing from collectors amounts received and deposited during the accounting period;

Compare the apportionments to the legal authority for compliance where more than one fund is permitted to share in the tax receipts;

Examine taxpayers' records, by collector or on a test basis by auditor, to determine that amounts paid were actually the full amounts due under the governing legislation.

Property Taxes

For local governments, property taxes on real estate and personal property are the largest single source of receipts. The preliminary audit activities of such taxes must include a thorough understanding of the methods by which property is assessed, the assessor's records are maintained, the billings are made and the collections are received and of the designated depository in which funds are placed.

In addition to generally accepted auditing requirements, the audit of property tax receipts should include such steps as:

A verification of the taxable property valuations and the tax rate set forth in the law;

A test of the appropriateness of total taxes billed by independently applying adjusted valuations and the tax rate to determine an estimate of gross revenues;

An independent confirmation by other governmental units from which monies were received or are due;

A determination that the taxes were properly levied, adjusted or collected; and

A confirmation of amounts paid or owned by taxpayers.

Licenses, Fees, Permits

All levels of government collect receipts pursuant to the issuance of licenses, fees and permits. Of concern to the auditor in examining these types of receipts is (1) the types of licenses, fees and permits issued, (2) the bases and rates charged or assessed by the governmental unit and (3) the appropriateness of the amounts collected.

An audit of such sources of receipts should consider that the administration of these taxes may be lax and the application of sound controls may be varied. In addition to verifying that the fees charged were in compliance with the legal criteria, tests should be made to establish the reasonableness of the gross receipts from these sources.

Fines, Forfeitures, Court Fees, Penalties, Settlements

Several categories of receipts are related to violations of legal requirements and court decisions. Receipts related to fines, forfeitures, court fees, penalties levied and court settlements cannot be related to a revenue base in the same manner as can income or property taxes.

In addition to the required verifications of records and tests to insure adherence to prescribed procedures, the audit must include an examination of the court dockets and of records of legal violations on file in the police or sheriff's department to assess the overall reasonableness of the receipts collected or waived.

Grants, Subsidies, Donations, Trust Deposits

Governmental units obtain significant receipts under grants from other governments, subsidies and donations, and trust deposits. For the most part, these receipts are restricted as to use, generally pursuant to a prior agreement.

Of particular concern to the auditor is the entitlement to the receipts. A determination generally must be made as to whether a receivable or a payable exists. The audit, among other concerns, must include:

An examination of the governing agreement concerning the receipt and expenditure of these types of receipts;

A verification that the funds were received and credited to the proper fund;

A confirmation that the original and all modifications to the governing agreement are available to the auditor; and

A verification of amounts paid or due to the governmental unit.

Enterprise Revenues

Many governmental units provide various types of services, such as transportation, water, electricity, gas, and recreational and public park facilities. In some units, separate accounting records are maintained, possibly by an independent authority. This is not always the case: the accounting could be done by the central administrative official of the government. In any event, financial records of such enterprises more closely parallel those of corporate organizations than those of governmental units. The audit requirements of such activities should be the generally accepted auditing standards.

As mentioned earlier, the revenues for such enterprises should be accrued in the same manner as a corporate organization.

Reporting of Revenues and Receipts

Illustrative financial statements and accompanying explanations relating to governmental revenue and receipts appear in Chapters 18 and 19.

Chapter 15
Expenditures and Expenses (Part I—An Overview)

Introduction
Auditing Requirements
Definitions
Classification and Classes
Requirements for Independent Audit
Accounting Principles
Obligations and Encumbrances
Statistical Sampling Procedures
Expenditure and Expense Audit Procedures

Introduction

Accounting for expenditures and expenses in the governmental sector requires an initial familiarity with the terminology related to these transactions. The government's liability usually is formalized with the incurrence of an *obligation* (at the federal level) or an *encumbrance* (at state or local government level). As goods and services are received, invoices accepted and payments made, the transactions are referred to by other descriptors—such as expenditures, cost, expenses and disbursements—reflecting the status or progression of transactions in the governmental accounting process.

262

Auditing Requirements

Governmental expenditures and expenses are subject to the same verification procedures as similar transactions incurred by a private enterprise or institution. An unique requirement, though, is the necessity to insure compliance with legal and fiscal restraints inherent in fund accounting. Each fund is an accounting entity, with separable assets, liabilities, fund balances and other transactions. Different tests are required to insure that monies are expended from funds only for authorized purposes and in authorized amounts, and that the integrity of the fund is maintained.

Published Guidelines

Proper preparation for auditing a governmental unit requires that the auditor be thoroughly conversant with the auditing standards and guides applicable to the public sector. The auditing criteria are set forth in several publications:

AICPA's *Statement on Auditing Standards;*

AICPA's *Industry Audit Guide—Audits of State and Local Governmental Units;*

National Council on Governmental Accounting's *Governmental Accounting, Auditing and Financial Reporting* (GAAFR)

U. S. General Accounting Office's *Accounting—Principles and Standards for Federal Agencies,* 1978;

U. S. General Accounting Office's *Manual for Guidance of Federal Agencies* (particularly Title 2—Accounting Principles and Standards and Internal Auditing Guidelines);

U.S. General Accounting Office's *Standards for Audit of Governmental Organizations, Programs, Activities & Functions;* and.

Specific audit guides and requirements published by governmental agencies relating to the acceptance and receipt of government funds or other assistance.

Each of these documents outlines general and specific internal control, accounting and auditing requirements applicable to the profession as a whole and to the audit of governmental units in particular. Since this information is comprehensive and generally available, only selected references have been made to these sources.

Definitions

Considerable commonality of expense and expenditure terminology exists among the various governmental levels. As illustrated in Exhibit 15-1, the acceptable definitions for various terms are similar.

Exhibit 15-1

Definition of Terms Related to Expenditures and Expenses

Federal Governmental Accounting *	State and Local Governmental ** Accounting
Obligations—amount of orders placed, contracts awarded, services received, grants issued, or similar transactions that will require the payment of money.	Encumbrances—obligations in the form of purchase orders, contracts, salary commitments, which cease to be encumbrances when paid.
Expenditures (or accrued expenditures) —goods received, services rendered, expenses incurred, grants earned, regardless of when payment is made or whether invoices received.	Expenditures—cost of goods delivered, services rendered, whether paid or unpaid.
Cash expenditures—not recommended terminology, but refers to cash disbursements of federal government.	Expenditure disbursements—not recommended terminology, but refers to payments for expenses when accounts maintained on a cash basis.
Expenses or costs (applied cost also referred to as accrued cost)—goods or services used or consumed in carrying out operations, functions or activity; payment may or may not have occurred.	Expenses or costs—charges incurred, whether paid or unpaid for operations, maintenance, interest, or other charges presumed to benefit period.
Disbursements—cash payments.	Disbursements—payments in cash.

Sources

*Planning, Programming, Budgeting and Systems Analysis—Glossary (1968)
*Frequently Asked Questions About Accrual Accounting in the Federal Government (1972 Reprint)
*GAO Manual for Guidance of Federal Agencies—Title 2: Accounting Principles and Standards and Internal Auditing Guidelines
*By the U. S. General Accounting Office, Washington, D. C.

**Governmental Accounting, Auditing, and Financial Reporting; National Committee on Governmental Accounting (1968)

Classification and Classes

The classification and classes of expenditures, costs and expenses by which accounting is performed differ slightly between the federal and the state and local governments.

Federal Government Classification and Classes

The General Accounting Office, in its manual, *Guidance of Federal Agencies* (Title 2 - Accounting Principles and Standards), requires that expenditures, costs and expenses be accumulated by the following classifications:

Appropriations or funds;

Major organizational segments;

Budget activities;

Agency program structures adopted under planning, programming and budgeting systems;

Capital or expenditures for acquisition of assets;

Current expenses or operating costs; and

Object classes.

The object classes are prescribed by the Office of Management and Budget and are uniform throughout the federal government for classifying expenditures for both budgeting and accounting purposes. The OMB Circular A-11 defines the object classes to be:

Personnel compensation—Class No. 11.0;

Personnel benefits—Class No. 12.0;

Benefits, former personnel—Class No. 13.0;

Travel, transportation of persons—Class No. 21.0;

Transportation of things—Class No. 22.0;

Rent, communications and utilities—Class No. 23.0;

Printing and reproduction—Class No. 24.0;

Other services (e.g., contracts)—Class No. 25.0;

Supplies, materials—Class No. 26.0;

Equipment—Class No. 31.0;

Investment—Class No. 32.0;

Investment, loans—Class No. 33.0;

Grant, subsidies, contributions—Class No. 41.0;

Insurance claims, indemnities—Class No. 42.0;

Interest, dividends—Class No. 43.0;

Refunds—Class No. 44.0; and

Administrative expenses for revolving and trust funds—Class No. 93.0.

Where an agency believes that further breakdown of classes is necessary, subentries may be used within each overall main entry. The amount of detail is left to the discretion of the individual agencies and depends upon the cost information desired to plan, control and appraise operations.

State and Local Government Classifications

In a similar manner, expenditures and expenses of state and local governments should be classified under several groupings. GAAFR prescribes the following categories for accounting and reporting of expenditures and expenses:

Fund—a fiscal and accounting entity, having a self-balancing set of accounts, which have been segregated for carrying on specific activities or achieving certain objectives.

Organization unit—the department, division, bureau or other administrative unit that makes the expenditure for carrying out its designated functions or activities.

Functions—the purposes for which expenditures are made and the types of work performed to accomplish the purpose or objective (see Exhibit 15-2 for a summary listing of the suggested functional and activity classifications).

Activity—a specific, distinguishable line of work performed by one or more organizational components for the purpose of accomplishing a function for which the governmental unit is responsible.

Character—the fiscal period benefiting from the expenditure:

(1) *current expenses*, primarily benefiting the current fiscal period;

(2) *capital outlays* benefiting both current and future fiscal periods; and

(3) *debt service expenditures*, or outlays for debt principal, periodic interest and related service charge payments received in prior, as well as for current and future, fiscal periods.

Object class—the commodity or services obtained. The object classes recommended by GAAFR for state and local governmental units are:

(1) *Personal services*—salaries, wages, related benefits;

(2) *Supplies*—articles and commodities consumed or altered in use, including small tools and minor equipment;

(3) *Other services and charges*—including: professional services, communications, transportation, advertising, printing and binding, insurance, public utility service, repairs and maintenance, rentals, aid to other governments and miscellaneous expenses (court costs, investigations, damages, taxes, etc.); and

(4) *Capital outlays*—including: land, buildings, improvements other than buildings, and machinery and equipment.

The labor costs and supplies used by a government in fabricating, rather than purchasing, a capital asset would be classified under other objects classes, such as personal services and materials and supplies.

Exhibit 15-2

Summary of GAAFR Expenditure Classification by Function

Suggested Account Number	Function and Activity
410	General government
411	Legislative
412	Judicial
413	Executive
414	Elections
415	Financial administration
419	Other (planning and zoning, data processing, research and investigation, general government buildings and plants)
420	Public safety
421	Police
422	Fire
423	Correction
424	Protective inspection
429	Other protection
430	Public works
431	Highways and streets
432	Sanitation
441	Health
444	Welfare
450	Culture-recreation

Requirements for Independent Audit

Within government, no uniform requirement exists for independent audits of expenditures or expenses.

The U. S. General Accounting Office is responsible for conducting audits of the executive agencies of the federal government. With few exceptions, however, the GAO does not make independent audits of an agency's financial statements and render an opinion thereon. Generally, an agency's reporting system and reports are audited by the internal audit staff on a cyclical basis, with an exception reporting made to management in the agency.

No audit is made of the financial condition of the United States government as a whole. Until 1976, when the Treasury Department issued prototype consolidated financial statements, there was no overall reporting of the financial status of the federal government. The prototypes were an attempt to apply the accounting principles of business to the business of government.

Like the federal government, states generally are required neither to make nor to have made independent audits on the overall financial status of this level of government. In contrast, many local government units, by law, require annual audits of the units' financial condition. Certified financial statements then are published for inspection by the public and others. The auditing organization varies. In some governments, the auditor may be an elected or appointed official, a permanent agency of the government staffed by governmental employees or a selected firm of independent certified public accountants.

Accounting Principles

At all levels of government, the accrual form of accounting has been prescribed. The implementation of the concept, however, has not been uniform.

Accrual Accounting Defined

While accountants may generally agree over the advantages of accrual accounting, the concept has not been generally applied in governmental finance. At all levels of government, however, the term has a similar meaning. For example:

At the federal level, the GAO stated, in *Manual for Guidance of Federal Agencies,* that the accrual basis of accounting consists of recognizing in the books and records of account the significant and accountable aspects of financial transactions or events as they occur. Under this basis, the accounting system provides a current systematic record of changes in assets, liabilities and sources of funds growing out of the incurrence of obligations, expenditures, costs and expenses, earning of revenues, disbursement of cash and other financial transactions.

GAAFR defines accrual accounting as the basis under which revenues are recorded when earned and expenditures are recorded as soon as they result in liabilities for benefits received, not withstanding when the receipt of revenue or payment of the expenditure may take place.

Accrual Accounting in the Federal Government

No financial concept has received more attention, analysis and discussion than the adoption of accrual accounting throughout the federal government. Since 1955 and the Second Hoover Commission, Congress has enacted laws, Presidents have issued directives, and the central accounting agencies (the General Accounting Office, the Office of Management and Budget and the Treasury) have published innumerable statements, instructions and regulations. In the 1970s, however, many federal agencies have yet to implement the accrual basis of accounting. Complementing the lagging implementation is the existence of varying definitions and understandings among federal financial managers as to the nature of the concepts inherent in the term "accrual accounting." In the federal government, the term could refer to either accrued expenditures or accrued costs and—in many instances, the distinction is not maintained among communicants.

Legal Requirements for Accrual Basis

The Budget and Accounting Procedures Act of 1950 requires that federal agencies adopt and use the accrual basis of accounting. Other legislation requires that the head of each agency maintain accounts on an accrual basis. The General Accounting Office, in its *Manual for the Guidance of Federal Agencies,* states that the accrual basis of accounting must recognize, in the books and records, the significant and accountable aspects of financial transactions or events as they occur. GAO recognized the importance of the accrual concept as providing more information than the cash basis (where financial transactions are recorded only when cash is received or disbursed) or the obligation basis (where financial transactions are recorded in the accounts primarily when obligations are incurred) when either of the two bases was used alone.

Timing Differences in Accrual Accounting

The principle distinction between classification of a transaction as an accrued expenditure or as an accrued cost is the emphasis on the time when the government recognizes the existence of a liability or consumes resources. There are a number of "steps" or "timing differences" in the status of funds through the life cycle of a transaction in federal accounting. An agency's system must be able to account for each phase: appropriation, apportionment, allotment, obligation, accrued expenditure, accrued cost and disbursement.

Exhibit 15-3 illustrates the general sequence or timing of a transaction and the differences that could occur because of financing arrangements in relation to periods of performance. Where there is no timing difference—in those instances where the obligation, accrued expenditure, accrued cost or disbursement is incurred, and payment is made immediately—timing differences are of no consequence for reporting purposes.

Exhibit 15-3

Illustrations of Timing Differences Under Federal Accrual Method of Accounting

Timing of the Recording of Purchase of Materials Under Accrual Method of Accounting

Transaction	Recorded in Accounting Records in Month in Which			
	Order is placed	Materials are delivered	Materials are used	Bill is paid
Placing an order for materials	*As an obligation*			
Materials delivered		*As an accrued expenditure*		
Materials used or consumed			*As an applied or accrued cost*	
Payment made for materials				*As a disbursement of cash*

Alternatives or Timing Differences in Relation to Periods of Performance

	First Period	Second Period	Third Period
1.	Obligation Incurred	Accrued Expenditure	Cash Disbursement
2.		Obligation Incurred Accrued Expenditure Cash Disbursement	
	Obligation Incurred	Accrued Expenditure Cash Disbursement	
		Obligation Incurred Accrued Expenditure	Cash Disbursement
	Obligation Incurred Cash Disbursement	Accrued Expenditure	

Source: *Frequently Asked Questions about Accrual Accounting in the Federal Accounting.* U.S. General Accounting Office, 1970.

If an entry is made for only the obligation and the cash disbursement, considerable accounting information will not be available, particularly for projects of long duration. Without an accounting for the changes in status, such as accrued expenditures and accrued costs, several fiscal periods could pass between the initial obligation and final disbursement, with no measure of performance or determination of interim liability.

Methods for Determining Accrued Expenditures

Various practices exist in federal agencies for determining accrued expenditures. For descriptive purposes, they may be titled the forecast method, the inventory method and the continual method. Not all of these practices, however, provide the same degree of accuracy or currency of information to agency management.

Forecast method. The least desirable practice of accruing expenditures is the method of forecasting the estimated liability to be incurred. During the fiscal period, cash payments are made against the forecasted balance; the amount remaining, or the unpaid balance, is considered to be the accrued expenditure. Implicit in this method is the assumption that the estimated liability is accruing at the same rate throughout the period. The method does not provide a continual, systematic accounting of performance or services or materials received.

Inventory method. A more desirable practice of recognizing accrued expenditures is the inventory method. As described by the General Accounting Office, in its *Manual for Guidance of Federal Agencies,* the inventory method requires that an inventory be made of unpaid bills and of open obligations at the beginning and at the end of the accounting period, and that the increases or decreases be related to the amount of accrued expenditures and obligations incurred during the period. This method obviates the need for maintaining an allotment ledger and an accrued expenditure register.

The inventory method is illustrated in Exhibit 15-4. This method, as recognized by the GAO, does not provide the same controls over expenditures and costs that would exist under a full accrual method of accounting. For example, in determining the obligations incurred under the inventory method, the exact, unobligated balance of allotments is determined only at the end of the accounting period. To obtain more precise control over the unobligated balances, additional records must be maintained during the accounting period; and, to obtain maximum benefit from the inventory method, the allotment structure must be maintained in a simplified form, thus minimizing controls.

Under the inventory method, accruals may be accounted for in one of two ways: (1) posting the end-of-month accruals in total or gross amounts and reversing the same entry at the beginning of the next fiscal period, or (2) posting only the net changes in the accruals from one fiscal period to the next, that is, adjusting entries only for the net decreases or increases.

Exhibit 15-4

Inventory Method of Determining Accrued Expenditures and Obligations Incurred

Item	Month of July	Last 11 Months of Fiscal Year	Total for Fiscal Year
(1) Total *cash disbursements* during current period	$41,250	$787,750	$829,000
(2) Increase or decrease of ending over beginning balance of accounts payable, determined by inventories of unpaid invoices and other liability documents:			
(a) Accounts payable, per ending inventory	350	1,000	1,000
(b) Accounts payable, per beginning inventory	—	350	—
(c) Increase (or decrease).......	$ 350	$ 650	$ 1,000
(3) *Accrued expenditures,* or liabilities incurred during the current period for assets and expenses (see Journal Entry Nos. 2 and 3 below).......	$41,600	$788,400	$830,000
(4) Increase or decrease of ending over beginning balance of unliquidated obligations, determined by inventories of purchase orders, contracts and other obligating documents:			
(a) Unliquidated obligations, per ending inventory	$35,000	$110,000	$110,000
(b) Unliquidated obligations, per beginning inventory	—	35,000	—
(c) Increase (or decrease).......	$35,000	$ 75,000	$110,000
(5) *Obligations incurred,* or purchase orders and contracts placed, and other obligating documents issued during the current period (see Journal Entry No. 1 below)...........	$76,600	$863,400	$940,000

JOURNAL ENTRIES:	JULY Debit	JULY Credit	LAST 11 MONTHS Debit	LAST 11 MONTHS Credit
(1) Unobligated allotments	$76,600		$863,400	
Unliquidated obligations (see Item No. 5 above)		$76,600		$863,400
(2) Unliquidated obligations	41,600		788,400	
Expended appropriations (see Item No. 3 above)		41,600		788,400
(3) Assets and expenses	41,600		788,400	
Fund balances with U. S. Treasury		41,250		787,750
Accounts payable (see Item Nos. 3, 1 and 2c above)		350		650

Source: GAO Manual for Guidance of Federal Agencies, "Title II—Accounting Principles and Standards and Internal Audit Guidelines," U.S. General Accounting Office.

Continual or full accrual method. The continual or full accrual method requires the continual processing, recording and accounting for transactions and events. The introduction of computers, along with the legal requirement to maintain comprehensive and integrated accounting and reporting systems, have facilitated the implementation of the full accrual concept in many agencies utilizing automated data processing. Under this method, receivables, inventories, payables, obligations, accrued expenditures and the changing status of transactions are promptly recorded in the accounting records.

Accrual Accounting in State and Local Government

Accrual Bases

The basis for accounting for expenditures and expenses of other governmental units varies and is related to the fund that the transactions affect and the purpose for which the fund was established. Generally, as is the case with revenues and receipts, the accounting bases are the accrual and modified accrual bases. The GAAFR identifies these bases with the following funds:

Funds, similar to commercial enterprises utilizing the accrual basis, also referred to as proprietary funds:

Enterprise funds;

Intragovernmental service funds; or

Non-expendable trust and agency funds.

Other governmental funds, utilizing the modified accrual basis, sometimes referred to as budgeting funds:

General fund;

Special revenue funds;

Debt service funds;

Capital projects;

Expendable trust and agency funds; or

Special assessment funds.

Pursuant to GAAFR, the accrual method of accounting requires that expenditures and transfers out be objectively and practicably measurable, and that the liability be recorded when it is incurred. The GAAFR's definition of accrual accounting does not include the recognition of depreciation in the course of expense measurement: depreciation and amortizations are allocations, not accruals. Under this concept, recognized exceptions would include:

Unmatured principal and interest on general obligation long-term debt may be recorded when due;

Interest expense on special assessment indebtedness, if offset by interest earnings on special assessment levies, may be recorded when due;

Inventory items may be expended when purchased or when used, but significant inventory balances should be reported in the balance sheet; and

Expenditures for insurance and other services extending over more than one accounting period need not be allocated, but may be expended when acquired.

Modified Accrual Basis

The AICPA's industry audit guide for state and local governments requires that expenditures be recorded on the accrual basis except for:

Disbursements for inventory-type items, which may be considered expenditures at the time of purchase or at the time the items are used;

Prepaid expenses, which normally are not recorded;

Interest on long-term debt, which normally should be an expenditure when due; and

The encumbrance method of accounting, which may be adopted as an additional modification of the accrual basis.

Expenditures benefiting more than one accounting period would be recorded as a prepaid expense under the full accrual method. In governmental accounting, such expenditures normally are not prorated among the different accounting periods, but rather are recorded as expenditures of the period in which the commitment is initiated. The interest expense, typically recorded in a debt service fund, is not accrued, but rather recorded on the date the interest is due.

Methods of Estimating Accruals

The accrual method of accounting requires the formal recognition of liabilities for work performed or goods received, which may be evidenced by invoices and other documents signifying completion. In addition, though, the accrual method requires the formal recording of expenditures for which no formal documentation has yet been received. In this latter instance, the amount of the accrual may have to be estimated to provide the reasonable disclosure. At the federal level, several methods have been suggested to governmental agencies by the General Accounting Office (*Illustrative Accounting Procedures for Federal Agencies—Accounting for Accrued Expenditures*, U.S. General Accounting Office, 1969) for determining the amounts to be accrued as expenditures. For example:

Unpaid invoices for shipments received should be used when available;

Receiving reports, whether for partial or complete shipments, are useful in determining the accrual when invoices have not been received;

Payroll, travel and other vouchers prepared but not yet paid also may be used for the accrual determination;

Personal services for days between the close of the latest payroll period and the end of the accounting period can be calculated on the basis of experience, plus other factors, such as overtime;

Rental, utility and similar costs might be estimated on the basis of experience for similar periods;

When an obligation has been recorded for an expenditure, which may accrue within the accounting period, the obligated amount may be the best estimate of the accrued expenditure;

In cases of fixed price contracts extending beyond the end of the accounting period and covering goods manufactured to government specifications, a statement from the contractor estimating a percentage of completion, including work performed by subcontractors, could be used for estimating the accrued expenditures;

For cost type contracts, monthly contractor reports showing unbilled costs for performance, including work performed by subcontractors, could be used to accrue the expenditure;

Similar monthly reports of performance received from grantees could be used to accrue expenditures for grants;

In the absence of contractor or grantee reports, estimates by governmental project managers and other officials knowledgeable of the progress or performance could be obtained; and

Sampling or other statistical methods susceptible to verification as to validity could be used, especially where amounts are small and the numbers of transactions large.

Other Methods of Accounting

The auditor may find federal, as well as state and local governmental units, maintaining financial accounts on a cash or hybrid accrual reporting basis in a manner similar to that used in accounting for revenues and receipts. Some units may account for transactions throughout the reporting period on a cash basis. Other units may use the cash basis during the accounting period, but may make adjusting entries at the end of the period to permit the accounts and financial statements to reflect the financial position on an accrual basis.

Obligations and Encumbrances

Definitions

At the federal level, and in many state and local governmental units, a special budgetary system, including formal journal entries, exists to insure that commitments, liabilities or other debts are made only pursuant to appropriation legislation. The budgetary accounting consists of making a reservation of the unexpended portion of the appropriation or fund balance each time a commitment is incurred. This reservation is known at the federal level as an *obligation,* at the state and local government level as an *encumbrance.*

The encumbrance or obligation method generally is used for accounting for transactions of governmental or budgetary funds (the general, special revenues, capital projects and debt service type funds). The recording of commitments or encumbrances against the available appropriation balance precludes the unintentional over-obligation of the authorized appropriation. This method requires that commitments (purchase orders, grants, contracts etc.), as well as expenditures accrued, be recorded. As the final amounts of the earlier commitments are known, adjustments are made to the earlier encumbered amounts. Where differences arise in the year of commitment, the adjustment is made to the accounts originally charged. If the adjustment must be made for a prior-year commitment, a current nondepartmental account should be charged.

In governmental accounting, knowledge of the status of the unliquidated obligations or encumbrances as well as of the accrued expenditures is necessary to determine the appropriation balance that is available for additional obligation or encumbering.

Fund Control

Generally, governmental units may not incur obligations or encumber fund balances unless there exists a previously approved appropriation. Appropriation legislation typically sets forth the amounts, purpose/and period for which an appropriation or fund will be available for obligation or encumbrance.

At the federal level, an unliquidated obligation remains available to settle the related liability pursuant to the appropriation legislation. In some instances, the obligated amount will lapse at the end of the fiscal year, unless expended. In other instances, the obligation might have to be liquidated within a legally mandated time period. Other obligations remain available to satisfy the liabilities of the agency indefinitely.

In state and local governments, specific legislation may dictate that the encumbered balance lapse at the end of the fiscal year. Alternatively, the encumbered balance may be considered as a part of the appropriation for the following year, pursuant to GAAFR. The AICPA's industry audit guide requires that an outstanding encumbrance be recognized as an expenditure and that the related obligation be carried until liquidated by replacement with an actual liability or by cancellation. The NCGA Interpretation No. 1, *GAAFR and the AICPA Audit Guide,* summarized the differences between GAAFR and the AICPA in the following manner:

> The (AICPA's) *Audit Guide* presents a significant difference from the concept of encumbrances contained in GAAFR. In the latter, encumbrances are treated as an element of the budgetary accounting system and, as such, represent the reservation of an appropriation for future payment. Encumbrances are not treated as expenditures. Funds reserved at year-end are used for payment of the outstanding commitments, and any necessary corrections or changes thereto are made by adjustment of the fund balance account. As an alternative, GAAFR also allows for the carryover of encumbrances as appropriations in the following year.

Transaction Analysis

At all levels of government, valid obligations and encumbrances should be supported by properly executed commitment documents that require the performance of a service or the delivery of supplies or materials or otherwise create a liability of the government.

At the federal level, the requirements or criteria for determining the existence of a valid obligation are described by law. Section 1311 of the Supplemental Appropriation Act of 1955 sets forth, among other items, the following criteria with respect to obligations:

No appropriation or fund that is limited for obligation purposes to a definite period of time shall be available for expenditure after the expiration of this period, except for liquidation of amounts validly obligated; and

Eight types of obligations may be validly incurred and must be supported by documentary evidence:

A binding agreement in writing between the parties, including the government, in a manner and form and for a purpose authorized by law, executed before the expiration of the period of availability for obligation of the appropriation or fund concerned for specific goods to be delivered, real property to be purchased or leased, or work or services to be performed;

A valid loan agreement, showing the amount of the loan to be made and the terms of repayment thereof;

An order required by law to be placed with a government agency;

An order issued pursuant to a law authorizing purchases without advertising when necessitated by public exigency or for perishable subsistence supplies or within specific monetary limitation;

A grant or subsidy payable (1) from appropriations made for payment of, or contributions toward, sums required to be paid in specific amounts fixed by law or in accord with formulae prescribed by law or (2) pursuant to agreement, authorized by, or plans approved in accord with and authorized by, law;

A liability that may result from pending legislation brought under authority of law;

Employment or services of persons or expenses of travel in accord with law, and services performed by public utilities; or

Any other legal liability of the United States against an appropriation or fund legally available therefor.

While no similar uniform legislation exists for all state and local government units, the GAAFR has defined "encumbrances" as obligations requiring specific documentation or form. Specific reference is made to purchase orders, contracts and salary commitments that are chargeable to an appropriation and for which a part of the appropriation is reserved. These commitments cease to be encumbrances when paid or when the actual liability is established or known.

Audit Considerations

A close examination should be made of the balance of unliquidated obligations and encumbrances at the end of the accounting period. A dual concern exists: (1) whether the balance reflects valid commitments of the government, and (2) whether all of the commitments are recorded in the accounts. Typically, the auditor has less concern with liquidated obligations and encumbrances because of the known controls that exist over the receipt, audit and payment of amounts liquidated by the recognition of the actual liability or the cancellation of the earlier commitment. Tests should be made to ascertain that:

Each amount represents a valid commitment of the government and is supported by a valid, properly executed document;

The balance of the obligation or encumbrance is for the proper amount, is recorded in the appropriate fiscal period and is for an authorized purpose in relation to the appropriation legislation;

The obligations or encumbrances are recorded against the proper appropriation or fund;

Sufficient inquiries and confirmations are made to ascertain that the recorded balance of obligations and encumbrances reflects the total unliquidated commitment of the government; and

No unrecorded commitment exists at the end of the fiscal period.

Statistical Sampling Procedures

The application of statistical sampling procedures to the audit of the governmental entities in much the same manner as is done in the audit of commercial organizations, is entirely appropriate. The guiding standards for sampling are set forth in the AICPA's Statement on Auditing Standards, No. 1:

Appendix A—Relationship of Statistical Sampling to Generally Accepted Auditing Standards (Section 320A); and

Appendix B—Precision and Reliability for Statistical Sampling in Auditing.

In the governmental sector, the U.S. General Accounting Office, pursuant to federal legislation (Public Law 88-521) permits the use of statistical sampling procedures in ·the examination of vouchers. The principal application of statistical sampling under this law is in the prepayment audit of vouchers within a government agency. Initially, adequate and effective statistical sampling procedures could be applied to disbursement vouchers of amounts of $100 or less. Subsequently, the amount has been raised to disbursement vouchers of $500 or less.

Expenditure and Expense Audit Procedures

General and specific audit procedures and tests relating to expenditures and expenses are discussed in Chapters 16 and 17.

Chapter 16
Expenditures and Expenses (Part II—Personnel, Travel and Transportation)

Internal Control Evaluation Criteria
General Audit Procedures
Audit of Payroll and Personal Services Expenses
Audit of Travel and Transportation Expenses
Reporting of Expenditures and Expenses

General and special audit procedures and techniques relating to expenditures and expenses for personnel services, travel and transportation are discussed in this chapter.

Internal Control Evaluation Criteria

As mentioned in earlier chapters, the AICPA's Statement on Auditing Standards, No. 1, relating to the evaluation of internal controls, is applicable to the audits of governmental units. Specifically, the following sections are applicable in their entirety:

Section 320—"The Auditor's Study and Evaluation of Internal Control";

Section 320-A—"Appendix A—Relationship of Statistical Sampling to Generally Accepted Auditing Standards";

Section 320-B—"Appendix B—Precision and Reliability for Statistical Sampling in Auditing."

These documents outline both general and specific requirements for the evaluation of internal controls applicable to the profession as a whole. Since this information is comprehensive and generally available, only selected references have been made to these sources.

General Audit Procedures

As mentioned earlier, the audit of governmental expenditures and expenses is subject to the same verifications as is a similar audit of a private enterprise or non-governmental institution. With few exceptions, the generally accepted auditing standards are applicable in total to governmental audits. The governmental audit requirements should be viewed as an addition to the tests normally applied in a commercial-type audit. Most comprehensive audit check lists, internal control questionnaires and detailed programs for the audit of expenses in commercial-type audits also are applicable to governmental audits. Other audit procedures, either unique to government or having an increased importance in public-sector audits, would include tests and examinations to insure that:

Pre-numbered, printed checks are controlled, properly voided and filed, and are coded by fund, organization, function, budget activity, program, type of expense and object class;

Signatures on authorizing documents, approval forms, checks and other documents are prescribed by the governing body, the responsible executive or some type of legislation;

Transfer documentation for inter-fund and inter-bank transactions, and the transactions of several deposit funds, is under proper accounting control;

Obligations, encumbrances and expenditures are continually monitored to insure that the total of such commitments does not exceed legal limits set forth in law or other requirements;

The balances of obligations and encumbrances at the end of the accounting period represent valid commitments, and tests are made to determine the extent of other unrecorded commitments;

Expenditures and expenses are authorized in legislation, approved by the appropriate official;

Supporting documentation, such as contracts, invoices, vouchers, receiving reports and other evidence, is marked or otherwise mutilated to avoid reuse and is properly coded (to account for the transaction by appropriation or fund, organization, budget activity, program, type of expense, and object class), and the content of such records is reconcilable with ledgers, books of original entry and other records;

Supporting documentation contains evidence that records were:

Properly prepared and the expenditure was for authorized purposes,

Annotated to show receipt of the services or goods,

Examined for accuracy of prices, quantity, arithmetic detail, correctness of amounts charged and propriety of services or goods received,

Consistent with legal requirements for advertising or otherwise obtaining competitive bids where appropriate,

Approved in advance for payment, and

Coded appropriately;

A continual review is made of the appropriation or legal budget for the year under audit to insure compliance;

A comparison is made of actual expenditures to the budget, appropriation legislation and other legal provisions to insure consistency; and

Obligations, encumbrances and other commitments, expenditures and expenses do not exceed the appropriation of the governmental unit or fund.

Neither the above general areas of concern, nor the considerations discussed in the following paragraphs, relating to specific expenditures and expenses, are intended to be all-inclusive; nor is there an intention to supplant the judgment of the auditor. These identified areas of concern should be viewed as tests of internal controls and audit checks, which may not be of equal importance in the audit of a non-governmental entity.

Audit of Payroll and Personal Services Expenses

Definition

The cost of personnel is the largest expenditure of most government agencies and is often of major concern to management and legislatures. Personal services may be defined as including compensation for services, fringe benefits, special living allowances, incentives, special awards and other types of remunerations for personnel services or performance.

Transaction Analysis

Generally, government employees can be hired only for positions authorized by the legislature or other governing body. Rates of compensation and amounts of annual increases and fringe benefits must be set forth in law, statute or ordinance. The budget for a governmental organization also generally sets forth the level and number of personnel that may be retained by an agency.

Conceptually, meeting the payroll in a governmental unit is generally quite systematized, and checks are issued on a routine basis. The exception payment basis typically is used—that is, the payroll department presumes that a check for the normal work period is due to all employees, unless notice or documentation is received to the contrary. Where exception documentation is received, a special payroll often is required. The difficulty of payroll accounting usually is the volume of records that must be updated and supporting documentation that must be established within a regular and definite time period.

Exhibit 16-1 provides an overview of the payroll process that exists in most governmental agencies. Non-payroll, but personal services-related, transactions such as awards, incentive payments and special allowances often are processed by the payroll function, but require special documentation and approval or authorization.

Internal Controls

In many respects, the controls over payroll and related transactions within government are similar to those prescribed for commercial and institutional organizations. For example, a sound system of controls would provide for:

Clearly defined and written procedures for

   hiring and severing personnel,

   placing personnel on the payrolls,

   recording attendance and absences,

   processing special payrolls and overtime compensation, and

   paying, recording, and accounting;

Approval of the payroll computation, authorization of payment of the payroll and distribution of paychecks or cash;

Segregation of duties of employees who review supporting documentation, reconcile payroll bank accounts, maintain payroll records, prepare payroll checks and authorize payment;

A system of audit to verify hours worked, rate of compensation and appropriateness of deductions; and

Appropriate control of unclaimed checks and wages.

Governmental agencies and legislatures generally require that other controls exist and that safeguards be monitored to insure compliance with legal or other imposed criteria. For example, it may be required that:

An approved salary schedule exist and be formally recognized by both the executive and legislative branches;

Budgets for governmental units be based upon the official salary schedule;

Ceilings and other controls be imposed to insure compliance with personnel limitations as to numbers, quality and compensation of personnel;

Payment for overtime generally requires special approval, on occasion by a legislative oversight group as well as from within the executive branch;

Exhibit 16-1
Overview of Personnel and Payroll Transactions and Documentation

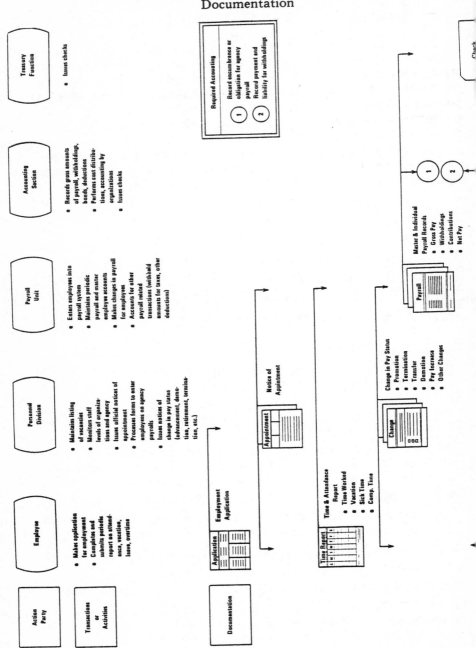

Policies and procedures exist relating to nepotism and to conditions regarded as conflict of interest;

Criteria exist concerning the type and level of outside employment permitted for governmental personnel or the gifts, honoraria or other remuneration that may be received.

Internal control questionnaires have been developed by professional organizations and associations and by many accounting firms for examining the quality of the controls of governmental organizations. Care should be exercised, though, to insure that questionnaires prepared for another governmental unit are applicable to the unit under audit. Often the authorizing and appropriation legislation and statutes are not uniform among governmental units. A questionnaire adequate for the review of one governmental entity may not be adequate to test the controls of another entity.

Audit Considerations

In the audit of commercial or institutional organizations, primary concern may be directed to the confirmation of payment and the appropriateness of the accounting for payroll disbursements. In the governmental sector, the compliance with legal and government-wide civil service requirements are of equal importance. Thus the scope of audit for governmental payrolls should encompass tests to:

Verify the arithmetic accuracy of the payroll;

Review the coding and bookkeeping procedures to insure that the required accounting has transpired, both from a fiscal and a cost accounting view;

Reconcile the total of payroll imprest account to the general operating fund disbursement control account;

Determine that disbursements for payroll and related personal services comply with federal, state and local laws and with civil service requirements;

Verify the validity of payments for overtime, incentive awards, bonuses and special allowances with respect to both amounts and appropriateness of recipients;

Verify the employment authorization and rates of compensation to appropriate criteria;

Compare the payroll to amounts authorized in the budget, with respect to number, quality and compensation of personnel;

Examine and reconcile the various documentation and records, such as attendance records, payroll listings, journals and entries and general ledger accounts to assure proper appropriation or fund and organizational cost accounting;

Witness a payroll on an unannounced basis, controlling unclaimed checks for specified period, cancelling checks and establishing a liability due to identified employees;

Verify payments made to terminated employees for salaries earned, termination pay, earned and due vacation or sick time, and for other authorized items.

Audit of Travel and Transportation Expenses

Definition

At the federal level, travel and transportation expenses have been defined uniformally for all agencies by the Office of Management and Budget's Circular A-7:

Travel and Transportation of Persons—includes transportation of government employees and other, their per diem allowances (i.e. lodging and meals allowance) and other incidental expenses incurred either away from the duty station or for local travel. Also included within this definition are contractual services for carrying persons from place to place, whether on land, in the air or on the water, and the costs for commercial or private carriers, vehicles or conveyances.

Transportation of Things—includes contractual costs for transporting employees' household effects, freight and mail.

Transaction Analysis

Expenditures for travel and transportation sometimes constitute a major element of a federal agency's budget and an expense for which controls are dutifully exercised. While the amount of these costs could be significant, the close monitoring more often is defended because of the opportunity for personal abuse. While state and local governmental units may spend funds for travel beyond the governmental jurisdiction, local travel costs—either for the use of public transportation or for the use of employees' vehicles for the conduct of government business—may be more significant than state travel costs.

For these reasons, expenses for travel and transportation are closely monitored. Often, the governmental procedures for these types of expenses require that (1) a formal request for authorization to travel be submitted; (2) a formal approval be obtained before any travel costs are incurred; (3) a formal accounting be made of all expenses once the travel or transportation costs have been incurred; (4) often, a prepayment audit be made of all travel and transportation vouchers.

While each federal agency must establish its own travel and transportation procedures for authorization, performance and reimbursement or payment of travel and transportation costs, such criteria must be consistent with the federal *Standardized Government Travel Regulations.* The SGTRs are often a condition precedent to the issuance of a contract or grant to state and local governmental units. The definition of travel and transportation expenses and the applicable regulations will vary by state or governmental unit. Thus, while no uniform travel and transportation regulations exist among the several states and local governmental units, many units have incorporated aspects of the SGTRs as part of their own regulations. Exhibits 16-2 and 16-3 provide an overview of the travel and transportation documentation and related transactions, respectively.

Internal Controls

Governments require approval and authorization of travel and transportation expenses before the obligation or encumbrance is incurred and again at the time a claim is made for payment. Typically, these procedures are more detailed than those found in commercial or institutional organizations. To insure that funds are expended only for travel and transportation, in accord with the governmental agency or unit policy, a detailed system of controls and procedures generally will exist. These controls often provide for:

Existence of clear and widely published written guidance relating to the authorization, performance and payment of travel and transportation costs;

Use of prescribed forms and obtaining specific approval in advance of performance of travel or incurrence of transportation costs;

Documentation that is controlled, numerically and physically, pursuant to prescribed fiscal procedures designed to minimize improper or duplicate payments and to insure timely payments;

Preaudit or testing, before payment, to provide assurance to the certifying government official of the propriety of the request to incur the cost or the payment made for cost incurred;

Procedures to control disbursements to claimants for either an advance or reimbursement for travel or transportation costs;

Proper accounting in the formal records of the governmental agency or unit for the transactions related to travel or transportation—the initial obligation or encumbrance, any advances, the liability for payment and the disbursement of cash;

Exhibit 16-2

Overview of Travel Transactions and Documentation

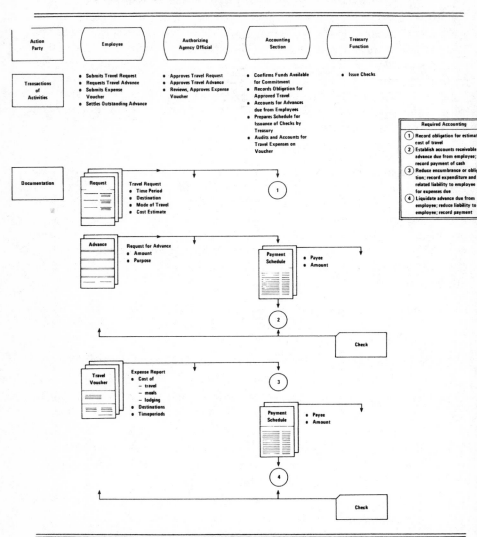

Exhibit 16-3

Overview of Transportation Transactions and Documentation

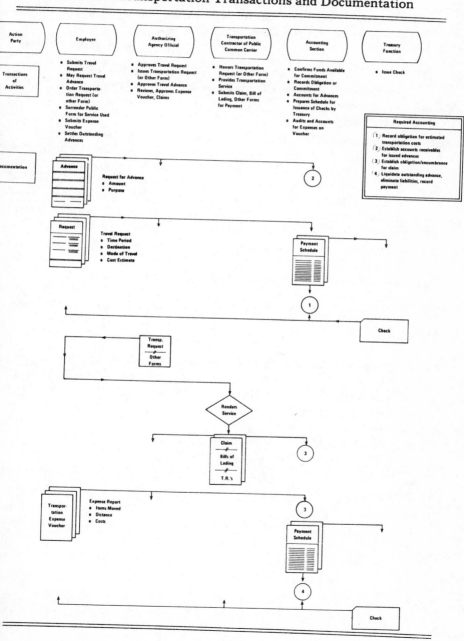

Administrative procedures for

Determining (prior to authorization) that travel or transportation is necessary and in the interest of the government,

Designing authorized itineraries to accomplish the objectives of the travel or transportation at minimum costs,

Authorizing (within governmental policy and regulations) a per diem rate that will most equitably compensate the traveler for costs, and

Authorizing the mode of transportation, the rate of reimbursement and the period allowed for the completion of the travel or transportation services.

Federal employees often are required to use *Transportation Request* forms, in lieu of cash, for payment of transportation services provided by a common carrier. These forms are highly negotiable and could be subject to misuse; therefore, considerable care must be exercised in controlling the supplies of these forms. A similar form may exist at a state or local governmental unit. State and local governmental employees may be permitted to use a federal *Transportation Request* to pay for travel to a federal supported activity.

Few internal audit questionnaires exist for assessing the adequacy of controls and compliance requirements with respect to travel and transportation. In the development of such a document, care should be taken to thoroughly review the regulations and administrative procedures and practices in existence for the individual governmental agency or units under audit.

Audit Considerations

The procedures for controlling travel and transportation expenses in a commercial or institutional organization are considerably less detailed and contain less formal approval steps than is the case in government. Often, in the audit of non-governmental financial statements, the concern with travel is minimal because of the relative insignificance of the expenses. Government controls are more detailed because of the continuing possibility that such expenses will be used to personal gain or benefit.

Additional specific audit procedures or tests that should be considered in examining the reasonableness of travel and transportation costs might include tests to:

Determine the validity of unliquidated obligations or encumbrances for travel and transportation in relation to formally authorized, but incomplete, travel and transportation activities to insure that funds are still committed for validly authorized reasons;

Determine compliance with governmental and agency policy, regulations and procedures through an examination of the amount, purpose, etc. of expenses and transportation vouchers paid;

Verify the manner of claiming and computing such travel and transportation costs as per diem costs, mileage expenses for personal automobiles, costs of automobile· rentals, costs of public transportation, costs for charters or other group arrangements and costs of contracts issued for transportation;

Verify that required management approval is obtained in advance of travel performance and that approval is obtained for all claims for payment;

Examine the practices of awarding, accounting, liquidating and settling travel advances and, where appropriate, the use and controls for forms such as *Transportation Requests;*

Determine the age of long-outstanding travel advances and the possibility of requesting a periodic settlement of all travel advances;

Reconcile the outstanding travel and transportation authorizations to the unliquidated obligations or encumbrances, and confirm that unliquidated encumbrances and advances are proper;

Reconcile the original authorizations to claims for payments and the payment support documents to the various journals and ledger accounts, including those used for appropriation or fund and other cost accounting purposes;

Assure, in the case of transportation of things, that the proper government bills of lading are completed and filed, that receiving reports exist, and that discounts and other payment terms are honored;

Examine the possibility of duplicate payments (particularly when payments have been delayed for extended periods and duplicate copies of billings have been received as follow-up claims, when vendors' invoices have been submitted to more than one location for payment and when adjusted claims are received after payment has been made);

Determine compliance of travel and transportation expenditures to the amounts authorized by approved budgets, legal limitations and any appropriation or fund restrictions; and

Verify that an adequate review or prepayment audit is made of all requests or claims for payments.

Reporting of Expenditures and Expenses

Illustrative financial statements and accompanying explanations relating to governmental expenditures and expenses appear in Chapters 18 and 19.

Chapter 17
Expenditures and Expenses (Part III— Contracts, Grants, Inter-Agency or Intra-Governmental Transactions)

Internal Control Evaluation Criteria and General Audit Procedures
Audits of Contracts and Purchases
Audit of Grant Expenses
Audit of Inter-Agency or Intra-Governmental Expenses
Reporting of Expenditures and Expenses

General and special audit procedures and techniques relating to expenditures and expenses for contracts, grants, and inter-agency or intra-governmental transactions are discussed in this Chapter.

Internal Control Evaluation Criteria and General Audit Procedures

As mentioned in the introduction to Chapter 16, the AICPA's statement relating to the evaluation of internal controls applies to the review of controls of a governmental unit.

The earlier Chapter also discussed several general audit procedures and considerations that either were unique to the audit of governmental units or were of increased importance in public sector audits.

These sections of Chapter 16 would apply to the audit of expenditures and expenses discussed in this Chapter as well.

Audits of Contracts and Purchases

For many federal, state and local governmental agencies, the expenditures made under contracts and purchase orders for services, supplies, equipment and material are significant. Often the amounts are of such magnitude that legislatures will specifically approve amounts budgeted for such expenditures. Special reporting may be required in such situation.

Definitions

All levels of government enter into contracts and issue purchase orders for equipment, supplies, materials and services. The terminology for contracts and purchase orders, while not uniform, is rather consistent among governmental levels. The basic terms include:

Contracts—commitments and transactions resulting from acceptance of an offer, issuance of notice of award, job orders, letter contracts, letters of intent and purchase orders calling for the construction or the delivery of such items as buildings, roads, other construction, equipment, services, supplies or materials.

Contract withholdings or payables—amounts withheld under contracts issued for construction, equipment, services or other acquisitions until final inspection and acceptance by the government. The amount of the withholding is often a part of the conditions of the contract.

Purchase order—a small contract (for less than $10,000 at the federal level) for services, supplies or materials, authorizing delivery and providing authority to bill the government for the delivered items.

Formal contracts, often competitively awarded, may be divided into two general categories. Cost type contracts are entered into when the precise scope of services to be performed is not definable; contractors are reimbursed for cost incurred plus a prenegotiated profit amount. Fixed-price or lump-sum contracts are issued for services that are definable; contractors accept such contracts for a fixed amount and must perform the services, regardless of the actual costs incurred. Any costs above the fixed price must be borne by the contractor; alternatively, if performance is accomplished at less than the fixed price or lump sum, the contractor is entitled to the full contract amount. Purchase orders are viewed as fixed-price in nature.

Transaction Analysis

At all levels of government, public policy dictates that contracts should be awarded as the result of an evaluation of competitive proposals from responsible organizations. The federal government has formalized the regulations concerning the issuance of contracts in a document titled *Federal Procurement Regulations.* At this time, no uniform codification of contracting regulations exists among the several states and local governmental units, but there have been efforts to develop regulations similar to the federal government's.

Exhibit 17-1 provides a general overview of the contractual process and a summary description of the activities often associated with the issuance of a contract. Exhibit 17-2 illustrates the procurement process often required for the purchase of equipment, supplies and materials.

Exhibit 17-1

Overview of Procurement or Contract Transactions and
Documentation

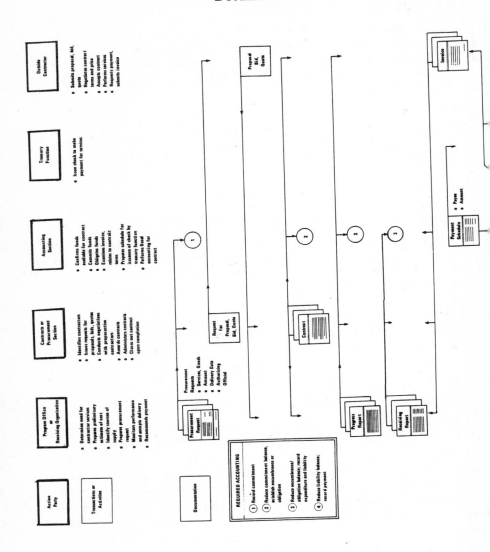

Exhibit 17-2

Overview of Equipment, Supplies or Materials Transactions and Documentation

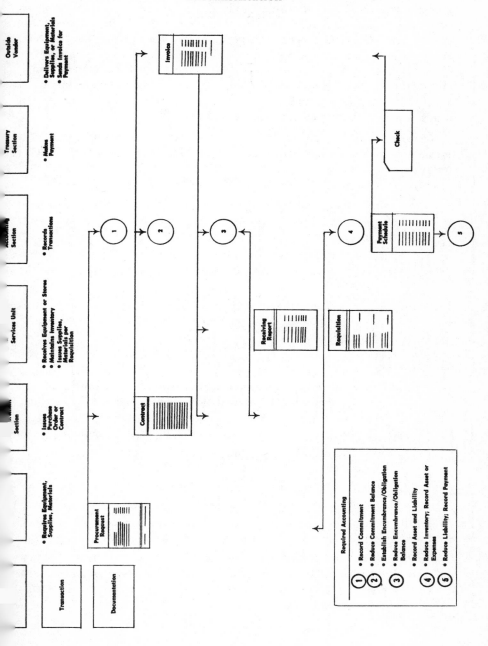

Internal Controls

The placement of the contracting function in government, or within a governmental agency or unit, varies. At the federal level, the more significant procurements, such as real estate, buildings, construction and larger or more expensive capital equipment, are generally the responsibility of a central agency, the General Services Administration. The individual agencies, however, also spend considerable funds for goods and services through the issuance of contracts and purchase orders. A similar condition exists at state and local government levels: the contracting function might be centralized in a government-wide procurement office or several department and agency heads might purchase goods and services individually.

Knowledge of the manner in which contracts are awarded and of the formalities of procurement policy and procedures must be acquired early in an audit to insure that all controls are examined properly. Whether decentralized or centralized, prudent procurement practices should include these controls:

Clear procurement policy and procedures should be written and disseminated to all responsible executives and procurement personnel;

Procurement policy and procedures should be consistent with the legislation and the mission of the agency or governmental unit authorizing the issuance of contracts;

Procedures should insure that procurements are made for goods or services only in compliance with the language of the appropriation or funding legislation;

Procurement function controls should include a description of procedures and practices relating to the solicitation of offerors, evaluation of offers, selection of the most advantageous offer, award of the contract, monitoring of contract performance and orderly close-out of contracts;

A system of prepayment audits should be established for verification of prices, quantity, quality, timeliness of performance and adherence to prescribed procurement procedures;

Controls should be designed to prevent or minimize the opportunity for duplicate payments to be made;

Specific guidance should exist relating to stamping or mutilating vendors' invoices and to filing support documentation in an orderly way;

Purchase order procedures, designed for efficient procurement of minor items, should be regularly monitored to insure that no abuses exist and that practices do not circumvent the more formal contracting process and controls;

Prescribed forms should be prepared and approved in advance of any government representative committing the agency or unit to the procurement of goods or services;

Documentation should be controlled (numerically and physically), prescribed fiscal procedures adhered to and payments made to all contractors and vendors in a timely manner;

Procedures should exist for inventorying contract property and providing an accounting and reporting on any variances with control records; and

Accounting in the formal records of the governmental agency or unit for the procurement transaction—the initial obligation or encumbrance, any advances to contractors, the disbursement of cash, the withholding of amounts until acceptance or performance, and the contract close-out—should be accounted for in the governmental agency or unit's formal records.

It should be noted that, while end-of-period contract withholdings or payables may exist, contract receivables also may exist. A government agency or unit may advance funds to the contractor; these advances or receivables must be liquidated in accordance with the prescribed formula.

The above controls are related to the issuance of contracts and purchase orders. Under certain conditions, the governmental agency or unit under audit may, itself, be a contractor. This condition could exist, for example, when a state or local governmental unit accepts a contract from the federal government or another governmental organization. Controls over these activities should include plans to:

Insure that the contractual liability is properly reflected in the formal accounting records;

Monitor the governmental unit to determine that the contract service or performance is consistent with the contract conditions;

Provide that money received in advance of performance or billed for services or performance rendered has been properly earned in accordance with the terms of the contract and that end-of-period receivables and liabilities are appropriately valued;

Insure that billings are made currently, collections are monitored and receipts are properly recorded; and

Provide that contract close-out procedures are adhered to and settlements are made in a timely manner.

Audit Considerations

The audit considerations relating to governmental contractual expenses differ somewhat from the procedures typically used in the audit of commercial and institutional organizations. For the most part, the governmental agency or unit is the issuer of the contract, while nongovernmental organizations generally are the recipients of contracts. Thus, the governmental audit procedures must include a test of controls and account balances resulting from the government's position as a recipient of services, rather than as a provider of services. As mentioned above, however, there will be instances when a governmental agency or unit could be the contractor or vendor of services.

Audit procedures or tests that should be considered in examining the reasonableness of contract and purchase expenses might include:

Reviews to determine that the procurement policies and procedures are consistent with applicable laws, statutes and regulations;

Tests to determine that the practices used to solicit proposals or bids from reputable contractors, examine offers, award contracts, make payments, accept services, and close-out contracts are consistent with prescribed policy and procedures;

Examinations to insure consistency of contracts, terms and conditions with governmental policy and procedures;

Tests to insure that contractual obligations or encumbrances, and the liquidation thereof, are proper and timely, and that unliquidated balances at the end of the period reflect the receivables or payables;

Tests to prove the arithmetic accuracy of contractual amounts (payments made, data on invoices received, status of any advances due, discounts taken or earned);

Reviews to assure the correctness of accounting for contract expenses with respect to appropriation or fund, organizations and other required cost accounting or expense distributions;

Examinations to reconcile support documentation (procurement requests, proposals received, contract, invoices, payment schedules, checks) to journal entries, amounts recorded in books of original entry and general ledger accounts;

Tests to ascertain whether purchase order procedures are being used to circumvent the more formal contract award and monitoring procedures;

Tests to determine whether deductions have been taken for taxes and other exemptions to minimize the costs to the governmental unit;

Tests to confirm the status of the contract—the conditions, amounts, payments made, changes or modifications, withholdings, performance or deliveries made and conditions for completion;

Inventory of open or active contracts at the end of period to verify the accuracy of amounts reflected as unliquidated contractual obligations or encumbrances, amounts withheld from contractors and payables due to contractors, and balances of any unliquidated advances due from contractors; and

Reviews to assess the reasonableness of physical inventories of contract-related property, observe counts and reconcile physical inventory to balances in financial accounts.

The following audit procedures might be considered as appropriate in those instances where the governmental agency or unit is a contractor to another governmental organization:

Examination of contract terms and conditions to establish the services or performance to be rendered and to determine the status of actual performance;

Comparison of contract performance and payments received to the reasonableness of the liability or receivables reflected in the formal accounting records;

Tests of costs incurred and charged to contracts for compliance with contract terms and conditions;

Verification that amounts due were properly billed, received, recorded and deposited, and that ending balances of liability or receivable accounts reflect contract status;

Test of close-outs to determine that contracts are closed out properly and promptly, whether the governmental agency or unit is the contractor or the contracting agent;

Examination of the reasonableness of any indirect cost allocation plans and determination of whether the plan is updated annually in support of any indirect costs claimed under federal grants and contracts (OMB Circular A-87);

Confirmation of the status of the contract with the issuer: the conditions, amounts, payments made, performance or deliveries made, changes or modifications, withholdings and conditions for completion; and

Review and confirmation of assets and other property furnished under the contract to assess the appropriateness of accounting and the adequacy of controls.

Audit of Grant Expenses

During the decade of the 1970s, the significance of grant-in-aid programs increased dramatically. Today, governmental expenditures under grant programs dwarf all other types of expenditures. At the federal level, alone, there exist over 1,000 grant programs, administered by over 50 departments, agencies, commissions and councils. Grant agreements often require the performance or delivery of services in much the same manner as do contracts. A formal document often is executed, terms and conditions are met, payments are made, delivery and acceptance criteria exist, and, in many cases, a formal process of grant close-out is required.

Definitions

The audit of grant expenses provides unique audit problems. For example, at the federal level, departments and agencies are typically grantors, responsible for the award and monitoring of grant funds disbursed to grantees. Whereas, at the state and local government levels, these departments and agencies simultaneously may be grantees of a federal program and grantors or subgrantors issuing grants to other organizations. Under these conditions, the audit procedures must consider the appropriate tests to be made of grantor and grantee roles in arriving at conclusions relating to the reasonableness of reported grant funds.

At the federal level, while the several federal grantor departments and agencies may have various implementing regulations, these regulations can not be contrary to the government-wide requirements issued by the Office of Management and Budget. These requirements are:

OMB Circular A-102 (also referred to as Financial Management Circular 74-7)—*Uniform Administrative Requirements for Grants-in-Aid to State and Local Governments.*

OMB Circular A-87 (also referred to as Financial Management Circular 74-4)—*Principles for Determining Costs Applicable to Grants and Contracts with State and Local Governments.*

At the federal level, pursuant to Circular A-102, the term "grant" or "grant-in-aid" means

> . . . money, or property provided in lieu of money, paid or furnished by the federal government to a state or local government under programs that provide financial assistance through grant or contractual arrangements. It does not include technical assistance programs or other assistance in the form of revenue sharing, loans, loan guarantees or insurance.

The term "local government" includes a county, municipality, city, town, township, local public authority, special district, intrastate district, council of governments, sponsor group representative organization or other regional or interstate government entity.

A similar definition of "grant" or "grant-in-aid" is prescribed for state and local governmental units by the *GAAFR:*

> A contribution by one governmental unit to another unit. The contribution is usually made to aid in the support of a specified function (for example, education), but it is sometimes also for general purposes.

With few exceptions, the conditions appearing in Circulars A-102 and A-87 are applicable to state and local grantees and to their subgrantees, to whom federal funds are transferred. Knowledge of these circulars is a prerequisite to the conduct of governmental audits, since compliance with their conditions is a determination necessary to an assessment of the allowability of costs received or claimed by state and local governments under federal grants.

Grants may be made for many purposes, including research, construction, studies and program operations. While several classifications of grants exist, the more common include:

Formula grants—issued pursuant to law, with the entitlement or amount being determined by the Congress; minimal discretion is exercised by the grantor.

Block grants—issued for broad program purposes (such as education, transit, employment programs).

Project grants—issued by grantors for specific services or performance, with conditions similar to contracts, for such purposes as research, pilot, training or planning programs.

Construction grants—awarded only for construction of such capital assets as buildings and of permanent facilities.

Each of these grants has differing terms and conditions that will govern the allowability and collectability of funds from the grantor. Typically, if a subgrantee is involved, specific monitoring responsibilities also are mandated upon the state or local grantee.

Transaction Analysis

In governmental finance, a state or lcoal governmental unit might be a grantee for a federal grant. However, the execution of an agreement to accept grant funds and make expenditures for grant purposes must be approved by the state or local legislature. All expenditures must be made pursuant to the statutes governing the grantee organization and must be in compliance with the specific terms and conditions of the grant agreement. Exhibit 17-3 illustrates the activities and documentation often required in issuing and accounting for a grant.

Inter-governmental grants often provide for a system of advance funding under the federal letter-of-credit procedures. The letter of credit, as defined in OMB Circular A-102, is an instrument, certified by an authorized grantor official, permitting a grantee to draw funds when needed from the U.S. Treasury. Letters of credit are used when there is a continuing relationship between grantees and a federal grantor agency for at least 12 months, and total advances will be above a prescribed amount. Under this method, grantors may withhold payments where (1) the grantee has failed to comply with program objectives, grant conditions or federal reporting requirements; or (2) the grantee is indebted to the United States, and collection of the indebtedness would not impair accomplishment of the objectives of the grant program sponsored by the federal government.

Exhibit 17-3

Overview of Grants Transactions or Documentation

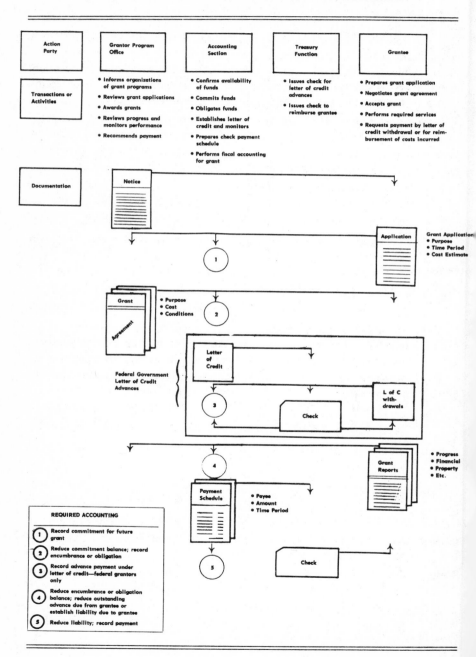

Internal Controls

The designation of a grantee department or of the appropriate fund under which a grant is to be monitored is dependent upon the conditions of the grant and the structure of the recipient government. A basic principle, though, is that controls and accounting procedure should be examined to insure that all costs charged to the grant are in strict accord with the grant agreement. Noncompliance with the grant conditions could jeopardize subsequent reimbursement and might ultimately lead to an actual disallowance of claims, thus affecting payments received and any outstanding receivables.

As mentioned, state and local government units may, in turn, be expected to exercise grantor-like responsibilities over their subgrantees. Controls therefore should exist to insure that subgrantee actions and accounting activities are consistent with the governing grantor's requirements.

Knowledge of the manner in which grants are awarded and of the existence of governing policy and procedures must be acquired early in the audit to insure that an internal control questionnaire addresses all pertinent aspects of the financial process.

An adequate system of controls for grant activities should, as a minimum, provide for:

Clearly written and widely disseminated policies and procedures relating to the award, acceptance, performance, monitoring, reporting, accounting and closing of grants;

Consistency of the governmental grant policy and procedures with any legal or administrative requirements and, to the extent possible, of grant practices with the grantee's overall management and financial requirements;

Procedures for the award and issuance of any grants to subgrantees, and the requirements for satisfactory performance by these organizations;

Sound practices, consistent with federal requirements, for withdrawing funds under a federal letter of credit;

A system of prepayment audits for verification of invoices, claims and other requests for expenditure of funds under grants with respect to compliance with the grant conditions;

Appropriate checks to prevent or minimize the opportunity for duplicate payments to be charged to grant accounts;

An orderly system for marking or mutilating and filing supporting documents;

Accounting, in the formal records of the governmental grantee and/or grantor, for the full cycle of the grant transaction (the initial obligations or encumbrances, advances, disbursement of cash, withheld amounts, close-out of grant project);

Procedures for end-of-period internal audit and review to confirm the accuracy of grant receivables and payables in compliance with the grant terms and conditions;

Procedures for inventorying grant property and providing an accounting and reporting on variances from the procurement or control records;

Procedures for depositing grant receipts immediately and intact; and

An indirect cost allocation plan, updated annually, pursuant to federal contract and grant cost principles.

Controls, similar to the above, that are applicable to state and local grantors also would have to exist at the federal grantor level. Other federal grantor controls might include:

Clearly written and widely disseminated policies and procedures for soliciting and evaluating grant applications;

Assessment of the adequacy of grant applications approval process, consistent with the intent of Congress and the criteria set forth in any authorizing or appropriation legislation;

A system by which the grantor continuously monitors the performance of grantees (in executing the grant conditions, meeting funding requirements, reporting activities and closing out the grant at completion);

A program of audit, providing for periodic on-site evaluations of grantees' performance and compliance with grant conditions;

An internal audit of the grantor's management and financial procedures and practices for monitoring the overall program achievements and preparing reports to the Office of Management and Budget and the Treasury Department; and

Accounting in the formal records of the federal grantor for the full cycle of the grant transaction (the initial obligation, advances made and outstanding, disbursements of cash, drawdowns under letters of credit, withheld amounts, property and other resources furnished to grantees, and close-out of the grant).

Careful assessments should be made by all grantees of the controls and other procedures required by the grantor for complying with the grant terms and conditions. Circumstances will exist where the normal controls of the grantee may be deemed inadequate by the grantor or not in strict accord with the grant requirements. In such cases, where possible, the grantee organization might be able to revise or refine the normal controls to better accommodate the grantor's requirements. If such an accommodation is not possible, the grantee should, when possible, obtain a formal waiver of such grant requirements from the grantor. A special condition is necessary to avoid subsequent discussions concerning the adequacy of controls and risking disallowances of otherwise proper claims.

Audit Considerations

The audit procedures for examining the reasonableness of expenditures for grants should be established from two perspectives: (1) those audit procedures required to assess the performance and financial position of a governmental grantor, and (2) those audit procedures required to assess the performance and financial position of grantees or subgrantees. While the federal government is almost always a grantor, state and local governmental units simultaneously could be a grantee of the federal government and a grantor of funds to other governmental units and organizations.

Audit procedures and tests that should be considered in examining the reasonableness of grant expenditures might include:

An examination of grant terms and conditions to ascertain compliance with authorizing and appropriation legislation;

A test of grant transactions related to selection of grantees, award of grant, control and monitoring of grantee performance, review of grantee reports and closing out of grant projects;

Tests to insure that grant obligations or encumbrances, and the liquidation thereof, are proper and timely, and that unliquidated balances at the end of the period reflect the receivables or payables of the grant project or program;

Proof of the arithmetic accuracy of grant amounts (payments made, status of any advances made, balances owed or due);

Confirmation of the status of the grant (the conditions, amounts, payments made or received, changes or modifications, withholdings, conditions for completion);

Reconciliation of supporting documentation (grant authorizations, executed grant agreements, payment schedules, reporting received, checks issued, records of outstanding balances) to journal entries, amounts recorded in books of original entry and general ledger accounts;

Determination of the correctness of the accounting of grant transactions with respect to appropriation or funds, organizations and other required cost accounting or expense distribution and the grant terms and conditions;

Tests of the appropriateness of receivables and payables due under the grant programs to ascertain that the balances are accurate and in compliance with the grant terms and conditions;

Tests to determine that acquisitions made under grant programs and projects were exempted from various federal and other taxes to minimize the cost to the grant;

Inventories of the balance of open or active grants at the end of the period to verify the accuracy of amounts reflected as unliquidated grant obligations or encumbrances and any amounts owed or due;

Tests of inventory balances, physical counts, and verification of assets in possession of grantors, grantees and/or subgrantees;

Examination of the reasonableness of any indirect cost allocation plans and determination of whether the plan is updated annually in support of any indirect costs claimed under federal grants and contracts (OMB Circular A-87).

Audit of Inter-Agency or Intra-Government Expenses

Definitions

At all levels of government, departments, agencies and units procure services from other agencies or units. Significant funds often are transferred between organizational entities and from one appropriation or fund to another. Typically, these inter-agency or intra-governmental transactions relate to space, facilities, equipment, supplies, transportation, utilities and, recently, computerized data processing assistance.

Transaction Analysis

It should be noted that, while this section emphasizes the nature of inter-agency services that could be rendered by one governmental unit to another, the same services can and often are secured, in many instances, from nongovernment sources as well. Further, depending upon the nature of the service being procured, the receiving governmental unit could reflect the transaction as an asset or an expenditure in its accounting records.

Methods of Financing Inter-Agency Transactions

There are several methods by which the agency receiving the service can make "payment" for or finance the goods and services received. These methods include:

Deposit accounts and advances—made to the agency providing the goods or services to assist that agency by making operating funds available. The funds advanced would be shown as a receivable by the advancing agency and as a liability by the provider agency until performance is completed.

Transfers to appropriation accounts—made from the appropriation or funds of the agency procuring the goods or services to the appropriation of the provider agency. The procuring agency transfers its authority to obligate and expend funds to the providing agency. Upon performance, the procuring agency then will reflect the assets, expenses and expenditures on its own accounts.

Reimbursements between agencies—require the performing agency to bill other agencies for the reimbursements for goods delivered or services performed. Appropriate receivables and liabilities a.e established until performance has been rendered and accepted by the buying agency.

Working Capital and Enterprise Funds

In many instances, the fund of the providing agency is referred to as a working capital fund or a revolving fund. These funds are distinguishable from enterprise funds in that the former provide goods or services only to governmental entities. Services of an enterprise fund, on the other hand, also could be provided to the public. Examples of the latter would include public utility-type services, such as water, sewerage, gas, electricity and other commercial-type activities (such as hospitals, airports, transportation, recreational facilities).

The GAAFR provides detailed descriptions on operations, budgets and preferred accounting for the activities provided by both intra-governmental or internal service funds and enterprise funds for state and local governmental units. At the federal level, the General Services Administration is often the providing agency, although some departments perform functions similar to the GSA for their constituent agencies. In another instance, the Civil Service Commission, the trainer of the federal government, provides services to other departments and agencies and is compensated by a transfer of funds to its appropriation account by the benefitting agencies.

Internal Controls

The controls for inter-agency or intra-governmental transactions generally must be the same as those for procurement transactions that involve nongovernment parties. In addition to the controls in existence for other expenditures, the following controls should be considered to monitor inter-agency, internal service or intra-governmental expenses:

A procedure for obtaining proper approval or authorization in advance of obligating or encumbering an agency's appropriation or fund for inter-agency transactions;

A procedure for completing, processing and controlling documents affecting fund transfers or payments;

A system of prepayment audit or review to provide the receiving agency's officials with some assurance as to the propriety of the requested payment or fund transfer;

Published procedures and policies to provide guidance to personnel on the use of these services and the method by which payment must be made; and

Formal agreements executed for goods and services not provided on a routine or regular basis, such as:

letters of agreements,

blanket contracts (under which work orders might be issued as required),

job orders for services as requested,

personnel arrangements for inter-agency loan of staff,

contracts for maintenance and other support services, and

formal requisitions provided by the performing agency.

The obligations or encumbrances for these transactions must be monitored in the same manner as is used for other transactions, since an over-expenditure or violation of an appropriation or fund ceiling would require the same reporting to government executives and the legislature as would other transactions of the government.

Audit Procedures

The audit criteria or cautions applied to inter-agency or intra-governmental transactions should not vary from those applied to the audit of other transactions. The reasonableness of the amounts reflected in the accounts can be suspected for the same reasons—poor controls, unauthorized procurements, improper accounting, diversion of goods or assets to personal use, or violations of appropriation or fund conditions. Thus, in addition to the normal audit procedures, an audit of inter-agency or intra-governmental expenses should consider:

A review of appropriation or fund legislation to ascertain the nature of inter-agency or intra-governmental activities that might be procured;

An examination of policy, procedures and other guidance to determine consistency with appropriation or fund legislation;

A test of transactions to assess whether the practices and the nature of expenses incurred are consistent with policy and the law;

A test of the appropriateness, accuracy and completeness of documentation to support the initial obligation or encumbrances, the later expenditure, asset or expense, and disbursement entries;

Tests of the correctness of the accounting for inter-agency or intra-governmental transactions with respect to the appropriation or fund, organizations and other required cost accounting or expense distributions;

A reconciliation of support documentation and transaction coding to journal entries, books of original entry and the general ledger accounts;

An examination of the formal documentation requesting services or goods (except routine services or goods) for definition of goods or services to be provided, quality and quantity, period of performance, unit and total cost to be incurred and acceptance conditions;

A confirmation from the providing agency of the quality and quantity of services delivered for comparison to the audited agency's receiving and inventory records;

A review of inventory records and, where possible, observation of the inventorying of supplies, materials and equipment;

A reconciliation of results of physical inventory to balances in financial accounts; and

A confirmation of the appropriateness of end-of-period receivables and payables due to or due from other agencies.

Reporting of Expenditures and Expenses

Illustrative financial statements and accompanying explanations relating to governmental expenditures and expenses appear in Chapters 18 and 19.

Part V
Reporting of Governmental Activities

Chapter 18
Illustrative Financial Statements—Federal Governmental Units

Introduction
Federal Governmental Reporting Requirements
Reporting by the Federal Government
Illustrative Agency Financial Statements
Publication and Audit of Federal Financial Statements

Introduction

The form and content of governmental financial statements vary between levels of government. Federal government agencies are required to comply with a few standard reports, related to monitoring compliance with appropriation laws and expenditures related to a single agency. State and local governments generally comply with the requirements of *Governmental Accounting, Auditing and Financial Reporting* (GAAFR), which has gained wide acceptance as the authoritative body of generally accepted accounting principles applicable to state and local governmental units.

At all levels of government, the accounting and reporting of legal compliance is essential. Although financial statements can be prepared in a manner to comply with both legal requirements and generally accepted accounting principles, there may be instances where the two are irreconcilable. In these instances, the reporting of legal compliance must take precedence over accounting conventions. Often, though, notes to the statements, separate schedules or other financial analyses will permit the expression of an opinion that the statements are consistent with generally accepted accounting procedure as well as in compliance with applicable laws.

312

Federal Governmental Reporting Requirements

There exists a considerable body of requirements relating to federal governmental accounting, auditing and financial reporting. The U.S. General Accounting Office is required by law to prescribe the accounting and reporting principles for government agencies. These requirements appear in the *GAO Manual for Guidance of Federal Agencies* (Title 2—Accounting Principles and Standards and Internal Audit Guidelines). The ability of an agency to meet these requirements is considered by the GAO when it approves the accounting systems design of an agency, another responsibility of the GAO. The general reporting requirements, set forth in Title 2, for all reports of federal agencies address a number of considerations, such as:

All essential facts relating to scope, purpose and time period of the report must be clearly displayed;

The financial data must be derived from accounts maintained on a basis consistent with the prior period, with material changes in accounting being clearly explained;

Bias, obscurement of facts and presentation of misleading information must be avoided;

Basis of data, other than the accounting system, must be clearly explained;

Consistent and nontechnical terminology must be used;

The content and form of reports of federal agencies must comply with specific requirements of laws and regulations; and

Reports containing classified information must comply with applicable national security restrictions.

Reporting by the Federal Government

Consolidated Financial Statements for Federal Government

In 1976 and 1977, prototype financial statements for annual recurring reporting on the financial condition of the federal government were published by the Treasury Department. These consolidated statements, though preliminary in nature, attempted to provide comprehensive financial statements covering the full range of federal government activities. The prototype statements included the accounts of all significant agencies and funds comprising the Unified Budget of the United States. While useful as an overview, these statements consolidated the financial results of many governmental agencies and merged the financial resources provided by many appropriations. It should be noted that no audit has been made of these statements, and that the methods of deriving the consolidated account values do not represent the results of applying generally accepted accounting principles. Considerable problems and issues must be resolved before comprehensive, consolidated statements can be prepared for the federal government in accordance with generally accepted accounting principles. A few of the significant, acknowledged problems and issues relate to such subjects as valuing assets, presenting liabilities for pensions, selecting appropriate methods of depreciation and valuing fixed assets, and determining procedures for properly accruing costs and taxes.

Federal Agency Financial Reports

Description of Required Financial Reports

The head of each federal department or agency is responsible for preparing financial statements reflecting the financial position, results of operations, sources and application of funds, status of appropriation balances and status of individual funds. The GAO has interpreted these reporting requirements to mean that the following statements or reports should be prepared:

Statement of assets and liabilities—a balance sheet on the program and activities of the agency, displaying assets, liabilities and the investment of the federal government.

Statement of changes in investment of the United States—a report on the fund balance of an appropriation or of several appropriations for which an agency is responsible.

Report on status of appropriations and fund balances—required by the Office of Management and Budget for agencies financed by appropriations and for revolving funds and trust funds.

Statement of operations—a statement disclosing revenues and costs for agencies carrying on business-type activities and programs or showing revenues classified by source and applied costs by budget activities for other types of agencies.

Statement of sources and application of funds—a report displaying all sources and applications of funds on a gross basis.

Report on agency transactions—required by the Treasury Department for cash and other transactions relating to the financial conditions and operations of the agency and to the appropriations for which an agency is responsible.

Other reports—as required by Congress, its committees, or other agencies of the government.

At the federal level, an agency may be responsible for more than one appropriation. Conversely, a single appropriation may finance the activities of more than one agency. In the latter instance, one agency may be responsible for the consolidated reporting of the appropriation, or each of the involved agencies may report only on their activities under the appropriation.

The fund accounting for the various appropriations should be integrated in a single accounting system for the agency. The integrated accounting system should be on the accrual basis, with the records reflecting the complete accounting cycle of transactions, including the status of the appropriations, apportionments, allotments, obligations, accrued expenditures, cash disbursements, cash receipts, cost of work performed or services rendered, property, liabilities, and any income and expenses.

Requirements for Financial Reports

The GAO has prescribed several requirements that must be met by the federal agencies in connection with the preparation and distribution of financial reports. These requirements generally refer to fund accounting and to the accurate reporting of legal appropriations for which an agency is accountable. Other requirements address specific issues that could result in misleading reporting, absent proper disclosure and explanation. The following listing is a summary of the GAO's requirements for financial reports as set forth in Title 2:

Inter-agency and inter-fund transactions should be separately identified in agency records and statements to permit proper treatment in consolidated financial statements;

Foreign currency, not readily convertible, may be stated in dollar terms, provided that there is disclosure that the amounts shown are not realizable in U.S. dollars;

Estimates of uncollectible accounts receivables should be separately disclosed in the financial reports;

Receivables, collectible in foreign currency and not freely convertible, may be stated in dollars at the appropriate conversion rate if there is proper disclosure that the receivables are not realizable in U.S. currency;

The nature of significant property values should be clearly disclosed;

Authorized, but undisbursed, loans should be disclosed;

The method of depreciation for major classes of depreciable assets should be disclosed;

Extraordinary items of revenue and cost should be shown separately from the results of operations or ordinary items;

Contingent liabilities of material amounts should be disclosed and explained;

Reports on federal insurance, pension and similar programs measured on an actuarial basis should disclose the accrued current costs and estimated liability to make future payments;

Major elements of federal investments should be disclosed and changes summarized for each fiscal period in a separate schedule;

The cost and related liability for accrued annual leave should be accrued and disclosed as of the close of each fiscal year;

Cost incurred and paid by other agencies should be separately identified;

Realized gains and losses on exchange transactions should be disclosed;

Unusual costs or nonrecurring losses should be separately classified;

The exclusion of significant costs applicable to an activity being reported upon should be clearly explained, with estimates provided of the amounts involved; and

Net increases or decreases in liability for annual leave should be classified as an operating cost for the year, at least at the appropriation level of reporting.

While the above requirements generally would be applicable to the financial reports of all federal agencies, specific laws, regulations and other requirements may not permit uniform compliance with these criteria. Care must be exercised when examining financial reports of federal agencies; and inquiries must be made related to the basis for reporting, the treatment of operating and capital expenditures and the possible existence of other costs that benefited the operations of the agency.

Illustrative Agency Financial Statements

Heads of federal agencies have the authority to prepare those financial statements that best meet the technical reporting requirements of the agency, the governing appropriation laws and the needs of such central agencies as the Office of Management and Budget and the Treasury Department. While financial statements are expected to meet management needs, other government-wide needs must be recognized in designing the statement structure and in defining the level of detail and content that will appear in the financial statements.

The illustrative statements, which appear in Exhibits 18-1 through 18-5, relate to an agency whose activities are financed primarily from appropriations and, minimally, from other sources of receipts. The statements are based on an illustrative case published in Title 2 of the *GAO Manual for Guidance of Federal Agencies*. Annotations and other inserts have been added for explanatory purposes. (Notes on the annotations follow each chart.) Fiscal year dates have been revised to reflect the fiscal year effective after October 1, 1978.

Statement of Assets and Liabilities (Exhibit 18-1)

The statement of assets and liabilities, with some minor exceptions, is comparable to the balance sheet prepared for commercial organizations and for governmental entities carrying on business-type activities. A major statement difference relates to the net worth section of this statement. In the federal government, the residual of total assets less total liabilities is referred to as the investment of the government.

Exhibit 18-1
An Agency Financed from Appropriations
Statement of Assets and Liabilities
September 30, 1979

Assets

Current Assets:

1	Fund balances with U. S. Treasury	$ xx,xxx	
2	Deposits in transit	x,xxx	
3	Undeposited collections	xxx	
4	Imprest fund	xxx	
5	Accounts receivable—repayments to appropriations	x,xxx	
6	Inventories	xx,xxx	
7	Prepaid expenses	xxx	
8	Travel advances	x,xxx	$ xx,xxx

Fixed Assets:

9	Buildings equipment	xx,xxx	
	Less accumulated depreciation	x,xxx	xx,xxx
	Total Assets		$ xx,xxx

Liabilities and Investment of the United States Government

Current Liabilities:

10	Disbursements in transit		$ x,xxx	
11	Accounts payable to others		xx,xxx	
12	Accrued liabilities		x,xxx	
13	Deposit fund liabilities:			
	Employee's bond deductions	$ xxx		
	Employee's tax deductions	xxx		
	Employee's FICA deductions	xx		
	Employer's share of FICA	xx	xxx	$ xx,xxx

Other Liabilities:

14	Liability for imprest fund advances	xxx	
15	Liability for accrued leave	x,xxx	x,xxx

Total Liabilities:

Investment of the United States Government

16	Invested capital	xx,xxx	
17	Unexpended appropriations	xx,xxx	xx,xxx
	Total Liabilities and Investment of the United States Government		$ xx,xxx

Assets

Assets of a federal agency have been defined by the GAO, in Title 2, as things of value owned, plus prepayments and deferred expenses that represent charges against future accounting periods. As in commercial organizations, assets are further classified as current, fixed and other assets. Current assets would include unrestricted funds and other assets convertible or available to support agency or governmental activities within a one-year period. Fixed assets are assets of a longer-term character, whose benefits will accrue to more than one accounting period.

Current Assets

1. **Fund Balances with U.S. Treasury.**—This account represents the balances of congressionally legislated appropriations and is available for disbursement in accordance with the governing legislation. The account is the governmental equivalent of the corporate cash balance. A separate account must be maintained for each appropriation for which the agency is responsible.

2. **Deposits in Transit.**—This account reflects the monies collected by the agency and transmitted to a governmental depositary for deposit on the date of the financial statement. This balance indicates that the agency has not received a confirmation of in-transit deposits from the authorized depositaries as of the reporting date.

3. **Undeposited Collections.**—This account reflects cash receipts, in the possession of the agency, but not yet submitted to the authorized depositaries.

4. **Imprest Funds.**—This account represents the balance of cash advanced by the U.S. Treasury Department to agency imprest fund cashiers. Within the federal government, such funds initially are financed by the Treasury Department. As disbursements are made, entries for these costs are made in the agency's records. These imprest fund balances must be replenished by charging expenditures to the agency appropriations. Each imprest fund must be offset by a liability account showing the amount due to the Treasury Department for imprest fund advances.

5. **Accounts Receivable—Repayments to Appropriations.**—This account reflects amounts due from other agencies for materials or services or for overpayments or advances made by the agency, for which repayment must be made.

6. **Inventories.**—This account may reflect the cost of materials or supplies, work in process or finished goods, depending upon the objective of the agency. The inventories typically are valued at cost, unless conditions or circumstances warrant an alternative valuation.

7. **Prepaid Expenses.**—This account reflects expenses paid during one accounting period that will benefit later accounting periods, such as rent, utility expenses or insurance. Many agencies may account for such assets as

expenses during the period of purchase or disbursement, rather than in the benefiting period.

8. Travel Advances.—This account reflects the amount of travel advances outstanding to employees. At the time of advance, the disbursement is not treated as an expenditure or cost to the appropriation. When an accounting is made by the employee, the advance is liquidated and settled, and the amount of the travel expense recorded.

Fixed Assets

9. **Buildings and Equipment** (less accumulated depreciation).—These accounts reflect the cost incurred by the government in acquiring or constructing such fixed assets as buildings and equipment. The cost of a building would include equipment and fixtures that normally are required for the type of building involved and that are permanently affixed. Machinery and other equipment, not a part of the realty, are recorded as equipment.

The Accumulated Depreciation account is charged for the sum of the depreciation related to depreciable assets. It should be noted that many federal agencies do not formally recognize depreciation in their financial statements.

Liabilities and Investment of the United States Government

The GAO, in Title 2, has defined liabilities in a manner similar to that used in the corporate sector. Under the accrual basis of accounting, liabilities have been defined as amounts payable to others, usually as a result of the receipt of funds, property or services. It should be noted that liabilities are distinguished from obligations of the federal government. Obligations best may be viewed as commitments or reservations of the agency's expenditure authority, which may mature into a liability in the future, but which presently represent anticipated services or work to be performed or undelivered orders.

Most federal agencies, financed by appropriations, are concerned with current and other liabilities. There is minimal opportunity for incurring long-term liabilities.

Current Liabilities

10. **Disbursements in Transit.**—This account reflects the amount of disbursement vouchers, which have been submitted to the U.S. Treasury Department, requesting that checks be issued, but for which notification of check issuance has not been received.

11. **Accounts Payable to Others.**—This account reflects the amount of the liability due to others for performance rendered or materials or supplies received by the agency.

12. **Accrued Liabilities.**—This account reflects the estimated amounts of liabilities outstanding at the end of the accounting period. Deliveries may

have been made or services rendered to the agency, but no billing has been received by the agency. Additionally, a billing may have been received, but, at statement date, a voucher has not been prepared authorizing payment.

13. **Deposit Fund Liabilities.**—These accounts reflect payroll-related liabilities for deductions and the employer's share of FICA. Such accounts would apply for those employees who are not under the federal retirement system. The accounting for civil service retirements would be included in the records of the U.S. Civil Service Commission.

Other Liabilities

14. **Liability for Imprest Fund Advances.**—This account reflects the liability due to the U.S. Treasury Department for funds advanced to the agency for imprest fund purposes. It is a contra-account to the current asset account, Imprest Fund.

15. **Liability for Accrued Leave.**—This account reflects the value of accrued vacation leave earned by current employees; when leave is taken, this account is charged.

Investment of the United States Government

GAO has defined the investment of the United States in the assets of a federal agency to be the residual equity of the government after accounting for all known liabilities and investments or equities of others. There could be several major elements of the investment of the government, consisting of additions and reductions. Additions to the investment would include such transactions as congressional appropriations, advances from the U.S. Treasury, property and services obtained by the government without reimbursement, donations received and the accumulated net income from any operations. Reductions of investment could be related to funds returned to the U.S. Treasury, property transferred to other federal agencies without reimbursement and an accumulated net loss from any operations.

Each of these elements, to the extent present during a fiscal period, should be separately disclosed and explained in the financial statements.

16. **Invested Capital.**—This amount is a summary of the several accounts comprising the investment of the government in the activities of the agency.

17. **Unexpended Appropriations.**—This account is a summary account of the several subsidiary accounts comprising the unexpended balance of the agency's appropriation. This account should be detailed further in supporting schedules.

Exhibit 18-2
An Agency Financed from Appropriations
Statement of Changes in the Investment
of the United States Government
For the Fiscal Year ended September 30, 1979

18	Balance of Investment of the United States Government, October 1, 1978		$ x
	Add—Increases:		
19	Appropriations		
20	Income	$xxx,xxx	
21	Transfers of property from government agencies	xx,xxx	
		x,xxx	xxx,xxx
	Less—Decreases:		xxx,xxx
22	Expenses		
23	Funds returned to U. S. Treasury	xxx,xxx	
		xxx	xxx,xxx
	Balance of Investment of the United States Government, September 30, 1979		$ xx,xxx
	Composed of:		
24	Invested capital		$ xx,xxx
	Unexpended appropriations		
25	Unapportioned appropriations	$ x,xxx	
26	Unallotted apportionments	x,xxx	
27	Unobligated allotments	x,xxx	
28	Unliquidated obligations	x,xxx	xx,xxx $ xx,xxx

Statement of Changes in Investment (Exhibit 18-2)

In some respects, the statement of changes in investment of a federal agency is comparable to the statement of changes in fund balances when accounting for funds of local governments. The statement attempts to portray the additions, decreases and residual balance of the government's investment in the agency's activities. In addition, the elements comprising the end-of-period investment balance usually are detailed.

18. **Balance of Investment of the United States Government.**—This account should reflect the government's investment as of the last day of the prior fiscal period. (The illustration presumes that the agency is a newly established entity, reporting at the end of the first fiscal year of existence.)

19. **Appropriations.**—This account is a summary of the subsidiary accounts, reflecting the amount of the funds appropriated by Congress to support the activities of the agency. The detailed records should provide for an account for each appropriation.

20. **Income.**—This account reflects amounts received by the agency for work performed or services rendered. This amount should be explained further in a separate schedule of income and expenses (if any). Depending upon the authorizing and appropriation legislation, these receipts may or may not be available for obligation and use to support the activities of the agency.

21. **Transfers of Property from Government Agencies.**—This account reflects the increase in asset value realized from receipt of property transferred to the agency by other government agencies. (The accounting for such property shall not be for a value that is less than its estimated useful value.)

22. **Expenses.**—This amount reflects the amounts expended by the agency for its operations. This amount should be explained further in a separate schedule of income and expenses (if any).

23. **Funds Returned to the U.S. Treasury.**—This amount reflects funds, received by the agency, which are not available to the agency for obligation and support of its operations. Unless funds are appropriated, or Congress authorizes and appropriates receipts or income of agency for use in its operations, an agency has no authority to expend this income. The income received then must be returned to the Treasury Department and reported to the Congress, the Treasury Department and the Office of Management and Budget.

24. **Invested Capital.**—This amount is a summary of the several accounts comprising the accumulated investment of the government in the activities of the agency.

In addition to the accumulated invested capital, the remainder of the investment of the government consists of the balance of the unexpended appropriations. The total amount of the unexpended appropriations usually will consist of:

unapportioned appropriations;

unallotted apportionments;

unobligated allotments; and

unliquidated obligations.

A separate set of accounts for the unexpended appropriation amount must be maintained for each appropriation or fund for which the agency is responsible.

25. **Unapportioned Appropriations.**—This account reflects the amount of the agency's appropriations, authorized by the Congress, for which the Office of Management and Budget has not, as yet, provided an apportionment. Until apportioned by the OMB, the agency is precluded from allotting, obligating or expending this portion of the appropriation.

26. **Unallotted Apportionments.**—This account reflects the portion of the agency's appropriation that is available for allotment to operations or other authorized activities. These funds have been apportioned by the OMB, and the allotment decision now rests with agency officials.

27. **Unobligated Allotments.**—This account reflects that portion of appropriated funds, allotted by agency officials to specific agency operations or activities, which has not, as yet, been obligated by program officials.

28. **Unliquidated Obligations.**—This account reflects the balance of the unliquidated obligations or undelivered orders or services to be received. For each amount, pursuant to law, a formal document or agreement must exist. The balance of this account will be reduced as performance, services or deliveries are received, regardless of when the agency actually is billed or makes payment. A separate accounting will continue to be made, by appropriation, for a period of two years after the expiration of the appropriation. After this time, the unliquidated obligations are merged into a single grouping of accounts referred to as the "M" or "merged" accounts. These amounts still remain available to meet all prior valid obligations of the agency, but the accounting and reporting effort is considerably reduced.

Statement of Status of Appropriations (Exhibit 18-3)

A statement of the status of an agency's appropriations often is required to provide details and further explain the total of the appropriated fund available to the agency for its operations or activities, and to give an accounting of funds expended during the fiscal period. The statement of an agency with multiple appropriations would be correspondingly more detailed or require additional supporting schedules. In practice, the Office of Management and Budget prescribes the format for appropriation status reports. This format will vary, depending upon instructions given to the agencies.

29. **Total Appropriation and Reimbursements.**—This amount reflects the total funds available under congressional appropriations for expenditure by the agency. In this illustration, reimbursements to the agency for work performed, services rendered or materials provided are available for reobligation and re-expenditure. Absent this reobligation and re-expenditure authority, any commitments and disbursements of these funds by the agency would be in violation of the Constitutional provision that funds may be disbursed only pursuant to an appropriation made by Congress.

30. **Unexpended Balance of Appropriation.**—This amount is comprised of the several accounts reflecting the status of unexpended funds. The status of these funds varies for several reasons, as indicated in Exhibit 18-2:

A portion of the appropriation has not been apportioned by the Office of Management and Budget (the unapportioned appropriation);

Another amount of the appropriation has yet to be allotted by the agency head to the various operating officials of the agency for obligation to support the agency's operations or activities (the unallotted apportionment);

Another amount, while allotted to operating officials has not been committed or obligated by these ófficials for expenditure for agency operations or activities (the unobligated allotment);

While some funds have been obligated, an amount of these obligations remains unliquidated or outstanding at the end of the accounting period (the unliquidated obligation).

Exhibit 18-3
An Agency Financed from Appropriations
Statement of Status of Appropriations
September 30, 1979

Current Fiscal Year Appropriation

Appropriation		$xxx,xxx
Reimbursements		xx,xxx
29 Total appropriation and reimbursements		$xxx,xxx
Less: Unexpended appropriation at September 30, 1979		
Unapportioned appropriation	x,xxx	
Unallotted apportionments	x,xxx	
Unobligated allotments	x,xxx	
Unobligated balance of appropriation	xx,xxx	
Unliquidated obligations (Undelivered orders)	x,xxx	
30 Unexpended balance of appropriation		xx,xxx
Current appropriation expended in current fiscal year		$xxx,xxx

31   Prior Fiscal Year's Appropriations

Unliquidated obligations, October 1, 1978	xxx	
Less: Unliquidated obligations, September 30, 1979	xxx	
Prior appropriations expended in current fiscal year		xxx
32 Total appropriation expenditures		$xxx,xxx

Depending upon the legislation, an agency may be required to obligate its appropriation within a specified time period, after which the authority to obligate or expend lapses and the funds are no longer available to the agency. Similarly, Congress also may require, by law, not only that the agency obligate the appropriated funds within a specified period, but also that the funds must be actually expended by a fixed date. Obligations or expenditures made after the expiration of these dates are illegal; and a detailed accounting is required to Congress, the President, the OMB, the Treasury Department and the General Accounting Office.

31. **Prior Fiscal Year's Appropriation.**—In federal accounting, the unliquidated obligations of the prior fiscal year represent carryover funds that generally are available for expenditure or settling of obligations in the next year. The unliquidated obligations would constitute an additional sum of funds that are available for expenditure in the accounting period. The balances of unliquidated obligations for several fiscal years must be accounted for and reported separately.

Exhibit 18-4
An Agency Financed from Appropriations
Statement of Operations
For the fiscal year ended September 30, 1979

Income:			
33 Sales		$ xx,xxx	
Other income		xx	
Total income			$ xx,xxx
34 **Expenses:**			
Direct costs:			
Direct labor		xxx,xxx	
Direct materials		xx,xxx	xxx,xxx
Salaries and wages		xx,xxx	
Travel		x,xxx	
Freight		x,xxx	
Telephone and telegraph		x,xxx	
Heat, light, and power		x,xxx	
Rent		x,xxx	
Printing		x,xxx	
Materials and supplies		x,xxx	
Expendable equipment		x,xxx	
Employer's share of FICA taxes		xxx	
Employer's share of group life insurance		xxx	
Employer's share of civil service retirement		x,xxx	
Depreciation		x,xxx	
Annual leave		x,xxx	
Other overhead expense		xx	xx,xxx
Total expenses			xxx,xxx
Net Expenses			$xxx,xxx

32. **Total Appropriation Expenditures.**—This amount is the total of expenditures made by the agency. All of the expenditures must be for earlier obligations, properly incurred.

Statement of Operations (Exhibit 18-4)

A statement of operations displaying any income and the operating costs and expenses incurred for the accounting period often is prepared by a federal agency. In many respects, this statement closely resembles the corporate profit and loss statement. The detailed records, in support of this schedule, must provide an accounting of each of the cost and expenses elements by the individual, congressionally approved, appropriation or fund. As presented, the report would represent the total costs and expenses of the agency for the fiscal period, regardless of appropriation source.

33. **Income.**—This amount consists of any receipts of the agency, that have been authorized by Congress. Typically, the receipts of most executive agencies are minimal. At the end of the fiscal year, the balances in these accounts are closed to the Invested Capital Account.

Among the executive agencies, the Internal Revenue Service and the Bureau of Customs are the principal collectors of receipts. Funds collected by these agencies—except for the funds authorized for expenditure by them in support of operations—are deposited in the general fund of the Treasury Department. As mentioned, income of a collecting agency does not automatically become available to that agency for obligation and expenditure. Such authority must be specifically provided by the Congress.

34. **Expenses.**—These amounts must be supported by additional records, detailed by appropriation or fund. Amounts reported should be, but may not be, on the accrual basis. At the end of the fiscal year, the balances in these accounts are closed to the Invested Capital Account.

To simplify reporting, many agencies classify expenses by the same terminology as required by the OMB for reporting expenditures by object classification, thus permitting a continual comparison of actual to budgeted expenditures.

Statement of Sources and Application of Funds (Exhibit 18-5)

The statement of sources and application of funds, similar to that required in the corporate sector, provides an accounting of the sources by which funds are provided and the items, operations or activities to which funds were applied.

35. **Funds Provided by.**—The total funds provided to an agency can be in excess of the funds appropriated to that agency by the Congress. For example, receipts collected by the agency may not be available as part of the appropriation for agency operations. Also, imprest funds advanced by the Treasury Department are not part of that agency's appropriation until the fund is replenished by the borrowing agency, at which time the expenses comprising the replenishment become charges against the operating agency's

Exhibit 18-5
An Agency Financed from Appropriations
Statement of Sources and Application of Funds
For the fiscal year ended September 30, 1979

35 **Funds Provided by:**

Appropriation from Congress	$xxx,xxx	
Income—sales	xx,xxx	$xxx,xxx
Sale of equipment		xxx
Advance from disbursing officer for imprest fund		xxx
Total funds provided		$xxx,xxx

36 **Funds Applied to:**

Cost of current year's operations:

Total expenses		$xxx,xxx	
Less:			
Depreciation on equipment	$x,xxx		
Leave earned but not taken	x,xxx	x,xxx	xxx,xxx
Purchase of furniture and equipment			xx,xxx
Funds returned to U. S. Treasury			xxx
Total funds applied			xxx,xxx

Increases in Working Capital	$ xx,xxx

The increase in working capital is accounted for as follows:

	Working Capital	
Current Assets:	Increase	Decrease
Fund balances with U. S. Treasury	$ xx,xxx	
Deposits in transit	x,xxx	
Undeposited collections	xxx	
Imprest fund	xxx	
Accounts receivable—repayments to appropriations	x,xxx	
Inventories	xx,xxx	
Prepaid expenses	xxx	
Travel advances	x,xxx	
Current Liabilities:		
Disbursements in transit		$ x,xxx
Accounts payable to others		xx,xxx
Accrued liabilities		x,xxx
Employee's bond deductions liability		xxx
Employee's tax deductions liability		xxx
Employee's FICA deductions liability		xx
Employer's share of FICA liability		xx
Subtotals	$ xx,xxx	$ xx,xxx
Increase in working capital		xx,xxx
Totals	$ xx,xxx	$ xx,xxx

appropriation. The imprest fund is available for expenditure and would be in addition to the appropriations provided by Congress.

36. **Funds Applied to.**—Funds may be applied to other than current costs and expenses. This is particularly true in those agencies where depreciation is recorded: such costs do not require the use of current-year funds. On the other hand, capital expenditures will require the use of current-year funds, but the costs will not be accounted for until later years through amortization or depreciation. Additionally, the agency may be required by law to return monies to the Treasury.

Publication and Audit of Federal Financial Statements

While the above statements are prescribed by the General Accounting Office, the systems of some federal agencies will not permit the periodic preparation of such reports. In addition, not all federal agencies maintain their accounts on the accrual basis. Most agencies, however, can provide, through adjustment or periodic inventories of appropriate transactions, financial statements on an accrual-equivalent basis. For the most part, the statements of a federal government agency are not published, although much of the information on agency performance is fully available in records of Congressional hearings and in the Budget of the United States. Aside from use by agency management, the other principal use of this information is to support financial presentations and requests for appropriations before the Congress and to make regular reportings to the Office of Management and Budget and the Treasury Department.

An independent audit generally is not made of federal agencies' financial statements, particularly those of agencies financed by appropriations. Frequently, the internal audit staff of the federal agency will conduct audits of selected financial statements and account balances as part of a programmed audit cycle.

Chapter 19
Illustrative Financial Statements—Local Governmental Units

Introduction

As mentioned in Chapter 18, fund accounting at the federal level often is equated with reporting for a single agency. In many ways, a similar agency-type structure and accounting exist in some state governments. With the exception of the experimental consolidated statements, no government-wide financial statements have been prepared for the operations of the federal government. In contrast, it has been the practice of some states and many local governmental entities to prepare government-wide statements to reflect the full scope of the activities supported by these governments. The diverse operations and activities of most governmental entities dictate the publication of a rather complete set of financial statements covering several types of funds and account groupings.

Fund Reporting

State and local governmental units generally comply with the requirements of *Governmental Accounting, Auditing and Financial Reporting* (GAAFR), which has gained wide acceptance as the authoritative body of generally accepted accounting principles for these governmental organizations.

The exposure draft of the *GAAFR Restatement Principles* (February, 1978) classifies the several types of funds into the following categories: governmental funds, proprietary funds, fiduciary or trust funds and account groups. The *Restatement* definitions of these categories are summarized in the following paragraphs.

Governmental Funds

Governmental funds are accounting segregations of current assets and expendable resources, the related current liabilities and the difference or fund balance (or deficit). The funds included within this category are:

general fund;

special revenues funds;

debt service funds;

special assessment funds; and

capital projects funds.

Such funds also have been referred to as expendable, government-type or budgetary funds.

Proprietary Funds

Proprietary funds are used to account for governmental activities that are similar to those of private sector or commercial-type organizations. Revenues are earned, expenses are incurred and net income accountability is required from these organizations. The accounting must include a reporting of all assets and liabilities, both current and noncurrent. The funds included within this category are:

enterprise funds;

internal or intra-governmental service funds; and

nonexpendable trust funds.

Such funds have often been referred to as income determination, or nonexpendable funds.

Fiduciary Funds

Fiduciary funds are used to account for assets held by the government in a trustee or fiduciary status. The funds included in this category may include funds otherwise classified as governmental and proprietary funds. For example, the category of fiduciary funds may include:

expendable trust funds (governmental funds category);

agency trust funds (governmental funds category); and

nonexpendable trust funds (proprietary funds category).

Account Groups

Account groups are not funds, in that the transactions of account groups do not involve financial resources. Account groups are maintained for management control and accountability of a government's general fixed assets, and unmatured general long-term debt. Two account groups may exist:

the general fixed-assets account group; and

the general long-term debt account group.

Note that fixed assets relating to the activity of a proprietary fund should be accounted for in such funds, and not as a part of the general fixed-asset account group. Similarly, the noncurrent liabilities of proprietary funds, special assessment funds, and certain fiduciary funds should be accounted for in those funds, and not as part of the general long-term debt account group.

Illustrative Financial Statements and Schedules

The generally accepted accounting procedures related to financial reporting for state and local governmental units have been the subject of study by the accounting profession for some years. The National Council on Governmental Accounting, the American Institute of Certified Public Accountants and, more recently, the Financial Accounting Standards Board are continuing in their research to establish the preferred basis of presenting financial statements for a governmental unit and the nature of the attestation that should accompany the audited statements. It is difficult to predict when, or if, a single reporting and attestation format will emerge as the generally accepted practice. At this time, the publications of professional organizations deliberating the issues include:

By the National Council on Governmental Accounting:

Governmental Accounting, Auditing and Financial Reporting, 1968.

Interpretation No. 1—GAAFR and the AICPA Audit Guide, 1976.

GAAFR Restatement, Introduction and Principles—Working Draft, 1976.

GAAFR Restatement Principles—Exposure Draft, 1978.

By the Municipal Finance Officers Association:

Disclosure Guidelines for Offerings of Securities by State and Local Governments, 1976 (copy in Appendix B).

Guidelines for Use by State and Local Governments in the Preparation of Yearly Information Statements and Other Current Information, 1978.

Procedural Statements in Connection With the Disclosure Guidelines for Offerings of Securities by State and Local Governments and the Guidelines for Use by State and Local Governments in the Preparation of Yearly Information Statements and Other Current Information, 1978.

By the American Institute of Certified Public Accountants:

Industry Audit Guide: Audits of State and Local Governments, 1973.

Statements on Auditing Standards, No. 1 and subsequent issuances.

By the Financial Accounting Standards Board:

Financial Accounting in Nonbusiness Organizations: An Exploratory Study of Conceptual Issues, 1978.

In addition, several public accounting firms have contributed to studies and have published papers on reporting and attestation.

The GAAFR suggests that the annual report of a governmental unit be viewed as pyramidal—(1) summary government-wide statements are further explained by (2) combining fund statements, which are analyzed by (3) individual fund and account group statements, with (4) supporting schedules to provide additional details.

The general purpose financial position and operating statements and schedules required by GAAFR for a governmental unit, as set forth in the *GAAFR Restatement Principles* (draft dated September 1978), are:

Balance Sheets:

A combined balance sheet for all funds and all account groups (Exhibit 19-1);

Combining balance sheets for all funds for each type of fund; and

Separate balance sheets for each fund and account group.

Operating Statements

A combined statement of revenues, expenditures and other changes in fund balances (or retained earnings) for all funds (Exhibit 19-2);

Combining statements of revenues, expenditures and other changes in fund balances (or retained earnings) for all funds for each type of fund (Exhibit 19-3);

Separate statements of revenues, expenditures and other changes in fund balances (or retained earnings) for each fund; and

Combined and/or separate proprietary fund statements of changes in financial position.

Account Groups

Statement of changes in general fixed assets (Exhibit 19-4);

Statement of changes in general long-term debt (Exhibit 19-5).

The illustrative statements, which appear as Exhibits 19-1 through 19-5, relate to a local government having activities requiring accounting under governmental, proprietary and fiduciary funds and account groupings for general fixed assets and general long-term debt. Notes on the annotations appearing on the several financial statements follow each exhibit.

Combined Balance Sheet (Exhibit 19-1)

The GAAFR defines the term "combined balance sheet" as a single balance sheet that displays the individual balance sheet accounts of each class of funds, and the account groups of a governmental unit, in separate, adjacent columns.

There is a clear distinction between the combined balance sheet of governmental units and the consolidated financial statements, reflecting inter-entity eliminations and consolidation entries. The combined statements reflect the fiscal and legal realities of the several governmental units. Consolidated statements, common in the private sector, require the elimination of inter-fund receivables or payables and of cash balances or other transactions that could result in an absence of full disclosure or could be in violation of law. It is for this reason that the "Combined Total" column must be clearly labeled "(Memorandum Only)," since the implication that all fund account balances are additive could be erroneous because of statute, legislative mandate or contract.

Fund and Account Groupings

1-13. Additional information concerning governmental and proprietary funds, and account groups (items 1, 2 and 3 of Exhibit 19-1) appears in Chapter 4. The nature of the fund type (items 4 through 13 of Exhibit 19-1) dictates the type of account balances that will be reflected in the columns of the combined balance sheet.

14. **Combined Total (Memorandum Only).**—As mentioned above, if a total column appears, there should be a clear annotation that the total column is only for memorandum purposes, since these totals generally will not appear in the financial records of the governmental unit.

Assets

The assets of a local government include all items of value (cash receivables, property and investments) owned by or due to the governmental unit.

15. **Cash.**—This account should reflect cash funds of the government. Diverse bank accounts may exist, cash may be commingled with accounts of officials of other than the executive branch, restrictions as to availability for expenditure may exist and should be identified. General, imprest and in-transit cash may be required to be separately reported. Also included would be currency, coin, money orders, bankers drafts and funds on-hand or on-deposit.

16. **Accounts Receivable.**—This account reflects amounts due to the government, or from customers in the case of an enterprise fund. This account would not reflect amounts due from other funds of the government.

17. **Taxes Receivable.**—This account reflects taxes and assessments due. Timing considerations, materiality and the availability of tax revenues should be examined in determining whether property taxes should be accrued.

Exhibit

A City Combined

All Funds and Account

	1				
Assets	General Fund (4)	Special Revenue Funds (5)	Special Assessment Funds (6)	Debt Service Funds (7)	Capital Projects Funds (8)
15 Cash	$xxx,xxx	$xx,xxx	$x,xxx	$xx,xxx	$xx,xxx
Receivables:					
16 Accounts receivable	xx				
17 Taxes receivable	xx,xxx		x,xxx	x,xxx	
18 Due from federal, state, local governments	xx,xxx	xx,xxx			x,xxx
19 Due from other funds	x,xxx				
20 Investments and accrued interest		x,xxx		x,xxx	x,xxx
21 Inventories	xx,xxx				
22 Land, buildings, equipment and other fixed assets, less accumulated depreciation					
23 Land held for redevelopment					
24 Amount provided for retirement of general long-term debt					
25 Amount to be provided for retirement of general long-term debt					
Total Assets	$xxx,xxx	$xx,xxx	$x,xxx	$xx,xxx	$xx,xxx
Liabilities, Reserves and Fund Balances/ Retained Earnings					
Liabilities:					
26 Vouchers payable	$ xx,xxx	$ x,xxx	$	$	$ x,xxx
27 Contracts payable	x,xxx				
28 Notes payable and accrued interest	xx				
29 Matured bonds payable and accrued interest	xx				
30 Contracts payable—Retainer					x,xxx
31 Accrued payroll and payroll taxes	xxx	xx			
32 Due to other funds	x,xxx	xxx			
33 Due to other governments	xx,xxx				
34 Long-term leases payable					
35 Taxes collected in advance	x,xxx				
Total Liabilities	xx,xxx	x,xxx	—	—	x,xxx
Reserves; Fund Balances/Retained Earnings:					
36 For taxes receivable	xxx,xxx		x,xxx		
37 For inventories	xx,xxx				
38 For encumbrances	xxx,xxx	x,xxx	xxx		xxx
Total Reserves	xxx,xxx	x,xxx	x,xxx	—	xxx
39 Appropriated balance	xx,xxx	xx,xxx		xx,xxx	xx,xxx
40 Unappropriated balance	xx,xxx	xx,xxx	x,xxx	x,xxx	
41 Investment in general fixed assets					
42 Contributed capital					
43 Retained earnings					
Total Fund Balances/Retained Earnings	xx,xxx	xx,xxx	x,xxx	xx,xxx	xx,xxx
Total Liabilities, Reserves, Fund Balances/Retained Earnings	$xxx,xxx	$xx,xxx	$x,xxx	$xx,xxx	$xx,xxx

19-1

Balance Sheet

Groupings June 30, 1979

| | 2 | | 3 | | |
Trust and Agency Funds (9)	Enterprise Funds (10)	Intragovernmental Service Funds (11)	General Fixed Assets Accounts (12)	General Long-Term Debt Accounts (13)	Combined Total (Memorandum Only) (14)
$xx,xxx	$ xxx	$ x,xxx	$	$	$
	x,xxx				x,xxx
					xx,xxx
xx,xxx					xx,xxx
		x,xxx			x,xxx
xx,xxx					xx,xxx
	xxx	xx,xxx			xx,xxx
x,xxx	xx,xxx	x,xxx	xxx,xxx		xxx,xxx
x,xxx			xx,xxx		xx,xxx
				xx,xxx	xx,xxx
				xxx,xxx	xxx,xxx
$xx,xxx	$xx,xxx	$xx,xxx	$xxx,xxx	$xxx,xxx	$x,xxx,xxx

	$ x,xxx	$ x,xxx	$	$	$ xx,xxx
					x,xxx
x,xxx				xx,xxx	xxx,xxx
				xxx,xxx	xxx,xxx
					x,xxx
	xx	xx			xxx
xx					x,xxx
				x,xxx	xx,xxx
					x,xxx
x,xxx	x,xxx	x,xxx	—	xxx,xxx	xxx,xxx
					xxx,xxx
					xx,xxx
	xxx	xxx			xxx,xxx
—	xxx	xxx	—	—	xxx,xxx
xx,xxx					xx,xxx
xx,xxx					xx,xxx
			xxx,xxx		xxx,xxx
	xx,xxx				xx,xxx
	xx,xxx				xx,xxx
xx,xxx	xx,xxx	xx,xxx			xx,xxx
$xx,xxx	$xx,xxx	$xx,xxx	$xxx,xxx	$xxx,xxx	$x,xxx,xxx

Additionally, material revenues otherwise not recorded should be accrued if the amounts should have been received before statement date. The balance of these receivables will be offset by a reservation of the fund balances.

18. **Due from Federal, State and Local Government.**—This account reflects amounts due from other governments. Where expenditure of funds is the primary factor in determining eligibility for contract or grant funds, the revenue may be accrued at the time of expenditure. In other instances, the validity of the receivable may be conditioned upon compliance with the specific terms of the individual agreements.

19. **Due from Other Funds.**—This account reflects amounts due from other specific funds of the governmental unit. Funds due from other levels of government would not be reported in this account.

20. **Investments and Accrued Income.**—These accounts reflect the investments and income owned or due. Investments could include securities and real estate. The income could include interest, dividends, rentals or other payments.

21. **Inventories.**—This account reflects amounts of supplies, materials and other stock to be consumed by the governmental unit in a future period. While recordable for enterprise-type funds, inventories may not be recorded for nonenterprise-type funds. In this instance, the balance of the inventory will be offset by establishing a reservation of the fund balance.

22. **Land, Buildings, Equipment and Other Fixed Assets.**—This account reflects the cost of fixed assets, less accumulated depreciation when the assets are related to an enterprise or service fund. All fixed assets not related to enterprise or service funds are entered in the General Fixed Assets Accounts, and no depreciation usually is recorded.

23. **Land Held for Redevelopment.**—The account reflects the cost of real estate acquired or reserved for specified purposes and is not part of the unrestricted real estate of the governmental unit.

24. **Amount Provided for Retirement of General Long-Term Debt.**—This account reflects funds provided to date in payment or liquidation of general long-term debt.

25. **Amount to Be Provided for Retirement of General Long-Term Debt.**—This account reflects funds to be provided in future fiscal periods necessary to liquidate the outstanding general long-term debt.

Liabilities

As in balance sheets for organizations in the private sector, the liability section of the balance sheet must summarize the unpaid obligations, outstanding debts and other amounts owed by the governmental unit.

26. **Vouchers Payable.**—This account reflects amounts owed to organizations and persons outside of the governmental unit for goods and services received.

27. **Contracts Payable.**—This account reflects amounts owed under contracts for assets, goods and services received by the governmental unit. Amounts withheld for outstanding contracts as guarantees for which performance must be received should be reflected in a separate account, such as "Contracts Payable—Retainers."

28 and 29. **Notes Payable and Accrued Interest Payable; Matured Bonds Payable and Accrued Interest.**—These accounts reflect the amounts owed for debts of the government that have maturity dates beyond a year from the date of issuance. The reporting varies according to the fund involved. Enterprise or service funds will perform the accounting for related long-term debt and obligations within those fund accounting structures. Other long-term debt of the governmental unit will be recorded and accounted for in the General Long-Term Debt Account Group.

30. **Contracts Payable—Retainers.**—This account reflects the amount of withholdings or retainers received by the government as guarantees for future contract performance.

31. **Accrued Payroll and Taxes.**—These accounts reflect the liability for salaries and wages and related taxes earned by employees in the period between the last payment date and the date of the financial statements.

32. **Due to Other Funds.**—This account reflects amounts owed to a specific fund by another fund of the governmental unit. Long-term obligations and funds owed to other levels of government would not be recorded in this account.

33. **Due to Other Governments.**—This account reflects amounts owed to other levels of government.

34. **Long-Term Leases Payable.**—This account reflects amounts owed by the governmental unit under terms of executed leases. Depending upon the terms, lease liabilities may have to be recorded; qualifying leases also should be included in the General Fixed Assets Accounts or in proprietary funds, where appropriate.

35. **Taxes Collected in Advance.**—This account reflects either taxes collected in advance of due date or overpayments that must be returned to or offset against amounts due from taxpayers.

Reserves and Fund Balances/Retained Earnings

In governmental accounting, the term "reserve" connotes a restriction or segregation of a portion of the otherwise free or available fund balance for the purpose of providing for some contemplated or expected future expenditures. The amounts reserved are not available for future commitment. Conceptually, the terms "fund balances" and "retained earnings" are similar and represent the net equity of the governmental fund.

36. **Reserve for Taxes Receivable.**—This account reflects the amount of taxes that have been levied, earned or otherwise due to the government, but that have not yet been collected and are not considered as received or available for use.

37. **Reserve for Inventories.**—This account equals the value of the inventory asset account and connotes that portion of the fund balance or retained earnings that has been expended in the past or current period and that is not available for expenditure or appropriation in the next fiscal period.

38. **Reserve for Encumbrances.**—This account reflects the amount of the unliquidated or outstanding encumbrances or obligations for which a portion of the fund balance must be segregated or restricted from future expenditure or appropriation.

39. **Appropriated Balance.**—This account reflects the current portion of the fund balance that is available for expenditure or obligation.

40. **Unappropriated Balance.**—This account reflects the portion of the fund balance that has not been appropriated by the legislature at statement date. These amounts may be available for future budget financing under certain specified circumstances or upon appropriation by the legislature.

41. **Investment in General Fixed Assets.**—This account reflects the total recorded value of the governmental unit's investment in general fixed assets. This amount does not include the value of fixed assets related to an enterprise or service fund, which records and depreciates the fixed assets within the accounts for those funds.

42. **Contributed Capital.**—This account reflects capital provided to underwrite the support of an enterprise, trust or agency service fund. Earnings and reimbursements of costs for services rendered by the fund to the public or to other agencies are intended to provide for the on-going financing of these funds.

43. **Retained Earnings.**—This account reflects accumulated earnings or net equity of enterprise trust or agency service funds. This balance is similar to retained earnings accounts of commercial organizations.

As noted earlier in this Chapter, a combining balance sheet also should be prepared for all funds comprising each type of fund. Additionally, a separate balance sheet should be prepared, or explanatory schedules should be included in the audit report, for each individual fund and each account group. With respect to comparative statements, the AICPA's *Industry Guide, Audits of State and Local Governmental Units,* cites Accounting Research Bulletin No. 43, which concludes that, in any one year, it ordinarily is desirable for the balance sheet, income statement and surplus (or retained earnings) statement to be presented for one or more of the preceding years, as well as for the current year. However, the Guide recognizes that a combined balance sheet of all funds, rather than separate balance sheets of individual funds, may be the more meaningful statement for presenting the financial position of a governmental unit. When the combined balance sheet is used, the Guide recognizes the possible impracticality of also presenting data in a comparative form.

Combined Statement of Revenues, Expenditures and Other Changes in Fund Balances or Retained Earnings

In the *GAAFR Restatement Principles,* the National Council on Governmental Accounting recommended that the combined statement of revenues, expenditures and other changes in fund balances should contain data categorized by major revenue sources and organizations, functions of expenditures (as well as by organization, activity, character and object class), and types of transfers or other changes in fund balances. The combined statement also should:

Provide a uniform basic operating statement format for all funds, and for governmental and proprietary funds;

Present all changes in the fund balance or retained earnings (or equity);

Provide an overview of such changes and a reconciliation of the beginning and ending balances in a single statement.

The GAAFR presentation embodies the all-inclusive approach, thus eliminating questions as to whether certain changes in fund balance or other equity should be reported directly in a statement of that account, while other changes are shown in a separate operating statement. It is intended that this format will eliminate the need for separate statements of changes in fund balances, retained earnings or other equity reserves.

Exhibit 19-2 illustrates reporting on governmental funds where a major objective is to present the fund balance at the beginning and end of the fiscal period. Like the balance sheet (Exhibit 19-1), this statement is presented in a combined format. A "total column" appears on the combined statement of revenue, expenditures and other changes in fund balances for memorandum purposes only. Generally, the amounts in this column will not be set forth in the accounting records of the governmental unit.

Fund Groupings

This statement reflects the changes in the fund balances of the governmental or expendable-type funds. Appropriations are passed by the legislature for obligation and expenditures by governmental funds (1), and by expendable fiduciary funds (2).

Exhibit

A City Combined Statement of Revenues, Expenditures

For the fiscal year

	General Funds	Special Revenue Funds	Special Assessment Funds	Debt Service Funds
Revenues and Other Additions				
4 **Revenues:**				
Property and sales taxes	$ x,xxx,xxx	$ xxx,xxx	$ x,xxx	$ xxx,xxx
Licenses and permits	xxx,xxx	x,xxx		
Service charges	xx,xxx			
Federal revenue sharing				
Other federal funds	x,xxx,xxx	x,xxx,xxx		
Fines and forfeitures	xxx,xxx			
Other operating revenues	xxx,xxx	xxx,xxx	xxx,xxx	xxx,xxx
Total Operating Revenues	xx,xxx,xxx	x,xxx,xxx	xxx,xxx	x,xxx,xxx
Other Additions:				
Note proceeds	xxx,xxx			
Bond proceeds				
5 Trust and agency fund additions				
6 Other transfers	xx,xxx	xx,xxx		xxx,xxx
Total Other Additions	xxx,xxx	xx,xxx		xxx,xxx
Total Revenues and Other Additions	xx,xxx,xxx	x,xxx,xxx	xxx,xxx	x,xxx,xxx
Expenditures, Encumbrances and Other Deductions				
7 **Expenditures and Encumbrances:**				
General government	xxx,xxx	x,xxx,xxx		
Public safety	x,xxx,xxx			
Health	xxx,xxx	xx,xxx		
Sanitation	x,xxx,xxx	xxx,xxx		
Parks and recreation	x,xxx,xxx	xx,xxx	xx,xxx	
Total general governmental expenditures and encumbrances	xx,xxx,xxx	x,xxx,xxx	xx,xxx	
8 **Other Expenditures and Encumbrances:**				
Debt service				x,xxx,xxx
Capital projects			x,xxx	
Total Other Expenditures and Encumbrances			x,xxx	x,xxx,xxx
Other Deductions:				
6 Transfers	xx,xxx	xxx,xxx		
5 Trust and agency funds disbursements				
Total Other Deductions	xx,xxx	xxx,xxx		
Total Expenditures, Encumbrances and Other Deductions	xx,xxx,xxx	x,xxx,xxx	xxx,xxx	x,xxx,xxx
Excess of Revenues and Additions over Expenditures, Encumbrances and Other Deductions	x,xxx,xxx	(xxx,xxx)	xx,xxx	xxx,xxx
Fund Balance July 1, 1978	xxx,xxx	xxx,xxx	x,xxx	xxx,xxx
9 Fund Balance June 30, 1979	$ x,xxx,xxx	$ xxx,xxx	$ xx,xxx	$ xxx,xxx

19-2

and Other Changes in Fund Balances

ended June 30, 1979

Capital Projects Funds	2 Trust and Agency Funds	3 (Memorandum Only) Inter-fund Eliminations	Total
$	$	$	$ x,xxx,xxx
			x,xxx,xxx
			xxx,xxx
	x,xxx,xxx		
x,xxx,xxx	xxx,xxx		x,xxx,xxx
			xxx,xxx
xxx,xxx	xxx,xxx		x,xxx,xxx
x,xxx,xxx	x,xxx,xxx		xx,xxx,xxx
			xxx,xxx
x,xxx,xxx			x,xxx,xxx
	x,xxx,xxx		x,xxx,xxx
xx,xxx	x,xxx	(xxx,xxx)	
x,xxx,xxx	x,xxx,xxx		x,xxx,xxx
x,xxx,xxx	x,xxx,xxx		xx,xxx,xxx
			x,xxx,xxx
			x,xxx,xxx
			xxx,xxx
			x,xxx,xxx
			x,xxx,xxx
			xx,xxx,xxx
			x,xxx,xxx
x,xxx,xxx			x,xxx,xxx
x,xxx,xxx			x,xxx,xxx
xxx,xxx	x,xxx,xxx	(xxx,xxx)	
	x,xxx,xxx		x,xxx,xxx
xxx,xxx	x,xxx,xxx		x,xxx,xxx
x,xxx,xxx	x,xxx,xxx		xx,xxx,xxx
xxx,xxx	(xxx,xxx)		x,xxx,xxx
xx,xxx	xxx,xxx		xxx,xxx
$ xxx,xxx	$ xxx,xxx		$ x,xxx,xxx

3. **Memorandum Only.**—The *GAAFR Restatement* permits the presentation of combined totals, with or without inter-fund eliminations. Should eliminations be made, explanatory notes should be included. Inter-fund revenues, transfers and expenses should be noted, particularly when there is an erroneous implication that all columns are additive, which may be contrary to statute, legislative mandate or contract.

Revenues and Other Additions

4. **Revenues.**—These accounts reflect all sources from which the government received revenues in the fiscal year. Generally, the legislature has provided appropriation legislation to permit these funds to be available for general or specific obligation and expenditure.

5. **Trust and Agency Fund Additions.**—These accounts reflect the additions or deductions to trust and agency funds resulting from actions of the government in its fiduciary capacity. Examples of transactions that could affect these accounts include: deposit funds, escrowed amounts, payroll taxes withholdings, pension funds, insurance funds and sinking fund deposits.

6. **Other Transfers.**—These accounts reflect inter-fund transfers. Funds are appropriated from one fund to support expenditures of other funds. All transfers should be in accord with established precedent or specific legislation to insure that such transfers are consistent with the intent of the appropriation legislation.

Expenditures, Encumbrances, Other Deductions

7. **Expenditures and Encumbrances.**—These accounts reflect the cost of goods delivered or services received (the expenditures) and outstanding obligations such as purchase orders, contracts, and salary commitments (the encumbrances, which have been established as a reserve against the fund balance). Where the governmental unit is not on the accrual basis, the expenditures would be synonymous with cash disbursements.

8. **Debt Service.**—This account reflects the amounts of revenues provided to meet the obligation of the government for the principal and interest payments due during the fiscal period on the general obligation debt, other than the debt payable from special assessment and other debt serviced by a governmental enterprise organization. In the latter two instances, these debt service costs must be accounted for as part of those fund's transactions.

9. **Fund Balance.**—This account reflects the amount of the fund balances at the end of the fiscal year. It should be noted that these balances may or may not be appropriated or available for obligation and expenditure in the next fiscal year. The status would depend upon existing legislation or expressed legislative intent. Information should be provided on the amount of any encumbrances or reserves that may exist, thereby limiting that portion of the fund balance that can be obligated in the next year.

As noted earlier in this Chapter, a combining statement of revenues, expenditures and other changes in fund balances should be prepared for all funds comprising each type of fund. There also should be a separate, similar statement or explanatory schedule for each individual fund. The AICPA's industry guide, *Audits of State and Local Governmental Units,* suggests that, in government, the most meaningful comparison in operating statements of budgetary funds, i.e., of expendable-type funds, frequently is of actual results against the budget. One mode of comparison would be a comparison of actual results with the budget and with the prior year's activity. Such a comparison should be made in the operating statements of the individual funds.

Exhibit 19-3 would be appropriate for use with proprietary or non-expendable governmental funds. The operations of these types of funds (enterprise and service-type funds) are similar to commercial organizations. Generally, the objective of these funds is to conduct activities on a basis that provides for a return of costs and, possibly, a minimal profit factor. The term "retained earnings" is used in lieu of "fund balance."

Statement of Income, Expenditures and Changes in Retained Earnings

As with other statements, Exhibit 19-3 is presented in a combined statement format. While the total column appears on this statement, it is for memorandum purposes only. Generally, the accounting records of the governmental unit will provide the financial status on each of the individual funds as aggregated in Exhibit 19-3.

Fund Groupings

This statement reflects revenues, expenditures, and changes in retained earnings for all enterprise (1) and service-type (2) funds. While revenues may be received from the general fund, operating revenues and reimbursements for services provided to other activities of the government typically provide the principal source of revenues from which expenditures will be met. Accounting for these funds should be on the accrual basis, similar to commercial organizations.

3. **Memorandum Only.**—The *GAAFR Restatement Principles* permit presentation of combined totals. Inter-fund revenues, transfers and expenses should be noted, particularly when there is an erroneous implication that all columns are additive, which may not be the case.

Operating Revenues

4. **Enterprise Funds.**—These accounts reflect revenues and other income earned by funds. Enterprise funds are established to perform such activities as acquiring, operating or maintaining governmental facilities on a self-supporting basis by user charges, fees, etc. (Examples may include water, gas, electric, transportation and transit utilities.)

Exhibit 19-3

A City
Combined Statement of Income, Expenditures and Other Changes in Retained Earnings
For the fiscal year ended June 30, 1979

	1 Enterprise Funds	2 Intra-governmental Service Funds	3 Total
Operating Revenues			
4 Enterprise Funds:			
Operating revenues	$xx,xxx,xxx	$ xxx,xxx	$xx,xxx,xxx
Other revenues	xx,xxx		xx,xxx
Total	xx,xxx,xxx	xxx,xxx	xx,xxx,xxx
5 Intragovernmental Funds:			
General revenues		xxx,xxx	xxx,xxx
Special revenues		xx,xxx	xx,xxx
Total			
Total Operating Revenues	$xx,xxx,xxx	$ xxx,xxx	$xx,xxx,xxx
6 Operating Expenses			
Personnel	xx,xxx,xxx	xxx,xxx	xx,xxx,xxx
Contractual services	xx,xxx	x,xxx	xx,xxx
Supplies, materials	xxx,xxx	xx,xxx	xxx,xxx
Other	x,xxx	x,xxx	xx,xxx
Total	xx,xxx,xxx	xxx,xxx	xx,xxx,xxx
7 Operating Income Before Depreciation			
Less: Depreciation	xx,xxx	x,xxx	xx,xxx
Operating Income	xxx,xxx	xx,xxx	xxx,xxx
Other Income or Expense			
Interest income	xxx,xxx		xxx,xxx
Interest expense			
Net Other Income (Expense)	xx,xxx	x,xxx	xx,xxx
Net Income (Loss)	xx,xxx	x,xxx	xx,xxx
Retained Earnings July 1, 1978	xx,xxx	x,xxx	xx,xxx
8 Retained Earnings June 30, 1979	$ xx,xxx	$ x,xxx	$ xx,xxx

5. **Inter-governmental Service Funds.**—These accounts reflect general and special revenues earned by the service funds. Such funds often are called working capital funds and revolving funds. These funds provide commodities or services to other agencies. Revenues and other income generally are the reimbursement paid by other agencies for these services.

Operating Expenses

6. **Operating Expenses.**—These accounts reflect costs necessary to maintain enterprise or service funds, including any merchandise costs, disposition costs and collection expenses related to fund activity.

7. **Depreciation.**—These accounts reflect depreciation expense of fixed assets in the funds. Unlike governmental or expendable funds, an accounting is made for depreciation of fixed assets used or devoted to support of enterprise and service funds.

8. **Retained Earnings.**—These accounts reflect the accumulated earnings of an enterprise or service fund retained by the fund that have not been appropriated for another purpose.

As noted earlier in this Chapter, a combining statement of income, expenditures and other changes in retained earnings should be prepared for all funds comprising each type of fund. As mentioned earlier, the AICPA, in its industry audit guide, suggests that a more meaningful comparative statement with respect to operations would be a comparison of actual results with the budget and also with the prior year's activity. Such a comparison should be made in the operating statements of the individual funds.

GAAFR Restatement Principles also require statements of changes in financial position for proprietary funds. Such combined statements should present separate data for each major proprietary fund in a columnar format and may contain a total column, with or without inter-fund eliminations. Any inter-fund eliminations should be clearly identified by headings or disclosed in footnotes to the statements.

Statement of General Fixed Assets

The general fixed assets of a governmental unit may be defined as those fixed assets that are not accounted for as part of an enterprise, service or trust fund. These accounts, the general fixed assets group of accounts, are self-balancing and show the nature of the fixed assets and the source from or by which the assets were acquired. Exhibit 19-4 illustrates a typical statement of general fixed assets for a governmental unit.

Statement in Changes in Long-Term Debt

The general long-term debt group of accounts reflects the long-term debt payable from the general revenues of the government. A self-balancing set of accounts generally is established to provide controls over this data. Exhibit 19-5 illustrates a typical statement for general long-term debt, showing the funds to be provided to liquidate or settle the debt and the total amount of the long-term debt.

Exhibit 19-4
A City Statement of General Fixed Assets
June 30, 1979

General fixed assets:	
Land	$ xx,xxx,xxx
Buildings	xx,xxx,xxx
Improvements	xx,xxx,xxx
Equipment	xx,xxx,xxx
Land held for redevelopment	x,xxx,xxx
Total fixed assets used in operations	xxx,xxx,xxx
Fixed assets held for investment:	
Sports arena and land	xx,xxx,xxx
Leased land	x,xxx,xxx
Total fixed assets held for investments	xx,xxx,xxx
Total general fixed assets	$xxx,xxx,xxx
Investment in general fixed assets:	
From capital projects funds	$ xx,xxx,xxx
From federal funds	x,xxx,xxx
From general fund revenues	xxx,xxx,xxx
From special revenue fund revenues	x,xxx
Donations	xxx,xxx
Total	$xxx,xxx,xxx

Exhibit 19-5
A City Combined Schedule of General Long-Term Debt
June 30, 1979

AMOUNT AVAILABLE AND TO BE PROVIDED
FOR PAYMENT OF GENERAL LONG-TERM DEBT

Serial bonds:		
Amount available in debt service funds	$ x,xxx,xxx	
Amount to be provided	xxx,xxx,xxx	$xxx,xxx,xxx
Leases:		
Amount to be provided for long-term lease		xxx,xxx
		$xxx,xxx,xxx

GENERAL LONG-TERM DEBT PAYABLE

Serial bonds payable	$xxx,xxx,xxx
Long-term leases payable	xxx,xxx
	$xxx,xxx,xxx

Part VI

Use of Computers and Electronic Data Processing in Auditing

Appendix A—*Program for Examination of Municipalities,* prepared by the Pennsylvania Institute of Certified Public Accountants

Appendix B—*Disclosure Guidelines for Offerings of Securities by State and Local Governments,* published by the Municipal Finance Officers Association

Chapter 20
Use of Computers and Electronic Data Processing in Auditing

Introduction

The size of even smaller governmental entities often is sufficient to require the use of computers and electronic data processing. The reporting requirements of governmental entities, in some instances, is dependent upon the application of complex and almost instantaneous recording and accumulation of data.

The changes in data processing have been revolutionary. The mere updating of computer files may destroy the historical record and simultaneously create a new file. In many computerized systems, books of original entry, journals and general ledgers—so familiar to auditors—no longer exist. Computerized systems are able to create journal entries, accumulate data and prepare reports. Automated accounting may be accomplished without leaving a verifiable audit trail or a hard copy record that permits visual examination. In the last few years, considerable changes have been experienced in both the method and medium of entering, processing, and retrieving data from computerized systems. In many instances, the governmental unit may do no processing of data itself, relying instead on a data processing service center. Such an organization presents even different audit considerations.

None of the above considerations are issues exclusively related to governmental organizations. The same challenge to historical auditing procedures exists in the corporate sector. Increasingly, it is the computer that must be audited; the earlier practice of "auditing around the computer" will not provide the necessary assurance of the adequacy of the electronic data processing controls and the reasonableness of the reported information. At one and the same time, the computer represents a new field of required expertise and a potential to perform broader, more comprehensive audit tests by utilizing the capabilities of electronic data processing.

Auditing Standards and EDP

General Audit Standards

Auditing standards, particularly those related to the study and evaluation of internal controls, apply to all methods of data processing, including electronic data processing. Depending upon the complexity of the computerized systems, the auditor must be capable of applying the specialized expertise of the computer sciences in order satisfactorily to perform the required audit procedures.

The first general auditing standard, set forth in the AICPA's Statement on Auditing Standards, No. 1, requires that the audit be performed by a person (or persons) possessing adequate technical training and proficiency as an auditor. Proficiency as an auditor, however, will not be attained if the audit staff is deficient in the expertise necessary to conduct a meaningful review and evaluation of a computerized system. In governmental auditing, the GAO *Standards for Audit* are more specific: the second general GAO standard states that the assigned auditors "... must collectively possess adequate professional proficiency for the tasks required." The GAO Standards address the special requirements of EDP in the following manner:

> If the work requires extensive review of computerized systems, the audit staff must include persons having the appropriate computer skills. These skills may be possessed by staff members or by consultants to the staff.

Impact of EDP on Accounting Controls

Two specific issuances of the AICPA highlight the integral relationship of electronic data processing and the accounting controls that must be evaluated by the auditor. The content of these publications applies to audits in both the private and public sector.

The AICPA's SAS No. 3 emphasizes that EDP systems may require organizational structures and control procedures that differ from manual or mechanical data processing systems. The AICPA's Statement on Auditing Standards, No. 3., "The Effects of EDP on the Auditor's Study and Evaluation of Internal Control," discusses both general controls (relating to all EDP activities) and application controls (relating to a specific accounting task, such as payroll).

General Controls

SAS No. 3 has defined general controls to include:

The plan of organization and operation of the EDP activity;

The procedures for documenting, reviewing, testing and approving systems or programs and the changes thereto;

Controls built into the equipment by the manufacturer, commonly referred to as "hardware controls"; and

Other data and procedural controls affecting overall EDP operations.

Application Controls

SAS No. 3 describes application controls as those controls relating to a specific task performed by the computer. The purpose of such controls is to provide assurance that the computer properly records, processes and reports data. Application controls also are described in such terms as input controls, processing controls and output controls. This publication also outlines several areas that must be specially considered when reviewing, evaluating and testing for compliance in an EDP system environment.

Another publication of the AICPA related to EDP is an audit guide, titled *Audits of Service-Center Produced Records.* The purpose of the guide is to assist auditors serving clients who use a service center to process financial information. The audit guide explains the application of auditing methods to this environment. The guide addresses such questions as: When should the auditor consider a review of controls at a service center? What types of controls are likely to be encountered? How should the review of controls at a service center be approached?

Governmental Standards Relating to EDP

The U.S. General Accounting Office has, for many years, been concerned with the impact of computers and the electronic processing of financial data. In its 1972 publication, *Standards for Audit of Governmental Organizations, Programs, Activities & Functions,* the GAO emphasized the significance and the integral nature of computers in relation to the work to be performed by auditors. In May, 1978, the GAO published three supplemental standards for audit work involving computer systems design, development and operations. The standards and related objectives cited in the publication appear in Exhibit 20-1.

These standards place a responsibility on the auditor to participate in design, development and subsequent modifications over the life cycle of a computer system. The standards also address the responsibilities of the auditor with respect to making reviews of both the general controls and the data processing applications in a computerized system.

Exhibit 20-1

Supplemental Standards for Computer-Related Audits of Governmental Organizations, Programs, Activities and Functions

Supplemental Standards	Related Objectives
First Standard The auditor shall actively participate in the design and development of new data processing systems (including software matters, as well as hardware configuration decisions) or applications, and significant modifications thereto, as a normal part of the audit function.	• To assure that systems/applications faithfully carry out the policies management has prescribed for the system. • To provide assurance that systems/applications provide the controls and audit trails needed for management, auditors, and operational review. • To provide assurance to management that systems/applications include the controls necessary to protect against theft and serious error. • To provide assurance that systems/applications will be efficient and economical in operation. • To assure that systems/applications are in conformity with applicable legal regulations. • To provide assurance that systems/applications are documented in a manner that will provide an understanding of the system required for maintaining and auditing the system.
Second Standard The auditor shall make a review of general controls in data processing systems to determine whether the controls' existence and operations are in accordance with management direction and legal requirements and are operating effectively to provide reliability of, and security over, the data being processed.	
Third Standard The auditor shall make reviews of installed data processing applications to assess their reliability in processing data in a timely, accurate, and complete manner.	• To determine whether the installed application conforms to standards and the latest approved design specifications. • To disclose possible weaknesses in the installed application through periodic audits designed to test internal control and the reliability of the data produced.

Source: An exposure draft issued by the U.S. General Accounting Office, Washington, D.C., May 9, 1978, supplemental to the GAO *Standards for Audit of Governmental Organizations, Programs, Activities and Functions,* issued 1972, reissued 1974.

Computer Audit Applications

An Audit Aid

The potential of the computer to assist in the performance of broader, more comprehensive audit tests exists in the public, as well as the private, sector. While review and evaluation of the computer requires that the auditor possess or obtain the necessary expertise in electronic data processing, it is just this field of knowledge that will permit the auditor to utilize the computer to expand audit in greater depth with the financial information produced by the EDP system. In addition to performing a myriad of clerical tasks (searching, retrieving, computing, comparing, sorting and summarizing, etc.), the auditor may use the computer to construct and select random samples of data, conduct tests and analyses of client files and transactions, and, to a degree, produce flow charts of selected aspects of the EDP system.

Computer Tools and Techniques

In 1977, the Institute of Internal Auditors, Inc., sponsored a research study on international data processing audit and control practices. The report of that study, *Systems Auditability & Control—Audit Practices,* described numerous audit methods, tools and techniques. Exhibit 20-2 outlines many of the tools and techniques cited in that study that are being applied to the audit of computerized systems, and lists several adaptations of existing data processing auditing techniques. In several instances, the IIA's study devotes entire chapters to the description of these auditing applications.

While this study was directed primarily towards the work of internal auditors, the concern over controls and over accuracy of results is no less in any other auditing field, including that of governmental auditing. A summary observation of the study, however, points out that, while an increasing number of internal auditors are using the computer, many still are auditing around the computer, thus providing a verification of historical data, but failing to evalute computer application program controls or to verify the operations of these controls.

Exhibit 20-2

Data Processing Audit Tools and Techniques

Tools and Techniques	Description
Audit Planning and Management • Audit Area Selection	Computer models to compare estimates of expected values to actual values to identify areas of significant differences warranting closer examination

Tools and Techniques	Description
Audit Planning and Management	
• Simulation/Modeling	Computer models permitting an analysis of variables to evaluate financial results between accounts and periods, used on a periodic basis
• Scoring	A manual rating procedure assigning numeric values to selected characteristics in order of risk importance to auditor, each factor weighted according to importance
• Multisite Audit Software	Centralized preparation and distribution of EDP audit software for decentralized use by audit staff to be used in several computer service centers
• Competency Center	A central data processing location receiving data files, executing audit software programs, distributing results to originating auditor
Computer Application Tests	
• Test Data Method	The exercise of computer application programs and systems using test data sets or test decks, verifying processing accuracy by comparison to predetermined results
• Base Case System Evaluation	Use of test data sets as part of comprehensive testing program, verifying processing accuracy by comparison to predetermined results with objective of verifying system operations before and after production acceptance
• Parallel Operation	Simultaneous operation of existing and new system to compare processing results
• Integrated Test Facility	The concurrent processing of test data sets through computer application systems with production processing, comparing test results with predetermined results
Selection and Monitoring of Transactions	
• Transaction Selection	Use of audit software to screen and select transactions for input to computer application system as part of regular production cycle
• Embedded Audit Selection	Use of audit software to screen and select input transactions and transactions generated within computer application system during production processing
• Extended Records	Gathering of data affecting the processing of individual transactions by means of special program(s), accumulating into single record the results of processing the transaction
Data Verification	
• Generalized Audit Software	General purpose software to access, extract, manipulate, and present data for verification by audit
• Terminal Audit Software	General purpose software to access, extract, manipulate and display data from on-line data bases using remote terminal inquiry commands

Tools and Techniques	Description

Audit Planning and Management

- Special Purpose Audit Programs — Computer programs specially tailored to extract and present data from a specific application system's files in variable formats

Analysis of Computer Application Programs

- Snapshot — Program instructions or subroutines recognizing and recording the flow of designated transactions through logic paths within computer application programs, providing documentary evidence of logic, control conditions and processing sequences

- Manual Tracing and Mapping — Manual tracing, mapping or flowcharting of transactions and associated application controls, including source document origination, approval, manual processing, data processing transaction entry, computer processing, distribution and use of data processing reports

- Computer-Aided Tracing and Mapping — Computer programs to identify program segments or subroutines used in processing test transactions. Computer-assisted tracing provides documentary evidence of program statements used to process specific transactions. Mapping is a technique providing evidence of processing sequences used at subroutine level rather than application program statement level. Purpose is to verify transaction processing logic and identify unused portions of computer programs

- Control Flowcharting — Use of computer flowcharting techniques to identify and present logic paths and control points within computer application systems

Audit of Computer Service Center

- Job Accounting Data Analysis — Procedure to select, extract and present job accounting information and monitor access to sensitive data files and application files permitting the identification of unauthorized or improper use of production files

- Audit Guide — The formal instructions for consistent, uniform, comprehensive review, evaluation and testing of specific areas as the computer service center or computer application systems

- Disaster Testing — Simulation of a disaster to evaluate effectiveness of contingency plans

Application System Development Techniques

- Postinstallation Audit — The review, evaluation and test of computer application systems and controls after implementation to determine that operations conform to specifications

- Control Guidelines for System Development — Joint development, between auditors and data process-personnel, of appropriate computer application system controls and audit features

Tools and Techniques	Description
Audit Planning and Management	
• System Development Life Cycle	Method of structuring the application system development process and later maintenance activities to establish a standard sequence of activities and checkpoints permitting the planning and scheduling of audit involvement
• System Acceptance and Control Group	An organization to monitor application system development on a continuing basis to insure the incorporation of appropriate control techniques, both manual as well as computer controls
• Code Comparison	Use of computer to compare two versions of computer application program for differences in coding to permit the identification of changes occuring between original design of application programs and any subsequent revisions

Source: Information used in this exhibit was excerpted, with permission, from the study titled *Systems Auditability & Control—Audit Practices,* prepared for the Institute of Internal Auditors, Inc., by the Stanford Research Institute, © 1977.

The breadth of this study (interviews at 45 organizations in many countries; 1,500 organizations, contacted through mail survey, including industry groups and government) to survey the state of the art in the audit and control of computer-based information systems and data processing probably makes the findings in Exhibit 20-3 equally applicable to practitioners auditing financial statements.

Other References Concerning Audit of Computerized Systems

Numerous texts and other reference works that discuss the effect the computer has had on the processing, transforming and reporting of financial information are available. Space does not permit the listing of many excellent sources of which auditors might avail themselves. However, because of their currency, direct relevance to the audit of financial statements or applicability to governmental operations, the following publications have been highlighted as worthy of consideration:

The 1977 study by the Institute of Internal Auditors, comprised of three volumes:

Systems Auditability & Control—Executive Report,

Systems Auditability & Control—Audit Practices and

Systems Auditability & Control—Control Practices;

The AICPA's audit guide, *Audits of Service-Center-Produced Records,* which includes a detailed bibliography of computer-related auditing applications and other references concerning service bureaus in particular;

Review Guide for Evaluating Internal Controls in Automatic Data Processing Systems, published by the U.S. General Accounting

Office, 1970, with a bibliography of references on computer applications; and

Guide for Reliability Assessment of Controls in Computerized Systems (Financial Statement Audits), published by the U.S. General Accounting Office, 1976, with bibliography.

Exhibit 20-3

Use of EDP Audit Tools and Techniques

EDP Audit Tool/Technique	Percentage Used in Auditing Developments and Modifications*	Percentage Used in Auditing Production Systems*
Generalized audit software	12.5%	32.6%
Manual tracing and mapping routines	22.9	31.2
Test data method (e. g., test-decking)	27.1	26.6
Parallel operation	32.2	23.1
Tagged transactions (flagging transactions in "live" operations through the flow of transactions)	12.0	20.9
Snapshot (picture-taking of selected transactions through the flow of transactions)	10.0	18.4
Systems performance monitoring and analysis (e. g., SMF, SCERT)	8.2	15.8
Program source code comparison	9.6	14.5
Control flowcharting	8.3	9.0
Program object code comparison	4.7	8.9
Integrated test facility (mini- or dummy company)	4.2	5.0
Modeling (simulation)	9.5	7.6
Automatic tracing and mapping routines (analysis of source language and logic to determine if any program segments are not being utilized)	3.6	3.9
Other	6.5	10.5

* Percentages are based on actual responses weighted to reflect the probable response distribution of all organizations in the sampling frame. See the appendix for further description of weighted procedures.

Source: Table 6-2, Chapter 6, study titled *Systems Auditability & Control—Audit Practices,* The Institute of Internal Auditors, Inc., © 1977, printed with permission.

Appendix A

The publication reproduced on the following pages, titled *Program for Examination of Municipalities of the Commonwealth of Pennsylvania,* was prepared by the Pennsylvania Institute of Certified Public Accountant's Committee on Local Government Auditing and Accounting.

This document, reprinted with permission from the Pennsylvania Institute, is an illustrative internal control questionnaire and audit program.

Program for the Examination of Municipalities of the Commonwealth of Pennsylvania

Committee on Local Government

Auditing and Accounting

PENNSYLVANIA INSTITUTE OF CERTIFIED PUBLIC ACCOUNTANTS

1100 Lewis Tower Building

Philadelphia, PA 19102

FOREWORD

PICPA's Committee on Local Government Auditing and Accounting appointed a subcommittee to prepare the accompanying audit program and questionnaire for evaluation of internal control. This audit program has been prepared to assist certified public accountants in their continuing examination of municipalities in the Commonwealth of Pennsylvania. It is intended as a guide and should be modified to fit the conditions and circumstances of each engagement. It is *not* intended to supplant the judgement of the independent certified public accountant.

The *American Institute of Certified Public Accountants* (AICPA) Industry Audit Guide, entitled "Audits of State and Local Governmental Units", has defined "generally accepted accounting principles" and "generally accepted auditing standards" as they apply to local government units.

The accompanying questionnaire for the evaluation of internal controls has been prepared to assist the auditor in identifying the strengths and weaknesses of the system employed by a municipality. Conclusions reached by the auditor form the basis for decisions as to the extent and timing of audit procedures to be employed. They also may lead to a supplemental report offering constructive suggestions for improvements in the accounting procedures and related system of internal control. The seriousness of the weaknesses to be commented upon should, of course, be considered before issuing the auditor's opinion on the municipality's financial report.

Audits of municipalities must be performed in accordance with generally accepted auditing standards established by the AICPA in Statement on Auditing Standards No. 1, "Codification of Auditing Standards and Procedures," (SAS 1). These standards are as follows:

General Standards:

1. The examination is to be performed by a person or persons having adequate technical training and proficiency as an auditor.

2. In all matters relating to the assignment, an independence in mental attitude is to be maintained by the auditor or auditors.

3. Due professional care is to be exercised in the performance of the examination and the preparation of the report.

Standards of Field Work:

1. The work is to be adequately planned and assistants, if any, are to be properly supervised.

2. There is to be a proper study and evaluation of the existing internal control as a basis for reliance thereon and for the determination of the resultant extent of the tests to which auditing procedures are to be restricted.

3. Sufficient competent evidential matter is to be obtained through inspection, observation, inquiries, and confirmations to afford a reasonable basis for an opinion regarding the financial statements under examination.

Standards of Reporting:

1. The report shall state whether the financial statements are presented in accordance with generally accepted accounting principles.

2. The report shall state whether such principles have been consistently observed in the current period in relation to the preceding period.

3. Informative disclosures in the financial statements are to be regarded as reasonably adequate unless otherwise stated in the report.

4. The report shall either contain an expression of opinion regarding the financial statements, taken as a whole, or an assertion to the effect that an opinion cannot be expressed. When an overall opinion cannot be expressed, the reasons therefore should be stated. In all cases where an auditor's name is associated with financial statements, the report should contain a clear-cut indication of the character of the auditor's examination, if any, and the degree of responsibility he is taking.

The overall objective of the audit of a municipality is stated concisely in the SAS No. 1, Section 110.01.

"The objective of the ordinary examination of financial statements by the independent auditor is the expression of an opinion on the fairness with which they present financial position, results of operations and changes in financial position in conformity with generally accepted accounting principles. The auditor's report is the medium through which he expresses his opinion or, if circumstances require, disclaims an opinion. In either case, he states whether his examination has been made in accordance with generally accepted auditing standards. These standards require him to state whether, in his opinion, the financial statements are presented in conformity with generally accepted accounting principles and whether such principles have been consistently applied in the preparation of the financial statements of the current period in relation to those of the preceding period."

Care should be taken that the municipality is not under the impression that audits are intended to discover fraud. The primary purpose of the audit is a determination as to whether or not the financial statements present fairly the financial position at the statement date and results of operations during the period under review.

SAS No. 1, Section 110.05 and .06 comment on detection of fraud as follows:

"In making the ordinary examination, the independent auditor is aware of the possibility that fraud may exist. Financial statements may be misstated as the result of defalcations and similar irregularities, or deliberate misrepresentation by management, or both. The auditor recognizes that fraud, if sufficiently material, may affect his opinion on the financial statements, and his examination, made in accordance with generally accepted auditing standards, gives consideration to this possibility. However, the ordinary examination directed to the expression of an opinion on financial statements is not primarily or specifically designed, and cannot be relied upon, to disclose defalcations and other similar irregularities, although their discovery may result. Similarly, although the discovery of deliberate misrepresentation by management is usually more closely associated with the objective of the ordinary examination, such examination cannot be relied upon to assure its discovery. The responsibility of the independent auditor for failure to detect fraud (which responsibility differs as to clients and others) arises only when such failure clearly results from failure to comply with generally accepted auditing standards.

"Reliance for the prevention and detection of fraud should be placed principally upon an adequate accounting system with appropriate internal control. The well-established practice of the independent auditor of evaluating the adequacy and effectiveness of the system of internal control by testing the accounting records and related data and by relying on such evaluation for the selection and timing of his other auditing procedures has generally proved sufficient for making an adequate examination. If an objective of an independent auditor's examination were the discovery of all fraud, he would have to extend his work to a point where its cost would be prohibitive. Even then he could not give assurance that all types of fraud had been detected, or that none existed, because items such as unrecorded transactions, forgeries, and collusive fraud would not necessarily be uncovered. Accordingly, it is generally recognized that good internal control and fidelity bonds provide protection more economically and effectively. In the case of fidelity bonds, protection is afforded not only by the indemnification for discovered defalcations, but also by the possible deterrent effect upon employees. The presence of fidelity bonds, however, should not affect the scope of the auditor's examination."

CPAs should have a working knowledge of the AICPA Industry Audit Guide "Audits of State and Local Governmental Units" and be aware of the various peculiarities in accounting in local government. You should also be aware of changing requirements of both state and federal agencies concerning information to be included in the auditor's report.

Entities that use Electronic Data Processing (EDP) in accounting applications will require different audit concepts. CPAs encountering an EDP system should consult the American Institute's SAS No. 3 on "The Effects on EDP on the Auditor's Study and Evaluation of Internal Control," as well as other sources including continuing education courses, data processing manuals, current textbooks and current professional literature on the subject.

There are a number of other publications which the auditor should have available in his library for both reference and guidance. The Municipal Finance Officers Association of the United States and Canada in its publication "Governmental Accounting, Auditing and Financial Reporting", published in 1958 by the National Committee on Governmental Accounting. This publication deals with the financial management and accounting records and procedures of governmental units and a thorough knowledge is a prerequisite of any auditor considering an engagement of a governmental unit.

The United States General Accounting Office has established evolutionary audit concepts concerning not only financial audits but extends the audit to include compliance, economy and efficiency, and program results. In audits of governmental units receiving directly or indirectly federal funds the auditor should obtain copies of audit requirements, if any, of the supervisory agency.

The auditor should also be aware that if he accepts an engagement and agrees to audit in accordance with standards or requirements other than generally accepted auditing standards he is bound to meet those requirements *in addition* to generally accepted auditing standards.

The subcommittee wishes to thank each member of the committee for the comprehensive review of the work.

Lastly the subcommittee would remind you that nothing can take the place of the auditor's own professional judgement. In preparing this report care was taken not to limit, restrict or expand the requirements, or to indicate the extent of examination required, feeling that this determination is better determined in each given situation after thorough analysis of the facts involved.

Subcommittee on Audit Program for the

Examination of Financial Statements

of Pennsylvania Municipalities

Donald F. Tonge, Chairman

Peter Geleta

Leon A. LaRosa, Jr.

Henry F. Sanville, Jr.

John R. Miller

Dennis S. Misiewicz

John B. Welsh

Lawrence E. Barger, Chairman

Committee on Local Government Auditing and Accounting

January 1977

QUESTIONNAIRE FOR EVALUATION OF INTERNAL CONTROL

MUNICIPALITIES

COMMONWEALTH OF PENNSYLVANIA

Name of Municipality———————————————————————

Prepared by———————————————————. Date——————.

In consultation with——————————————————. Unless
otherwise noted in Remarks Column

Reviewed by——————————————————. Date——————.
Note:

It is not intended that this checklist for evaluating internal control must be used on all examinations. However, where the checklist is omitted, adequate memoranda explaining procedures and segregation of duties, audit steps performed and related conclusions as to the effectiveness of the system of internal control must be clearly indicated in the working papers.

When this checklist is used the question should be answered yes, no or not applicable (Y, N or N/A). In addition the auditor should indicate whether the questions were answered by the auditor (A) or the client (C).

	Yes	No	N/A	Audit Program Reference
Cash—General				
1. Is the co-mingling of cash in the various funds prohibited?				
2. Are the depositories instructed not to cash checks or money orders payable to the earned or other income tax collector?				
3. Is the person reconciling the bank accounts:				
a. Independent of other cash procedures including handling currency, receipts and signing of checks?				
b. Obtaining the bank statements (Including documents) unopened from the bank?				
Cash Receipts				
1. a. Are cash receipts controlled immediately upon receipt by proper registration devices?				
b. Are cash receipts reconciled to the totals of cash registers or other devices?				

	Yes	No	N/A	Audit Program Reference
c. Is the cashing of checks out of cash receipts prohibited?				
d. Does someone other than cashiers prepare and/or review the bank deposits?				
2. a. Is the mail opened by someone independent of other cash and record keeping functions?				
b. Is a record prepared by the person opening the mail for the checks and cash received?				
c. Is the record of cash and checks received given to someone independent of record keeping functions for verification of the amount recorded and deposited?				
d. Are incoming checks restrictively endorsed immediately upon receipt?				
3. a. Are receipts deposited intact daily?				
b. Is a duplicate deposit ticket after authentication by the bank, received by an employee independent of record keeping functions and of the person who makes the deposits and compared with:				
(1) Record of incoming remittances?				
(2) The cash book?				
4. a. Are deposits or collection items subsequently charged back by bank (because of insufficient funds, etc.) delivered directly to an employee independent of those:				
(1) Preparing the deposit?				
(2) Keeping the books?				
b. Are such items investigated by a person independent of those responsible for receipt or entry of cash?				
5. Are unsatisfactory remittances under adequate control and properly followed up?				
6. Are all bank accounts authorized by the governing board?				
7. Are bank accounts properly collateralized in accordance with the various codes?				
8. Are banks advised not to cash checks payable to the municipality?				
9. Are proper procedures in effect to insure the proper and prompt reporting of miscellaneous receipts, i.e., receipts from lost book fines, vending machines, sale of tickets, etc.?				
10. Are change funds maintained on an imprest basis?				
11. Are all receipts supported and reconciled by detailed analysis and by documentary evidence?				

	Yes	No	N/A	Audit Program Reference
12. Is the cash receipt book posted daily from supporting documents?				
13. If receipt forms are used:				
a. Are they pre-numbered?				
b. Are the issued numbers accounted for?				
c. Are unissued forms under adequate control?				
14. Are the duties of personnel who receive over the counter collections independent of other cash functions and bookkeeping?				
15. a. Is the receipt of currency relatively insignificant, as opposed to checks or drafts?				
b. If not, are the controls over such currency adequate?				
16. Are each day's receipts recorded promptly in cash receipts journal and taxpayers' accounts?				
17. Are total postings to taxpayers' accounts reconciled periodically to recorded cash receipts?				
18. Do the cash receipt records provide for:				
a. Identification of all sources of cash receipts (i. e., interest, tax, penalty, etc.)?				
b. Classification of tax receipts by year of assessment?				
19. Are records in condition to readily ascertain:				
a. Taxpayer's delinquency?				
b. Amounts receivable from other taxing jurisdictions for taxes collected under joint collection or reciprocal agreements?				

Cash Disbursements

	Yes	No	N/A	Audit Program Reference
1. a. Are checks pre-numbered and pre-printed with the name of the municipality, including proper identification of funds?				
b. Is the stock of unused checks under adequate control?				
2. Are voided checks kept and filed?				
3. Is the sequence of check numbers accounted for when reconciling bank balances?				
4. Is a check protector used?				
5. Is a check register prepared simultaneously with the preparation of the check by mechanical device?				

	Yes	No	N/A	Audit Program Reference
6. Are authorized signatures limited to those prescribed by the governing body and various legal provisions?				
7. Is the signing of checks in advance prohibited?				
8. Is the practice of drawing checks to the order of "cash" prohibited?				
9. Are inter-bank and inter-fund transfers under adequate accounting control?				
10. Are balances on the bank statements compared to ledger?				
11. Are checks returned by the bank compared with lists of those outstanding at the beginning of the period and with bank statements with which they were returned?				
12. Is the practice of examining paid checks for date, name cancellations and endorsements followed by those reconciling bank accounts?				
13. a. Are all invoices and supporting data submitted to the municipality for approval in accordance with the various codes?				
b. Are invoices examined by a responsible officer or employee to ascertain completeness of attachments and various required approvals?				
c. Does an approved payment list accompany the checks when they are submitted for signatures?				
d. Is there a definite (supported by evidence) responsibility for checking invoices as to:				
(1) Prices?				
(2) Extensions?				
(3) Freight charges?				
(4) Discounts?				
(5) Quantity?				
(6) Description of goods or services?				
14. When a mechanical check signer is used:				
a. Has approval been received for the legality of its use in accordance with the various laws?				
b. Is the signature plate under adequate control by persons independent of those responsible for preparing the checks?				
15. Are invoices and supporting data effectively cancelled?				
16. Are checks mailed without returning them to those involved in check preparation?				

	Yes	No	N/A	Audit Program Reference

17. Is the cash disbursements book posted simultaneously with the preparation of the check?

18. Are checks, which are outstanding for a long period of time investigated and/or restored to cash?

19. In regard to earned income tax:

   a. Does the tax collector maintain satisfactory records of cash receipts and disbursements?

   b. Does the tax collector remit collections to the taxing districts on a timely basis?

   c. For refunds:

     (1) Is supporting detail required for all refund payments?

     (2) Is approval required for all refund payments?

     (3) Does the approved refund voucher and supporting evidential matter accompany the checks when presented for signature?

   d. Are controls in effect to readily ascertain liabilities to other taxing jurisdictions for tax as collected under joint collection or reciprocal agreements?

Petty Cash

1. Is there a petty cash fund?

2. Is the fund on an imprest fund basis?

3. Is responsibility for each fund vested in only one person?

4. Is the custodian independent of employees who handle receipts?

5. Are the accounting records inaccessible to the custodian?

6. a. Does the custodian obtain a formal voucher for all disbursements made from the fund?

   b. Are such vouchers executed in ink or otherwise in such manner to make alterations difficult?

   c. Are the vouchers approved by a department head or some responsible employee?

   d. Are the items contained in the fund of current and usual nature, i. e.: No post-dated checks or stale-dated vouchers?

7. Are checks for reimbursements made out to the order of the custodian?

8. Are reimbursement vouchers and attachments cancelled at, or immediately

	Yes	No	N/A	Audit Program Reference

following, the signing of the reimbursing check, so that they cannot be misused thereafter?

9. If imprest fund is represented in whole or in part by bank account, has bank been notified that no checks payable to the municipality should be accepted for deposit?

10. Are petty cash funds restricted as to:
    a. Amount not exceeding requirements for disbursements for a reasonable period of time?
    b. Expenditures of petty nature not exceeding a certain fixed amount?

11. a. Is the cashing of accommodation checks prohibited?
    b. If not, are such checks drawn to the order of the custodian?

12. Is there an adequate internal audit or review of disbursement vouchers and attachments before reimbursement is made?

Inventories

1. Does the annual inventory summary indicate under whose supervision and direction the inventories were taken?

2. Are the procedures and instructions adequate?

3. Are quantities determined by actual weight, count, or measurement?

4. Are recount procedures required?

5. Do the instructions provide for indication of obsolete or damaged inventory?

6. Are inventories taken at least annually and supporting records adjusted?

7. a. Are perpetual inventory records maintained?
    b. If so:
       (1) Are perpetual records in lieu of physical inventories?
       (2) Are perpetual records supported by physical inventory?

8. Are adjustments of both detail and control records made in the period to which they applied?

9. Are inventories maintained under proper safeguards?

10. When applicable are issuance procedures of inventory adequate?

11. Are inventories covered by insurance and can proof of loss be readily established?

	Yes	No	N/A	Audit Program Reference

Investment Securities

1. Are securities adequately safeguarded?

2. If kept in safe deposit box, is it necessary for more than one person to be present to open the box and, if so, are such persons authorized by the governing board?

3. Are securities in the name of the municipality?

4. Are securities periodically inspected or confirmed?

5. Is a record maintained of each security, including certificate numbers?

6. Are purchases and sales of securities:
   a. Authorized by the governing body?
   b. Recorded in approved minutes?
   c. Legal investments for municipality?

7. For investments purchased with co-mingled monies of various funds, is each fund's portion of principal and interest readily determinable and accounted for?

8. Do the investment records contain the following information:
   a. Nature of security.
   b. Number of units.
   c. Serial number.
   d. Name of issuer.
   e. Face value or par value.
   f. Premium or discount.
   g. Term.
   h. Date of maturity.
   i. Interest or dividend rate.
   j. Interest or dividend dates.
   k. Accrued interest at close of period.
   l. Date of default, if any.
   m. Whether registered.
   n. Date of purchase.
   o. Cost.
   p. Market value at close of period.
   q. Physical location.

Property, Plant and Equipment

1. a. Are detailed ledgers or other records maintained?
   b. Are any properties owned by related authorities but operated by the municipality insured?
   c. Are periodical appraisals made for insurance purposes?

2. Does the municipality have a well defined policy, based on the provisions

	Yes	No	N/A	Audit Program Reference

of the various codes, to govern accounting for capital additions as opposed to maintenance and repairs?

3. a. Is approval by the governing body required to scrap or to sell items?

   b. Is control of such items maintained to assure receipts of the sales proceeds?

4. Is a satisfactory system in effect for the safeguarding of small tools and maintenance supplies?

5. a. Is depreciation being recorded in the general fixed asset group of accounts?

   b. If not, are memo entries or other work papers used for cost reimbursements purposes, where applicable?

6. Are assets which have been fully depreciated but which are still in use retained in the accounts?

7. Are depreciation and replacement policies and accounting closely coordinated?

Notes Payable

1. Are borrowings authorized by the board and in accordance with the various codes?

2. Are retired notes properly cancelled and accounted for?

3. Are sinking funds maintained?

4. Are schedules of borrowing maintained, and, if so, do they contain the following information:

   a. Date.

   b. Name of payee.

   c. Amount.

   d. Due date or dates.

   e. Payments made.

   f. Outstanding balance.

   g. Balance past due.

   h. Interest rate.

   i. Accrued interest.

   j. Prepaid interest.

   k. Date and amount of original debt.

   l. Collateral.

   m. Endorsements.

Bonded Debt

1. Are schedules maintained for bonded debt, and, if so, do they contain the following information:

   a. Date of issue.

	Yes	No	N/A	Audit Program Reference

b. Description of issue and property pledged.

c. Denominations and numbers of bonds authorized and issued.

d. Discount or premium at which issued.

e. Table of amortization of bond discount or premium.

f. Dates of maturity.

g. Denominations and numbers of bonds retired.

h. Denominations, numbers and locations of bonds held in other funds.

i. Name and address of trustee and registrar.

j. Sinking fund:

   (1) Name and address of trustee.

   (2) Amount which should be on hand according to trust indenture.

   (3) Amount on hand.

   (4) Composition of fund.

   (5) Sinking fund income.

   (6) Sinking fund reserve.

   (7) Interest rate on bonds.

   (8) Coupon dates.

   (9) Accrued interest.

   (10) Interest on default.

   (11) Endorsements.

2. Are capital outlay bond funds kept separate from other funds?

3. Are disbursements of bond funds subject to normal disbursing controls?

4. Has a separate sinking fund account been authorized?

5. Are bond registers maintained?

6. Are paid bond and interest coupons properly accounted for and cancelled?

7. Does the trustee issue timely statements of trust fund transactions in reasonable detail including an accounting for investment securities on the statements of trust fund transactions?

Lease Obligations

1. Are leases authorized by the board and in accordance with the various codes?

2. Are rental payments properly approved and accounted for?

3. Are leases and related transactions periodically reviewed by a responsible official to insure compliance with the terms of the agreement?

	Yes	No	N/A	Audit Program Reference

4. Does the board receive and review audited financial statements of related authorities at least annually?

Revenues

Real Estate Taxes

1. Does the municipality prove the real estate assessment as furnished by the appropriate county official by:

   a. Adding individual assessments and comparing to certificates of total assessments as furnished by the county?

   b. Accounting for all changes in the original assessments?

2. Do review procedures provide for extending each assessment contained in the tax duplicate by the tax rate, totaling the taxes, thus determined, and comparing the gross yield determined by applying the tax rate to the total assessed valuation as determined in 1 a?

3. Does the municipality post all transactions to a copy of the tax duplicate?

4. Are collections from each tax collector promptly deposited to the credit of the municipality?

5. Does the municipality independently prove the tax collector's monthly reports?

6. Does the municipality audit the accuracy of the tax collector's final settlement?

   a. Deducting taxes collected from the gross yield as adjusted for authorized changes?

   b. Comparing result with total of uncollected taxes returned to the county commissioners or filed as liens in an office of the prothonotary?

   c. Comparing uncollected taxes as reported in detail by the tax collector with uncollected taxes as reflected on the municipality's copy of the tax duplicate?

   d. Requesting the county commissioners to confirm the total of uncollected taxes returned?

   e. Requesting individual taxpayers to confirm that taxes were unpaid as reported by tax collectors?

7. Does the tax collector settle the prior year's duplicate prior to being furnished with the current year's duplicate?

8. Are adequate controls maintained of uncollected taxes as such relate to subsequent collections, exonerations, etc.?

	Yes	No	N/A	Audit Program Reference

Per Capita Taxes

1. Are proper controls and procedures in effect to reasonably establish that each resident or inhabitant subject to per capita tax has been included in the assessor's lists of such taxables?

2. Does the municipality post all collections to a copy of the tax duplicate?

3. Are the collections from the tax collector deposited promptly to the credit of the municipality?

4. Does the municipality independently prove the tax collector's monthly reports?

5. Does the municipality prove the accuracy of the tax collector's final report?

6. Are uncollected taxes properly exonerated or otherwise accounted for?

7. Are adequate controls maintained of uncollected per capita taxes not exonerated or otherwise settled?

Additional Taxes

1. Are adequate controls maintained to enable the municipality to prove the collections and accountability for taxes as reported by the tax collector?

2. Are the policies, scope and administration of the tax clearly defined in the governing ordinance or resolution and the rules and regulations?

3. The tax rolls:

   a. Are the tax rolls established by methods which will most likely result in reasonable comprehensive lists of potential taxpayers?

   b. Are procedures in effect for revising and updating the tax rolls to provide reasonable assurance that:

      (1) New taxpayers are added?

      (2) Accounts of taxpayers no longer liable are deleted?

      (3) Taxpayers' addresses are correct?

      (4) Evaders are detected?

   c. Is evidential matter in support of deletions from the tax rolls retained?

   d. Are tax rolls adequately safeguarded to prevent unauthorized alterations or removals?

4. Method of assessment:

   a. Are reasonable methods employed to provide that taxpayers receive tax notices, including investigation of notices returned by the post office?

	Yes	No	N/A	Audit Program Reference

5. Do the forms of tax notice:
   a. Clearly advise taxpayer of his responsibility to file a return?
   b. Describe the method of preparing the forms?
   c. Provide for listing of pertinent information, including estimated taxable income (if a declaration), taxable income and tax?
   d. Instruct taxpayer as to when, how and where to return the forms and remittances?
   e. Prescribe method for obtaining refund of overpayment of final tax liability?

6. Are reasonable methods employed to determine that employers within the taxing jurisdiction withhold, remit and report taxes of employees?

7. Enforcement:

   a. Are tax returns audited by the tax collector as to:
      (1) Comparison of tax returns with tax notices mailed?
      (2) Mathematical accuracy?
      (3) Analysis and substantiation of net profit returns?
      (4) Substantiation of wage returns for which tax was not withheld?
      (5) Reconciliation of employers' remittances with amounts reported on employees' tax returns?
      (6) Reconciliation of estimated tax payments with amounts claimed on final returns?
      (7) Review of returns for comparability of income reported with that of prior year?

   b. Are adequate records of delinquent taxpayers maintained?

   c. Are policies set forth in governing ordinance, rules and regulations strictly enforced as to:
      (1) Notification of delinquency in payments or filing returns?
      (2) Assessment of interest and penalties?
      (3) Prosecution of evaders and delinquents?

Revenues from State Sources

1. Are receipts of such revenues reconciled by the municipality to claims and applications filed?

	Yes	No	N/A	Audit Program Reference

2. Are proper controls maintained of uncollected revenues from state sources?

3. Are accounting procedures adequate to facilitate the preparation of the prescribed reports to state authorities?

Revenues from Federal Sources

1. Are all applications for federal reimbursements and appropriations adequately supported by work sheets and prescribed forms?

2. Are revenues from federal sources properly segregated in the accounting records as such segregation is required?

3. Are procedures in effect to assure disbursements of the funds in accordance with the terms of approved grants and on a timely basis?

4. Are proper controls maintained of uncollected and/or refundable revenues from federal sources?

5. Are the accounting procedures adequate to facilitate the preparation of the prescribed reports to federal and state authorities?

6. Does adequate documentation exist to support the receipt and/or valuation of the non-federal share or in-kind contributions?

7. Did the grantee maintain a rate of contribution for the non-federal share as required as the grant agreement?

8. Are procedures adequate to assure compliance with the contract and regulations of the federal grant/program?

Enterprise Fund Revenues

1. Does the enterprise fund derive revenues from the following sources:
   a. Assessments?
   b. Connection fees and permits?
   c. Charges for service? (if yes, explain).
   d. State and federal grants?
   e. Lease rentals?
   f. Other? (if yes, explain).

2. Are proper controls and procedures in effect to reasonably assure the control of revenues?

3. Are revenues reconciled to independent source data (such as assessment rolls prepared by engineers, metered consumption furnished by other utilities, current fixture surveys, plumbing and building permits, etc.)?

	Yes	No	N/A	Audit Program Reference

4. Are charges for service checked against:
   a. Meter readings?
   b. Current rate schedules?
   c. Master billing control?

5. Are adequate records maintained on uncollected revenues?

Miscellaneous Revenues

1. Are proper procedures in effect to insure the reporting and accounting of miscellaneous revenues?

2. Does the board establish rent rate structures if applicable?

Purchases and Expenditures

1. Are open purchase orders reviewed periodically?

2. Are purchase orders approved by a responsible employee?

3. Is purchasing centralized?

4. Are purchase requisitions used to originate purchasing activity?

5. a. Are purchases made on the sole basis of purchase orders?
   b. Are purchase orders pre-numbered?
   c. Is numerical control maintained on all purchase orders?

6. Are the purchasing and receiving functions entirely separate?

7. a. Are receiving reports prepared for all goods received?
   b. Are such reports under numerical control?
   c. Is a list or copy of all receiving reports maintained?
   d. If a copy of the purchase order is used as a receiving report, are quantities deleted from the copy first used as a receiving report?

8. a. Are invoices paid, where applicable, only upon the strength of:
   (1) Purchase orders?
   (2) Evidence of receipt?

9. Is a register of all approved vendors maintained?

10. a. Are accounting distributions established by responsible employees?
   b. Are such distributions reviewed at, or prior to, the time vouchers are approved by the governing body?

11. Is proper provision made to insure that only original invoices are processed for

	Yes	No	N/A	Audit Program Reference

payment, i. e., as opposed to statements or duplicate invoices?

12. Are vendors' statements regularly reconciled to recorded payables?

13. Are detailed accounts payable records maintained and periodically reconciled with control accounts?

14. Are unpaid invoices under proper accounting control?

15. Are checks prepared only for approved vouchers or check requests by designated persons?

16. Are returned purchases, shortages and damaged materials accounted for in order to insure proper credit?

17. a. Are purchases made for the account of employees prohibited?

   b. If not, are such purchases properly controlled?

Payrolls

1. Are individual personnel files maintained?

2. Is an approved salary schedule made a part of the regular minutes of the governing body and in agreement with the approved budget?

3. Are all changes in rates, additions and dismissals approved in the minutes of the governing body?

4. Are methods of accumulating time and recording absences satisfactory?

5. Are clerical operations in preparation of payrolls double checked before payment?

6. Does the governing body or designated official approve the payroll computation?

7. Are duties of those distributing the payroll rotated?

8. a. Are employees paid by check?

   b. If so:

      (1) Are payroll checks signed by someone who does not participate in:
         (a) The preparation of the payroll?
         (b) Custodianship of cash funds?
         (c) Maintenance of accounting records?

      (2) Are payroll disbursements made from an imprest bank account?

      (3) Are payroll checks distributed by someone other than employees

	Yes	No	N/A	Audit Program Reference
who participated in the preparation?				
(4) Are checks written on machines with automatic totals?				
(5) Is adequate control exercised in preparing, signing, and distributing checks?				
(6) Is proper control exercised over back pay and unclaimed wages?				
(7) Are reconciliations of payroll bank accounts made by employees whose duties are unrelated to those preparing the payrolls?				
(8) Do the procedures followed when reconciling payroll bank accounts include the checking of names on payroll checks against payroll records and the examination of endorsements on checks?				
9. a. Are employees paid by cash?				
b. If so:				
(1) Are receipts obtained from employees?				
(2) Does the municipality employ the services of an independent pay agent (i. e., armored car or other service)?				
(3) Are paymasters rotated?				
(4) Are paymaster's duties independent of payroll preparation?				
(5) Is paymaster accompanied by a person who is independent of nothing to do with the preparation of payroll?				
(6) Is proper control exercised over unclaimed wages?				
10. Are individual pay records maintained?				
11. Are individual records periodically reconciled to control accounts?				
12. Are personnel policies established in writing?				
13. As a minimum, do the personnel and/or payroll records provide support for personnel actions, attendance, leave, and earnings, for full-time as well as part-time employees?				
14. When employees are first hired, do procedures provide for reference checks and confirmation of prior salary?				
15. When employees work overtime are there procedures to provide for:				
a. Authorizing and paying overtime only to employees entitled to receive overtime pay?				

	Yes	No	N/A	Audit Program Reference

b. Recording earned and used compensatory time in lieu of overtime pay?

c. Limiting accumulation of compensatory time?

16. When duties require employees to spend considerable working hours away from their offices, do they prepare reports for their supervisors disclosing their daily activities (e. g., number of persons contacted, interviewed, referrals)?

17. Has the municipality made appropriate withholding and payment of applicable federal, state and local taxes, including where appropriate, the following:

a. Federal income taxes?

b. State and local income taxes?

c. Social Security taxes (FICA)?

d. Federal unemployment compensation taxes (FUTA)?

e. Workmen's compensation insurance?

18. Are payroll records reconciled to applicable quarterly/yearly report by a person independent of their preparation?

19. Are periodic reviews made to determine that payment for employee benefits are in accordance with the provisions of the plans?

20. a. Does the municipality have written personnel policies prohibiting employment of individuals which result in:

(1) Nepotism?

(2) Conflict of interest?

(3) Discrimination?

21. Does the municipality have written policies to prohibit employees, governing body and members of their immediate families, from accepting gifts, money, or gratuities from beneficiaries of the program, contractors, or persons who are otherwise in a position to benefit from the actions of any employee or member of the governing body?

General

1. Are officers' and employees' duties reasonably fixed as to responsibility (organization chart, job description, etc.)?

2. Are employees' duties rotated?

3. Are all employees required to take vacations?

4. a. Are all public officials and employees in positions of trust bonded?

	Yes	No	N/A	Audit Program Reference
b. Has the adequacy of bonds recently been reviewed and approved by the board?				
5. Are known relatives so employed as to make collusion improbable?				
6. Do books of account include a general ledger?				
7. Are all postings to general and subsidiary ledgers required to be supported by entries in books of original entry or journal entries?				
8. Are ledger entries:				
a. Clearly referenced to indicate their source?				
b. Standardized for content and identification?				
c. Supported by readily identifiable data?				
d. Reviewed and approved by responsible official?				
9. Are the duties of the personnel responsible for the preparation of journal entries, etc., independent of the posting and financial statement preparation functions?				
10. Is access to accounting records limited at all times to persons whose duties require such access?				
11. Is there a chart of accounts supplemented by definitions of items to be included in the accounts?				
12. Are there written instructions as to the recording of accounting transactions?				
13. Are books of account:				
a. Posted on a current basis?				
b. Balanced at least monthly?				
14. Is there continuing supervision and review to determine that:				
a. Prescribed policies are being carried out?				
b. Procedures are not obsolete?				
c. Corrective actions are taken promptly?				
15. a. Do internal reports to the governing body appear to be adequate to bring to light abnormal financial figures and other discrepancies and and are they submitted on a timely basis?				
b. Do financial reports contain comparison of budget to actual?				
c. Are financial reports submitted on a timely basis and in accordance with the provisions of the various codes?				

	Yes	No	N/A	Audit Program Reference
16. Does a responsible employee periodically review all insurance coverage?				
17. Is the governing body independent of business enterprises with which the municipality does business?				
18. a. Is the annual budget supported by adequate documentation?				
b. Are the requirements of the various codes, as they apply to budgetary control of expenditures, strictly adhered to?				
c. Is the governing body furnished with a budget status report each month?				
19. Does the governing body and/or other municipality officials take prompt remedial action with respect to audit findings of representatives of the state?				
20. Are there any accounts in the name of employees' associations, etc., which are not recorded on the books?				

CONCLUSION

NOTE: After careful and serious study, the auditor should comment concisely on matters revealed by the questionnaire. Separate comments should be made for each fund, i.e., general fund, special revenue fund, utility fund, etc., with respect to each of the following matters:

1. Required changes in the audit program (extension or restriction of audit tests or altered timing of audit procedures).

2. Suggested changes in accounting system and procedures to achieve satisfactory internal controls.

3. Suggested changes in accounting system and procedures to achieve greater efficiency and improved financial reports and internal controls.

4. Suggested changes to reduce audit time requirements.

5. Other pertinent comments.

AUDIT PROGRAM

GENERAL

A. Obtain an engagement letter from the municipality outlining the scope of the engagement, funds to be audited, type of financial report required and any additional services to be performed.

B. Adequately plan the engagement. Consideration should be given to timing of audit procedures, control and scheduling of time, supervision of work, etc.

C. Review the system of internal accounting control by inquiries and observation.

D. Develop or revise the audit procedures based upon the review of internal control.

E. Become familiar with the legal requirements of the municipality and fund under review.

F. Minutes

    1. Review and abstract pertinent recordings and relate to books of accounts and financial statements.

    2. Obtain certification that Minutes reviewed were the official Minutes of the municipality.

G. Budgetary Control

    1. Review the laws or rules governing the appropriate budget functions.

    2. Review procedures relating to the execution and control over the budgets as adopted.

    3. Examine evidential matter as to the approval of both the budget originally adopted and any subsequent revisions.

    4. Compare final budget amounts with actual expenditures to determine whether the budget has been violated by over-expenditure.

H. Review any audit reports issued by federal or state agencies for disclosure of special financial reporting implications, e.g., disallowance of expenditure that will require a refund.

I. Insurance, public officials' bonds (including tax collectors) and Fidelity Bonds.

    1. Analyze accounts in which premiums for insurance coverage, etc. have been recorded.

    2. Prepare schedule of coverage and relate to premium payments.

    3. Examine policies and bonds noting restrictive or qualifying endorsements.

4. Inquire as to adequacy of coverage giving consideration to applicable legal provisions.

5. Relate coverage to approval by governing body and to insurance appraisals.

J. Books of account

1. Verify by appropriate tests, footings of the various books of original entry.

2. Trace footings so tested to the general ledger accounts to establish accuracy of the postings.

3. Review journal entries made during the period under review.

K. Review transactions and events occurring in the period between the date of the financial statements under examination and the date of the opinion to determine whether either adjustments of the accounts or disclosure is necessary for fair presentation.

L. Obtain letter from solicitor as to pending litigation, contingent liabilities, legal matters of any other matter which might materially affect the financial condition of the governmental unit.

M. Obtain letters from the governing body or responsible officials indicating that, to the best of their knowledge and belief, the financial report reflects financial position and results of operations for the year.

N. Prepare letter of comments and recommendations with respect to weaknesses in internal controls, accounting and operating procedures and financial reports observed during the course of the examination of the general and other funds. Much of the substance of such a letter would be developed in answering the questionnaire for evaluation of internal control.

ASSETS

The assets of a governmental unit are subject to verification in much the same manner as the assets of a private enterprise or institution. The auditor must also remember the essentials of fund accounting, particularly, that each fund is a separate entity and that the assets of each fund must be separately accounted for and available only for the purposes for which the particular fund was created.

A. Cash

Audit Objectives:

The auditor should determine that the cash balances are maintained in different accounts, if required, that the depositories are legally acceptable, that all municipal funds are recorded in the books and records, and are in the name of the municipality. He should further verify collateral, if required, and its sufficiency during the period. He should also review investment policy for idle cash balances. Some audit procedures for cash are:

1. Refer to the portion of the Internal Control Questionnaire which relates to cash receipts and petty cash. Note the weaknesses in internal control affecting the accounts covered by this Program. Consider additional audit procedures in light of these weaknesses.

2. Request confirmation as of balance sheet date from all depositories, including bank where certificates of deposit and Treasury Bills were purchased, with whom Municipality did any business during the period under review. Include in the confirmation requests for pooled collateral under Act 72 and authorized check signers.

3. Arrange to obtain bank statements and cancelled checks directly from banks after balance sheet date.

4. Ascertain that the cash disbursements cut-off is reasonable by performing the following:

   a. Obtain at balance sheet date, from the Municipality's records, the numbers of the last checks drawn prior to the close of the period under review.

   b. List and examine at balance sheet date checks drawn prior to the close of period under review but not issued at balance sheet date.

   c. In light of findings from previous two steps, ascertain at later date that cash disbursements cut-off as of balance sheet date is proper.

5. Ascertain that the cash receipts cut-off is reasonable by performing the following:

   a. Compare receipts per cash book with credits per bank statements for a period of time prior to and subsequent to the end of the balance sheet date.

b. Obtain Municipality's copies of deposit slips for a period prior to the balance sheet date, (an authenticated copy, if available) and compare the individual items thereon with the detailed items in cash receipts.

6. From the Municipality's records, tabulate transfers between bank accounts (for all funds) for a period of time before and after close of period under review, and ascertain that both sides of these transactions have been properly recorded on the books.

7. Obtain and check (or prepare) bank reconciliations for all bank accounts as of balance sheet date and reconcile book balance with general ledger.

   a. Trace balance per bank as shown on bank reconciliation to year end and cut-off bank statements, and also to confirmations.

   b. Trace deposits in transit to cut-off bank statement.

   c. Foot bank reconciliation prepared by Municipality.

   d. Trace book balances to general ledger.

   e. Investigate checks to unusual payees, banks, officials, cash, etc.

   f. Note that other reconciling items were properly accounted for.

8. Upon receipt from banks of bank statements and cancelled checks as of cut-off date:

   a. Ascertain that checks recorded in the cash disbursements book as of period prior to balance sheet date are listed as outstanding on the bank reconciliations. Note that check was endorsed by payee and cleared in a reasonable period.

   b. Examine bank endorsements of checks dated after reconciliation date noting they did not precede audit date.

   c. Ascertain that cancelled checks and debit/credit memos which were received with cut-off bank statements and represent transfers between bank accounts, are included as transfers between bank accounts.

   d. Ascertain that outstanding checks which are material in amount and did not clear the banks within a reasonable period are proper.

   e. Ascertain that reconciling items other than outstanding checks and deposits in transit are proper.

9. Upon receipt of confirmation from bank:

   a. Check balances confirmed to reconciliations.

   b. Ascertain that all other matters confirmed are reflected in the books and statements.

  c. Ascertain that pooled collateral under Act 72 is sufficient to collateralize all bank balances including savings accounts and certificates of deposit.

10. Prepare proof of cash transactions for test period, reconciling book entries with entries recorded on the bank statements.

11. Trace proof of cash totals and cash book totals to the books of account and test mathematical accuracy of footings of cash journals.

12. Ascertain that cash and investment balance at the end of the year is sufficient to cover unexpended federal program funds if applicable.

13. Determine that all checks and/or warrants outstanding at the beginning of the period under audit have been accounted for.

14. Determine that cash receipts are deposited intact on a daily basis.

15. Determine that separate bank accounts are properly maintained for the various funds, if required by law or bond indentures.

16. Reconcile Treasurer's cash balances with the governmental unit's accounting records.

B. Cash on Hand

1. Ascertain locations, custodians, and probable amounts of cash funds and undeposited receipts. Consider whether funds and undeposited receipts should be counted.

2. Check significant cash funds as follows:

  a. In presence of custodian, count currency and reconcile with general ledger.

  b. List the details of vouchers, checks, collections, etc.

  c. Ascertain that non-cash items are properly approved and that supporting data is adequate. If significant, consider recording unentered disbursement vouchers.

  d. Obtain explanations of differences and exceptions from custodian.

  e. Have custodian sign count sheet and acknowledge return of fund intact.

  f. Have a responsible official (other than the custodian) of the client review for irregular items the list of vouchers, checks, etc. included in the count.

  g. Have client deposit checks included in the count. Supervise the mailing or delivery of deposit to bank.

  h. Ascertain whether any of the checks are subsequently dishonored, and investigate.

  i. Trace deposits to bank statements.

j. Obtain from custodians of funds not counted, confirmations showing composition of funds.

3. Ascertain that checks said to represent undeposited receipts have been entered in the cash book under a current date, and are later deposited; take such steps as may be necessary and possible under the circumstances to guard against substitution of other receipts in making the deposit.

4. Ascertain that checks said to have been cashed have been entered in the cash book.

5. Ascertain that reimbursement checks included in the cash balance have been entered as disbursements, or, in the case of simultaneous verification with cash on deposit, that they are included in the reconcilement as outstanding. Also, in either case, ascertain that they are properly supported by vouchers, etc.

6. Determine whether any cash funds are restricted.

7. Determine whether all persons handling cash are bonded in reasonable amounts.

8. Examine all cash advances or other items carried as cash but not represented by cash or current checks. (The auditor should follow up these items and report them if they are not cleared during the course of the audit).

9. Ascertain the reason for holding checks not deposited immediately and see that they are cleared before the audit is completed, or consider mention of them in report.

10. Determine that all petty cash funds are authorized and set up in the accounts as assets.

C. Receivables

The auditor should verify the existence and propriety of receivables for the municipality in much the same manner as those of a commercial enterprise, recognizing the various laws, ordinances, resolutions and other restrictions which may offset receivables in the municipality. Some audit procedures to be considered are:

1. Taxes Receivable

   a. Review procedures for various taxes in section on revenues and receipts.

   b. Ascertain that any allowance made for uncollectible taxes is proper.

2. Notes and Accounts Receivable

   a. Review notes and accounts receivable supporting documents and authorization.

    b. Request confirmation of selected balances.

    c. Ascertain that any allowance made for uncollectible items is proper.

    d. Trace inter-fund receivables and payables to applicable funds.

D. Investments

The procedure for verification of the investments of a governmental unit should be the same as that for a private enterprise. One phase of the procedure should be emphasized. The auditor should obtain or make a complete list of the investments at the beginning of the period. With this list, he should account for all investments disposed of and add all investments acquired during the period. The authority for both the disposition and acquisition of investments should be determined. He should make inquiries concerning the rules and regulations relative to the custody of the investments.

The auditor must also satisfy himself that any special requirements with respect to the acquisition and disposition of investments for the account of the various funds holding investments are complied with. He should ascertain particularly that the investments examined are of the character specified by legal requirements.

Interest coming due during the period should be ascertained and care should be taken to see that interest is properly recorded.

Some audit procedures to be considered are:

1. Examine and count securities. Verify that unmatured interest coupons are attached or accounted for.

2. Determine that investments are recorded properly.

3. Verify that purchases and sale of investments during the period were at market prices and authorized.

4. Ascertain that income on investments has been properly accounted for in the proper funds.

5. Determine that investments owned which matured or have been sold during the period under examination have been properly accounted for.

6. Determine that the investment program complies with authorizations and the requirements of the various laws.

E. Inventories

The auditor should determine the physical existence and ownership of materials and supplies included in the assets of various funds verifying these assets in the same manner that similar assets of a private enterprise are verified.

1. Observe the taking of inventory of the governmental unit, if considered appropriate.

2. If material, or necessary, make test counts of quantities and test pricing, extensions, and footings.

3. Examine procedures employed in receiving, storing, and issuing supplies.

4. Apply appropriate auditing procedures to establish fairness of evaluation at statement date and procedures in effect for control of inventories.

F. Prepaid Expenses and Deferred Charges

Ordinarily, a unit does not undertake to equalize the incidence of expenditures by prorating them over the period of benefit. However, certain expenses are prorated in some funds, such as utility and other enterprise funds. Where this is true, the auditor should verify the prepaid expenses and deferred charges in the same manner that he would verify similar items of private enterprises and institutions. Some audit procedures to be considered are:

1. Test computation of balances as usual in commercial engagement.

2. Review nature of accounts, determining validity of prepayment or deferral, compliance with statutory provisions, value of asset, and propriety as to classification.

3. Old balances should be investigated and charge-offs considered.

4. Charge-offs during the period should be reviewed for authorization.

5. Consider whether comment on material amounts should be made in report.

G. Fixed Assets

The auditor should use the same procedures and care in examining the unit's expenditures for fixed assets as he would use in examining such expenditures of a private enterprise or institution.

In the case of acquisitions of real property, the auditor should see that deeds are on hand and are properly recorded. In the case of personal property, he should ascertain, as far as possible, that the items purchased were used exclusively for official business or rented out at an appropriate rental, and that they have been maintained in good condition.

Fire insurance policies and other indemnity contracts incident to the ownership and operation of fixed assets should be examined.

All dispositions of fixed assets should be checked as to the authorization therefor and as to the consideration received. There should be a realistic method of removing assets disposed of from the asset accounts.

Rentals of Property and Equipment. Leases, contracts, and other documents covering the use of municipal property by others should be examined and the amount of rents received and receivable verified.

Depreciation policy as and where required by G.A.A.P. or local policy should be reviewed taking into consideration useful life and salvage value.

1. Determine if annual inventory of fixed assets has been taken and obtain a copy.

2. Review consistency of method of valuation of fixed assets in the accounts and property records.

3. Examine vouchers, construction contracts, and other documents reflecting additions to fixed assets during the period to determine whether such additions were properly recorded.

4. Verify that disposals of fixed assets were authorized and recorded properly in the accounting records. Trace cash receipts from disposition into the treasurer's records.

5. By inquiry of appropriate officials, determine basis of recording additions to and retirements of property, plant and equipment and criteria for differentiating between repairs and maintenance and additions and improvements.

6. If recorded by the governmental unit, a check should be made of basis of depreciation used.

7. Review insurance policies for coverage, endorsements, and co-insurance clauses.

8. Vouch additions and improvements and examine contracts, deeds, titles and other evidence of ownership of current year's acquisitions. Verify that deeds have been recorded on real estate purchased or otherwise acquired.

9. Review and vouch, if considered necessary, maintenance, repairs, replacements and capital outlay accounts (note items which may have been misclassified).

10. Determine that expenditures have been made from proper funds and that proceeds of sales have been accounted for in accordance with applicable statutory provisions.

11. By inquiry, reference to minutes, etc. substantiate retirements.

12. Substantiate carrying value of property leased from municipal authorities by reference to authority's audited financial statements or by examination of applicable authority records.

LIABILITIES

Liabilities are generally similar to commercial or profit oriented enterprises, except for certain terminology differences. Care should be taken in classifying the various liabilities in the various funds. If the encumbrance method of accounting has been adopted the encumbrances outstanding should be shown on the balance sheet on a line between liabilities and fund balance. Care should be taken to determine that all liabilities are recorded. The audit procedures in examining liabilities of a municipality are similar to those of any other type of enterprise.

A. General

1. Review authority for and trace the cancellation or adjustment of any liabilities during the period under audit.

B. Payroll Accrual and Related Withholdings

If any salaries and wages are payable at the end of the period under audit, the auditor should ascertain the amount thereof.

1. Substantiate the accuracy of the computation of payroll accrual at the year end.

2. Determine, by appropriate test, that unremitted withholdings are fairly stated, comparing remittances subsequent to the year end to copies of reports or tax returns which accompany payments.

C. Accounts and Vouchers Payable

It is often the practice of governmental units not to account for purchase obligations until the bill for the goods or services is paid; consequently, there may be no control of accounts payable. In cases where purchase orders are issued, it is a relatively simple matter to verify the accounts payable, particularly if the purchase orders are recorded as encumbrances when issued. When purchase orders are not issued, the auditor should request the chief accounting officer of the unit to preserve the statements received from vendors at the end of the period under audit. The auditor should also consider requesting statements as of the balance sheet date from other vendors and suppliers. Subsequent payments, minutes and other data should be examined for unrecorded liabilities and, if material, they should be recorded.

The auditor should be particularly careful with respect to cut-off of disbursements and the possibility of delayed or advanced dating of invoices. Some audit procedures to be considered are:

1. Obtain or prepare a listing or trial balance of accounts payable; foot and compare the total with the general ledger control account.

2. Determine that obligations incurred during the period under audit are properly recorded in the accounts and that they are recorded in the proper accounting period.

3. Compare entries in the purchase journal, voucher record or cash disbursement journal immediately before and after the balance sheet

date to supporting vouchers to determine whether significant items are reported in the correct accounting period.

4. If circumstances warrant, confirmation of amounts payable directly from creditors with whom the governing board normally does business may be requested.

D. Other Payables (due to other funds or governmental units, prepayments etc.)

The auditor should use procedures similar to those he would use in a commercial enterprise.

Usually all the facts about interfund accounts will be found in the records of the governmental unit. In reviewing these accounts, the auditor should ascertain the authority for each inter-fund transaction. In no case should interfund receivables be offset by inter-fund payables, or vice-versa, unless properly authorized entries pertaining thereto have been made in the records. Some audit procedures to be considered are:

1. Analyze transactions in the accounts to determine their nature and propriety.

2. Trace inter-fund accounts payable and receivable to applicable funds.

3. Old balances should be investigated and analyzed.

E. Notes, Contracts, and Tax Anticipation Loans Payable

The auditor should determine that these liabilities are properly authorized in accordance with legal requirements, that sufficient resources are available to service the debt and that monies required for debt service have either been disbursed or set aside according to legal requirements.

The auditor should determine that proper amounts have been received from the issuance of debt during the current period.

1. Analyze loans incurred or repaid during year.

2. Determine that transactions have been authorized by the board.

3. Determine that loans are in accordance with the requirements of the various laws.

4. Consider confirming balances with noteholders.

F. Judgments

1. Confirm with the counsel of the governmental unit amounts due under court judgments.

2. Ascertain that the accounting records properly reflect judgments due.

G. Deposits

1. Determine that deposits are properly recorded.

H. Accrued Expenses

1. Ascertain that liabilities for expenses incurred but unpaid at the end of the period under audit are recorded properly.

I. Revenues Received in Advance, Taxes Held in Escrow, Returnable Deposits, etc.

1. Ascertain that amounts so recorded are properly classified and fairly stated.

2. Confirm with applicable parties, if considered necessary.

J. Bonded Indebtedness

1. Check the bond issues outstanding to records of elections approving issue or resolutions of board authorizing issue, approvals by state authorities and opinion of bond counsel.

2. Ascertain that bonds sold or retired during the period under audit are properly recorded.

3. Verify that bonds and interest coupons redeemed have been cancelled or disposed of in accordance with proper authorization.

RESERVES AND EQUITY ACCOUNTS

The auditor should determine that reserves and equity accounts are properly classified and restricted in accordance with budgetary, legal and other considerations. He should also determine that reserves are adequate to meet items not appropriated.

Some audit procedures are:

A. Reserves

1. Ascertain that amounts reserved are properly classified and accounted for in the manner prescribed by various laws.

2. Review transactions during the audit period.

B. Equity Accounts

1. Reconcile beginning of year balances in fund equities with closing balances in preceding year's auditor's report.

2. Analyze and substantiate changes in fund equities during the year.

3. Ascertain that the fund balance of each fund is separately stated and that the unexpended balance of any special fund is properly accounted for.

4. Determine that reserves are set up for items which are not available to meet appropriations, such as inventories of materials and supplies, petty cash and change funds, encumbrances, and long-term advances to other funds.

REVENUES AND RECEIPTS

The revenue of the average unit comes from a number of sources and is of many kinds. Ordinarily, the principal source of revenue is the general property tax. In addition, there are various types of other taxes, special assessments, business and professional licenses, fees, permits, fines, forfeitures, rents, interest on bank balances, interest on investments, franchise fees, and revenues from utilities or other enterprises.

There is no uniformity of administrative organization for the receipt and custody of municipal revenues and other receipts. Practice varies all the way from the requirement that all payments to a government be made to a single officer and all monies collected by held by a single officer to the requirement that different classes of revenue and other receipts be collected and held by different officers. Thus, the auditor may encounter a variety of practices as to the receipt and custody of money. Before beginning the audit of revenues, therefore, the auditor must ascertain who is supposed to collect each class of revenue, who is actually collecting it, who is actually holding it, and exactly what the collection routine is.

Some audit procedures are:

A. General

1. Refer to the portion of the internal control questionnaire which relates to revenues. Note the weaknesses in internal control affecting the accounts covered by this program. Consider additional audit procedures in light of these weaknesses.

2. Ascertain that money collected has been turned over to the treasurer promptly and credited to the proper funds.

3. Ascertain that money received by the treasurer has been deposited promptly to the credit of the governmental unit.

4. Review legal provisions with reference to the protection of funds handled by officials in an ex officio capacity.

5. Review the accuracy of cash receipts records, determine whether cash, or its equivalent has been received for receipts issued.

6. Review cash transactions between funds and between the governmental unit under audit and other governmental jurisdictions for propriety. and authorization.

7. Review authorization for exonerations, remissions, adjustments, or abatements of revenues.

8. Review journal entries involving revenues and receipts.

B. Real Estate Taxes

The auditor should review the propriety of the valuation of assessable property by the records of the assessor or corresponding agency independent of the treasurer or other tax-collecting officer. He should verify that the tax rate used in preparing tax statements agrees with that in the tax levy ordinance. The auditor should examine abatements and refunds of taxes. The procedure for obtaining an abatement or refund is ordinarily fixed by law. The auditor should ascertain that this procedure is followed.

It is customary practice to impose a penalty and to charge interest on taxpayers for failure to pay their taxes within the time required by law. The auditor should ascertain whether such penalties and interest have been collected and properly accounted for and if interest and penalties are accrued on the books, that the proper amounts have been accrued.

The auditor should determine that bills have been mailed timely, that receipts have been recorded properly and promptly and check the propriety and collectibility of taxes receivable.

The audit should also determine procedures for recording of tax liens and sales.

Some audit procedures to be considered are:

1. Verify the tax assessor's records of taxable property valuations and test the accuracy therof.

2. Determine that the tax rate is within the legal limit applicable to the governmental unit under audit.

3. Determine that the board passed an appropriate resolution in support of tax rate.

4. Request confirmation of original assessed valuation of real estate from the appropriate county office.

5. Obtain change notices of corrections and adjustments to original assessed valuations.

   a. Adjust original assessed valuation accordingly.

   b. Request confirmation of changes from appropriate county office.

6. Apply tax rate to adjusted valuation to determine gross yield.

7. Determine that the tax collector's bond was in force and adequate in amount.

8. Determine that discounts were properly allowed and that penalties were properly collected.

9. Apply tax collections to gross yield to determine amount of uncollected taxes to be returned to county commissioners as of the first Monday of May of the year following levy.

    a. Obtain tax collector's listing of returned taxes and prove mathematical accuracy of total.

    b. Reconcile total to amount determined by applying collections to gross yield.

    c. Request confirmation by county commissioners of the total of taxes returned, as reconciled.

    d. Request confirmation by taxpayers of unpaid taxes per the tax collector's list of returned taxes.

10. Trace tax collections into the treasurer's record of cash receipts.

11. Determine that funds collected for other governmental units are properly segregated and remitted.

12. In cases where the tax collector of another governmental unit collects taxes for this unit, arrangements should be made to secure confirmation from the collector of amounts collected for and remitted to this unit.

13. Check distribution of tax collections to proper funds.

C. Interim Assessment of Real Estate Taxes

1. Obtain assessment lists, as certified to by the board.

2. Determine, by appropriate tests, that taxes were properly levied and calculated.

3. Apply receipts to total interim taxes assessed to determine the amount of uncollected taxes at year end.

4. Consider requesting confirmation of uncollected taxes with taxpayers.

D. Delinquent Real Estate Taxes

1. To the beginning balance of uncollected delinquent taxes, add taxes returned by the collector, and deduct collections remitted by the county, to arrive at current outstanding delinquent taxes.

2. Request confirmation of collections during the year from the county treasurer.

3. Determine that interest and penalties are collected on delinquent taxes.

4. Prove commission paid to, or withheld by, the county.

5. Request confirmation of delinquent taxes in total with county, if practicable, with individual taxpayers, if considered necessary.

E. Income Taxes (Refer to Audit Guide for Earned Income Tax Collectors)

The auditor should determine that the application of the program of taxation is to all individuals subject to the tax. He should also review data for the correctness of returns and adjustments to returns filed. He should also check for proper and timely collection of receipts and application to appropriate accounts.

1. Test internal audit procedure for checking of income tax returns and collections.

2. Verify by test of taxpayers' lists and other available records that all returns required by law were filed.

3. Review calculations on income tax returns and ascertain compliance with applicable rules and regulations.

4. Trace tax computation indicated on tax returns to cash receipts records and deposits.

5. Review apportionment to multiple funds and other governmental units.

6. Where income taxes are owed but have not been paid by the end of the audit period they should be recorded as receivables and confirmed on a test basis with taxpayers.

7. Substantiate the reasonableness of the collector's records. This should be done in the light of the internal control over tax rolls. Names obtained from independent sources may be compared to names listed on the records of the collector. Such sources would include voter registration lists, per capita assessment rolls, school district census, superintendent's report of new students, current telephone directories, utility accounts, etc. An explanation should be obtained with respect to any names not included in the collector's records. These names should be included on a test basis in the circularization referred to in step "8" below.

8. Select a representative number of current and delinquent taxpayers and request confirmation of payments, if any, made during the year.

9. Select a representative number of businesses withholding taxes from employees' pay and request confirmation of amounts paid to the collector during the year.

10. Check the mathematical accuracy of selected final tax returns and compare the amounts of the tax with amounts collected per the individual taxpayer's accounts.

11. Review a representative number of taxpayer accounts and trace payments shown thereon to cash receipt records.

12. By appropriate tests:

a. Add receipt duplicates (or other form which serves as the remittance advice) for selected days and agree totals with cash receipt records.

b. If numbered receipts are used account for numerical sequence of receipt duplicates.

    c. Compare the amount of the tax and interest and penalty, if any, per the receipt duplicate (or other appropriate form) with the distribution in the receipts record. Check the allocation of the collections to the taxing districts.

    d. Trace details per receipt duplicates (or other appropriate form) to the individual taxpayer's accounts.

    e. Compare collections as recorded with bank statements, noting that deposits were made promptly and that collections were deposited intact.

13. Compare current collections with prior years (for the year and by periods, as appropriate in the circumstances) and investigate significant differences.

14. Review delinquent accounts and ascertain if appropriate collection efforts are being instituted on a timely basis.

SPECIAL NOTES REGARDING EARNED INCOME TAXES:

Act 511 requires, among other things, that, except in cities of the second class, the governing body of the political sub-division shall appoint a certified public accountant, a firm of certified public accountants, a competent public accountant, or a firm of independent public accountants to make not less than one examination each year of the books, accounts and records of the income tax collector.

In the event the auditor of the municipality is not the duly appointed auditor of the earned income tax collector, the following audit procedures are suggested:

a. Obtain and review latest report on examination of the earned income tax collector as a basis for reliance thereon.

b. Relate recorded income to reports submitted by tax collectors.

c. Request confirmations of receipts with the tax collectors.

It is recommended that the auditor's report include a statement as to the limitation of the scope of the examination of earned income taxes, if material, when the audit of such income is performed by other auditors.

F. Local Tax Enabling Act, Act 511, 1965, as Amended (except per capita tax)

Determination of additional taxes authorized under Act 511 and their proper collection and administrative procedures should be made by reference to minutes, ordinances, resolutions, and inquiry. Determination of timeliness of collection and application to appropriate accounts should be made on an appropriate basis.

Some audit procedures to be considered are:

1. Determine if any additional taxes are levied. Determine that such taxes are in accordance with the applicable sections of the law.

2. Relate recorded income to reports submitted by tax collector.

3. Verify receipts from such taxes.

4. Request confirmation of receipts with the tax collector.

G. Per Capita Tax

The auditor should determine the procedure for assessment and applicability of per capita tax to all persons covered by the resolution.

Some audit procedures to be considered are:

1. Obtain assessment roll and determine number of taxables.

2. Determine the tax rate is in accordance with applicable law and resolution of the board of governing body.

3. Extend taxables by rate to determine gross yield.

4. Determine that discounts were properly allowed and that penalties were properly collected.

5. a. Account for exonerations of tax collectors by reference to section of the board of governing body.

   b. Review basis for exonerations as to reasonableness.

6. Deduct collections and exonerations and reconcile balance to list of uncollected taxes submitted by the tax collector to the governing body.

7. By appropriate selection methods consider requesting confirmations of uncollected taxes with taxpayers.

8. a. Review controls maintained of uncollected delinquent per capita taxes.

   b. Account for collections of delinquent per capita taxes.

H. Licenses, Fees and Permits

Licenses:

The typical governmental unit issues a great variety of licenses. The basis of the license fees and the rates thereof are numerous. The auditor, therefore, must determine what licenses the unit issues and the bases and rates applicable to them. This information can be obtained from the record of the proceedings of the unit's legislative body and appropriate licensing officials.

The administration of license laws may be lax in that the unit relies upon the licensee to supply the data necessary to establish the bases upon which his license is computed.

Some units control and assure the maximum return from licenses by having inspectors visit the places of business of licensees and verify the bases reported by licensees. Revenue from licenses may be controlled by using prenumbered and manifold license receipts, so that licenses issued can be checked with collections therefrom.

Fees and Permits:

The average unit also has a variety of fees and permits. The auditor should ascertain what fees and permits the unit imposes and make such a check of the revenue of each class of fee and permit as the records will allow.

Some audit procedures for the above items are:

1. Obtain a schedule of the rates of all licenses, permits, inspections, recordings, and other fees.

2. Check rates charged against ordinances.

3. Trace collections into the treasurer's record of cash receipts.

I. Fines, Forfeitures, and Court Fees

The auditor should determine that fines and forfeits are collected timely and that there are prescribed conditions for waiving fines and forfeits.

Some audit procedures to be considered are:

1. Review the docket or other original court records for:

    a. Fines and fees collected.

    b. Payment of fines by the serving of jail sentences.

2. Review police traffic violation procedures and policies, test control of traffic tickets issued, and determine method of voiding tickets.

3. Review collections and waivers of police department fines and fees.

4. Trace collections into the record of cash receipts.

J. Rentals of Property and Equipment

1. Review internal audit procedure on lease agreements.

2. Review schedules, rates, leases, and other data to determine the use of property by others.

3. Verify the amounts or rents billed and collected and trace collections to the cash receipt records.

4. Review authorization of rates charged.

K. Interest on Bank Balances

1. Review agreements with depositories and ascertain that they conform with applicable laws and regulations.

2. Review interest earned calculations and trace amounts to records.

3. Based on the analysis of investment transactions and savings accounts determine that income from temporary deposits and investments have been properly accounted for.

4. Trace collections of interest into the treasurer's record of cash receipts.

L. Other Revenues from Local Sources

1. Analyze other revenues from local sources and, where practicable, relate income to independent sources, such as leases, permits, agreements, minutes, etc.

2. Determine or review amounts indicated to be receivable and evaluate their collectibility.

3. Request confirmation, if considered necessary, of amounts collected and/or receivable.

M. Grants and Subsidies from Other Governmental Units

The auditor should ascertain from what other units of government the unit is entitled to receive grants and subsidies and obtain from these units statements of amounts paid during the period under audit. He should also see that these payments have been received and credited to the funds to which they should have gone. Moreover, in auditing the expenditures from these funds, he should ascertain that these revenues, as well as other revenues of the fund, have been spent only for the purpose for which the funds were established and are being maintained.

Some audit procedures to be considered are:

1. Confirm with other governmental units the amounts collected for and transmitted to this unit.

2. Trace receipts into the treasurer's record of cash receipts.

3. Determine that grant funds have been or are being used only for authorized purposes.

4. Obtain and review copies of the grant documents and/or application for funds, including amendments and the notification of approval by the appropriate state or federal agency.

5. Obtain and review copies of the fiscal reporting forms and ascertain that they were prepared and filed in accordance with statutory and/or grant requirements.

6. Account for income received or receivable and, if the project is completed, amounts which may be refundable.

N. Special Assessments

Generally speaking, special assessments are those made for public facilities or improvements against the property owners particularly benefitted by the installation of such facilities or improvements. Such assessments usually are computed by the department or agency of the unit that installs the improvements, after which they are certified by that department or agency to the assessing authority. The auditor should check the special assessments certified in the department where they were computed and certified.

The auditor should check the expenditures for special assessment improvements to determine whether assessments have been made and their relation to the expenditures. He should see that surplus or deficits resulting from variations in the cost of improvements are properly disposed of. He should note whether any special improvements were completed in prior periods that should have been assessed in the current period.

Unit records should be kept of each piece of property on which assessments have been levied. These records will show the total amount of assessments due, the number of installments, the amount of each installment, and interest on installments, if the assessments are payable in installments, and the payments received on account of assessments and interest. The auditor should see that the total of the balance carried in each of these records agrees with the corresponding control accounts in the general ledger. If assessments are payable in installments, he should see that installments have been properly calculated and the proper amount of interest charges to assessment payers on outstanding assessment installments.

The auditor should determine the statutory requirements for doubtful accounts. If practicable the assessments should be classified as (1) current, (2) delinquent, and (3) deferred, not due.

The auditor should check interest and penalties. He should see that property acquired at a sale for unpaid special assessments is properly recorded on the books as an asset in the assessment fund. As in the case of taxes receivable, he should verify cancellations, remissions, or adjustments, as to their legality and authority.

Some suggested audit procedures are:

1. Reconcile current, deferred, and delinquent assessments with general ledger control accounts.

2. Review interest and penalties received or receivable.

3. Trace collections of assessments, interest, and penalties into the treasurer's cash receipts records.

4. Ascertain the authority for each special assessment project. Analyze expenditures for special assessment improvements to determine if the assessments therefore have been made. Correlate assessments to expenditures.

5. Ascertain that any improvements completed in prior periods that should have been assessed in the current period have been properly assessed.

6. Confirm receivables directly with owners of the property.

7. Confirm collections on current and delinquent assessments in the hands of collection agencies.

8. Verify authorizations for cancellations or adjustments as to their legality.

9. Check the interest on deferred installments charged.

10. Review authorizations and procedures for write-offs of uncollectible accounts and review any write-offs which have occurred.

O. Refunds of Prior Years' Expenditures

  1. Analyze transactions recorded in this account.

  2. Determine items contained within the account are properly classified.

  3. Review of correspondence to determine whether such refunds have been properly recorded.

P. Incoming Transfer Accounts

The auditor should review the minutes to determine the propriety of transfers and for a determination of application to proper funds.

Some suggested audit procedures are:

  1. Examine agreements establishing amounts contributable to other units, etc. and determine that revenues have been properly received.

  2. Request confirmation from participating units, etc. of amount received and receivable.

Q. Enterprise Revenues

Enterprise activities provide various types of services, transportation, electric, water and/or sewer, recreation, etc. Enterprise funds are more closely allied with commercial type enterprises than with municipalities and require audit procedures similar to commercial enterprises. The auditor should determine that revenues and expenditures are reported in a manner to permit determination of income and expense. The accrual basis of accounting is used by all enterprise funds.

The auditor should review user charges and collections to the various ordinances, rate schedules, contracts, and laws governing the enterprise.

The auditor will sometimes be called upon to determine compliance with the bond ordinance.

Some audit procedures are:

  1. Review rate schedule and authority for charges.

  2. Where charges are based on volume of usage, or other variable quantities, test usage records.

  3. Review rates charged and compare with those authorized.

  4. Check billing computations.

  5. Trace collections into record of cash receipts.

  6. Confirm on a test basis accounts receivable.

  7. Review authorizations and procedures for write-offs of uncollectible accounts.

  8. Review computation and support for unbilled revenues.

OTHER RECEIPTS

In municipalities and other local governmental units there are a number of other considerations, not normally found in commercial enterprises, of which the auditor must be aware.

Receipts from issuance of bonds and notes should be reviewed for legality, proper authorization by the municipality and application of the receipt to the proper fund. He should also determine that requirements for repayment are adhered to, that taxes assessed for repayment are applied properly and that coverage required in ordinances or indentures is complied with.

Receipts from sale of investments should be reviewed for date deposited and interest earned.

Sale of fixed assets should be verified by a review of the minutes. The auditor should also determine that sales are properly recorded in the asset accounts. He should also review controls over idle assets to make certain they have not been converted improperly.

Some audit procedures are:

A. Sale of Investments.

1. Review investment register and review authority for sales.

2. Ascertain that interest accrued to sale date has been collected.

3. Trace collections from sale of investments to the treasurer's cash receipts records.

B. Sale of Bonds or Notes

1. Review the authorization for sales and obtain and review trust indenture for restrictions.

2. Check discounts, premiums, and accrued interest involved in the sales of bonds.

3. Confirm the number of bonds printed with the printer. Obtain affidavit concerning printed bonds sold and unsold from the broker.

4. Trace receipts into the treasurer's cash receipts record.

5. Earnings of the bonds and notes

a. Review transactions in temporary investment of excess cash. Confirm investments owned at the year end with the custodian.

b. Determine that such investments were legal for the fund and that the transactions were authorized by the board.

c. Substantiate income earned on investments.

6. Contributions or Grants-in-Aid

    a. Account for receipt of proceeds of contributions or grants-in-aid by reference to underlying agreements or claims.

    b. Confirm directly amounts received and/or receivable.

C. Sale of Fixed Assets

    1. Review authority for sales of fixed assets.

    2. Review fixed asset records and verify sales prices.

    3. Trace receipts into the treasurer's cash receipts records.

D. Notes Payable, Tax Anticipation Notes

    1. Ascertain authority for sale of notes.

    2. Trace receipts from sales of notes into the treasurer's cash receipts records.

E. Taxes and Other Receipts Collected for Other Governmental Units

    1. Verify amounts and authority for payments made to other governmental units.

EXPENDITURES, PURCHASING, DISBURSEMENTS

The auditor should ascertain, by appropriate tests, that the purchases were made in accordance with procedures prescribed by law; that the goods were actually received; that they were what was ordered and paid for; that the prices paid were no more than those shown in the related purchase orders, bids, and contracts; that all discounts were taken; that such purchases were not paid for more than once; that they were charged to the proper appropriation accounts; and that no expenditures were made in excess of the balance to the credit of the appropriation account to which it was chargeable. The auditor should see that there is an itemized invoice or other formal evidence for every purchase, that a copy of the purchase order is attached thereto, if the unit follows the practice of issuing purchase orders, and that there is also attached a receiving report or proper record of receipt. He should also determine that prices, extensions, and footings have been checked, and that the proper officer or officers have taken such other steps as are necessary to enable them to justify the payment of the charge.

A. Review and gain an understanding of the system of internal control.

    1. Determine that expenditures were authorized and incurred and properly charged to the appropriate fund.

    2. Determine that expenditures are supported by itemized invoices, vouchers, contracts, or other supporting documents and that they are marked so that they cannot be reused.

B. Test of transactions

1. For selected representative vouchers (statistical or judgment sample)

    a. Compare voucher with appropriate books or original entry and supporting documents.

    b. Examine supporting documents for:

      (1) Properly prepared and authorized purchase orders.

      (2) Evidence of receipt of goods.

      (3) Evidence of verification of prices, quantities, extensions, etc.

      (4) Correctness of account charged.

      (5) Propriety of material or service purchased.

      (6) Evidence of legal compliance in regard to advertising for or soliciting quotations for prices, where applicable.

      (7) Approval for payment.

      (8) Effectively cancelled.

      (9) Account distributions are reasonable (charged to the correct fund and budgetary classification).

      (10) Agree with contract provisions, where applicable.

    c. Compare invoices to minutes or other evidence of approval for payment by the board.

2. For selected representative paid checks (preferable corresponding to vouchers selected).

    a. Compare check with appropriate books of original entry and supporting documents (vouchers).

    b. Scrutinize the endorsements and cancellations on checks and warrants.

3. Check the mathematical accuracy of disbursement and voucher records.

4. Trace postings to general ledger.

5. Check non-cash expenditures represented by inter-departmental transactions. Determine that all such transfers are supported by vouchers, properly authorized, and that charges have been made to the proper accounts.

6. Review the purchasing procedure and determine that it complies with applicable legal provisions.

7. Determine if appropriation accounts are encumbered for purchase orders and that subsequent payments are properly recorded.

8. Note vendors' names and watch for irregularities such as fictitious names and names of public officials and employees.

C. Appropriations

1. Review budget for the year under audit.

2. Determine if the budget and appropriation ordinances comply with governing legal provisions.

3. Check appropriation amounts and purposes.

4. Note whether appropriations are properly encumbered and determine if expenditures plus encumbrances are within appropriations.

5. Scrutinize transfers as to propriety.

D. Other Disbursements

1. Check adequacy of monies available for bonds and coupons due but not paid.

2. Examine bond indentures to determine compliance with debt service and other requirements.

E. Payroll

The auditor should determine that persons on the payroll are authorized both by position and budget. That their pay rate, deduction and fringe benefits are in accordance with wage and salary plans negotiated and/or various laws. He should also determine that distribution is made to proper accounts and that payments are made only in return for services rendered.

1. Check mathematical accuracy of payrolls.

2. If a separate payroll account is maintained, compare total payroll with the amount deposited in the payroll account and with the general fund disbursing check.

3. Compare individual earnings records with approved salary list for:

   a. Authorization of employment.

   b. Rate of pay.

   c. Minimum salary requirements established by the Commonwealth of Pennsylvania and federal government.

4. Check schedules of rates and fees for compliance with the salary and appropriation ordinances of the governing body and regulations of civil service commission or personnel department.

5. Check payroll receipts or payroll checks against the payroll journals and scrutinize endorsements.

6. Check payroll deductions for withholding taxes, retirement, insurance, and other authorized purposes. Determine that such deductions have been credited to the proper accounts or funds.

7. Determine if methods of delivering payroll checks provide for proper internal control.

8. Check amounts and disposition of unclaimed wages.

9. Check changes in rates, employment and dismissals of personnel by reference to approvals by the salary board or governing body.

10. Check basis for payments to supporting records, such as:

    a. Time cards.

    b. Absentee records.

11. Review pro-ration of employees' time to ascertain reasonableness of payroll allocations.

12. Compare salary list with W-4 withholding exemption slips on file.

13. Review withholding procedures and related reports and tax returns for the period under examination to determine whether they seem adequate; check such procedures to assure they are functioning properly.

14. Determine that payments have been made to the state or other retirement funds in accordance with requirements and determine adequacy of funding requirements.

15. Consider an observation of a payroll distribution on an unannounced basis, properly identifying each employee by obtaining signatures for comparison to personnel files or by other means.

OTHER EXPENDITURES

As in the case of receipts, there are expenditures which are not entirely analogous to commercial enterprise and which deserve special mention.

The auditor should review the minutes for mention of major construction, retaining architects and engineers and other items indicating a building program or other capital expenditure. He should relate this to the issuance of bonds or notes. He should determine that the municipality has adequate control over the project during acquisition or construction. He should also determine that they are properly recorded in the general fixed asset group of accounts or other fund accounts as appropriate.

He should relate payment of bonds and interest to the liability accounts and the revenue restricted to repay debt. He should review bonds or notes retired before maturity to determine the method used and the appropriateness as related to legal and other considerations.

Some audit procedures to be considered are:

A. Construction Contracts

1. Determine that the construction contracts were awarded to the lowest responsible bidder after due public notice for competitive bids was given.

2. Determine that contractors have given bonds with sufficient surety in amounts fixed by the governing board for the faithful performance of the contracts and for assurance of payment of materials and labor.

3. Determine that insurance coverage required under the contracts has been provided and is in force, if required, at the audit date.

4. Determine that changes to the original contract amount have been approved by the local board, its engineers or architects, and are supported by properly executed change orders.

5. Examine payments to the contractors to approved progress billings.

6. Confirm status of contracts at audit date directly with the contractors, including such information as original contract amount, approved change orders, adjusted contract amounts, payments to date, amount retained and balance payable.

7. Send copies of such confirmation requests to the engineers or architects, requesting their agreement of the data submitted and also their estimate of cost to complete such contract as well as compliance by the contractors with the items and specifications of the contracts, particularly as to agreed completion dates.

8. Architects' or Engineers' Fees

    a. By reference to agreements, substantiate fees paid and payable.

    b. Confirm, if necessary, with architects or engineers the agreed fee scale, payments to date and balance payable.

9. Other Expenditures (land, rights-of-way, equipment purchases, legal and financing costs, etc.)

    a. Relate to approved supporting invoices.

    b. To the extent necessary, confirm such payments directly with the payees, establishing the status of progress billings, if any. Should the minutes or other records indicate difficulties concerning settlements for rights-of way or land condemnation costs, request clarification from the solicitor with particular reference to his estimate of the amount of unsettled liabilities.

10. Long-Term Leases with Building Authorities, etc.

    a. Examine leases, abstract pertinent provisions, and determine that rentals and other obligations have been properly paid.

    b. Determine that government unit is not in default under the terms of the leases.

    c. Substantiate computation of aggregate amounts payable in future years.

B. Federal Programs

1. Obtain the approved project budgets, including amendments, and ascertain that expenditures and encumbrances conform therewith.

2. In the course of voucher examinations tests apply appropriate procedures for federal program expenditures to ascertain compliance with special requirements imposed by law. Also ascertain that the expenditure is appropriately identified with the specific program charged.

3. Review expenditures of each project required to be separately reported upon to ascertain that the regular invoice examination accomplished an appropriate test. Expand the tests on a project basis, as necessary.

C. Payment of Bonds and Interest

1. Review schedules of maturities and ascertain that principal and interest payments have been made.

2. Ascertain that bonds and coupons have been cancelled or voided after payment has been made.

D. Petty Cash Funds

1. Verify that vouchers are submitted for all reimbursements to the petty cash fund.

2. Ascertain that the amount of petty cash on hand, plus unreimbursed vouchers, equals the total authorized amount of petty cash fund.

E. Notes and Contracts Payable, Tax Anticipation Notes

1. Ascertain if payments are in accordance with contract or agreement.

2. Prepare a schedule of notes which are due and unpaid.

3. Review to make sure that tax anticipation notes have been retired in accordance with legal requirements.

4. Determine that the collections of special assessments have been used to pay the principal and interest of the obligations payable from such special assessments.

OTHER PROGRAMS

The PICPA has issued a number of audit programs specifically designed for certain programs. These programs should be used in the connection with auditing these programs or funds. The committee has however attempted to include certain steps in this program to enable the auditor to start his audit of these funds, while recognizing that these are not complete nor intended to be complete.

These limited audit procedures are:

A. Revenue Sharing (refer to revenue sharing audit guide)

1. Determine that funds granted from the department of the treasury were used within the prescribed time period for which check is applicable (used means "expended, encumbered, obligated or appropriated").

2. Determine that any interest earned from the investment of funds was appropriately used.

3. Determine that revenue sharing funds were only used for appropriate categories.

4. Determine that revenue sharing funds were deposited in a separate bank account.

5. Perform an audit of the ending cash balance utilizing the cash audit program included herein.

6. Confirm entitlement payments with the office of revenue sharing.

7. Confirm any investments held with outside independent custodian and make appropriate tests of interest income.

8. Obtain from minutes appropriating revenue sharing funds the amount of each appropriation and check to the accounting records.

9. Make appropriate tests of outstanding encumbrances.

10. Make appropriate tests of payrolls, vouchers and other documents charged against revenue sharing funds.

11. Determine that municipality has filed the appropriate reports with the department of treasury.

12. Inquire of the regional office of Revenue Sharing - Compliance Division to determine if there are any current complaints filed, and the nature and status of any such complaints.

B. Liquid Fuels Tax (refer to audit guide for liquid fuels tax by PICPA)

1. Determine that liquid fuels tax funds were deposited in a separate bank account.

2. Perform an audit of the ending cash balance utilizing the cash audit program included herein.

3. Confirm entitlement payments with Pennsylvania Department of Transportation.

4. Confirm any investments held with outside independent custodian and make appropriate tests of interest income.

5. Review copies of audit reports and correspondence from Penn DOT. Determine that municipality has complied with recommended changes or statutes from these reports.

6. Determine that municipality has filed the following reports with Penn DOT.

   a. Municipal budget.

   b. Report of state funds expenditures.

   c. Report of checks - state fund account.

7. Ascertain that highway aid funds are expended only for the following:

   a. Maintenance and construction or reconstruction of public roads, including bridges, culverts and drainage structures.

   b. Acquisition, maintenance and operation of traffic signs and traffic control systems.

   c. Funds expended in "1" and "2" above used for labor, hiring of equipment, purchase of construction materials and supplies, and repair parts for equipment, small tools, road drags, snow fence and street signs.

   d. Purchase of road machinery and equipment limited to 20% of total annual allocation.

8. Make appropriate tests of outstanding encumbrances.

9. Make appropriate tests of payrolls, vouchers and other documents charged against liquid fuels tax funds.

Appendix B

The publication reproduced on the following pages, titled, *Disclosure Guidelines for Offerings of Securities by State and Local Governments,* was published by the Municipal Finance Officers Association, copyright 1976.

This document, reprinted with permission from the Municipal Finance Officers Association, was prepared by MFOA as suggestions of information that may be disclosed in securities offerings by state and local governments.

413

Disclosure Guidelines for Offerings of Securities by State and Local Governments

Municipal Finance Officers Association
December 1976

Second Printing, April 1977

Copyright © 1976
by the Municipal Finance Officers Association

Library of Congress Catalogue Card Number 76-52521

Printed in the United States of America for the
Municipal Finance Officers Association of
the United States & Canada
1313 East 60th Street
Chicago, Illinois 60637

Acknowledgements

The Municipal Finance Officers Association of the United States and Canada expresses its appreciation to the following committees and individuals for their help and participation in the development of these guidelines:

Members of the Revision Drafting Committee:

Donald J. Robinson, Esq., **Chairman,** Hawkins, Delafield & Wood, New York City

J. Chester Johnson, Vice President, Morgan Guaranty Trust Company of New York, New York City

Richard Laird, Chief Accountant, Columbus, Ohio

Anthony Mandolini, Partner, Peat, Marwick, Mitchell & Co., Chicago, Illinois

David G. Ormsby, Esq., Cravath, Swaine & Moore, New York City

Staats M. Pellett, Vice President, Bessemer Trust Company, NA, New York City

William R. Snodgrass, Comptroller of State Treasury, Nashville, Tennessee

Peter C. Trent, Executive Vice President, Shearson Hayden Stone Inc., New York City

John M. Urie, Director of Finance, Kansas City, Missouri

Members of the MFOA Committee on Governmental Debt and Fiscal Policy:

Joe E. Torrence, **Chairman,** former Director of Finance, Metropolitan Government of Nashville & Davidson County, Nashville, Tennessee

Andre Blum, Director of Administration, Madison, Wisconsin

Harlan E. Boyles, State Treasurer, Raleigh, North Carolina

Daniel B. Goldberg, Esq., New York City

Lennox L. Moak, Director of Finance, Philadelphia, Pennsylvania

William J. Reynolds, Town Comptroller, Greenwich, Connecticut

John M. Urie, Director of Finance, Kansas City, Missouri

John T. Walsh, Director of Finance, Hartford, Connecticut

James V. Young, Collector-Treasurer, Boston, Massachusetts

Michael S. Zarin, Chief, Finance Division, Law Department, The Port Authority of New York and New Jersey, New York City

Members of the Disclosure Procedures Special Committee:

William J. Reynolds, **Chairman,** Town Comptroller, Greenwich, Connecticut

Gerard Giordano, Esq., Reed, McCarthy & Giordano, New York City

Donald R. Hodgman, Esq., O'Melveny & Meyers, Los Angeles, California

Robert Todd Lang, Esq., Weil, Gotshal & Manges, New York City

James W. Perkins, Esq., Palmer & Dodge, Boston, Massachusetts

Special appreciation goes to Robert W. Doty, MFOA General Counsel and Director of Fiscal Policy, and John E. Petersen, Director, Center for Policy Research and Analysis, National Governors' Conference, for their coordination of the guidelines project.

In addition, the following groups have contributed much time and energy to the project: American Bar Association, American Institute of Certified Public Accountants, Dealer Bank Association, Securities Industry Association Public Finance Council, Association of the Bar of the City of New York, National Association of Counties, National Association of State Auditors, Comptrollers and Treasurers, National Conference of State Legislatures, National Governors' Conference, National League of Cities, U.S. Conference of Mayors, and the many other public interest, professional and governmental organizations who participated in the development of the guidelines.

MFOA particularly wishes to thank the National Science Foundation for funding which enabled this project to be executed. (Grant #APR 75-17227)

Preface

During the past two years, disclosure on municipal bond offerings has been a topic of much discussion. The Municipal Finance Officers Association (MFOA) anticipated this issue and in 1974, they began work under a National Science Foundation Grant to study a variety of disclosure questions. One area of this project was designed to culminate in a set of disclosure standards. MFOA intended that these standards would provide greater protection to investors through increased disclosure and through standardization of disclosure practices. In November 1975, an exposure draft of *Disclosure Guidelines for Offerings of Securities by State and Local Governments* was released for public discussion and comment.

The draft guidelines received wide dissemination, and there was strong interest in their improvement and ultimate market acceptance. During 1976, MFOA sponsored a series of seminars for discussion of the guidelines and of a broad range of disclosure issues. A digest was prepared of the many excellent written comments that were received by MFOA. A Revision Drafting Committee, consisting of representatives of issuers, dealers, investors and professional groups, was appointed to review the comments and to revise the draft. The MFOA Committee on Governmental Debt and Fiscal Policy worked closely with this Revision Drafting Committee and with the MFOA Executive Board in producing the present guidelines.

The guidelines in this publication were approved and commended for use by municipal bond issuers on December 4, 1976, by the MFOA Executive Board. They are suggestions of information which may be disclosed in offerings of municipal securities. These guidelines are not intended to be legally binding. Rather, they represent information that usually should be included in official statements because it would be relevant to investors on most occasions for most issues.

The draft has been revised in a number of respects throughout the entire document. But the principal revisions are:

(1) Restructuring of the guidelines for a more readable and better organized document;

(2) Specification of the financial data suggested for presentation;

(3) Condensation of the introductory material; and

(4) Deletion of explicit positions regarding informational availability and underwriting data.

These guidelines represent an industry consensus on disclosure, and are a significant improvement over the exposure draft. They will be subject to periodic review and updating as experience is gained in their use.

Donald W. Beatty

Executive Director

Municipal Finance Officers Association

Introduction to
Disclosure Guidelines

These guidelines are designed for use in providing information to investors in connection with offerings of securities of state and local governments. In most cases, such information is provided to investors by state and local governments through investment dealers and dealer banks that purchase securities for reoffering. The information suggested in these guidelines is intended to produce an official statement which will be acceptable for such purpose. It is not intended, however, to create disclosure requirements or a legal obligation to disclose any or all items of information that are suggested.

The guidelines suggest material which an investor might consider of importance in making an informed investment decision. Such data is generally found in financial reports, budget documents, and other accessible material. Information in the issuer's records or which can be obtained from another source, such as U.S. Government census reports, normally should be obtained, compiled and reported. There should be an appropriate indication of the source of the information, if the source is other than the issuer. It is possible that other information, not suggested herein, may at times be material and in such cases should be provided. Certain types of issuers or circumstances might require additional information in order to give an adequate description of such issuer or circumstances. However, there may also be cases in which some of the suggested information is unnecessary or irrelevant. For instance, matters bearing principally on the long-term prospects of the issuer, such as demographic or economic data, may not be material in the sale of certain short-term obligations. The overriding consideration is to provide a complete, accurate, and objective description of those factors that relate to the securities being offered and that are necessary to make an informed investment decision.

The order of presentation suggested in the guidelines should not necessarily be deemed to recommend a specific order of presentation of information in the official statement. The information set forth in the official statement should be presented in a concise, understandable fashion. Consideration should be given to setting forth material in a manner which will give appropriate emphasis to such material in view of its relative importance.

Some sections of these guidelines are more appropriate for offerings of general obligation securities, while others are more appropriate for offerings of revenue securities or of special obligation securities. Certain sections are not applicable to obligations of state governments. In some cases, a particular security may combine characteristics of a general obligation security, a revenue security, or a special obligation security. For example, revenue sources from an enterprise or enterprises (as used in these guidelines, "enterprise" means any undertaking or activity relating to the construction, acquisition, operation, or maintenance of facilities or services or otherwise performing governmental functions which are expected to generate revenues which are to be a material source of payment for the principal of and interest or premium on the securities) or a specific tax may be the primary source of payment and security for an issue of bonds, while additional security is furnished by the general taxing power of the issuer. Under these circumstances, consideration should be given to providing the appropriate information suggested as to both types of securities. These guidelines may not be appropriate for disclosure in official statements for offerings of obligations issued for the purpose of providing pollution control or industrial facilities where the payment of the securities is solely dependent upon payment by the private entity involved in the offering.

Provision should be made to assure the availability of the official statement to prospective purchasers of the securities. However, in the case of direct negotiations with sophisticated purchasers, an official statement may not be necessary where the purchasers acknowledge that they have sufficient access to facts and have made such investigation as they deem necessary to decide whether to purchase the obligations.

These guidelines are not intended to establish standards of legal sufficiency. No implication is intended that previously prepared documents have been inadequate, or that any offering document prepared in the future is inadequate solely because it does not comply with suggestions in these guidelines. However, it should be emphasized that those preparing the official statements should take great care to see that they are accurate, complete and not misleading. Responsibilities of the various participants with respect to the development of information in the official statement should be described in the official statement. Where appropriate, the various participants or attesting officials should consider the necessity of certifying to the accuracy and completeness of the material they have prepared.

SECTION I
Cover Page of the
Official Statement

A cover page is sometimes used to describe certain details of the securities being offered. In these instances, the details which may be set forth include the following:

(1) The total principal amount of the securities.

(2) The name of the issuer (with appropriate identification).

(3) The type or title of issue being offered (e.g., general obligation, water revenue, etc.).

(4) The date of the obligations, interest payment dates, and the date from which interest is paid.

(5) The denominations in which the securities are being offered.

(6) Registration and exchange provisions.

(7) Trustee and paying agents.

(8) Redemption features, if any, including sinking fund provisions.

(9) Maturity date and principal amount by maturity in columnar form. (In the reoffering, interest rates, yields or prices should be specified. In the case of a public sale, it is suggested the issuer should provide space for such interest rates and reoffering yields or prices.)

(10) A statement of the tax status of interest on the securities being offered.

Additional information sometimes set forth on the cover page includes:

(11) Ratings by the various rating agencies (see "Miscellaneous").

(12) Designation of new issues.

(13) Brief statement of the authority for issuance.

(14) Anticipated date and place of delivery.

(15) Summary statement of the security or source of payment.

SECTION II
Introduction to the
Official Statement

The purpose of the introduction to the official statement is to set forth, in summary form, the salient portions of information with respect to the identification of the issuer; the statutory, constitutional or other basis pursuant to which the securities are being issued; the purposes for which the securities are being issued; and the security and source of payment for the securities. In addition, special circumstances that are of importance to the making of an informed investment decision and their possible consequences for investment risk should be described. The issuer should be briefly described as well as the project which is to be undertaken. The purpose for which the securities are issued should include a description of the application of proceeds, including the payment of costs of acquisition or construction; the making of deposits in debt service or capitalized interest funds; and the payment of costs incidental to the financing. The security and source of payment for the securities should be briefly described and reference to more specific information concerning such security and source of payment should be made. Appropriate references to more detailed information contained elsewhere in the official statement should be included.

SECTION III
Securities Being
Offered

Provide the following information to the extent relevant regarding the securities being offered and regarding the authorizing and governing instruments:

A. Consideration should be given to setting forth those items, 1-9, that appear on the cover page. Amplification of such items should be presented, where appropriate. In any case, set forth such items where they do not appear on the cover page.

B. Describe the pertinent provisions of the state constitution, statutes, resolutions and such other documentation that authorize the issuance of the securities.

C. State the principal purposes for which the net proceeds of the offering are authorized or proposed to be used and the approximate amount authorized or proposed for each purpose. Furnish a brief description of any program of construction or addition of equipment to be financed from the proceeds of the sale of the securities. If any material amounts of other funds are to be used in conjunction with the proceeds, state the amounts and sources of such other funds. If more funds are needed to accomplish the stated purposes, indicate the projected sources of such funds. State whether such other funds will be definitely available upon completion of the offering, and if not, describe the conditions which must first be satisfied. If the proceeds may be used for other purposes, describe the other purposes and amounts which may be used. If 15% or more of the proceeds has not been allocated for particular purposes, a statement indicating the amount of such unallocated proceeds should be given. If the aggregate expenses of the offering to be paid by the issuer, other than underwriting commissions, are 5% or more of the net proceeds of the offering, state the aggregate amount of all such expenses in connection with the issuance and distribution of the securities.

D. Describe provisions with respect to the security and sources of payment for the securities. State the relationship of the priority of payment or lien to any outstanding securities or other obligations of the issuer. If the securities are secured by physical properties, assets or revenues, such physical properties, assets or revenues and the provisions for their release or substitution should be described. If payment of the principal of or interest or premium on the securities being offered is guaranteed or insured in any respect, name the guarantor or insurer, state the terms and conditions of the guaranty or insurance and furnish such financial and other information as to the guarantor or insurer as may be appropriate. Describe any known claim of the guarantor or insurer which may be asserted as a defense in a suit on the guaranty or insurance.

E. Describe provisions regarding (1) the flow of funds from enterprise revenues, including any restrictions thereon, (2) the creation or maintenance of reserves, and (3) maintenance or insurance of properties. Describe any proposed investment of the proceeds or the reserves. Describe the parties who will hold and control the proceeds of the securities and the method by which such proceeds will be expended.

F. Describe the purposes for which additional debt may be issued, including provisions permitting or restricting the issuance of additional securities or the incurrence of additional debt. Describe legal requirements, such as voter approval, which must be met in connection with debt issuance. In offerings of revenue securities, describe the enterprise's authority to borrow funds for various purposes and the conditions under which the enterprise is empowered to issue varying types of indebtedness.

G. State the name of the trustee or fiscal agent, if any; summarize the rights and duties of the trustee or fiscal agent; and state the important conditions and the percentage of securities which would require the trustee or fiscal agent to take any action. Describe any indemnification the trustee or fiscal agent may require before proceeding to enforce the rights of holders of the securities. Indicate any business relationship of the trustee or fiscal agent with the issuer as security holder, depositary or otherwise. If the trustee or fiscal agent acts in the capacity of trustee or fiscal agent for the holders of other securities of the issuer, discuss such relationship or capacity.

H. Describe pertinent provisions of the state constitution, statutes, or judicial decisions that could affect the status of or priority for the bondholder.

I. State whether the terms of the securities, including provisions with respect to security or source of payment, may be modified.

J. Summarize provisions in the securities being offered, the indenture or other authorizing or governing instruments regarding specified events which constitute defaults and the remedies therefor under the securities and whether any periodic evidence is required to be furnished as to the absence of default or as to compliance with the terms of such securities, indentures or instruments. If the issuer cannot be sued for failure to perform its obligations to the holders of the securities or if judgments resulting from such suit are not enforceable against the issuer, such facts should be disclosed.

SECTION IV
Description of
Issuer and
Enterprise

A. Issuer. The information suggested herein would normally apply to offerings of general obligation securities which are payable from ad valorem taxation or other taxes.

Data should be given to provide sufficient background and general information regarding the issuer. Investors should generally be informed of factors which indicate the ability of the issuer to impose and collect, and the ability of its citizens to pay, taxes and other receipts which can be used to discharge the issuer's obligations. The information presented herein would normally include the issuer's range and level of services and the capacity of the issuer to provide such services. In addition, under most circumstances, a discussion of important population, economic, and educational data should also be presented.

Examples of the types of information which may be appropriate are:

(1) A statement indicating the year in which the issuer was established; the name of the state or other jurisdiction under the laws of which it was established; the form of government, such as mayor-council or city manager; the important powers and the governmental organization of the issuer; and relationships to and areas of shared responsibilities with other governmental entities.

(2) A list of the executive officials of the issuer. Discuss the manner in which the principal officials of the issuer are chosen, their respective terms, and the authority and method by which policy and program decisions are made.

(3) A brief description of (a) the principal governmental services performed by the issuer; (b) services which the issuer is required to perform; (c) the revenue sources for the services, and the degree of self-support of any service activity, described pursuant to (a) and (b); (d) the extent to which similar or differing governmental services are performed by or performed in conjunction

with other governmental entities; and (e) any recent major changes or interruptions in such services.

(4) A discussion of the general character of the principal facilities of the issuer. The material should allow the investor to appraise the ability of the issuer's principal facilities to continue to provide issuer services. Describe the capital improvements plan which indicates future construction requirements of the issuer and the currently projected methods of financing such expenditures.

(5) A statement or description of historical and current data concerning and estimates of the issuer's population, per capita income, median age, education levels, school enrollment, and unemployment rate.

(6) A statement or description of historical and current data concerning commercial and residential construction, commercial and savings bank deposits, property valuation, and values in housing stock.

(7) A statement or description of historical and current data concerning (a) the principal industries, commercial and governmental entities, and other employers in the issuer's immediate geographical area; (b) the number of persons employed by such industries, entities, or employers; (c) the economic stability of such industries, entities, or employers; and (d) the economic effects of any recent addition or loss of major industrial, commercial or governmental entities, or other employers.

(8) The numbers of persons presently employed and the percentage of employees of the issuer who belong to unions or other collective bargaining groups. Characterize employee relations.

B. Enterprise. The following information normally should be disclosed in offerings of revenue securities which are secured from the earnings of an enterprise. However, to the extent that the sources of revenues to pay debt service on the securities are dependent on the viability of a service area, certain material suggested in the preceding section should be set forth. Generally in the case of securities which are paid from a multiplicity of similar facilities or sources, such as obligations of a state housing authority or a student loan authority, the information suggested in this section is not necessary regarding each such facility or source on an individual basis.

(1) State the year in which the enterprise was organized, its form of organization (such as "a corporation," "an unincorporated association," "a department of the issuer" or other appropriate statement) and the name of the state or other jurisdiction under the laws of which it was organized. Name the municipalities, counties, and states in which the enterprise is located and describe the service area.

(2) List the executive officials of the enterprise. Discuss the manner in which the executive officials of the enterprise are chosen, their employment

over the past five years, their respective terms, and the authority and method by which policy and program decisions are made.

(3) Describe the location and general character of the principal facilities of the enterprise. If any property is leased or otherwise not held in fee or is held subject to any major encumbrance, discuss briefly the important factors in this regard. Provide sufficient information so that an investor may be able to appraise the ability of the enterprise to continue to provide its services. Such information should be furnished that will inform investors of the extent of utilization and the productive capacity of the enterprise's facilities. Itemization and detailed description of the facilities generally need not be given. Describe the capital improvements plan which indicates future construction requirements of the enterprise and the currently projected methods of financing such expenditures.

(4) If the proceeds of the offering will be used for the construction of all or part of the enterprise, briefly describe the new facilities, including their proposed purposes, productive capacity, anticipated life, and nature of construction. State the dates proposed for the commencement and completion of the construction; the dates proposed for the commencement of operations in the new facilities; the construction arrangements and principal contractors, engineers or other parties participating in the construction; the amount and location of the land on which the facilities are to be located; and the rights of the issuer or the enterprise in relation to the land, such as whether the land is held in fee, is leased, is held subject to encumbrances, or must be condemned or otherwise acquired before use.

(5) If the proceeds of the offering will be used for construction of all or part of the enterprise, reference should be made to any relevant engineer's or financial feasibility reports or studies on the feasibility of such construction as a part of the enterprise's operations. Name the parties preparing the reports or studies and whether the consent to the reference to such reports or studies has been obtained. Reference should also be made to any other reports or studies which may have a bearing on the conclusion of feasibility. All references should describe the material conclusions of the reports or studies, insofar as such conclusions relate to the use of proceeds as set forth in the official statement. If no such report or study has been made, a statement should be made to that effect, together with an explanation of the reasons therefor.

(6) Describe the operations performed and intended to be performed by any new or existing enterprise and the general development of such operations during the past five years, or such shorter period as the enterprise may have been engaged in operations. The description should include, but not be limited to, information as to matters such as the following areas (if the enterprise is engaged or will engage in more than one activity, provide appropriate documentation and description for each of the principal activities):

(a) The principal services rendered or to be rendered by the enterprise, and the principal users of, or service area for, including any reliance on seasonal factors related to, such services. Describe recent significant changes in the kinds of services rendered, or in the users or area served.

(b) Whether the enterprise has or will have an exclusive position in its service area, and if not, a description of the competitive conditions in the service area and the present and proposed competitive position of the enterprise, if known or reasonably available to the issuer.

(c) The numbers of customers of the enterprise at present and as proposed after the completion of construction into categories according to major sources of revenues, and an appropriate categorization of ranges reflecting amounts paid or to be paid by customers for the enterprise's services. If an important part of the operations is or will be dependent upon a single customer or a few customers, the loss of any one or more of whom would have an adverse effect on the operations or financial condition of the enterprise, give the names of the customers, their relationship, if any, to the enterprise, and significant facts regarding their contribution to the operations of the enterprise. Describe also any federal, state, or local governmental program which provides an important part of the enterprise's revenues.

(d) The parties responsible for determining and modifying rates, together with related limitations on the powers of such parties and rights of review of the enterprise or others; and any rate covenant or similar agreement on the part of the issuer or the enterprise, and the degree to which such covenant or agreement is designed to provide for debt service, and operating and any other important expenses.

(e) The sources and availability of raw materials essential to the enterprise's present and proposed operations.

(f) The status of licenses, permits and franchises required to be held by the enterprise. Describe any federal, state or local governmental regulation of the operations of the enterprise, including significant environmental protection requirements, and the effects of such regulation on the enterprise's present and proposed operations and on new construction.

(g) The numbers of persons presently employed and to be employed after completion of construction, and the percentage of employees of the enterprise who belong to unions or other collective bargaining groups. Characterize employee relations.

(h) If the enterprise has not received revenues from operations for the entire fiscal year prior to the date of the sale of the securities being offered, provide an analysis of the enterprise's current year's plan of operations, including a description of any results that may have been experienced at the time of the offering and a discussion of known factors and important assumptions related to operations for the next fiscal year. If such information is not available, the reasons for its not being available should be stated. Disclosure relating to any plan should include such matters as:

(i) A statement in narrative form indicating the enterprise's plan of construction. The schedule for completion and categories of expenditures and sources of cash resources should be identified.

(ii) Any anticipated large acquisition of plant and equipment and the capacity thereof.

(iii) Other matters which may be important to the enterprise's construction and operations.

SECTION V
Debt
Structure

The following suggested information is intended to describe various important factors related to the debt structure of the issuer or enterprise, including authority to incur debt, debt trends, the size of prospective debt burden, and rates of retirement. The tax related information is suggested for general obligation securities. Sufficient information should be provided by the issuer or enterprise so that an investor will be able to evaluate tax and other revenue sources in relation to the obligations or commitments of the issuer or enterprise.

A. Furnish the information of the type suggested by the following table as to appropriate categories of long-term and short-term securities and other indebtedness of the issuer or enterprise:

Category of indebtedness	Amount authorized	Amount outstanding as of [date] (less sinking fund installments paid to such date)	Amount to be outstanding
	$	$	$

The "appropriate" categories of indebtedness will vary from issuer to issuer and from enterprise to enterprise. Generally, the purpose of the indebtedness, or the maturity of the indebtedness, e.g., short-term debt, may be used as a basis for categorization. The description should also include a separate section on other commitments, such as long-term leases, lease-purchase obligations, installment purchase obligations, guaranteed debt, moral obligations, other contingency forms of debt and other forms of "off balance sheet" indebtedness.

Debt should be regarded as "authorized" when all legal steps have been taken by the issuer for its authorization for issuance, such as required approval by the city council or the voters. However, actions requiring only minor administrative performance normally should not be regarded as a stage for the authorization of debt.

The amount of indebtedness outstanding should be as of the latest practicable date, within the previous 120 days, with any major changes in debt position including any new obligations issued during the interim appropriately indicated. In stating the amount to be outstanding, give effect to the securities being offered including the retirement of outstanding debt with proceeds of such securities and, in addition, give effect to required or permitted debt retirement from existing funds.

B. Furnish a debt service schedule of the outstanding indebtedness of the issuer or enterprise including required payments of principal and interest, and where appropriate, authorized indebtedness to the final maturity date of all outstanding securities. Debt payable from different tax or revenue sources should be shown in separate columns as well as in the "Total" column. Include in the schedule debt service on the securities being offered. Indicate in footnotes to the schedule any assumptions, such as interest rates on authorized but unissued debt, on which information in the schedule is based. The schedule may be presented in substantially the following tabular form:

Fiscal year ending [date]	Principal	Interest	Total
19—	$	$	$
19—			$
19—			$
.			.
.			.
.			.
(year)			$

C. Furnish the information called for by the following table as to indebtedness of overlapping governmental entities. The information should be as of the latest practicable date, within the previous 120 days, with any major changes in debt position during the interim appropriately indicated. Unless inappropriate, the information in the last column should be based upon the estimated true valuation of real property in the respective jurisdictions.

Name of overlapping entity	Amount of authorized debt	Amount of outstanding debt (less sinking fund as of [date])	Percent of outstanding debt chargeable to persons or property in issuer's boundaries
	$	$	%

D. Give information as of the end of each of the issuer's last five fiscal years with respect to the issuer's (1) debt per capita; (2) debt expressed as a percentage of total assessed valuation of taxable real and personal property; (3) debt expressed as a percentage of total estimated true valuation of taxable real property; and (4) debt per capita expressed as percentage of estimated per capita income of individual taxpayers residing in the jurisdiction.

E. State the amounts of long-term and short-term indebtedness of the issuer or enterprise outstanding as of the end of each of its last five fiscal years.

F. Describe any legal debt or tax limit of the issuer or enterprise, the legal source of the limit, the indebtedness or tax rates chargeable to the limit, and the unused borrowing or taxation margin.

G. If any securities of the issuer have been in default as to principal or interest payments or in any other material respect at any time in the last 25 years, state the circumstances giving rise to such default, including descriptions of the relevant provisions of the securities and authorizing and governing instruments and the amounts involved. State whether such default has been terminated or waived, and if so, the manner of such termination or waiver.

SECTION VI
Financial
Information

The suggested information that follows is intended to disclose important factors related to the financial condition and results of operations of the issuer or enterprise. The section is divided into two parts: first, there is suggested information that would summarize the financial practices and recent results of operations of the issuer or enterprise; the second part sets forth the information to be presented as the financial statements of the issuer or enterprise for the last two fiscal years.

A. General Description of Financial Practices and Recent Results of Operations:

(1) Furnish in comparative columnar form a summary of operations for the fund/account groups which would provide information pertinent to the securities being offered. Such information should be provided for each of the last five fiscal years and, in the case of enterprises and in those unusual circumstances where it is otherwise appropriate, for the latest practicable date for interim periods of the current and prior fiscal year if the official statement is dated more than 120 days after the last fiscal year.

Information regarding the operations of enterprise and intragovernmental service funds should be presented separately from information regarding the operations of the general and other funds of the governmental entity.

(a) Information regarding operations of the general and other fund/accounts may be presented on a combined basis as appropriate. Such summary should include major categories of actual revenues and expenditures and comparable budgeted amounts.

In addition, beginning and ending fund balances and transactions reported as adjustments to fund balances should be included.

(b) Subject to appropriate variation to conform to the nature of the operations of an enterprise or intragovernmental service fund, the summary and discussion should include: operating revenues; operating expenses; interest expense; income from continuing operations; income from discontinued operations; extraordinary items; the cumulative effects of changes in accounting principles; and net income or loss. The summary should also include the amount of any changes in retained earnings other than net income or loss, and the amount of retained earnings at the end of each of the fiscal periods presented.

(c) Following each summary of operations, include a discussion of the material trends and changes and the reasons therefor, related to the components of such summary. For example, if debt service, as a percentage of total expenditures, has increased significantly in recent years, describe the conditions which contributed to the trend. Furthermore, if certain revenues or expenditures are dependent on the financial policies or practices of another governmental entity, state the amounts involved and describe the relationship of such other entity to such issuer or enterprise. In addition, such discussion should include the effect of the change in accounting principles or procedures during any of the years presented.

(d) Describe any known facts which would significantly affect any financial information presented or the future financial operations of the issuer or enterprise.

(2) Describe generally the accounting practices of the issuer or enterprise. Indicate any important deviations (and the effects thereof, if quantifiable) from generally accepted governmental accounting principles, as presented and recommended in the National Council on Governmental Accounting (formerly National Committee on Governmental Accounting) publication, *Governmental Accounting, Auditing, and Financial Reporting* and the Industry Audit Guide of the American Institute of Certified Public Accountants, entitled *Audits of State and Local Governmental Units,* as such generally accepted governmental accounting principles are supplemented and modified from time to time. The information recommended herein may be cross-referenced to the Notes to the financial statement.

(3) Describe the issuer's or enterprise's budgetary processes. The description should include matters such as: the parties responsible for the development of operating and capital budgets; the processes by which the budgets are approved and adopted; legal requirements for balancing such budgets and institutional mechanisms to assure achievement of that goal. Summarize the pertinent current operating and capital budgets. State whether the issuer or enterprise has conformed to such budgets to date, and if not, the significant variations which have occurred or are expected to occur. Describe the reasons for any material differences between the budgets and the actual financial results for the last five fiscal years and the current fiscal year.

(4) If the securities being offered are payable only from particular receipts of the issuer, such as a particular tax or assessment, describe the receipts and

give sufficient historical and other data to indicate the reliability of such receipts to meet debt service on the securities.

(5) If the obligations are secured in whole or in part by taxes of any type, describe briefly the manner in which such taxes are levied and collected. Where appropriate, describe briefly the manner in which property valuations and assessments are determined. Include descriptions of (a) the manner in which delinquent taxes are collected and the result of such collection efforts; (b) the interest and penalty charged on delinquent taxes; (c) important changes during the last five years in tax assessment, levy, or collection practices; and (d) the reasons for such changes. State the value of total tax title liens owned by the issuer as of the end of each of its last five years and as of a recent date. Describe briefly the procedures followed in foreclosure. Describe the priority of tax claims of the issuer over other indebtedness of taxpayers.

(6) Give in tabular or other appropriate form with respect to the issuer, as of the end of each of its last five fiscal years and as of a recent date, information as to (a) its assessed valuation of taxable real property; (b) its estimated true valuation of taxable real property; (c) its assessed valuation of taxable personal property; and (d) the assessed valuation of taxable real property expressed as a percentage of the estimated true valuation thereof. Segregate such information as to industrial, commercial, utility, and residential properties. State in tabular or other appropriate form the total tax levy and the accumulated amount of delinquent taxes as of the end of each of the issuer's last five fiscal years and the tax delinquency rate for each of such fiscal years and for the current fiscal year to date. Describe recent borrowing against such delinquent taxes and any anticipation of collection of delinquent taxes in budgets for current or future years. State the accounting policies applied in writing off delinquent taxes. For taxes and other revenue sources other than property taxes, include descriptions of the significance thereof to the issuer and recent volume of activity generating such funds.

(7) A table setting forth the ten largest taxpayers of the issuer, where appropriate and not prohibited by law, should be presented. State the amount of taxes paid by each such taxpayer, the percentage of the total tax levy or tax collections represented by such amount, and in the case of property tax levies the assessed valuation of taxable real property of each such taxpayer.

(8) With respect to interim borrowing for operational purposes such as revenue anticipation notes or tax anticipation notes, present the appropriate anticipated cash flow.

(9) If the proceeds from the sale of any securities (other than revenue anticipation notes or tax anticipation notes issued against revenues or taxes of a current fiscal year) or any nonrecurring revenues have been used for current operating expenses at any time in the last ten years, describe the

circumstances giving rise to such use, including the amount used in each of such years.

(10) If payments on outstanding securities or other obligations have been met through loans from other governmental fund sources, indicate the sources, the amounts involved, the purpose (as for payment of principal, interest, or operating cost), and any commitments for repayment of the loans.

Describe briefly any federal, state, or other legislation, program, or procedure which would apply specifically to the issuer in times of financial emergency.

(11) Describe briefly the issuer's or enterprise's pension or other public employee retirement plans and the methods and basis (e.g., actuarial funding or "pay-as-you-go") on which such plans are financed. State any adverse trends or factors in the financing or operation of such plans as they relate to the employer's contributions or liabilities to the plans. To the extent that there are unfunded accrued liabilities, state the amount of such liabilities as of the most recent actuarial study or estimate and indicate the date of such study or estimate. Information concerning the pension plan contained in the financial statements included in the official statement should be cross-referenced.

Liabilities and costs pertaining to other employee benefits such as vacation and sick leave may be material. When that is the case such liabilities and pertinent details should likewise be disclosed.

B. Financial Statements

Uniformity in the presentation of financial information and the consistent application of accounting principles are essential for adequate financial reporting. To that end, it is suggested that financial statements be prepared and presented in accordance with generally accepted governmental accounting principles (as contained in the following authoritative sources: *Governmental Accounting, Auditing and Financial Reporting* (1968) published by the National Council on Governmental Accounting (NCGA); *Audits of State and Local Governmental Units* (1974) published by the American Institute of Certified Public Accountants (AICPA); other pronouncements of the NCGA and AICPA; and pronouncements of the Financial Accounting Standards Board), as modified from time to time, and that examinations and reports on such financial statements conform with generally accepted governmental auditing standards (as contained in the *Statements on Auditing Standards* (1976) published by the American Institute of Certified Public Accountants; and in *Standards for Audit of Governmental Organizations, Programs, Activities and Functions* (1972) published by the U.S. General Accounting Office and *Audits of State and Local Governmental Units* (1974) published by the American Institute of Certified Public Accountants).

If financial statements are prepared in conformity with laws applicable to the issuer and their presentation does not conform with generally accepted governmental accounting principles, the material differences between such laws and generally accepted accounting principles should be disclosed and, if practicable, the effects of such differences should be stated. It is suggested that financial statements be examined and reported upon by an independent certified public accountant, an independent licensed public accountant, or an independent governmental audit organization. If such an examination and resultant report does not conform with generally accepted governmental auditing standards, the nature of the audit and how it differs from such standards should be disclosed.

Consent of the Certified Public Accountant or other independent auditor should be sought if the name of the independent auditor is used in any way in connection with the financial statements or financial data included in the official statement. If such consent is not obtained, such fact and the reasons therefor should be disclosed.

The financial statements should be included in the official statement for those funds and account groups which would provide information pertinent to the securities being offered. The information would normally include financial statements for those funds which will provide the resources to discharge the issuer's obligations to the holders of the securities being offered and for other funds or account groups which would provide information material to such funds. In all cases, if some fund other than the fund with the primary obligation either requires substantial financing from or furnishes substantial financing for the fund with the primary obligation, financial statements for the other funds should be included. Generally, the financial statements of an issuer or enterprise will appear at the end of the official statement.

The financial statements for each fund and account group included in the official statement should be presented for two years and should include all basic financial statements. Depending upon applicability to the respective funds, the basic financial statements would include balance sheets, statements of revenues and expenditures, statements of changes in fund balance, statements of income, statements of retained earnings, and statements of changes in financial position.

(1) *General Obligation Debt.* Normally, when general obligation debt is being offered, financial statements should be included for the general fund, special revenue funds which provide revenues to pay a substantial portion of the total expenditures of the issuer and which relate to major governmental functions, debt service funds, and general long-term debt group of accounts. In addition, if an enterprise or other fund either requires substantial financing from the funds relevant to the securities being offered or furnishes substantial financing for such relevant funds, financial statements for such enterprise or other funds should be included.

(2) *Debt Other Than General Obligation Debt.* When the source of the resources to discharge the issuer's obligations to the holders of the securities being offered is limited to a particular fund, e.g., revenue of an enterprise fund, normally, only the financial statements of that fund need be presented. Such financial statements should disclose pertinent restricted and unrestricted accounts as provided in existing bond indentures, ordinances or similar instruments. When the source is primarily a particular fund but the obligation is also payable from another fund, the financial statements of both funds should be included in the official statement. If the issuer also pledges its full faith and credit, all financial statements relevant to the source of payment for the securities being offered should be included.

(3) Full disclosure in accordance with generally accepted governmental accounting principles requires that financial statements be accompanied by footnotes which supplement or clarify the data contained in the financial statements. Typical footnotes provided with a governmental entity's financial statements include the following:

A summary of significant accounting policies.

Principles of accounting.

Identification and definition of included funds.

Basis of accounting.

Budgetary policies.

Accounting policies for specific accounts.

Fixed assets.

Bond indenture provisions relating to accounting and reporting.

Long term debt provisions.

Leases and other commitments.

Provisions of public employee retirement systems, including costs, liabilities, unfunded obligations, actuarial assumptions and most recent valuations.

Contingencies.

(4) Supporting schedules to financial statements should be included to provide significant detail where necessary to further disclose the financial position or results of operations of the various funds (groups of funds) included in the offering statement.

SECTION VII
Legal
Matters

A. Describe any pending legal proceedings which may materially affect the issuer's or enterprise's ability to perform its obligations to the holders of the securities being offered, including the effects of the legal proceedings on the securities being offered and on the source of payment therefor. Include the name of the court or agency in which the proceedings are pending, the date instituted, the principal parties thereto, a description of the factual basis alleged to underlie the proceedings, and the relief sought. In appropriate cases, include or summarize, with the consent of counsel, an opinion of counsel as to the merits of the legal proceedings. Provide similar information as to legal proceedings which have been threatened to a degree which constitutes a material possibility that they will be instituted. An opinion of counsel with respect to such legal proceedings may, with the consent of counsel, be included or summarized in the official statement. State the name of such counsel.

B. With the consent of bond counsel, include or summarize the approving legal opinion of bond counsel regarding the issue of the securities, or indicate that such an opinion will be furnished with the securities. State the name of such bond counsel.

C. Describe the tax status of the securities and the interest thereon. With the consent of counsel, include or summarize an opinion of counsel as to such tax status. State the name of such counsel.

D. It is customary for the issuer or enterprise to indicate that at closing a certificate of no litigation will be provided and will state that no litigation is pending to, among other things, (1) restrain or enjoin the issuance or delivery of the securities, (2) contest the authority for, or validity of, the securities, or (3) contest the corporate existence or powers of the issuer or enterprise.

SECTION VIII
Miscellaneous

A. Ratings. If ratings for the securities being offered have been received, state all ratings of the securities being offered and the names of the rating agencies. If no ratings have been obtained or a rating refused for any such securities, a statement should be made to such effect. Changes in any ratings of any securities of the issuer during the preceding two years should be described.

It is suggested that the discussion indicate that (1) such ratings reflect only the views of such agencies and either set forth an explanation of such ratings as described by such agencies or refer the prospective purchaser to such agencies for an explanation of such ratings; (2) there is no assurance that such ratings will continue for any period of time or that they will not be revised or withdrawn; and (3) a revision or withdrawal of the ratings may have an effect on the market price of the securities.

Consideration may be given to stating the ratings in the body of the official statement rather than on the cover page.

B. Interest of Certain Persons Named in Official Statement. If any person named in the official statement as having prepared or certified an engineering report, feasibility study, or similar analysis included or referred to therein was employed for such purpose on a contingent basis, furnish a brief statement of the nature of such contingent basis. If any such person was or is connected with the issuer as an underwriter, financial advisor, security holder, member of the governing body, executive official, or employee, describe such connection.

C. Additional Information. Efforts should be made to make available to underwriters and investors specimens or copies of any indenture and other authorizing or governing instruments defining the rights of holders of the securities being offered, or preliminary forms thereof. The availability may be upon request or upon payment by the underwriters or investors of a reasonable copying, mailing and handling charge. The official statement may inform underwriters and investors of the availability of the information and the means of obtaining it. In such event, the description of the terms of the securities being offered may be qualified by reference to such additional information.

Bibliography

Chapter 2

Office of Management and Budget, Washington, D.C.:

The United States Budget in Brief—Fiscal Year 1978, 1978.

Circular A-11, Preparation and Submission of Budget Estimates.

Circular A-34, Instructions Relating to Apportionments and Reports on Budget Status.

U.S. General Accounting Office, Washington, D.C.:

Glossary for Systems Analysis—Planning, Programming, Budgeting, October 1969.

Title 7, Standardized Fiscal Procedures, Manual for Guidance of Federal Agencies, 1970.

Office of Economic Opportunity, Washington, D.C.:

Planning, Programming, Budgeting System Procedures, 1970.

Planning, Programming, Budgeting System, 1968.

Committee on Governmental Accounting and Auditing, *Industry Audit Guide: Audits of State and Local Governments,* American Institute of Certified Public Accountants, 1973, New York.

Tierney, Cornelius E., *Federal Grants-In-Aid: Accounting and Auditing Practices,* American Institute of Certified Public Accountants, 1977, New York.

Moak, Lennox L., and Killian, Kathryn W., *A Manual of Techniques for the Preparation, Consideration, Adoption and Administration of Operating Budgets,* Municipal Finance Officers Association, 1974 (fifth printing), Chicago.

U.S. Congress, Congressional Budget Act of 1974, Washington, D.C.

Constitution of the United States.

Chapter 3

U.S. General Accounting Office, Washington, D.C.:

Title 2, Accounting, Manual for Guidance of Federal Agencies, 1972, revised 1978.

Title 7, see citation under Chapter 2, this Bibliography.

Accounting Principles and Standards for Federal Agencies, revised 1972.

Frequently Asked Questions About Accrual Accounting in the Federal Government, 1970.

Manual for General Government Matters, Federal Appropriations, 1972.

Office of Management and Budget, Washington, D.C.:

Circular A-11, see citation under Chapter 2, this Bibliography.

Circular A-34, see citation under Chapter 2, this Bibliography.

Federal Legislation:

Anti-Deficiency Act (Section 3679, Revised Statutes).

Budget and Accounting Act, 1921.

Budget and Accounting Procedures Act, 1950.

Supplemental Appropriation Act of 1955 (Section 1311).

U.S. Constitution.

U.S. Department of Treasury, *Receipts, Appropriations and Other Fund Account Symbols and Titles,* Washington, D.C.

Tierney, Cornelius E., and Hoffman, Robert D., *Federal Financial Management: Accounting and Auditing Practices,* American Institute of Certified Public Accountants, 1976, New York.

Chapter 4

Municipal Finance Officers Association, Chicago:

Governmental Accounting, Auditing and Financial Reporting, 1969 (third printing).

Interpretation No. 1—GAAFR and the AICPA Audit Guide, 1976.

GAAFR Restatement Introduction and Principles—Working Draft, 1976.

GAAFR Restatement Principles, Draft, September, 1978.

Committee on Governmental Accounting and Auditing, *Industry Audit Guide, etc.,* see citation under Chapter 2, this Bibliography.

Freeman, Robert J., Ph.D., Professor of Accounting, University of Alabama, paper titled *Overview of Governmental Funds and Nonfunds Account Group,* Tuscaloosa, Alabama.

Oliver, Fred M., paper titled *Classification of Accounting Characteristics of Fund and Groups of Accounts,* Salt Lake City, Utah.

Lynn, Edward S., and Freeman, Robert J., *Fund Accounting Theory and Practice,* Prentice-Hall, Inc., 1974, Englewood Cliffs, New Jersey.

Chapter 5

U.S. General Accounting Office, Washington, D.C.:

Suggested State Auditing Acts and Constitutional Amendments, 1974.

What GAO Is Doing to Improve Governmental Auditing Standards, 1974.

Internal Auditing in Federal Agencies, 1974.

Audits of Government Contracts, undated.

Letter, dated September 15, 1970, from Comptroller General of the United States to all federal agencies, on qualifying criteria when outside auditors are employed to express opinions on financial statements.

Office of Management and Budget, Washington, D.C.:

Financial Management Circular 73-2, Audit of Federal Operations and Programs by Executive Branch Agencies.

Circular A-73, Audit of Federal Operations and Programs, March, 1978.

Joint Financial Management Improvement Program, *Financial Management Functions in the Federal Government,* September 1974, Washington, D.C.

U.S. Congress, The "Inspector General" Bill (P.L. 95-452), 1978, Washington, D.C.

Freeman, Robert J., report titled *Governmental Auditing in Alabama,* University of Alabama, Tuscaloosa, Alabama.

Williams, James M., "Governmental Auditing," *Governmental Finance,* November 1976, Municipal Finance Officers Association, Chicago.

Tierney, Cornelius E., see citation under Chapter 2, this Bibliography.

Ethics Division, *Guidelines for Reporting Substandard Audit Reports,* American Institute of Certified Public Accountants.

Committee on Relations with the General Accounting Office, *Auditing Standards Established by GAO—Their Meaning and Significance for CPAs,* American Institute of Certified Public Accountants, 1973, New York.

Chapter 6

U.S. General Accounting Office, Washington, D.C.:

Standards for Audit of Governmental Organizations, Programs, Activities and Functions, 1974 reprint.

Letter from Comptroller General to heads of federal departments and agencies on qualifications of public accountants engaged to perform governmental audits.

Letter, dated May 28, 1975, from the Comptroller General to the Chairman, Committee on Government Operations, U.S. Senate (Decision B-148144).

Questions and Answers—On Standards for Audit of Governmental Organizations, Programs, Activities and Functions, September 1974.

American Institute of Certified Public Accountants, New York:

Auditing Standards Executive Committee, *Statement on Auditing Standards, No. 1* and subsequent statements, 1973.

Committee on Relations with the GAO, see citation under Chapter 5, this Bibliography.

Committee on Governmental Accounting and Auditing, see citation under Chapter 2, this Bibliography.

Board of Directors, Policy Statement on Guidance Relating to Independence of Governmental Auditors Conducting Financial Audits, March 1978.

Municipal Finance Officers Association, Chicago, Illinois:

Governmental Accounting, etc., see citation under Chapter 4, this Bibliography.

Interpretation No. 1, see citation under Chapter 4, this Bibliography.

Chapter 7

Office of Management and Budget, Washington, D.C.:

Circular A-87, Principles for Determining Costs Applicable to Grants and Contracts with State and Local Governments (also referred to as Financial Management Circular 74-4).

Circular A-102, Administrative Requirements for Contracts and Grants with State and Local Governments.

U.S. Department of Health, Education and Welfare, Washington, D.C.:

A Guide for State and Local Government Agencies—Cost Principles and Procedures for Establishing Cost Allocation Plans (OASC-10).

Grant Administration—Staff Manual.

Tierney, Cornelius E., see citation under Chapter 2, this Bibliography.

Environmental Protection Agency, *Audit Guide for Construction Grant Program,* 1976, Washington, D.C.

Tierney & Hoffman, see citation under Chapter 3, this Bibliography.

Chapter 8

U.S. General Accounting Office, Washington, D.C.:

Standards for Audit, etc., see citation under Chapter 6, this Bibliography.

The Audit Survey—A Key Step in Auditing Government Programs, 1978.

Questions and Answers, etc. see citation under Chapter 6, this Bibliography.

Audit Guidelines for Audits of Financial Operations of Federally Assisted Programs, 1977.

Auditing Standards Executive Committee, *Statements on Auditing,* etc., see citation under Chapter 6, this Bibliography.

Chapter 9

Tierney & Hoffman, see citation under Chapter 3, this Bibliography.

U.S. General Accounting Office, *Internal Auditing in Federal Agencies— Basic Principles, Standards and Concepts,* 1974, Washington, D.C.

Chapter 10

American Institute of Certified Public Accountants, New York:

Suggested Guidelines for the Structure and Content of Audit Guides Prepared by Federal Agencies for Use by CPAs, 1972.

Management Advisory Services Executive Committee, *Guidelines for CPA Participation in Government Audit Engagements to Evaluate Economy, Efficiency and Program Results.*

Environmental Protection Agency, see citation under Chapter 7, this Bibliography.

U.S. General Accounting Office, *Standards for Audit,* etc., see citation under Chapter 6, this Bibliography.

U.S. Department of the Treasury, Office of Revenue Sharing, Retention of Workpapers Policy.

Chapter 11

U.S. General Accounting Office, Washington, D.C.:

Standards for Audit, etc., see citation under Chapter 6, this Bibliography.

Internal Auditing in Federal Agencies, see citation under Chapter 5, this Bibliography.

Comprehensive Approach for Planning and Conducting a Program Results Review, 1978.

American Institute of Certified Public Accountants, Management Advisory Services Executive Committee, see citation under Chapter 10, this Bibliography.

Chapter 12

U.S. General Accounting Office, *Standards for Audit,* etc., see citation under Chapter 6, this Bibliography.

American Institute of Certified Public Accountants, New York:

Auditing Standards Executive Committee, *Statement on Auditing Standards, No. 16, The Independent Auditor's Responsibility for the Detection of Errors or Irregularities,* January 1977.

Auditing Standards Executive Committee, *Statement on Auditing Standards, No. 1, Codification of Auditing Standards and Procedures,* November 1972.

Chapter 13

American Institute of Auditing Standards, New York:

Auditing Standards Executive Committee, see citation under Chapter 6, this Bibliography.

Committee on Governmental Accounting and Auditing, see citation under Chapter 2, this Bibliography.

Accounting Principles Board, Opinion No. 8, "Accounting for Cost of Pension Plans."

Accounting Standards Division, Statement of Position No. 75-3, "Accrual of Revenues and Expenditures by State and Local Governmental Units."

Municipal Finance Officers Association, *Government Accounting,* etc., see citation under Chapter 4, this Bibliography.

U.S. General Accounting Office, Washington, D.C.:

Title 2, see citation under Chapter 3, this Bibliography.

Standards for Audit, etc., see citation under Chapter 6, this Bibliography.

Chapter 14

American Institute of Certified Public Accountants, New York:

Auditing Standards Executive Committee, see citation under Chapter 6, this Bibliography.

Committee on Governmental Accounting and Auditing, see citation under Chapter 2, this Bibliography.

Office of Management and Budget, *Circular A-11*, see citation under Chapter 2, this Bibliography.

U.S. General Accounting Office, *Accounting Principles and Standards*, etc., see citation under Chapter 3, this Bibliography.

Municipal Finance Officers Association, *Government Accounting*, etc., see citation under Chapter 4, this Bibliography.

Chapter 15

American Institute of Certified Public Accountants, New York:

Auditing Standards Executive Committee, see citation under Chapter 6, this Bibliography.

Committee on Governmental Accounting and Auditing, see citation under Chapter 2, this Bibliography.

U.S. General Accounting Office, Washington, D.C.:

Accounting Principles and Standards, etc., see citation under Chapter 3, this Bibliography.

Title 2, see citation under Chapter 3, this Bibliography.

Standards for Audit, etc., see citation under Chapter 6, this Bibliography.

Glossary, etc., see citation under Chapter 2, this Bibliography.

Frequently Asked Questions, etc., see citation under Chapter 3, this Bibliography.

Office of Management and Budget, *Circular A-11*, see citation under Chapter 2, this Bibliography.

Tierney & Hoffman, see citation under Chapter 3, this Bibliography.

Chapter 16

American Institute of Certified Public Accountants, Auditing Standards Executive Committee, see citation under Chapter 6, this Bibliography.

Office of Management and Budget, Circular A-7, *Standardized Government Travel Regulations, Revised*, Washington, D.C.

Chapter 17

Office of Management and Budget, Washington, D.C.:

Circular A-102, Uniform Administrative Requirements for Grants-in-Aid to State and Local Governments.

Circular A-87, Principles for Determining Costs Applicable to Grants and Contracts with State and Local Governments.

General Services Administration, *Federal Procurement Regulations,* Washington, D.C.

Municipal Finance Officers Association, *Government Accounting,* etc., see citation under Chapter 4, this Bibliography.

Tierney, see citation under Chapter 2, this Bibliography.

Chapter 18

Municipal Finance Officers Association, *Government Accounting,* etc., see citation under Chapter 4, this Bibliography.

U.S. General Accounting Office, *Title 2,* see citation under Chapter 3, this Bibliography.

U.S. Department of Treasury, prototype financial statements, Washington, D.C.

Chapter 19

Municipal Finance Officers Association, Chicago:

Government Accounting, etc., see citation under Chapter 4, this Bibliography.

GAAFR Restatement Principles, see citation under Chapter 4, this Bibliography.

Chapter 20

American Institute of Certified Public Accountants, New York:

Auditing Standards Executive Committee, see citation under Chapter 6, this Bibliography.

Audit Guide: Audits of Service-Center Produced Records.

U.S. General Accounting Office, Washington, D.C.:

Standards for Audit, etc., see citation under Chapter 6, this Bibliography.

Review Guide for Evaluating Internal Controls in Automatic Data Processing Systems, 1970.

Guide for Reliability Assessment of Controls in Computerized Systems (Financial Statement Audits), 1976.

Institute of Internal Auditors, Inc., *Systems Auditability & Control—Audit Practices,* prepared by the Stanford Research Institute, 1977.

Index

Date Due